The Sound of the Machine

My Life in Kraftwerk and Beyond

For Bettina

The Sound of the Machine

My Life in Kraftwerk and Beyond

KARL BARTOS

Translated by Katy Derbyshire

OMNIBUS PRESS

London / New York / Paris / Sydney / Copenhagen / Berlin / Madrid / Tokyo

ISBN 9781913172640
Signed edition 9781913172879

A catalogue record for this book is available from the British Library.

Typeset by Palimpsest Book Production Ltd, Falkirk, Stirlingshire

Printed in the Czech Republic.

www.omnibuspress.com

CONTENTS

PROLOGUE:
A LIFE IMMERSED IN SOUND

Clang! – 'It's been a hard day's night, and I've been working like a dog . . .' It was this song that changed my life – the Beatles' 'A Hard Day's Night'. Back then I was 12 years old and in the middle of puberty, and even though I didn't understand much English, the music spoke to me. That was the moment when sound took on a new meaning for me and I knew I wanted to become a musician.

When I began to teach myself the guitar not long afterwards, I soon couldn't imagine how my life would be without music. I didn't have a plan, just a wish to get better at it and play the music I was drawn to. That lent order and purpose to my life.

A little later, I learned the percussionist's craft at the Robert Schumann Conservatory in Düsseldorf, so that I could perform the masterpieces of classical music in an orchestra and make them come to life. I met extraordinary people along the way. My teachers were outstanding, passing on not only theoretical and practical knowledge but also dedication to music. Not by holding long lectures and recommending reading, but by letting me join the orchestra of the Deutsche Oper am Rhein without much ado, for example, and allowing me insights into their lives. That was the time when I began to think deeply about music, and I have not stopped to this day. This book is the story of my life, the story of my sound biography, and for that reason it is also a book about music.

1

Through an enquiry to my teacher at the conservatory, I unintentionally ended up in the music industry, which had grown into a multi-million-dollar business over the second half of the twentieth century. This book is therefore also about the band Kraftwerk, placing the music we made together in the context of its time.

I remember very well how I fell under the spell of electronic music and became part of what's known as Kraftwerk's classic line-up. To begin with, my job was playing electronic percussion. My contributions were apparently useful enough to make me a co-author of all our compositions from the *Man-Machine* album up to the point when I left the band. It was during this period above all that I regarded myself as a band member. My contribution, I thought, was audible and visible for both insiders and outsiders. After all, I brought plenty of life and music into the Kling Klang Studio. I remember our writing sessions and 'sound rides' as if they were yesterday, and the amazing feeling of being part of a community where the whole was more than the sum of its parts. Or that's how it seemed to me at the time.

Innovations and musical ideas rarely fall fully-formed from heaven. When I read musicians' biographies, I always find it interesting to learn about the inspiration for their various songs. So in this book, I'll be taking you along inside the Kling Klang Studio, showing you some of the sources for our ideas, providing context and background information, and describing how we created our music using compositional craft, dedication, emotion and a pinch of intelligence.

Over almost sixteen years, I worked on six Kraftwerk albums – plus one maxi-single about a French sporting event that was to be the basis for another album. Nonetheless, for the public I only became visible and audible when I left the band.

After my years in the Kraftwerk cosmos, I had to start by reinventing my life and asking myself: What does Karl Bartos sound like? Along that path, I was fortunate enough to meet and work with fantastic artists like Johnny Marr, Andy McCluskey, and Bernard Sumner.

My time as a guest professor of Auditory Media Design in the Sound Studies master's programme at Berlin's University of the Arts was another source of inspiration and development in my work.

Naturally, journalists and interviewers have always brought up my past. But the events that took place in the Kling Klang Studio were too complex to explain in just a few words. A rush-job autobiography in the form of an early evaluation seemed an inadequate response. I wanted to take a few steps back and look at the bigger picture to form my opinion from a distance. One day, I told myself, I would return to the project in detail.

Over thirty years after leaving Kraftwerk, I'm now holding the finished manuscript in my hands – *The Sound of the Machine*. Happily, I neither have a drawer full of unpaid bills, nor do I owe anyone a favour nor feel obliged not to comment for any other reason. I am independent, which means I can tell the whole story as I experienced it. Much of what happened in those years has been forgotten or was never known, due to the unusual conditions we worked under in Kraftwerk. In this book, I write about the creation of our music, look at our social behaviour, let you share our communications as far as I can, and try to describe how things developed over time. If I manage to lend a new perspective on Kraftwerk's music and perhaps encourage you to think about the nature of music in general, I will have achieved my goal. I certainly hope I do.

Ever since I heard that famous opening chord of 'A Hard Day's Night' I have been immersed in music. The mysterious thing about music is that it sounds different to every one of us, and means something different as well. For some of us it is divine, while others want merely to escape their everyday lives with its help. Some say it can teach us something of life. I know someone who can't understand that people perceive anything other than sound in music, while philosophers define it using metaphysical and psychological terms.

Coming out of a concert a few days ago, I heard admiring conversations peppered with adjectives such as 'great', 'amazing', 'marvellous' and the like. When we ask why someone finds a particular piece so extraordinary, it becomes clear how difficult it seems to be to say something more engaging about music.

And yet it is possible to talk about music – or at least it's worth trying. We can represent it and study it in the form of musical notation. Nor is depicting its frequency spectrum in three-dimensional form a problem, so as to analyse it over time. And computers – the most universal machines of our day – enable a very precise inside view of musical content in the form of data. But I'm afraid I have to disappoint anyone who assumes it's possible to even approach explaining what music really is. Only music itself can do that.

Karl Bartos, Hamburg, 31 May 2022

4

1

CHILDHOOD IN POST-WAR GERMANY

Back to the Beginning. Haus Kederlehen. The Little Reich Chancellery. The Berghof. Headquarters US Army 1945. Gasthaus zum Untersberg. Auf Wiedersehen Berchtesgaden. Düsseldorf on the Rhine. Unterbilk. How I Met Maximilian in the Education System. A Happy Family. The World in My Head. My Life Gets a Soundtrack. Radio and Television.

Back to the Beginning

I glance in the rear-view mirror, change down a gear and hear the engine killing the car's speed. On the way into the valley, where the road curves to the right, I hold my breath. Ahead of me the mighty peaks of the Watzmann rear up into the Upper Bavarian sky, and below me lies Berchtesgaden with its church towers, streets and houses. It's exactly as if I'd driven straight into a picture postcard. My birthplace of Marktschellenberg is embedded in the breathtaking landscape of a world-famous national park a few minutes' drive from Berchtesgaden. The area on the edges of the Alps in southern Bavaria is so beautiful that it looks strangely artificial, almost.

To help me write this book, I've come back to where my life

started out, to compare the images in my mind with the real settings as they are today.

Haus Kederlehen

Once I've dropped my suitcase off at the Hotel am Luipoldpark, I drive a few kilometres further northeast alongside the turquoise-flowing Berchtesgadener Ache towards Untersalzberg. About a hundred metres above the valley floor, on a wide green hill, is Haus Kederlehen. The Alpine panorama is unique – you can see the majestic peaks of the Watzmann, Hochkalter, Reiter Alpe, Untersberg and Kehlstein mountains from here. A light wind carries the resinous scent of the forest.

Here I stand, right in front of the archetypal Bavarian farmhouse. Whitewashed walls on the ground floor, above them brown wood panelling up to the roof. Not to forget a flourishing crop of geraniums on the balconies and wooden shutters, something I've associated with country life since the first visits I remember to Bavaria. In the forest – which begins directly behind the house – a mountain stream tumbles down Untersalzberg into the Ache river. It's clear enough to drink from, I think as I preserve its sound[1] on my recorder. Aside from the splashing of the stream, I hear not a single noise up here.

Haus Kederlehen – a farm as old as the hills, first mentioned in documents from the fourteenth century – is now a guesthouse. You can rent rooms and spend your holidays here, but it's no stretch for me to imagine chickens, pigs and cows and a cockerel crowing on the dung heap. Until the early 1940s,

Josef and Elisabeth Lankes ran a farm here with their four children – Hans, Josef, Rosa and Elfriede. The two sons Hans and Josef helped with the hard work. When the Second World War began, they were called up to the military. That made life difficult for the family, now lacking the labour to make their living. It spelled the end of the Lankes' marriage; they divorced and the farm was put up for sale.

Their daughter Elfriede was very young at the time and stayed with her mother. Little is known about her life. Her older sister, fourteen in 1940, had to leave school and take a job on the domestic staff of the Reich Chancellery's Berchtesgaden branch office. Rosa Lankes was the girl who would one day be my mother.

The Little Reich Chancellery

After my tour of Kederlehen, I get back behind the wheel and drive down to the valley, past Berchtesgaden station and a few kilometres northwest to Bischofswiesen-Stanggaß, number 26 Urbanweg. Here – directly below the Watzmann massif – is the building that once housed the Reich Chancellery branch office. I stop in the car park outside, get out of the car and take photos to help me with my writing later on. I'm amazed to see the entire complex survived the war completely unharmed and still looks exactly like in old photos. Only the swastika clutched in the talons of the Reich eagle has been chiselled off.

Berchtesgadener Land was always a well-known part of Germany. But it first came to fame – albeit in an unbearably sad way – with the rise of Adolf Hitler. The building known as the Little Reich Chancellery became Hitler's second seat of government in the 1930s, for when he was staying at the Berghof, his house on Obersalzberg. Foreign guests or the Wehrmacht High Command often stayed here, in town for political gatherings or meetings. My mother Rosa never told me whether she ever met Hitler. She did talk about waving little flags from the side of the road with other children and young people when motorcades and parades passed by.

I walk slowly around the house a few times, taking photos and imagining Rosa cycling up in the morning, tidying the guests' rooms, helping in the kitchen and watering the geraniums in the chancellor's house. Outside the building is a large sign that reads: 'Former Reich Chancellery from 1936 to 1945 – US Headquarters from 1945 to 1996 – private homes since 2001'.

There's not a soul to be seen. But the building is on public land and I've no idea why I'm creeping around like this, constantly looking over my shoulder for fear of getting told off. My imagination runs wild: Hitler, SS, Nazis. Nothing happens, and I drive the five minutes back to Berchtesgaden with my pictures. In the Goldener Bär inn, I order a Bavarian bread board with cured ham, radish, *obatzda* cheese spread and dripping. Berchtesgaden.

The Berghof

The mountain air ensures I get a good night's sleep and when I look out of the window early next morning, the Watzmann is hidden behind a wall of mist. I upload yesterday's photos and sound recordings to my laptop, pack a few things and set out for the Obersalzberg. That's the mountain where Hitler's Berghof home used to be.

It's September; the worst of the summer heat is over and the temperature is a pleasant 16 degrees. Unlike Kederlehen and the Little Reich Chancellery, there's a lot going on here.

The Berghof building was almost entirely destroyed shortly before the end of the war, but the state of Bavaria opened the Obersalzberg documentation centre on the site of the former guesthouse in 1999, examining Germany's Nazi past. Whole busloads of tourists come here. Of course, they want to find out about the Nazi dictatorship. But there's also a tiny bit of a thrill. So this was where the man lived who set the whole world on fire.

Hitler had discovered Berchtesgaden and Obersalzberg in 1928, renting Haus Wachenfeld at a thousand metres above sea level. In 1933 he bought the house, renamed it 'the Berghof' and had it rebuilt as an official residence. As a result, other Nazi politicians built homes inside the restricted area around the Berghof, plus a guesthouse, an SS barracks and a farm with a large greenhouse. The underground bunker system has survived and is now a popular tourist destination.

Hitler spent several months a year on Obersalzberg, conducting government business from Berchtesgaden. He received numerous state guests at the Berghof or in the Reich Chancellery, including Chamberlain, Mussolini and the Duke of Windsor, the former King Edward VIII, head of the United Kingdom and emperor of India for a year, at least, before his 1936 abdication. The photo and film footage from that time is well known, showing Hitler with statesmen or surrounded by his vassals. The colour films recorded privately by Eva Braun present a banal idyllic lifestyle. On 25 April 1945, the Royal Air Force put an end to Hitler's summer retreats in Bavaria with a few hundred Lancaster bombers, reducing the entire complex to rubble. Berchtesgaden in the valley below, however, remained almost completely intact.

I decide against taking photos up here. All that Hitler tourism/ fetishism crap makes me sick. Instead, I drive back down to the valley and onto the Alpine road to Untersberg.

Headquarters US Army 1945

The war ended on 8 May 1945 with Germany's unconditional surrender. Germans often refer to that date as the 'Zero Hour'. Rosa, by that time 19 years old, went on working at the Little Reich Chancellery, but her new employer was the US Army. She was a pretty girl. Her green eyes and dark curly hair made her look almost Mediterranean, thanks to her father Josef's Italian roots. Whether she saw the Americans as occupiers or saviours, I can't say.

What I do know is that she met a GI, Elmar, and that had consequences – she got pregnant. Her first child, Marietta, was born in Bischofswiesen on 23 July 1946. Elmar went back to the USA before the birth; my mother never saw him again. And she never talked about him either. At the age of 20, Rosa was solely responsible for her child. She left the army head-quarters and found a new job as a chambermaid at the Gasthaus zum Untersberg.

Gasthaus zum Untersberg

From Obersalzberg, I follow the course of the Ache until I reach Marktschellenberg a few minutes later. Where the river slows at a weir, I turn left and find myself outside Gadringers Gasthaus zum Untersberg.

The building is vacant these days, but it doesn't look neglected to me. Everything's still in working order, as if people had only just moved out. Walking around the building, I find myself in the former dance garden, a large mural on one wall illustrating how it once was. Beneath the heading 'Untersberg Inn – Rooms – Own Butchery – Owner A. Gadringer', a monk, a few men and women and three children are sitting at a table, holding beer mugs and having what looks like a lively conversation. A zither player is making music. Sausages, chickens and pretzels hang from strings above the heads of the jolly group, and the Untersberg is visible in the background. You can't get much more Bavarian than this.

I take a seat on a wooden bench and imagine what it must have looked like on a weekend in 1946 when Rosa was working here as a chambermaid: GIs' jeeps parked halfway onto the pavement outside. The inside and the garden have space for three hundred or more people. A small local orchestra in traditional dress plays Bavarian music, taking turns with a swing band that covers Glenn Miller and Benny Goodman songs. Bavarian mingles with American vocabulary – dirndls and lederhosen with uniforms. Waitresses bustle into the garden, laden with beer mugs. The soldiers whose marching orders brought them to Berchtesgaden certainly got lucky: bingo!

To entertain the troops, the owners booked not only bands but also other artists. One young man who appeared here with a theatre troupe in 1947 caught Rosa's eye. His name was Hans-Joachim – and he was to be my father.

Hans-Joachim Bartos – born in 1923 – had ended up in show business during the chaotic post-war years. Something about the stage had always fascinated him. He'd had piano lessons in his youth and worked as an extra at the Leipzig State Opera. An old passport describes his appearance in brief – Face shape: oval. Eye colour: blue. Height: 1.78 metres. Distinguishing features: none. He wore his brown hair cut short and combed back out of his face. Hans-Joachim was slim and good-looking.

Like most young men of his generation, he had seen his plans for the future destroyed by the war. He was drafted into military service on the Eastern Front in 1943 and captured by the Russians. My father never spoke about the war or his time in the prisoner-of-war camp. He was released in 1945 at the age of 22. Hans-Joachim was free but he remained marked by the experience for the rest of his life, never really recovering from the hardships of war and life in the camp. Much more than the frostbite on his feet and the severe malaria attacks he struggled with for years after the war, he suffered the psychological effects of his time as a soldier and a prisoner. These days, we'd call it post-traumatic stress disorder. Back then, it was a collective condition.

To earn his living, Hans-Joachim joined a small theatre troupe. It was in 1947, at a performance in the Gasthaus zum Untersberg in Marktschellenberg, that he met Rosa Lankes. I don't know a great deal about their first meeting. In the few photos from that time, they look like they were made for each other. They clearly fell in love and became a couple. I can well imagine Hans-Joachim persuading pretty Rosa to join his artists' ensemble.

And so, Rosa and Hans-Joachim were not only an item in their private life, they also worked together on the stage. The two of them went on to their next engagement in Munich in January 1948. That was the first time Rosa ever left the Berchtesgaden region. On 28 February 1948, Rosa and Hans-Joachim married in Leipzig, where his parents, Martha and Alfred Bartos, lived.

The Bartos family had emigrated from Hungary to Poland and then to Germany in the late nineteenth century. The Hungarian name was originally pronounced 'Bartosh' but soon became Germanized as 'Bartos'. Alfred Bartos worked as a train driver for the German Army during the First World War and was taken on by the Reichsbahn railway company after 1918. In the 1920s, he married Martha from the Riesengebirge moun-tain region, now part of Poland and the Czech Republic, and their only child, Hans-Joachim, was born in 1923. The family moved to Leipzig in 1930. During the Second World War, both father and son were drafted into the Wehrmacht.

I only ever saw my grandfather smartly dressed: suit, shirt and tie, fur-collared coat. He wasn't a great conversationalist, which didn't stop him from railing at the television later in life – especially with Social Democrat politicians, who he considered communists. My grandmother, Martha, was a few years younger than Alfred and much more alert. She loved getting dressed up and she made sure they took part in public life and didn't get stuck at home. She took piano lessons and signed her son, Hans-Joachim, up with her teacher.

But back to the newlyweds Rosa and Hans-Joachim. After their wedding in Leipzig, they had more variety troupe jobs in Munich from July to November 1948, and from 1949 the young family lived there full time. I didn't discover this episode in my parents' lives until long after their death, looking through their papers. Why on earth did they never tell us about it?

In 1951 Rosa and Hans-Joachim gave up their stage jobs and returned to Rosa's origins near Berchtesgaden. Hans-Joachim's parents also moved there, wanting to stick together. The whole Bartos family found a new home in Marktschellenberg. Hans-Joachim's father, however, at 53, couldn't find work. But needs must, and the family soon got hold of a machine for making woollen clothing, and set up a company. The Schellenberg Sock Knitting Company advertised 'production, mail order and sale of socks of all kinds'. The knitting was done at home in Marktschellenberg and they then opened a shop in Berchtesgaden. I soon put in an appearance to boost the team. I was born in the company headquarters at number 33 Kirchgasse in Marktschellenberg, on 31 May 1952. About time too!

I have no idea how long I've been sitting in the garden at Gasthaus Untersberg – probably several hours. The next stop on my journey into the past is Kirchgasse. Only a few metres up the hill, I spot the house of my birth.

It was easy enough to find a name for the new family member – according to legend, the Emperor Charlemagne and his retinue are waiting in a magnificent cave inside the Untersberg. His name in German is Karl, so that was to be mine too. My grand-parents preferred the name Heinz, and so my parents reached a compromise – can you guess? Karlheinz.

Auf Wiedersehen Berchtesgaden

I spend a few more days in Berchtesgaden, roaming around the town, looking at the churches, listening to the Franciscan monks singing in the monastery and reading the names on the stones in the graveyard. And I head back to the place where I bought one of my first records, at some point in the sixties – 'Get Off of My Cloud' by the Rolling Stones.

Of course, I don't miss the chance to go to the Königssee lake for the first time in years, to listen to the famous echo. No photos of the echo, please, the guide on the tour boat jokes – and then he grabs his flugelhorn and lets rip. Between notes, I really do hear an echo with a long but quiet feedback. As always, I've got my sound recorder with me. Being a real whizz with gadgets, I stupidly forget to switch it out of standby mode to record. So there's nothing to take home with me, but I did hear it – which means that moment will remain unique and unrepeatable.

On my last evening, I catch a concert by an authentic Bavarian brass band right next to the Goldener Bär. Then I head back through Berchtesgaden and Marktschellenberg to Salzburg, where I take the next flight to Hamburg – with the start of my autobiography in my head and an ambivalent *Heimat* feeling in my heart.

Düsseldorf on the Rhine

My parents' post-war knitting business never really picked up. People didn't want to buy new socks, it seems. Despite my tantrums in protest, my family decided to move up to North-Rhine Westphalia. It would be easier to earn a living in booming Düsseldorf, so we set off with all our belongings in November 1954. Our first flat was in Bilk, a working-class neighbourhood near the Rhine, on the third floor of a building on the corner of Friedenstrasse and Bilker Allee. But three rooms were not enough space for six people in the long run. So we breathed a sigh of relief when my grandparents moved into a flat of their own.

From the ages of 3 to 17, I grew up in Unterbilk. The area was the centre of my childhood, with the nearby streets making up my world. I wouldn't go as far as calling our neighbourhood picturesque, but it was certainly lively. The old buildings with their backyards, the many bomb sites and building sites. German corner pubs with bullseye panes in the windows or once-white net curtains, the cobbles that shone in the rain, the advertising columns with their commercials. Sometimes I'd even hear the sound of a barrel organ, pushed through the streets by an organ grinder.

Our building was new and boasted all the mod cons of the fifties. There were now four of us sharing sixty or seventy square metres. A bathroom and central heating were major improvements on our old home in Marktschellenberg.

In the beginning, my young parents tried to continue making a living with the knitting machine, but they eventually gave up. It didn't work at all without a shop. But it was the time of Germany's 'economic miracle' and it wasn't hard for my father to find a job. And my mother soon got sewing commissions from a tailor's shop, which she could do at home. She liked her work. I listened happily as she sang her Berchtesgaden songs at the sewing machine.

16

The Rhineland gradually became our home – most of all for me. We began mixing our dialects, saying 'Hello' with the southern 'Grüss Gott' and 'Goodbye' with the northern 'Tschüss'. Even today, my language has a hint of the Rhineland to it – at least, that's how a journalist once described it in an interview.

Unterbilk

I loved roaming the streets of my neighbourhood. Before I started school, I'd often go shopping with my mother. There was a Kaiser's coffee purveyor but supermarkets had not yet sprung up. A large shop on the ground floor of our building drew the crowds with neon lettering: 'Radio & Fernsehen Mende'. But radios and TVs weren't the only things Herr Mende sold. He also had record players, records and kitchen appliances. One very special place was the greengrocers on Bilker Allee. It was impossible to overlook, with displays of fruit and veg that were very generous for the time. It held a particular draw for Marietta and me, because the shopkeeper kept two horses in a stable in the backyard: Iron Bill and Sinai. Marietta was crazy about horses and had permission to take care of them both. She would take them to a nearby field regularly, and was even allowed to ride them.

Towards Kronprinzenstrasse on Bilker Allee, there was a little shop for everyday needs. It sold tobacco, newspapers and drinks, the equivalent of a British newsagents. I can't say how many 10-pfennig surprise bags I bought there during my childhood. One of our favourite pursuits was swapping the content of the bags. But we'd also buy marbles there and cubes of sherbet, which we mixed with spit and slurped out of our palms.

The bicycle shop opposite had pushbikes and washing machines, plus a few special highlights: Kreidler mopeds. What a thrill! We were most infatuated with the 'Florett' model, staring at it over and over. The older boys in the neighbourhood already had similar vehicles. Interestingly enough, they'd give girls a lift on the back seat. Mhmmm! Later, when I had a bike of my own, I tried to spruce it up like their mopeds, with coloured spirals on the brake cables and a foxtail. It didn't have quite the same effect.

The inescapable first day of school, in 1958, left no mark on my memory to speak of. The only proof it ever took place is a photo showing me clutching a huge cone full of sweets, like all children starting school in Germany. But things did change in my life from then on.

How I Met Maximilian in the Education System

The Protestant primary school was co-educational, but boys and girls were taught separately. Our classrooms were full to bursting. All the pupils came from Unterbilk, most of them from modest backgrounds like me. The school was just under ten minutes' walk from home, at least.

I never felt comfortable during lessons. Sometimes I wonder if I was even there in the first place. We had slates to learn reading and writing on – and everything else. Our first teacher was Herr Maas. He was a man with a penchant for tweed; he liked all things British. We also soon made the acquaintance of Maximilian, his rattan cane, about sixty centimetres long. Anyone caught daydreaming, being noisy or impertinent had to stand up and hold out his hands to the teacher – palms down. Then he'd get a few whacks from Maximilian. Other sophisticated educational methods were cheek pinches and ear-pulling. Herr Maas was an expert on all that.

And then there was my first encounter with music as a school subject. Our teacher's vain attempts to get us to read notes would probably make a great comedy sketch. Sadly, none of us boys had the slightest interest in the five lines with the black dots and their funny little flags. What were they for? That first, entirely theoretical approach, divorced from our senses, didn't bring me any closer to music. It went right over my head.

A Happy Family

At home, I shared a room with my sister and we generally got on well. Marietta is six years older than me and took good care of her little brother. She was baptised a Catholic and I'm a Protestant. Religion didn't really play much of a role in our family, but our different confessions meant we ended up at different schools, with Marietta at the Catholic primary school.

That had certain advantages, though – as a Catholic, she had access to the parish library at the Church of Peace. My sister would borrow a new book after morning mass every Sunday and read it to me untiringly. That was how I came across Enid Blyton's Famous Five and the Five Find-Outers. And then of course Karl May's cowboy books: *Winnetou* books 1 to 3, *Old*

Surehand, The Treasure in Silver Lake and so on and so on. I was incredibly impressed by Marietta's reading skills.

Looking back, those days seem like a fairy tale to me. Everything was just the way it should be. In the photo albums from the time, we look like a happy family. And we were.

The World in My Head

When I was given an electric model railway for Christmas in 1961, I was enthralled, like almost every little boy. 'All aboard, doors closing' was my favourite announcement. But my interest in the trains soon faded, eclipsed by the joy of designing the landscape of my model world. The hill without which no tunnel was possible, a lake, the station, the surrounding houses and of course the miniature Elastolin figures that populated the station and the pathways.

These tiny people in all kinds of situations fascinated me. I could use them to set up scenes and tell stories. Then I discovered other figures in my favourite toyshop. The characters from the Karl May novels looked really good, and I soon added Old Shatterhand, Winnetou, Old Surehand and the rest to my collection. There was another category, a set of Prince Valiant figures: knights, knaves and damsels. Then there were soldiers of various armed services and all kinds of tanks, trucks and jeeps from the German Wehrmacht, the Red Army and the US forces.

It wasn't the collecting itself I was most interested in. What really captivated me was a wooden chest with three drawers, in which I built three different landscapes. At the top was the Wild

West, in the middle a desert with Rommel's Africa corps, and at the bottom a great hall with Prince Valiant and several knights of the Round Table. I didn't actually play with the figurines – what I cared most about was having these secret landscapes in the drawers.

Gradually, reading Enid Blyton developed into another, rather specific leisure activity. Like the hero of the Five Find-Outers series, Fatty, I wanted to be a detective. From a theatre hairdresser, I got hold of make-up, a fake moustache, special glue and padding for my cheeks. I also rustled up a whole extra wardrobe of outfits. To make sure I looked really convincing, I even studied a book about make-up artists at the opera. Then I'd go out on the street in my disguise, tail passers-by for a couple of blocks and write copious notes on what they got up to. I'll leave it to my readers' imaginations to picture the scene in detail. But I was absolutely convinced nobody would recognize me.

I had a good life. I pursued whatever projects I was interested in at any given time, and school wasn't overly challenging. As long as my report cards were OK, my parents let me do whatever I liked – all I had to do was get home on time in the evening. It may sound strange but I almost think no one noticed me, really. I slipped through the gaps everywhere – at school and at home with my parents – as if I was invisible. It's not that they didn't love me, but our lives went on as though drawn with a stencil. My parents knew nothing but their work, days off and their annual holiday.

In the summer, we would drive the still relatively empty autobahn down to my mother's old region. From 1960 on, we spent our summers there for several years in a row, on a kind of farm holiday. I may have grown up and been socialized in the Rhineland, but I'll still always feel tied to the Berchtesgadener Land.

My Life Gets a Soundtrack

In retrospect, there was no soundtrack to my childhood up to this point. Or was there? Naturally enough, I perceived a large part of the noises and sounds of my environment via my hearing, as acoustic information, without thinking about it. But when did I start to become consciously aware of sound?

Like in every family, it was my mother who sang me my first songs. That's the way it's always been, and presumably it'll always stay that way. It is part of our human culture all over the world. When I think back to my childhood, the very first thing I hear is my mother Rosa's voice and then . . . what do I hear then?

The bells of the nearby Church of Peace in Bilk – I remember listening even as a little boy as a single bell began chiming slowly. Then a second and a third would join in at different intervals, intermingling, speeding up, intensifying and then sounding out simultaneously in an utterly unpredictable way, only to grow slower after a while and finally fall silent again.

Then there were the trams that passed by regularly, with their jangling, juddering, screeching and rattling. They seemed to travel loudly back and forth along Bilker Allee untiringly.

The girls' choir at the Konkordia School is another musical memory from my childhood. I was impressed by their high-pitched voices, but also the orderly nature of the performance, a communal act. Then there was the organ music during the school church services our class attended every Thursday.

The role of the marksmen's clubs in the Rhineland is not to be underestimated. There are marksmen's festivals a few times a year where visitors shoot at targets, followed by copious celebrating or drowning of sorrows. Before and after that, marching bands like to promenade around town, preferably in the early hours of the morning – playing piccolo, glockenspiel, marching drums, snare drums, bass drums, marching cymbals and bell trees.

Remembering the sound of my childhood, the 'Rheinische Karneval' ('Rhineland Carnival') is another essential ingredient. Local children can't avoid growing into this annual festival with its fixed rituals. This is the so-called 'Fifth Season', ending at the start of Lent, the über-party, an affirmation of life and a one-of-a-kind mega-ritual of its own. But it's also an effortless violation of the boundaries of everyday life and good taste. Sexual freedom and unpunished promiscuity are all part of the package. For us children, what counted more was the fun of dressing up. I would usually turn myself into an Apache with the requisite bow and arrow, wig and make-up. In this get-up, we'd play in the park, attacking lonely cowboys and the Confederate Army. Once our work was done, we'd go and watch the 'Rosenmontag' ('Rose Monday') parade in town. In my memory, the marksmen's bands played the jolly tune 'Freut euch des Lebens' uninterrupted and in all variations. But in truth, other songs are also sung and played at 'Karneval' – there's no escaping them when a whole city is singing along. Even as a child, you automatically learn the words to numerous 'Karneval' songs without even realizing.

Radio and Television

The medium of those days was still radio, to start with. But I didn't regard the radio as a transmitter of music or news; it just stood on the sideboard and made sound, somehow. What the content of that sound was didn't really seem important to me. It was more a question of 'radio on – radio off'. The device didn't make much of an impression on me.

Then came the day when my father surprised us with a black-and-white television set. American series flickered across the screen: *Lassie*, *Fury* and *77 Sunset Strip*. Or the German children's programmes, crime shows and kitschy films: *Jim Knopf und Lukas der Lokomotivführer*, *Samstagnachmittag zu Hause*, *Stahlnetz*, *Ein Platz für Tiere*, *Die Mädels vom Immenhof* and the ever-popular *Sissi* trilogy.

From 1961, the sports programme *Sportschau* was essential viewing, first on Sundays and, after the Bundesliga began, on Saturdays too. That was on the first German public channel, ARD, but the second channel, ZDF, followed two years later with *Das aktuelle Sportstudio* on Saturday evenings – classic weekend entertainment to this day. I find it remarkable, incidentally, that the show's title tune – 'Up to Date' played by Max Greger and his orchestra – is still in use today and has become part of Germany's musical canon.

Then at the age of 11 or 12, I experienced the advent of the big Saturday evening entertainment shows. I'd usually appear in the living room freshly bathed and combed in my pyjamas, and we'd all gather in front of the TV to watch these almost sacred shows: *Einer wird gewinnen*, *Vergißmeinnicht* and *Der goldene Schuss*.

Alongside entertainment, the new medium brought something else into our home: adverts. These brief messages – with their jingles and slogans for product brands – seem to have etched themselves onto my memory for all time; I can still call them up today. If I read one of the old catchphrases, the matching tune immediately pops into my mind – the cheerful strings of the HB cigarettes ad, something more sophisticated for Underberg bitters and the saccharine vocals praising Bärenmarke tinned milk.

Just like in the USA, Germany's advertising industry grew to huge proportions, fired on more and more by the 'economic miracle'. The 1960s economy was booming. West Germany had full employment and all the families in our building on Friedenstrasse could afford a car, telephone, washing machine and television. The Eberstallers on the second floor had two sons, Martin and Michael. In 1963, Martin and I were both 11. As we were playing, he asked as an aside: 'Want to hear something really great? Mika's got a record collection – he's crazy about this new music.' His brother Michael was a couple of years older than us and obviously a music fan. To be precise, he loved rock'n'roll. 'There's this singer from America,' Martin told me, 'he's brilliant – his name's Elvis Presley.' 'Never heard of him,' I admitted. Martin went right ahead and put a 7-inch single on the record player, then lowered the needle. We listened to Elvis's 'Jailhouse Rock', 'Blue Suede Shoes' and 'Return to Sender' and also 'Ready Teddy' by Cliff Richard – 'Oh, that's this other one,' Martin explained. He only played the beginning of each record, perhaps a minute, before he put the next one on. He was an absolute beginner of a DJ. And after this brief acoustic interruption, we went back to our toys and watched the neighbourhood lads out of the window as they tuned their Kreidler mopeds. My mother called them 'half-pints', the German equivalent to hooligans.

And the music? Yes, I did think the whole rock'n'roll thing was quite interesting. Perhaps partly because Martin's big brother was such a fan? Who knows? But it didn't get through to me. It seems my receptors weren't yet tuned in to it.

NOTES

1. I use the term 'sound' in the sense of the Canadian composer and scholar R. Murray Schafer's expanded concept of the soundscape, which includes the entire range of voices, tones, language and noises in an environment or landscape.

2
A CHORD CHANGES MY LIFE

Brits at the Bartos Abode. The Music of the Sixties Speaks to Me. Help! A Winter in Berchtesgaden. Real Life? How Do I Become a Band? Bedroom Photo Session. Franz, Klaus and Me. Band Seeks Guitarist and Drummer. Beat Music in Düsseldorf. In the Psychedelic Volkswagen Van. Drum Lessons with Otto Weinandi. My First Love. The Jokers. Leaving Home.

Brits at the Bartos Abode

1964 got off to a turbulent start for us when Marietta got lost on a trip to the forest. Having wandered hopelessly until darkness fell, she saw a light in the distance, walked towards it and came to an army barracks housing British forces. As luck would have it, Lance Corporal Peter Hornshaw was on duty that night. Opening the door and finding Marietta in tears outside, he fell in love at first sight, as he told me much later.

We'd been very worried all evening, so we were all the more relieved when the doorbell rang at around eleven and two British soldiers, looking rather impressive in their military police uniforms, delivered my sister unharmed. Peter and Terry – as they introduced themselves – got the best tea Rosa had in the house, and every one of us thanked them at least a thousand times over in halting English: 'Thank you, thank you very much.'

27

Over the next few weeks Pete, as everyone called him, came by suspiciously often to ask how Marietta was doing. I knew what was up right away. Or I had an inkling, at least . . . And the two of them did indeed get closer as the weeks passed. Rosa and Hans-Joachim were relaxed about it – they had no objections to warm-hearted Pete. He also made a great effort to get me on his side, Marietta's little brother, and he soon managed it. When he took me for a ride in a British military police Land Rover, I was well and truly won over.

Only 21, Pete brought a welcome breath of northern English fresh air into our family. I don't know how often he came over for tea or supper with Terry. Sometimes they would bring along something from the NAAFI supermarket, flowers for my mother, a bottle of whiskey for my father or a bar of Cadbury's chocolate for me. They were both great lads – I really liked the way they spoke English and their sense of humour.

Nobody doubted that something serious was building up between Marietta and Pete. But there was something else on the horizon, which would have a fundamental effect on my life and change it forever. Rosa had been talked into joining the Bertelsmann book club by a sales rep who came to the door. He told her she could get cheap books there. Members had to buy at least one product every three months. But as well as books, they also had record players and records. The timing was perfect. A record player seemed like the ideal birthday present for Marietta, along with Cliff Richard's 'Living Doll' and Elvis's 'Return to Sender'. We'll take it! The new Philips device had a cream-coloured case and a turquoise turntable and pick-up arm. It was connected up to our Grundig radio via a cable with two jack plugs. It sounded just right for us. Now Marietta and my mother started ordering music every month from Bertelsmann. We listened to the German singer Ronny's translated versions of American hits 'Hundert Mann und ein Befehl', 'Geisterreiter' and 'Es hängt ein Pferdehalfter an der Wand',[1] Leonard Bernstein's *West Side Story*, or Max Greger's *Kellerparty*, a whole album of swing music to accompany 'sophisticated drinks and dancing' at basement bashes. But that's not the big change I'm referring to. That took a bit longer – but when it came it hit me unexpectedly, full on.

The Music of the Sixties Speaks to Me

On one of his next visits, Pete brought along a new record. He put it on the turntable with the words 'Listen to the new Beatles album', lowered the needle to the groove on the black vinyl and turned to face us in anticipation. It started with a slight crackle, but then it kicked in: Clang! – 'It's been a hard day's night, and I've been working like a dog . . .' We listened to the songs on the A-side. Pete sang along here and there. Marietta moved very oddly to the music, I thought. The three of us kept laughing all the way through. I remember to this day how impressed I was by the music's lightness. I was especially into the faster, upbeat numbers. The drums beat urgently, the guitars sounded incredibly fresh, and the vocals – loud and confident – seemed to be addressed directly at me. I couldn't yet speak English so the words were pure sound to me, but I understood the expression in the voices.

We turned the record over and went on without stopping until the last track, 'I'll Be Back', then flipped it a second time and listened to it all again – over and over. I'd never heard anything like it, it was incredible!

I had no idea who these people were who called themselves the Beatles. The album cover didn't help all that much either. Alright, they were English boys with funny haircuts, that much was clear. But I didn't find their identity all that important. I simply listened – nothing else. That guy Elvis Presley's music had also interested me in a way. But the Beatles were a whole different ball game – they were a group, a gang, a band. Something inside me had switched to 'receive'. And yet it was only the sound of the music played back from the record. That sound had no story behind it, there was no context for me other than that Pete had brought it along. He wasn't trying to get me into the music, explain it to me or sing its praises and convert me. I think he just didn't want to listen to German songs about cowboys every time he came to visit.

Not long after that, I swiped our music equipment for myself, and the Philips record player and our radio moved into the room Marietta and I shared. Marietta went on working at Foto Geller after she finished her apprenticeship there, so she didn't get home until the evenings, which meant I could listen to music all afternoon. Like most kids did at the time, I bought 7-inch singles with my pocket money and my record collection began to grow and grow.

For many young people of my generation, beat music was a kind of rebellion against their parents or the authorities of post-war society. In our family, though, it never caused any arguments. Although I felt the seismic social and cultural changes of the sixties, I wasn't consciously aware of them. I was young and innocent and amazed by the sensations this new music awoke in me. Marietta liked the Beatles' sound and my mother loved their slow songs. We never fought over what music to listen to. Quite the opposite, in fact – we ordered all sorts of records together from Bertelsmann, including *The Rolling Stones No. 2* (1965) and *Aftermath* (1966). Pete also got hold of other albums by the Liverpool lads for us, probably *Please Please Me* (1963), *With the Beatles* (1963) and *Beatles for Sale* (1964). If there was one moment when I felt music really speaking to me for the first time in my life, it was that equivocal chord from the start of 'A Hard Day's Night'. It was both wake-up call and invitation in one. But for what?

Help!

It must have been 1965 when Pete one day received marching orders for a military operation in northern Africa. We were all upset and didn't know what to do. Marietta was in a state of shock. The precise details of the mission were confidential. I have no idea what went on there, but Pete received an injury to his temple while on duty and was taken to a field hospital. He had the great fortune to survive, and after five long weeks of uncertainty, he was back with us again. He didn't talk much about the mission but it had definitely left its mark on him. Shortly after that he left the army. Pete never wore a uniform again for the rest of his life.

Over the 1965 Christmas season, the Rex cinema at Düsseldorf main station was showing the Beatles' second film: *Help!* – with the ridiculous German title of *Hi-Hi-Hilfe!* I was allowed to go and see it with Marietta and Pete. The movie almost tore me out of my seat. It wasn't the plot – it seemed to be trying too hard to be funny for my taste – it was seeing

31

the actual band members singing and playing their instruments for the first time.

I was hypnotized by the group dynamics of their performance. Before that, I had seen making music as an activity carried out by anonymous professionals, for instance the musicians in a big band for a television show format. All that changed now. The Beatles were four individuals, John, Paul, George and Ringo, who played their music with their own sound. And they did it with a unique attitude – serious and humorous at the same time. After the film, we happened to pass Musik Kunz on Karlstrasse. The instruments in the shop window – guitars, bass guitars, drum kits, microphones, amps – suddenly had a totally different effect on me. Everything suddenly made sense; these inanimate objects had been given a new meaning by the Beatles. They became musical instruments for me – I could almost hear their sound through the glass. It must be amazing to play in a band, I thought. My mind revolved around nothing else now.

Marietta and Pete's wedding was a turning point, as you might expect. My beloved sister packed her things and moved out. But there was one thing she left behind, an early impulse buy – her guitar. 'It was something to do with Elvis Presley,' she explained to me later. For a year or two, the instrument hung decoratively on the wall on what had been her side of the room. After the Beatles film, I saw even this dust-coated guitar in a new light. It was really just a simple dark brown sunburst archtop guitar with f-holes and a white scratchplate. But if I attached a Schaller pick-up, I thought, maybe I could play it through an amp. I took it down from the wall, dusted it off and . . . well, what now? The six strings were all in place, but it sounded awful. How did you tune a guitar? Marietta had no idea so she couldn't help me. My father knew the standard E-A-D-G-B-E tuning from somewhere, but what came after that? I got hold of all the information at Musikhaus Jörgensen on Berliner Allee, the largest music shop in Düsseldorf. The place felt like the promised land – the wind department boasted saxophones, trumpets, trombones, clarinets and flutes. There were countless guitars and bass guitars hanging on the walls or leaning against stands. Drum kits from various makers were on display on the first floor, with organs from Philicorda, Farfisa and Hammond lined up beside them.

For some reason, the sheet music department held a particular magic for me. They had the latest Beatles and Rolling Stones songs in book form. I couldn't yet read notes but the fingering charts for guitar said something to me. That seemed to be one way to do it. Like many German beginners in my generation, I learned the chords from the charts in the two volumes of *Grifftabellen für Schlaggitarre*. I tried my best to get by at home with sheet music, fingering charts and lyrics. After a while I noticed that the songs' structure began to make sense to me, if I followed the lyrics and kept an eye on the chord symbols. The sheet music and my record collection were my first references. I wasn't just listening to music – I was playing along as best I could and trying to use the fingering charts to understand how music is made. As I did so, I soon realized that I could sing not only the standard tune over the chords of a certain song, but also another melody that I came up with myself. Alongside my autodidactic practice sessions, I went back to Musikhaus Jörgensen regularly, simply to spend time in the surroundings, looking at instruments, having a go at playing them and flicking through the sheet music.

I wasn't conscious I was going through puberty, of course, but presumably I reacted so strongly to music because I was in that phase when my hormones were turning my life inside out. Two things happened to me: my view of girls changed, and at the same time music hit me with this never-before-experienced sensuality – and the two went together.

At that time, the brand-new beat music was on the air, literally. Along with the soldiers' broadcasters BFBS and AFN, Radio Luxembourg was the hot station of the minute. Word soon got around that they played the hippest tunes. And there really was a whole lot of great music on the station, including from other bands I'd never heard of before. Sadly, I never got very good reception, but the sound quality was at least good enough to hear parts of the songs in between the atmospheric disturbance: 'Pretty Woman', 'House of the Rising Sun', 'Stop! In the Name of Love', 'Wooly Bully', 'Mr Tambourine Man', 'Like a Rolling Stone', 'Help Me Rhonda', 'I Got You Babe', 'Hang On Sloopy', 'Tired of Waiting for You' and the Stones' 'The Last Time' and 'Satisfaction' – what a sound! And of course the Beatles' latest hits: 'I Feel Fine', 'Eight Days a Week', 'Rock and Roll Music', 'Ticket to Ride' and 'Long Tall Sally' . . . At some point the television stations could no longer ignore the fact that beat music was dominating the German hit parade more and more, and on 25 September 1965 the television show *Beat-Club* first aired on Radio Bremen (confusingly enough, a public TV broadcaster).

The Beatles' *Rubber Soul* came out in early December 1965, plus the double A-side single 'Day Tripper'/'We Can Work It Out'. The riff on 'Day Tripper' seemed to me like the epitome of the whole new music thing, a man-made acoustic miracle.

What I heard was new, raw and emotional, but it also wondrously followed certain rules and principles – which I didn't yet understand, but I wanted to learn all about.

Music very swiftly became the centre of my life. And another thing became clear: I didn't want just to listen to music, I wanted to make it too. There was absolutely no alternative. For some reason, I was certain of that from the very beginning.

A Winter in Berchtesgaden

Over Christmas and New Year of 1965/66, my parents and I made another trip to Berchtesgaden in our Ford Taunus 17M, to visit Uncle Sepp and his wife, Liesel, on Hintersee Lake. One evening, I was walking through their snow-covered village in the dark, when I stopped abruptly outside a record shop. They had the new Stones single in the window: 'Get Off of My Cloud'. Not thinking it over for a second, I invested my entire pocket money in the record. The stupid thing was, I couldn't even listen to it, seeing as Uncle Sepp didn't have a record player. It didn't matter though. It was the Rolling Stones and those guys would hardly bring out anything second-class after 'Satisfaction'. Every time I bought a new record and made it my own, I was overcome by a very special feeling – like an upload to my system. I remember us sitting in Uncle Sepp and Auntie Liesel's kitchen that evening, around a huge, tiled stove. Sepp played the zither and sang Bavarian folk music with my mother. I followed the scene with excited fascination. I'll never forget that wonderful unrepeatable moment, the enthusiastic way they looked at each other as they sang and laughed, and then hugged once the last note was played, and Rosa cried tears of joy. Of course, it wasn't the same music as the Beatles or the Rolling Stones, but I was very touched by the devotion with which they played and sang.

Real Life?

I was due to leave school in March 1966. Long before I finished, it had been decided that I'd do an apprenticeship as a telecommunications engineer and get a lifelong job with the post office. My grandfather Alfred, the former train driver, had been the driving force behind this idea. I can still hear him to this day: 'A secure income and a secure pension.' I didn't have an alternative suggestion to my parents' and grandparents' plan. Music set the tone of my everyday life, but even if I'd thought as far as becoming a professional musician, I had no model to follow for how to get there.

I wasn't really aware that I was at the beginning of a career track that would determine the rest of my life. I was far too busy thinking about music. That may sound overconfident or even arrogant, but it was precisely as simple as that: I wanted to get familiar with music, understand what I was hearing and at the same time try to play a few matching notes on the guitar. I would sing the melodies and translate the chord symbols into guitar fingering. At that point, E minor, G major, A major and A minor were just random chords that happened to have those names. I didn't know how they were related to each other, what functions they had. How was I to know a thing like that?

How Do I Become a Band?

One day, we talked about the new beat music in class. Our teacher, Herr Maas, asked us what was so special about the music and why we liked listening to it so much. I wish I could experience that situation all over again – it would definitely make a good example of how difficult it is to talk about music. I made a real mess of it. In any case, it ended with me reciting a verse from the Who's 'My Generation' like a poem: 'People try to put us down' – as the famous first line goes, and my classmate Achim piped up spontaneously with 'Talking 'bout my generation'. Achim clearly shared my taste, had the same blood group and knew what was going down. He added something like: 'It's our own music.' We left out the line 'Hope I die before I get old' . . .

After school that day, I walked home with Achim. We became friends, even something like accomplices, and from then on we started talking to each other about pop music. Achim was a fan of the Who. He liked their bassist John Entwistle. Or rather, he liked his role in the band. And now he wanted to be a bassist too.

'I'm saving up for a Framus bass,' he told me, fired with enthusiasm. 'My parents might give me some extra money and then I could afford a bass for my next birthday.'

Achim's chances looked good. His father was a music lover who let a skiffle band rehearse in his garage, and we were allowed to listen in. They played Dixieland jazz like 'Alexander's Ragtime Band' – a great tune. The lads were amazing! Their music was loud and exciting. I was most interested in the banjo and the washboard. And that feeling of a group interaction made the leap over to me once again. The musicians' body language. I wanted to experience it at first hand. Playing in a band and making music with other people was my dream.

Bedroom Photo Session

At school and in the neighbourhood, I asked around to see if anyone wanted to start a band. Heiko from school told me he liked the idea. And Karl, who lived on the first floor of our building with his parents, wanted to join in as well. A guitarist, Jürgen, lived a couple of streets away and also showed an interest. He was much better at guitar than me, and explained he was taking lessons from a professional musician.

As a precautionary measure before we'd even met up for a single practice, I arranged for a photo session in my bedroom with my sister as photographer. It had to be done – bands always needed photos. Marietta gave us instructions and we posed for her camera. The photos from that first session reveal how creatively I had pasted pictures of musicians and bands all over my walls, mainly the Stones in all sorts of variations. But you can also spot Donovan, a certain Barry McGuire and the Kinks. After that first 'promo shoot' we were still at a loss for a good band name. I hope it wasn't me who came up with 'The Hotbacks'. We definitely weren't thinking of sexy vertebrae – more something like hot guys. I'm afraid what sounds these days like irony was meant absolutely seriously back then.

As well as a band name, our line-up needed a drummer. That was a law of nature; every band had a drummer. So I begged and pleaded with my parents until they gave in and bought me a drum kit. I had already had a look around and discovered an affordable

Teka kit in the window of Musik Kunz. I believe Teka was short for Theo Kunz, an own-brand product. My first set was made up of bass drum, tom-tom, snare drum, hi-hat and two cymbals. In turquoise. For obvious reasons, I wasn't allowed to practise in my room, so I put cushions on the drums, sat down on the stool and whacked the cushions, producing clouds of dust. But I couldn't decide once and for all whether to be the Hotbacks' drummer, so I kept practising the guitar and learning the lyrics to our songs.

For some reason, the original line-up broke up due to artistic differences and we regrouped before our first rehearsal: Karlheinz Bartos – now on vocals and rhythm guitar; Adolf Krebs – lead guitar; Achim Bauer – bass guitar. We couldn't find a replacement drummer, so we practised without drums in the coal cellar of the building where Adolf lived. Sometimes Achim would come and visit me with his Framus bass, which he really had been given by his parents. The two of us would go through a few songs until my mother, Rosa, knocked on the door and asked: 'Who'd like a tomato sandwich?'

I spent every free moment practising the guitar and drums. And I also enjoyed meeting up with the boys from the band. All I wanted was to play the songs I heard on the radio or had on my records.

Franz, Klaus and Me

On 1 April 1966, my apprenticeship as a telecommunications engineer began in the training department of Telephone Exchange 2 on Fürstenwall. Over the three and a half years of the apprenticeship, I was to go through various sections, such as the devices, soldering, telecommunication and substation workshops, and also learn the basics of electrical engineering and circuit technology – or at least that was what was on the syllabus. It started off with nine months of metalworking. Filing, turning, sawing and drilling fittings, or something like that. At the end of the day, my apprenticeship was very like school: about twenty boys in blue work suits – each at his workbench – fiddling around at their fittings and getting up to all sort of nonsense on the side. To be honest, filing away at a piece of metal just didn't suit me – I have two left hands. It was clear I'd ended up in completely the wrong job. But I had no idea how to get out of the whole thing. My only consolation was that I'd return to my real life at 4:30 every day and start making music.

Thankfully, that schizophrenic lifestyle only lasted a couple of weeks. One morning, someone from the director's office showed up in our workshop and asked whether any of us played a musical instrument. They were assembling a band from the ranks of the apprentices to perform at a ceremony of some kind. I immediately reported to the director. It looked like I was the only apprentice in my year who could play an instrument, or at least claimed he could. There were also Franz-Joseph Krähhahn and Klaus Rybinski from the second year, already waiting in the office. I looked at the two of them and thought: This might work out. When I heard they both played guitar I heard myself saying, in a flight of megalomania: 'I'm a drummer.' How on earth did I come to say such a thing? But I'd be more useful on the drums than at the workbench, that much I knew.

The director fancied himself something of an impresario, beaming from ear to ear. And we three lads arranged to meet the very next day to rehearse. We were actually released from our normal duties – from then on, our only task was to work on the programme for the works party. The next morning, I transported my drum kit to the exchange, set it up in an empty room we'd been allocated for our rehearsals, and waited for my bandmates. They soon showed up with their instruments and amps.

Klaus was friendly and modest, and he was absolutely sure of himself in all things music-related. As we soon discovered, he had the most developed musical skills out of the three of us. He played all kinds of chords on his Höfner electric guitar that I didn't even know existed. Then he suggested a couple of songs from his extensive repertoire, which we practised. Franz went on lead vocals. I remember him singing us David Garrick's saccharine 'Dear Mrs. Applebee', which had just got into the German charts, playing along on his electric guitar. A workmate who'd already finished his apprenticeship would join us occasionally on clarinet. At our first gig, he played a few tunes like 'Petite Fleur' from Acker Bilk's repertoire.

And then? It all went well – the works party was a complete success and we soon became the showpiece band of Telephone Exchange 2. From that point on, everything was fine. We would practise several times a week during work hours, as part of the youth support programme, and we pretty much got a free ride out of it.

It wasn't long before we had a set we could perform for longer than an hour, including songs like 'I Saw Her Standing There', 'Then I Kissed Her', 'Black Is Black', 'San Francisco' and instrumentals like 'Apache'. Klaus, Franz and I took a purely functional approach to our music. We never talked about the bands whose songs we covered, or about the music or what the lyrics meant. They were simply popular tunes, songs or numbers we liked and were able to play in our line-up. For us, the Shadows went with the Beatles, Herman's Hermits went with the Kinks and the Beach Boys went with the one-hit-wonders Los Bravos. Just like in the hit parade. We were so naive we couldn't even tell the difference between the musicians' attitudes or their lyrics. I didn't have the faintest idea what 'Drive My Car', 'Day Tripper' or 'Norwegian Wood' were about.

We had no ambitions to write our own music. That was a different dimension. All we wanted was to cover the latest hits well. And exactly that was a whole lot of fun! Our first gig outside of the telephone exchange soon came along – we played at a dance on Bilker Strasse in the old town centre, and we even got paid a real fee, no matter how modest it was.

Band Seeks Guitarist and Drummer

It must have been one day in 1967 when Franz read out a small ad in Düsseldorf's largest local paper, the *Rheinische Post*: 'The Anthonies' String Group seeks guitarist – who sings – and drummer.' It sounded interesting. Franz made the contact, played them two songs – 'San Francisco' and 'Then I Kissed Her' – and got the job. Not long after that he brought me into the band, and the two of us were soon regularly taking the bus to our rehearsals in the Düsseldorf suburb of Itter.

Günther Hilgers was a pretty wily fox with well-honed business instincts, which made him predestined for his job as band leader. Günther played a Fender Jaguar, owned an Echolette vocal amp and made a very professional impression in his dark green velvet jacket, like he'd jumped straight out of the movie

Blow-Up. The dark timbre of his voice sounded pleasant and mixed well with Franz's lightness. Their harmonies on 'Needles and Pins' were not bad at all. The other band member was Jörg 'James' Hünsche, who played a Fender jazz bass. He was the only one of us with a proper Beatles haircut. Günther had set up a rehearsal room in his father's 'hobby cellar'. It was a large space, clean and warm, and we could practise as if under live conditions with the set-up down there.

On 1 June 1967, the Beatles released *Sgt. Pepper's Lonely Hearts Club Band* and turned everything on its head. I was totally enthusiastic about this great music – although at the age of 15, I couldn't yet grasp the album's psychedelic elements. Even the meaning of 'Tomorrow Never Knows' on their last record had flown way over my head, like the wondrous tape loops on the track. The drugs in our world weren't marijuana, hashish or LSD, they were a few beers or whiskey and Coke at most. We tried out a couple of the songs. 'With a Little Help from My Friends', 'When I'm Sixty-Four' and 'Lovely Rita' stayed in our repertoire for a while. At that point, I was practising in parallel with the telephone exchange band (FA2-Band), the Anthonies' String Group and the Hotbacks.

Beat Music in Düsseldorf

A premiere for the Hotbacks: we played our first gig on 10 October 1967 at the Jugend-Tanzcafé, a dance venue for teens. In our new line-up I was the lead singer, strummed at my Höfner guitar and instantly sang myself hoarse. But Adolf on lead guitar did a decent job and Achim performed a great John Entwistle impersonation on his Framus bass and supported me with his vocals on the choruses. A guest drummer completed the band. People seemed to like our show and we were booked then and there for 14 November. I'd rather not imagine what our music sounded like. Thankfully, there's no sound to go with the photos taken that evening.

By the second half of the sixties, beat music had become firmly entrenched in the Düsseldorf scene and various live clubs were set up. Bands sprang up like mushrooms. One local popular group at the time was definitely Spirits of Sound, with Michael Rother on lead guitar, who later moved on to Neu!, Harmonia and a solo career. The line-up also included Wölfi Riechmann and the legendary Houschäng Nejadepour, the son of a Persian carpet merchant. The man behind the Ludwig drum kit for a while was Wolfgang Flür.

I gradually began expanding my radius and listening to a lot of bands – if I could afford the entrance fee. British bands played every evening in the Liverpool Club, such as Casey Jones and the Governors, who were touring Germany with their hits 'Jack the Ripper' and 'Don't Ha Ha'. In comparison to the German bands, they sounded tough as nails and incredibly loud. Their hard-hammered rhythm had a mechanical quality to it. I also saw Houschäng's new band The Smash at Studio B. The crazy Persian played 'Jeff's Boogie' by the Jeff Beck Group and Cream's 'Strange Brew' and was a virtuoso guitarist. I was only a couple of metres away from him and I couldn't believe my ears. He played right in front of a Marshall tower, transforming the whole place into a sounding box for his guitar riffs.

Düsseldorf's music scene was pretty exceptional at the time. There was something happening all over the city . . .

In the Psychedelic Volkswagen Van

Things were moving along nicely with the Anthonies' String Group as well. We got our first gigs and I started saving up for a professional drum kit. I soon took my Teka set back to Theo Kunz's shop as part-payment and ordered the original 1964 Ludwig kit, in black oyster pearl finish with Zildjian cymbals. I even had enough money for cases from Premier. My new instrument sounded incredible and its cult status was unquestionable. I couldn't imagine a better drum kit. It made me feel like I'd moved up to a different league.

Günther worked hard as manager of the Anthonies' String Group. We took part in the *Chance 67* beat competition at Stadthalle Neuss and even made second place. Then in 1968 things really kicked off. We were performing almost every weekend. Günther had bought a second-hand Volkswagen 'Bulli' van for the purpose, which was painted just as you might expect of the flower power era. We built up our repertoire and got better at playing it. Seeing as we played in British Army barracks, we needed a good command of British chart hits or we'd have been laughed – or booed – off the stage.

Incidentally, I was in the third year of my apprenticeship, but thanks to the FA2-Band I was more or less constantly busy making music. Franz, Klaus and I could get away with anything at work. While our colleagues followed the syllabus, we performed at qualification ceremonies for apprentices and foremen or festivities on the director level. The Hotbacks had gently drifted into inactivity but I was still practising the guitar like crazy.

It was around my 16th birthday that the new Rolling Stones single came out, 'Jumpin' Jack Flash'. I first heard it on the radio – what a revelation! Once I'd rushed out and bought the record, I played it pretty much uninterrupted for several days on end. That was the last straw – there was no going back now. Music gave me purpose and meaning and nothing else brought me further in life, nothing else interested me.

Gradually, an interesting side effect was becoming apparent, something I hadn't thought about before: I was earning money with the Anthonies' String Group. In the sixties there weren't yet any discotheques where DJs played records. On the week-ends, young people went out to municipal halls, youth clubs, bars, pubs or clubs to dance. We were usually booked for Friday, Saturday and Sunday. We'd play for thirty minutes, take a ten-minute break and then carry on that way for five or six hours until one in the morning. Our drinks were free and there'd be a sausage with potato salad or something similarly nutritious at some point in the evening. For a gig at the Rheydt British Army barracks or the News Club, we'd get a hundred marks each – which was a lot of money back then! And not just for me, a 16-year-old apprentice.

I invested my earnings straight back into more instruments: a used Farfisa organ and a second-hand Höfner bass – yes, Paul McCartney's violin bass. That meant I had the basic instruments for a rock band and played guitar, bass, organ and drums.

Everything was going well but I started wondering what would happen after my apprenticeship, when we'd have to leave the protected space of our musical biotope. What then? Would everything collapse? Would life really turn serious? And if so, what would that look like? Would I be locked into a boring

46

eight-hour-a-day job at the telephone exchange, doing something that had nothing to do with my interests? That was a nightmare. What I needed was the opposite. Words like 'professional musician' began to make an appearance in my considerations. In those days, to me that meant musicians who played from sheet music in dance orchestras, combos or big bands. I realized reading notes was the basic prerequisite for changing my path in life – and I had to take that hurdle. At Musik Kunz, buying a pair of drumsticks, I discovered by the by that they also arranged music lessons. I wanted to try it out; thanks to our gigs, I could afford it. On the spur of the moment, I contacted my new drum teacher.

Drum Lessons with Otto Weinandi

Otto Weinandi taught at his home. Entering his first-floor flat, I found myself in the middle of the kitchen, which he also used as a living room. Next to the window was a 1950s Resopal cabinet, like in every German kitchen in the sixties. Opposite it was the table with a corner bench, where we sat on the plastic cushions. The drumming happened on a round black practice pad from Premier. I had to get myself one for practising at home.

I can still picture Otto Weinandi to this day, with his pleasant voice and his circle of dark, slightly too long hair around a bald pate that revealed his deeper side. He clearly lived alone and he earned his money by playing at weddings, parties and functions, and teaching the drums. In his mid-50s, Weinandi usually wore a shirt with a dark-grey cardigan over it. During the lesson, he would take off the cardigan, put it back on and then remove it again, depending on the difficulty of the étude, which he introduced by playing it to me himself.

Over the next few lessons, we worked our way through the snare-drum textbook *Knauer Schule für kleine Trommel*. First of all, as is right and proper, how to hold the sticks and adopt the correct posture: 'Always practise seated, by placing the drum at a slant on a chair (or drum stand). Sit up straight and relaxed, without bending your back.' An illustration showed a young man with neatly cropped hair and short trousers, playing a snare drum on a chair. OK, the method came across as fairly old-school. I had to take a couple of deep breaths. It was very strange but also kind of cool in a way, because it dated back to a different time and so had absolutely nothing to do with pop music. Instead, it represented a different, closed system: the world of classical music.

My drum teacher tried to explain to me how note values worked. Semibreves, minims, crotchets, quavers, semi-quavers and so on. I didn't understand much of what he said, to be honest: tempo, metre, bar, cadence, note values, syncopation, triplets . . . the terms rolled off his tongue and got tangled in my brain. Although the transmitter and the receiver weren't really compatible, I miraculously learned to play what it said in the notes. I didn't understand the connection intellectually, but intuitively I did. The eighth notes have a little flag or a bar and the sixteenth notes have two flags or bars, and an arrangement of the graphic symbols sounds this way or that in 4/4 time. On the last pages of the textbook were what was called 'orchestral studies for snare drum', all of which looked pretty complicated, but they had names like *Fra Diavolo, Scheherazade* or *Rienzi* and that really stimulated my imagination. I liked musical notation from the very beginning. The system's five lines weren't prison bars that took away my freedom, but a window into my future.

And then there was the drum roll. That moment when the slow, consciously performed drum beats – two with the right hand, two with the left – speed up and bounce back and segue into a flowing movement was a pretty high hurdle. But I basically did nothing else but practise my drum roll for days and weeks on end, until it got faster and more even and started to roll off my sticks. As you might expect, Weinandi taught me the old-fashioned hold with the left hand – the traditional grip where the drumstick rests between the third and fourth fingers.

Meanwhile, Günther Hilgers was still working hard and getting us good promotion. I've no idea how, but he managed to interest the legendary Gerda Kaltwasser – the big-name journalist on the *Rheinische Post* – in the Anthonies' String Group. She showed up for an interview at our practice room in Itter with a photo-grapher in tow. The headline of her article was: 'Looking for Fame with Vocals and Guitar – Anthonies' String Group Wants to Learn a Lot More'. She wrote: 'Jörg is the only one who can read notes. Drummer Karlheinz is taking lessons but can't yet "read all the little dots."' I carefully cut out the first press report to mention my name and stuck it in a photo album . . .

My First Love

At Easter of 1969, the Anthonies' String Group played at Stadthalle Wegberg. We drove the forty kilometres from Düsseldorf towards the Dutch border in our psychedelic Volkswagen van – which was known for having the odd mundane, non-psychedelic breakdown. No doubt about it, the civic centre had the unmistakeable flair of provincial insignificance. It was no effort to imagine the space housing local council sessions, marksmen's festivals, jumble sales and rabbit-breeder meetings. In other words, it wasn't exactly an important gig and I wouldn't mention it in my chronology if there hadn't been a girl dancing in black clothes right in front of the stage.

She was a real beauty with short dark hair, big eyes and an unselfconscious smile, but she was obviously also very young. How strange, I thought; she seems to be interested in my drum kit, because she kept looking in my direction during our set. Our eyes met a couple of times. Girls usually acted like I didn't exist, but this girl down on the dance floor was looking directly at me, smiling and laughing. That was a new experience. Once we'd finished playing she and I got talking. 'My name's Margot and I'm nearly 15,' she informed me.

The next day – Easter Monday – we played in the Wegberg civic centre again, and things came to a head: Margot Heimbuchner became my first real girlfriend. At 16 years of age, I was utterly inexperienced with girls, and so the two of us innocents experienced our first touches over the next few weeks. We were in love and free and unashamed, and knew we were doing the right thing. We stayed together for several years.

At Musik Kunz, paying for my drumming lessons, I met Reiner, Theo Kunz's son. We got talking about music lessons and at some point he mentioned the 'Con', where you could study music. 'The Con?' I asked. 'Yeah, the conservatory,' Reiner answered, and added in a serious tone: 'If you want really good training, you have to study music there.'

I'd never heard of this 'Con' before. And neither had I ever thought about studying classical music. Me? There were the orchestral studies at the back of my drumming textbook, though I didn't know when we'd get to them in my lessons, but aside from that? Well, aside from that it was an unknown world, out of my reach. I had never been to a classical concert in my life. My parents couldn't show me the way into that world – they didn't know it themselves. Classical music consisted only of vague ideas in my mind. But my interest was piqued and I wanted to know more about it, for instance what requirements they had. Did I even have enough talent? And wasn't it only the gifted wunderkind type that studied classical music? I had to find out more.

So I came to a decision all on my own and sent a handwritten letter to Düsseldorf's Robert Schumann Conservatory, asking if I could apply to join the percussion class. I didn't mention any of it to my parents. After only a week, I received an answer: I was more than welcome to apply to study percussion. However, I was to learn the basics first and take an audition in September. Rather amazed to find out it was that easy to get invited, I did everything to pass the audition. From that day on, I went to my lessons at Otto Weinandi's place with a whole new attitude. I wanted – no, I really had to grasp the concept of musical notation and especially to perfect my drum roll. I had six months' time and I was determined to use it.

In parallel, the Anthonies' String Group was still speeding around to local gigs in the Volkswagen van. Günther's younger sister, Brigitte, had joined us as a singer by that point. She had a very delicate voice and unfortunately that pushed our repertoire drastically towards German sway-along pop hits. The second article about us in the press – this time in the *Neue*

Rhein Zeitung – was headlined accordingly: 'Beat Profile: Anthonies' String Group. Brigitte is the Highlight.' And underneath: 'They've been playing for a year now. Their repertoire includes all facets of entertainment music, from beat to pop, soul and classic dance music. It's no wonder they're booked up almost every weekend.'

In every band with a female singer, sooner or later the question arises: who will she get together with? Brigitte and Franz . . . well, all of a sudden, they were a couple. That in turn changed the atmosphere between us all. OK, we had plenty of jobs on the weekend and we were making money – but, then again, our repertoire was getting increasingly smooth and boring. I started losing interest.

The Jokers

The cards were reshuffled in July. I was one of the estimated five to six hundred million television viewers who watched the *Apollo 11* landing and Neil Amstrong taking the first walk on the moon in the history of space travel, uttering the immortal words: 'A small step for man . . . a . . . giant leap for mankind.' It was that very summer that Klaus Rybinski from the FA2-Band decided to buy himself an organ at Musik Kunz. Looking back, that proved to be a giant leap for all of us. Klaus was actually a pianist and accordionist who'd strayed to the guitar, and now he was finding his way back to the keyboard.

Klaus seemed like a genuine wunderkind to us. A virtuoso on keys who knew every song in the world – and how to play it. He read notes, was a fabulous arranger and could also improvise – a real musical genius. The organ he bought at Musik Kunz was a Farfisa. I assume Reiner made him an offer the instant he heard him playing it, asking him to join his band the Jokers as an organist. That was just how things worked in those days. Klaus told Franz and me about the offer, and we were fascinated. So when he wanted to go and see the band a few days later – they were playing in a pub somewhere – we went along with him. We didn't want to miss the opportunity to satisfy our curiosity.

The place was almost empty when we arrived. It smelled rather musty. Our eyes instantly alighted on the equipment on stage: lead guitar, rhythm guitar, bass guitar – all Burns brand and all in white, just like the Shadows. Two Vox AC30 amps were placed on wooden chairs. Next to them on the floor was the Vox bass amp, a huge box. Ludwig drum kit, of course, the same one I played. Three Sennheiser MD 421 microphones and an Echolette vocal amp with tape delay rounded off the set-up. Nothing less than the full set of equipment needed to perform everything that was in at that time. Extremely impressed, we took our seats.

The Jokers played the last three songs of their set: 'Carrie Anne', 'I'm a Believer' and 'Help!' Wolfgang Keller, the lead singer and lead guitarist, did an absolutely brilliant job. He was an amazing guitar player and sang in perfect English with excellent intonation. His repertoire – as I later found out – included the classic rock'n'roll songs of Elvis, Carl Perkins, Little Richard, Jerry Lee Lewis, Chuck Berry, and also Beatles numbers. He came across as absolutely authentic, whatever he played. On top of that, he was tall, dark and handsome – the kind of guy girls get major crushes on. But Wolfgang was definitely a serious person, not a slimy womanizer. When he wasn't playing music on stage, he worked in a photo laboratory. The band also had Reiner Kunz on bass, a rhythm guitarist and a drummer.

In the break, Reiner and Wolfgang joined us at our table, treated us to a round of altbier, and we had a laid-back music-nerd chat about equipment. I kept fairly quiet, trying my best to look cool. Then we listened to their next set. By the time we said goodbye, we'd well and truly realized we were playing in the regional league, and the Jokers were a cut above us. Shortly after that, Klaus did join them on the organ and the most astounding thing happened: he brought Franz and me into the band as well. I could hardly believe my luck. The new line-up had a definite advantage: Wolfgang and Franz both had quite large vocal ranges, hit the notes and were really good lead singers. In other words, we could play all white pop songs in their original key. Reiner, Klaus and I sang the harmonies and chorus parts. I think Günther Hilgers was very, very angry with us when we took our leave from him and the Anthonies' String Group.

We now practised one or two evenings a week with the Jokers, in amongst all the instruments at Reiner's dad's music shop. All I did was tap quietly on the snare, hi-hats and one cymbal. The amps were turned right down and the vocals were acoustic. We got better and better at playing together all the time, so I never saw our rehearsals as anything like work. As I write this, I realize that I used to look out of the front window of Musik Kunz onto Mintropstrasse while we practised. The street with a strange roller door outside house number 16.

We had our first job with the Jokers at the Ranch House in Kettwig on 4 July 1969. It was a month-long engagement – we performed there every Saturday and Sunday in July. After that, the Düsseldorf-based pop singer Sven Jensen unexpectedly booked us as his backing band for a TV appearance for the *Drehscheibe* show on ZDF. While we were accompanying him on a few gigs around the German provinces, I totally failed to register the Woodstock Music and Arts Fair making history in the USA in August 1969.

I had to postpone the audition for the Robert Schumann Conservatory from September 1969 to March 1970, because my apprenticeship exam awaited me. When I qualified as a tele-communications engineer on 5 September 1969, our band was of course playing for the occasion, so I missed the chance to shake the director's hand and receive my certificate because I was busy on stage with 'Apache', 'Peter Gunn' or 'Wipe Out'.

Leaving Home

On 28 September 1969, I went out to buy the new Beatles album *Abbey Road*, and was instantly gripped by 'Come Together' fever. The song had a magical effect on me as I listened transfixed, over and over. When Ringo leads into the solo with one of his typical drum fills and switches to the cymbal, creating an almost non-stop white noise interrupted only by a few fills, I totally flipped out. This rhythm had a completely new quality, gliding almost seamlessly ahead. All this euphoria over the new album was abruptly punctured the next day, however. My father, Hans-Joachim, and I ended up having a huge row.

My parents didn't know I'd applied to the Robert Schumann Conservatory. They would never have let me study music, I was sure of that. Instinctively, I knew I had to make that kind of decision on my own. I was planning to tell them about it that Saturday afternoon. In my room, I showed my father all the correspondence with the conservatory so far. He gave me a questioning look. And then I confronted him with my ideas and the plan for my path in life: 'I can't imagine working in telecoms for the rest of my life, Dad. OK, I managed to finish the apprenticeship, but the job doesn't really suit me at all. It was a mistake to train for it. The work makes me sick.' My father listened, incredulous. I continued: 'Music makes me happy, that's where I see my future.' To finish off, I announced that I'd be going to an audition at the conservatory next spring, and summed it up for him: 'Try to understand – I want to be a musician!'

This unexpected independence and also the determination I showed was too much for my old man – who wasn't even all that old, at 46. He naturally saw my criticism and my actions as a violation of his authority and made it unmistakeably clear that I couldn't make a decision like that at the age of 17. He was right, technically, because in 1969 you didn't come of age in Germany until you turned 21.

For him, work had nothing to do with fulfilment and happiness; it was a duty you had to perform to earn your living. My wish to become a musician seemed nothing less than utopian to him. To be perfectly honest, I wasn't capable of convincing him. The situation was far too much for both of us – rhetorically and emotionally. 'I'm going to be a musician whether you let me or not,' I argued stubbornly. My mother was crying and sobbing in the kitchen. Eventually, my father lost control of himself and lashed out at me. But I didn't feel the slightest inclination to turn the other cheek, and I defended myself. In the end, I had to leave the flat to prevent our fight from escalating further. As I walked out, from the corner of my eye I saw my father kicking in the soundboard of my brand-new acoustic guitar, which was on the floor. 'I'm leaving!' I yelled. And I slammed the door behind me.

That Saturday afternoon in September was the dramatic climax – or rather the absolute nadir – of our family history! I pounded the streets of Unterbilk like a headless chicken, not feeling safe again until a gig with the Jokers that evening.

There was no going back after such an extreme row. I had to leave home. In my desperation, I talked to my grandparents about the whole mess. Strangely enough, the fact that I wanted to be a musician didn't trouble them at all. They understood my problem; they knew their son, after all. Martha made a pragmatic suggestion. There was an empty room on the attic floor of their building on Rethelstrasse – I could live there for the time being. I was only 17 but it would be fine; they lived just downstairs and could keep an eye on me. That was the emergency exit I needed! Martha convinced my parents it would be the best thing for all of us if I moved into the attic room. And then my father and I declared a ceasefire for the next few weeks, avoiding each other at all cost. We never spoke about the incident again, to his dying day.

NOTES

1   Ronny's songs were cover versions of 'The Ballad of the Green Berets', Stan Jones's '(Ghost) Riders in the Sky' and Carson Robison's 'Bridle Hanging on the Wall'.

3

CONSERVATORY, OPERA, POP MUSIC, LSD

The Seventies. The Robert Schumann Conservatory. A Different Idea of Music. LSD. Vocals, Guitar, Bass, Drums. Recording Session in Conny's Studio. Commune. Oh Happy Day. The Force of Destiny. Movie for the Ears. My First Orchestra Rehearsal. Life in a Song. Around the Old Town. On Tour with Lester Wilson and the Extremes.

The Seventies

My new address: 32 Rethelstrasse, fifth floor. The landlord had let out the three rooms of the attic flat separately. All three tenants shared the toilet at the end of the corridor. My room was no more than 15 square metres in size. There was a washbasin directly next to the door and on the other side a radiator, which would occasionally start thudding out of the blue. For a few minutes, a mechanical pulse would fill the room – about 60 to 80 beats per minute – before gradually dying down and disappearing into the atmosphere. To evade the sound, I turned the central heating off when I was at home. I had a fridge with a motor that also piped up at certain intervals, and on top of it an electric hotplate. Fresh air came through a hatch in the slanting roof, which could be opened and held in place with a rod. The glass was so scratched I couldn't see through it, but the gap revealed a tiny slice of the sky above Düsseldorf. Aside from the strange fridge noises and the sounds from the other rooms, it was quiet up there with the heating off. My rent was 80 marks a month.

To take a shower or a bath, I had to go down to my grandparents' place on the first floor. My grandma charged me 50 pfennigs for a bath, and I could also wash my dirty laundry there, in the bathtub. By the cold light of day, my living conditions weren't exactly optimal, but I can still only describe my basic mood in my first own place as 'infinitely optimistic.' I had taken control of my life and nothing in the world would keep me from my plan of studying at the Robert Schumann Conservatory.

However, after finishing my apprenticeship I'd been automatically taken on by the post office telecoms service and put into a team in charge of local phone cables, the Ortskabel-Messtrupp – OKM for short. The gang was made up of the boss, an engineer, his deputy, and two teams of two men. I soon realized I was actually surplus to requirements – my apprenticeship director may well have put in a good word for me. The main task of the OKM was finding the cause of disruptions on the line. From my point of view, it was a first-rate workplace – because we basically had nothing to do. And when a fault report did come in, the lads were eager to get out of the office at last and scrambled for the jobs. That gave me plenty of scope to prepare for my drum lessons with Otto Weinandi on the practice pad in a back room every free minute. I was making good progress. At last I could play a decent drum roll, as I proved at every opportunity – much to my workmates' dismay.

One day, after a Jokers rehearsal, Reiner Kunz suggested we

visit a friend of his in Bochum, who was a student at the university, had a large record collection and knew a hell of a lot about music. He lived in a student hostel, in a room just big enough for a bed, chair and desk – plus a record player. We squeezed into the remaining few centimetres and proceeded to smoke a joint, awkwardly. That, I was told, was the prerequisite for *really* experiencing music. So now I was making the acquaintance of the psychedelic era, with some delay and in a rather amateur fashion. But still: the hashish's effect made the music seem incredibly spatial. As if another, previously concealed dimension had suddenly emerged.

The Robert Schumann Conservatory

Then came the day of my audition for the percussion course at the Robert Schumann Conservatory. I entered the white administration bungalow with knees like jelly, paid the ten-mark fee in cash and then had to wait in the corridor for a few minutes. There were notices about recitals, concerts, exams and semester breaks pinned to the wall, and also the timetable for the orchestral school. As if hypnotized, I read the names of the subjects: aural theory, harmonics, musical scores . . . It all looked pretty mysterious but also full of promise. 'If they accept me,' I vowed, 'I'll put all my energy into learning.' I couldn't imagine exactly where that would take me. But I knew one thing: this is it, this is where I want to be!

A few minutes later I was called into the dean's office. Professor Jürg Baur was a renowned composer. He welcomed me and introduced me to Konni Ries, telling me he was a chamber musician and the principal percussionist with the Düsseldorf Symphony Orchestra, as well as one of the conservatory's percussion lecturers. Ries was in his 50s, about my height, with an amiable face. He was wearing a dark suit. My eyes instantly fell on his burgundy waistcoat, which I later learned was something like his trademark. A white shirt, silver tie and polished shoes rounded off his fancy outfit. Good grief! Was I incredibly underdressed in my jeans, sweater, cord jacket and duffle coat? What I didn't know was that Konni Ries taught at the conservatory in the afternoons and was already in costume for his evening performance at the opera house.

I informed the two gentlemen that I'd been taking lessons on the snare drum with Otto Weinandi and just *had* to study music at the Robert Schumann Conservatory. My formulation really was that drastic. It would mean the world to me, I emphasized. In a gentle voice, Professor Baur enquired about my knowledge of musical theory: 'How about the basics? Let's take the baroque dance suites, for example. Are you familiar with them?' Instantly, I broke out in a sweat; I wasn't prepared for this. 'No, I'm afraid I don't know,' I admitted. As I attempted to look as calm as possible, I wished I was invisible. In the end, Konni Ries rescued me by asking: 'So you've been taking lessons on the snare drum. That's good. Would you like to play something for us – just something very short?'

He pointed at a drum with a metal shell. Now I was in my element: 'Yes, I've brought my textbook along,' I replied, placed the book on the music stand and flicked through for an étude. As I was about to start, Konni Ries pulled a neatly ironed and folded handkerchief out of his pocket and placed it on the drumhead, close to the edge. 'That will just make it sound better,' he explained with a wink. I played the étude as quietly as I could. It was a good day for me, and the drum really did sound very subtle thanks to the handkerchief's damping. Out of the corner of my eye I noticed Konni Ries reading the sheet music, checking my posture and giving a faint smile.

'That sounds pretty good already,' he said when I was done. After a moment's pause he continued: 'How about we give you a go in a trial semester?'

'Oh yes, that would be great,' I answered with huge relief. I could have hugged him. After my humiliation with the dance suites, I was delighted they hadn't thrown me out on my ear.

As I left, Professor Baur recommended a book by Willy Schneider: *Was man über Musik wissen muss – Musiklehre für jedermann*. It was a music theory book written for laymen, and it would fill the gaps in my knowledge. 'By the way,' he added, 'the dance suites are called Allemande, Courante, Sarabande and Gigue.' 'I'll work my way through the book,' I promised. At the end of my interview, I left the white bungalow with a huge weight off my chest. Now I knew for certain: today is the first day of my new life.

Four weeks later, my dream became real – the summer semester started on 1 April 1970. The conservatory's main building was at that time the Villa Engelhardt on the corner of Homburger Strasse and Kaiserswerther Strasse. The nineteenth-century building harboured a very special atmosphere. The sound of pianos, violins, woodwind and brass rang out from every room. Through a gap in a ground-floor door, I saw a lecture being held. A string quartet was practising in the room next door. Everything in the place was lively and made all kinds of noises. Even the floor and the stairs creaked as I walked on them. A student carefully carrying a strange-looking long red-brown wooden tube came from the lower level, crossed the corridor and dashed past me up the stairs. In a small room next to the entrance sat Herr Riem, the janitor, who gave me a quizzical look through his window . . .

My timetable included an hour a week of percussion lessons with Konni Ries, who taught me how to play the snare drum in an orchestra. I got the first piano lessons in my life, half an hour a week, from Ernst Göbler – starting with the C major scale. And in Elementary Music Theory, Heinz Bernhard Orlinski introduced me to the foundations of music for another hour a week. We soon got to the circle of fifths, and it turned out that the small, plain book Professor Baur had recommended really did contain everything I needed to know about music, as its title suggested.

That might not sound like much work in terms of teaching hours, but I had to practise and also try to grasp the theory, which was entirely new to me. For the first time in my life, I really wanted to learn something. When I started my studies, my life was divided into several areas: I studied music, turned night into day at weekends with the Jokers, and I had my day job with the telecoms team. By that point I was free to do what I liked at work. Everyone knew I'd be handing in my notice as soon as I could. But the lads and even the boss were very relaxed about it. They let me attend my lessons at the conservatory during work hours – something inconceivable these days.

A Different Idea of Music

Klaus Drieb was one of my OKM workmates; we got on well. One day he came out with it: 'Listen, there's this guy in the flat next door to mine, he makes music like you. His name's Marius and he plays in the band Harakiri Whoom – they're pretty famous, they were even in a film. I really have to introduce you to him.' None of that meant much to me but it made me curious. The next day, we took the grey VW van from work to visit this Marius guy. The doorbell said Müller-Westernhagen. I suspect Klaus had told him we'd be coming. Marius's room was rather luxurious in comparison to my garret. On the bed, very conspic-uously arranged, were a telephone, a tray with a teapot and cup, magazines, a German-English dictionary and an annotated script. Marius told us he happened to be learning his lines for a radio play.

Then Klaus cut to the quick and announced I was studying percussion at the 'Con'. Marius gave me an interested look and without hesitation, he suggested we should play together as soon as possible. I replied with something like, 'Yes, sure, let's do a session,' and that was that. We talked a bit more about pop music, did a bit of namedropping, compared our taste and decried the countless idiots running around the music world. To finish off, we arranged to meet in a couple of days' time, to continue our conversation.

At our age, pop music was a key subject. Marius had also got caught up in it, and had already made a name for himself in the scene. He had been performing with the band About Five at music clubs and school parties in and around Düsseldorf since 1967. What he really wanted was to be an actor, though. He'd been getting small roles in radio plays, TV productions and theatres since the early sixties. An offer to play the lead in a film about a beat band brought the two worlds together. And that's how About Five became the four-man band Harakiri with

Marius Müller-Westernhagen, Bodo Staiger, Patrick Verreet and Alan Warren. Incidentally, Klaus Dinger also appears at the end of the short film *Harakiri Whoom* as a stand-in drummer. After the production was shown on the WDR channel, the boys kept the name Harakiri Whoom. They gave a legendary performance at a school party in Kaiserswerth. Once the musicians had opened their set with an ear-splitting crash, Marius strode from the back of the school hall to the stage in a wolf-skin coat, firmly establishing his reputation as an eccentric pop star. Not much later, though, the band folded.

Soon after our introduction, I met Marius in the old centre of Düsseldorf. He suggested going to a rehearsal space in Golzheim – and we promptly climbed into his green BMW. It was a snazzy sports car with a leather steering wheel and all sorts of technical extras. I watched in amazement as he pulled on driving gloves and shot out of the parking space. The rehearsal room was in the technical college on Josef-Gockeln-Strasse. The caretaker was a music fan and let a few musicians practise there. As we arrived we heard guitar chords and a long loud screech of feedback, even from outside. It sounded suspiciously like Jimi Hendrix. The basement rooms were directly next to the boiler room; it was incredibly hot down there. Inside, we found Bodo Staiger, the guitarist from Harakiri Whoom, holding his Gibson Les Paul up to an amp and testing various methods of creating feedback. His shoulder-length dark hair was parted in the middle, and he was wearing a polo-neck sweater despite the heat. We sat down together and chatted, the way musicians do.

LSD

The next weekend, I had a date to meet up with Bodo. It was supposed to be a 'listening party'. Putting on records together and discussing the bands and their songs was a widespread ritual back then. I'd brought along my favourite albums, of course. And to add a little contemporary pep to the auditive occasion, we wanted to experiment with acid. I'm not claiming to remember all the details – it's more than fifty years ago now – but some sequences of my first LSD experience are still fresh in my mind.

The drug began to take effect unnoticed. Bodo sat cross-legged on the flokati rug and strummed at his Les Paul. Even without an amp, his playing sounded remarkably clear. The six strings of his guitar appeared to be made of a kind of steel rubber. It seemed to me as if the notes were moving around the room, tangibly reflected by the walls. After a while, he carefully put the guitar back in its case and picked an album out of the pile of records on his left: Jimi Hendrix's *Electric Ladyland*. And then things really kicked off.

As described in the pharmaceutical textbook, the music began to trigger explosions of colour in my brain. The next thing I felt – and I was certain it was all reality, not an illusion – was flying absolutely weightless through a never-ending space. Or more precisely: the music transformed into this space that I floated through. I was inside the music itself. In this apparently infinite space, countless paisley-patterned shapes unfurled, and I slid right through them. These organic patterns altered along with the music, constantly flowing into new forms. The laws of physics and acoustics, according to which music makes the air vibrate, appeared to have been temporarily suspended. The music spoke to me in all the world's languages at once, and I understood its message down to the very last frequency. Never before, it seemed, had the essence of music been as clear to me as in that instant. But not only that. Basically, I finally understood 'what holds the innermost world together', or at least as long as the drug was still working. Whether that perception lasted seconds, minutes or hours, I couldn't tell. Time had stood still for me.

Apparently out of nowhere, Bodo put on a new record. The beat was astoundingly simple but effective. A voice articulated in a kind of chant: 'Doo right, yoo doo right, doo right, yoo doo right . . .' The rest of the night and the day that followed have slipped my memory. Later I found out the track we'd listened to was 'Yoo Doo Right' from the Can album *Monster Movie*. Just recently, so many decades later, I listened to it again and I was surprised by how much it reminds me of 'Autobahn'.

Vocals, Guitar, Bass, Drums

In July, I passed my driving test thanks to the OKM – the lessons were free. I'd saved up three thousand marks and I spent it on my first car, a grey second-hand Citroën 2CV. It may have been a bit wobbly, but as soon as you came to terms with the strange gears it was a great student car.

Bodo had left his grammar school and got a casual job with a haulage company at the freight station. He lived in an apartment not far from me. I would often pick him up there and drive us to our jam sessions at the technical college. By this point we were now meeting regularly in our rehearsal room with our new bassist Peter Wollek. Peter had dark curly shoulder-length hair and a friendly, upright character. He was studying electrical engineering to keep his father happy. Years later, he switched subjects and followed me to the Robert Schumann Conservatory to study electric bass. Now we were a quartet: Marius, Bodo, Peter and me. We played together like in a work-shop. These days we'd call it a 'project'. Perhaps it was a laboratory for free musical experiments or experimental sound design. Something along those lines. Our premise was not to cover other bands' songs but to develop our own music. That was very much in the air at the time.

In the sixties, pop music exploded. The short 7-inch single format developed into a veritable art form. At the same time, the design of the album changed so that songs were seen as different chapters of a book following an overarching concept. In my opinion, the Beatles composition 'Tomorrow Never Knows' (1966) introduced this development, continuing via *Pet Sounds* (1966) by the Beach Boys and *Sgt. Pepper's Lonely Hearts Club Band* (Beatles, 1967). 'A Day in the Life', the last track on *Sgt. Pepper's*, which closes the album with an E major piano chord, may only last five and a half minutes, but it's made up of two song fragments linked together with great compositional skill, creating a complex musical form with their transitions. Some artists took their lead from jazz and placed greater value on improvisation. Their music grew more experimental, lasting longer and longer – the arrangements soon filled one complete side of an LP. Jimi Hendrix broke the usual time frame in 1968 on several tracks on *Electric Ladyland*, as did the British band King Crimson with their debut album *In the Court of the Crimson*

68

King (1969). On *Hot Rats*, Frank Zappa brought out the almost 13-minute track 'The Gumbo Variations' that same year, and 'Yoo Doo Right' (also 1969) was over 20 minutes long. In California, the Grateful Dead became famous for playing their single 'Dark Star' in endless versions at their live gigs, something I experienced first-hand with Bodo in Düsseldorf's Rheinhalle venue. The albums that had the greatest influence on me in 1970 were both double LPs, significantly: *Third* by Soft Machine – all four tracks on the album are just under twenty minutes long – and Miles Davis's *Bitches Brew*, the title track going on for a whole 27 minutes. At that point, I didn't yet have Pink Floyd on my radar.

Recording Session in Conny's Studio

That August, Bodo met the sound engineer and producer Conny Plank in the rehearsal room. One of the places Conny worked was the Rhenus Studio in Cologne-Godorf, with various German pop artists. His freelance job left him enough time to go out in search of interesting music projects with his colleague, Hans Lampe, to produce them in the hours when the studio wasn't booked up.

A few days later, Conny invited Marius, Bodo, Peter and me to a recording session at the Rhenus Studio. We didn't know what we'd record but we didn't care. Everything was left to chance; it never crossed our minds that we might fail. Conny sat behind his mixing desk in the control room like a big bear, motivating us with suggestions: 'Just start with drums and bass,' and that kind of thing. Marius reported from the recording room with a request for an echo effect on the mic to make his harmonics sound a bit more unreal. Bodo spent hours tuning his guitar that evening, but then Conny uttered his catchphrase 'The tape is rolling,' and we kicked off. Marius came up with his lyrics live, and I have to say he was pretty good at it.

The original tape from the session disappeared mysteriously and was forgotten. Decades later, Peter Wollek happened to find it in his attic. We listened with bated breath. What can I say? We simply hadn't come up with anything – not even with Conny's help. For some reason beyond my understanding, the recording got lost again after that. I'm sure musical history will forgive its disappearance, though.

Without a doubt, Conny Plank was a great catalyst for the German music scene – if not the greatest. He had a unique, pure energy, unbridled enthusiasm and a whole lot of enterprising spirit. He must have organized countless sessions with as-yet unknown bands and musicians during those years. For a long time, I didn't know that Conny had recorded five tracks in the Rhenus Studio in December 1969 with another group and produced a record by the name of *Tone Float*. When we were doing our session with Conny in August 1970, the British RCA label released *Tone Float* by the German band Organisation, unnoticed by us and the rest of the world.

Commune

The last time I saw Marius for a while was when we went to Bavaria together. His BMW was in for repairs and he asked me to drive him to Munich in my 2CV, to get him to an important appointment with an acting agency. My Citroën limousine reached a top speed of 100 km/h, and when it got that fast it felt like plummeting to the ground in an out-of-control Messerschmitt ME-109. It took some getting used to. Once we arrived in Munich late in the evening, Marius directed us to the Schwabing neighbourhood, where he said he 'knew a few people'. That was how I met the German counterculture icons Uschi Obermaier and Rainer Langhans. Marius had arranged for us to stay overnight in their commune.

Uschi was sitting cross-legged on the floor in the middle of the room, rolling a joint and looking pretty overwhelming. Perhaps it was because she had next to nothing on. Rainer turned out to be an amiable host. We chatted for a while, as Indian music played in the background and one of the commune members danced, swaying her arms above her head in snake-like movements like the goddess Shiva. Despite all that, we were exhausted from the long drive and retired to the guest room. The next morning, Marius took his photos and documents to the agency and we set off for home again. That was to be the last thing we did together. For some reason, we didn't manage to rehearse any more, but it wasn't a big deal. All of us had plenty of other projects to pursue, which gave us the fulfilment we needed. I didn't hear from Marius again for years. These days, he's one of Germany's most successful singers and composers.

Oh Happy Day

I earned my living on the weekends with the Jokers – and it was really great fun. At the Bochum Press Ball in the Ruhrland-Halle in January 1971, we alternated sets with Paul Kuhn and the SFB Dance Orchestra on the big stage. The gala's music programme featured Katja Ebstein, Sven Jenssen, Günter Keil, Helen's Afro-Beat Dancers and the star of the night: Lester Wilson.

The 29-year-old African-American singer and dancer had made his career in sixties America and was now a familiar face in Germany, thanks to several sensational TV appearances. He also made records that sold pretty well. In 1977 he came to worldwide fame as the choreographer for *Saturday Night Fever*, working with John Travolta.

At the beginning of the seventies, he was an early live performer of something that was to be repeated ad nauseam a few years later in countless videos: formation dance. Essentially, it was an old revue format with music, dance and spoken elements, like in Broadway musicals. That evening in Bochum, he was on stage with Helen's Afro-Beat Dancers. Lester Wilson's act was greeted with furious enthusiasm – an unexpected performance. He boogied across the stage in a fringed one-piece suit, light as a feather, with almost acrobatic moves, and sang a couple of classics like the Temptations' 'Get Ready'. The SFB Dance Orchestra had worked with Wilson before and knew the ropes. The drummer – an American professional – suddenly started grooving like crazy. An hour before, performing a German pop hit about the alleged lack of beer in Hawaii, he'd been an entirely different person. The biggest moment of the night, though, was when 'Reverend' Wilson covered the Edwin Hawkins Singers' 'Oh Happy Day' with us, the Jokers. The whole auditorium freaked out.

My curiosity piqued, at the end of the set, I headed backstage, where the dancers were taking off their make-up and getting changed. Professional dancers are known for their cheerful demeanour, and I wanted to catch them in person. Lester Wilson came straight up to me, now without his afro wig, and told me he had some great stuff I'd definitely be into. With a grin, he showed me at least a kilo of hash cookies in a biscuit tin. And then – a completely new experience for me – he came on to me, fairly unabashed. That made me wonder: how must girls feel in similar situations? In this case it was fine, he didn't go too far. I told him I had to go back on stage to play our next set. In the end I gave him my phone number to make up for it – but that was it with Lester for the time being.

The Force of Destiny

And now for something completely different: the conservatory. I was actually only there on a trial basis, but that was soon forgotten. I was accepted into the second semester without comment, so my studies continued. One day after class, Ernst Göbler asked me if I fancied helping out with the music at the opera.

Göbler, I now learned, not only taught piano and percussion at the conservatory, he was also the principal timpanist with the Düsseldorf Symphony Orchestra, the city's concert orchestra that played at the Deutsche Oper am Rhein. A top-class ensemble. The job, which had come up at short notice, consisted of two drum rolls in Giuseppe Verdi's *La forza del destino*. He'd clearly had a chat with Konni Ries – they saw each other every day at the opera house – and heard that my drum roll was at least good enough for stage music.

'You can do it,' he encouraged me when he noticed my hesitation. 'In one scene, two drummers enter the stage and play two short rolls on their marching drums on set. Have you got a snare drum with a strap?'

'Sure I have!' I fibbed.

'It's the day after tomorrow. Fritz Haus – an experienced percussionist – will be on with you and tell you what to do.'

Even in my wildest dreams, I had never imagined performing on an opera stage. But I still said yes. I was sure to find some way to attach my snare drum to a belt and deliver the drum rolls – there was no doubt in my mind.

And so I set foot in an opera house for the first time in my life, through the stage door – a great feeling. Fritz Haus was already expecting me. We descended a narrow metal staircase past the orchestra pit to the canteen and started off with a cup of tea. The place was a constant bustle: soloists, choir members and countless extras – in costume and greasepaint – stage-hands, firemen, make-up artists and other staff flooded in and out, drinking, eating, chatting loudly. Anyone at a loose end for a few minutes came down to the canteen. Before the interval, Fritz Haus and I left our table. We went up a couple of floors to the costume department, where we changed and got made up.

We waited behind the curtain for several minutes, and then we were on. A stagehand showed us the way. I stuck close to Fritz Haus and found myself unexpectedly a few metres above the stage on top of a wall – in reality, a piece of scaffolding disguised with papier mâché. For the first time, I looked down at the audience. The view didn't make me particularly nervous, but Giuseppe Verdi's music, the power of the staging, the huge spectacle, the incredible machinery operated here by so many people – all of it caught hold of me in that instant. Then Fritz

Haus gave me a sign: Here we go! And we played the drum roll. And again. It all went fine; exit Haus and Bartos.

Ernst Göbler and Konni Ries were happy with me. Things were going great at the conservatory and I decided to reduce my hours on the telecoms team to half-days. I simply couldn't quite manage to stop working there, to cut the umbilical cord to my petit-bourgeois origins.

Movie for the Ears

Bodo, Peter and I met up regularly at our practice room in Golzheim. We were now calling ourselves Sinus, a name that fitted with the times. German bands were giving themselves unusual to downright bizarre names to distinguish them from their Anglo-American cousins: Amon Düül, Faust, Guru Guru, Grobschnitt, Popol Vuh, Kraan, Kluster, Kraftwerk . . .

None of us were keen to take over the vacant position of lead singer. Bodo came up with the idea of getting a flautist or saxophonist to join us. The current fusion of jazz and rock meant the sound of wind instruments cropped up on many productions. Peter put his ear to the ground in grammar-school circles, and in the end, Rainer Sennewald was recommended to him. Rainer looked exactly the way I imagined a saxophonist or flute player: shoulder-length brown hair and glasses. Like me, he had just turned 18. His father had introduced him to classical music at a young age, but more importantly to jazz. At last we had a line-up we could work with: saxophone/flute, guitar, bass and drums. We spent a lot of time together. Rainer and Peter still lived with their parents; that was OK for them but Bodo and I started thinking about how we could improve our living conditions. I remembered my trip to Munich and suggested: 'Marius and I went to this commune and it was pretty laid-back. Why don't you and I share a flat?'

Bodo didn't need much convincing and we soon found a place to share on the top floor of a new building on Nordstrasse, in the Derendorf area. Fortunately, it had a lift. At that time, Nordstrasse was a bustling street with plenty of restaurants, cafés, shops and even a cinema just around the corner. It was as lively as in the big city. The location proved to be ideal: the conservatory, the Hofgarten, the opera house, the old town centre and the Rhine were all about a ten-minute walk away. And the rent for the sixty square metres was also affordable. The place was perfect. With all due respect, Bodo didn't look anywhere near as amazing as Uschi Obermaier – but he was a much better guitar player than her. And so, we both moved in on 1 March 1971. It didn't take us long; we didn't really own much and my drum kit was best off kept in our practice room, anyway. In its place, I got hold of a second-hand piano for my composition exercises. The flat became our headquarters and a frequent meeting place for our friends.

Bodo contributed records by Marvin Gaye, Isaac Hayes, Curtis Mayfield, Sly and the Family Stone, Santana and Jimi Hendrix to our pool. And also Pink Floyd. He owned the coolest albums. I remember *Ummagumma*, *Atom Heart Mother* and *Meddle*. All around my record player, our LPs leaned up against the wall after we'd listened to them. Over time, the result was a playlist for our listening evenings, authorized by both of us. I don't think it's too far-fetched to assume that the happening means of 'mind-expansion' at the time encouraged the production of extended instrumental tracks and the use of electronic effects. Another thing we found out was that LP covers – aside from protecting records – were very well suited for building the next joint. In our flat, I believe most of them were rolled with *Electric Ladyland* on our laps. What on earth would we have done if music had already been available on CDs, MP3s or from streaming services?

When Pink Floyd played in Düsseldorf's Philipshalle on 4 July 1971, I was part of the huge audience. What a show! What impressed me most was the staging and the out-there sounds. The crew had installed special speakers to play effects like in a radio play. Footsteps, voices and other noises moved around the space in ways I'd never heard before. Phenomenal! Several times over the course of the evening, Roger Waters banged a huge gong that seemed to be floating on air, burning. They were quite odd, those Pink Floyd fellows. Their music was too slow for my taste and I couldn't hear any songs, any cool riffs, any singable tunes . . . and yet it hit the right spot. They had something to say. Perhaps it was that evening when I became aware of how sounds communicate when you place them in a musical context. Without a doubt, their performance was major aural cinema.

In contrast, our own efforts came across like modest Super-8 screenings for family get-togethers. We really couldn't compare ourselves to Pink Floyd – the technical equipment they had was unattainable for us. Plus, we were aiming for more of a fusion of jazz and rock. That gave rise to our first joint compositions, with titles like 'Steps', 'Dictator', 'Return' and 'Vacuum'. A few gigs soon came along. Things were starting out well. We plastered all of Düsseldorf with our posters in night-time guerrilla campaigns and even made what would these days be called a flyer.

My First Orchestra Rehearsal

In the summer semester of 1971, Konni Ries stopped teaching at the conservatory and I switched to Ernst Göbler for my main subject. He instructed me on timpani technique, the most important percussion instrument in the orchestra. Alongside, we also worked on études and orchestral studies for mallet instruments. I loved the sound of the xylophone and glockenspiel. And it was during that semester that I was accepted into the conservatory orchestra. We were playing Franz Schubert's *Symphony No. 9 in C Major* and I was put on timpani.

Slightly nervous, I turned up for my first orchestra rehearsal in the Robert Schumann Hall. I took a pair of felt mallets out of my case and tuned the two timpani to C and G. The other orchestra members were also tuning up or chatting; the atmosphere was relaxed. One thing I noticed, though, was that people only seemed to be communicating within the instrument groups. A brass player wouldn't exchange words with a cellist. The only percussion instruments used in Schubert's great symphony are timpani – which meant I had nobody to talk to.

General Music Director Trommer strode in, bounced up to the conductor's desk and tapped his baton against it until everyone was looking at him. 'We'll play the first movement, andante – allegro ma non troppo,' (fast but not too fast) he said, looked towards the woodwind and signalled at the horns to start the symphony. During the rehearsal, Trommer focused on the separate instrument groups in turn and worked out details. When I followed the parts in isolation I also understood them better in the full version – all of a sudden, everything seemed much more transparent to me. A melody that begins with the woodwind, gets picked up by the strings and taken to its climax by the brass section, altering its position in the room as time goes on, was something I'd never heard in such clarity. I'd certainly come into contact with classical orchestral music before – on the radio, records or TV. But it sounds different from speakers than played by instruments in a room. Plus, Schubert didn't compose his ninth for loudspeakers, he wrote it for performance in a concert hall; that's the difference. I don't think I'd be exaggerating if I said: on that Friday afternoon on the stage of the Robert Schumann Hall, my perception of sound altered.

In an orchestra, the main objective is to reproduce a composed piece. Usually – leaving aside contemporary music or premieres – it is the sound of a different age. Schubert's *Symphony No. 9 in C Major* was first performed in 1839 and we were practising it in 1971, over a century later. The traditional medium for recording music in written form is musical notation. However, the system has considerable shortcomings. Old works often lack important parameters like precise tempo information, length of the general rests, articulation, volume ratios or instrumentation. Naturally, instrument construction and thus their sound has also changed over time. That means performing old music is always an interpretation under present-day conditions. What the Europeans achieved was to invent a method of documenting music on paper. That enabled the spirit of the music – though not its sound – to stand the test of time.

Life in a Song

On the weekends of May, June and early July, we had a lucrative engagement with the Jokers at Club Romantika near Aachen. It was a gigantic club with a large stage to match and a capacity of several hundred. The dancefloor was always packed. Along with standards and rock'n'roll classics, we played the latest hits: 'Venus', 'The Letter', 'Yellow River', 'Aquarius', 'Good Morning Starshine', 'Proud Mary', 'My Sweet Lord' and all the rest. In the meantime, Holger Clausen had taken Reiner Kunz's place on bass. He was a trained jazz pianist and a fantastic musician with a soul voice fit for songs by Fats Domino, Ray Charles and Georgie Fame. Hank Hauf had also joined us, an American saxophonist well versed in anything going in the R&B and soul scene – plus of course the evergreens that got audiences dancing.

I could have been satisfied with playing the pop and entertainment canon at a high level and making an easy living that way. But I was gradually becoming aware that entertaining people with music is akin to performing a service. For Ray Charles, the song 'What'd I Say' is part of his life. But the Jokers had no relation to it, of course. All we did was borrow his words, chords and melodies to keep people happy on the dancefloor. The Beatles, Stones and Kinks also played their heroes' songs. For all bands in the post-war generation, covers were the first step towards their own identity and into the music business. The money to be made back then came from the live business, not from recordings. The second step was synthesizing their role models. That leads to compositions 'in the style of . . .' and then to the third step, letting your own biography influence the material. The Beatles are a prime example of this process. The Jokers never aimed for that kind of development, though. We were more like an updated version of the entertainment bands that used to perform in music halls or variety theatres.

Much later, Franz once reminded me of how, while we were unloading and loading our equipment for the Romantika gig, I talked about writing a song about my car. It was going to be called 'It's My Car' – most likely more to do with 'Drive My Car' than any idea of my own. But it appears that the wish to translate my life into music was already on my mind back then.

Around the Old Town

Everything was business as usual in our flatshare. Bodo and I had our rituals, like our short stroll through the Hofgarten into the old town centre. We usually headed for the Ratinger Hof for a cup of tea. In the first half of the seventies, the 'Hof' seemed to me like a Dutch hippie café. Oriental rugs on the tables, palm trees vegetating in the corners, fairy lights and joss sticks. Guests sat daydreaming on ragged sofas, while others played chess or a round of billiards. People had plenty of time. If you were hungry you'd order a bowl of muesli at the counter. On warm summer evenings, it was great to stand outside in the crowd, clutching a glass of altbier or export and watching the sun set on the other side of the Rhine.

From the 'Hof', Bodo and I would turn onto Neubrückenstrasse. We'd occasionally meet our trusted hash dealer in the small car park outside the old county court. Then we'd mosey past the

Kunsthalle gallery to Carlsplatz, our destination being a tiny ice-cream parlour with three tables and a TV. There, we'd savour our sundaes while watching the new political magazine show *Kennzeichen D*. The editors had chosen the song 'Ruckzuck' by a band called Kraftwerk as its title tune. Everyone was talking about the group with the markedly German-sounding name. Their odd record with a traffic cone on the cover was a veritable subcultural hit. The TV show's opening titles were pretty crazy. You saw the mechanized production process of a car registration plate in conjunction with percussive flute sounds – a perfect audio-visual combination. Once we'd polished off our ice creams we'd set off for home in slow motion.

There was one surprise during this time, though. The conservatory administration office asked me whether they could start giving me 250 marks a month from the winter semester onwards. The Friends of the Robert Schumann Conservatory had recommended me for a stipend. Pardon? I couldn't quite believe it! With this support and my income from the Jokers and the opera house, I'd have my costs covered and could now concentrate entirely on my studies. So I cut the ties to my former life and handed in my notice at the OKM. Psychologically, that brought me closer to my goal of becoming a musician, a whole lot closer.

Bodo and I saw out the eventful year of 1971 with another LSD trip – my second. A third one was to follow, but then I put a stop to my hallucinogenic experiments. The drug's long-term effect started to worry me.

On Tour with Lester Wilson and the Extremes

Early in 1972, the grey-and-white telephone in our hall rang. 'Hi, Lester Wilson here. How're you doin'? We're heading up to Düsseldorf – can we meet?'

Wow – Lester! I couldn't believe it! And lo and behold, a few days later he showed up at our flat – bringing along his boyfriend and colleague Michael Peters. The two of them greeted us effusively like old friends and made themselves at home in our living room. Then – does it even need to be said? – the guys got out their grass . . .

Lester and his dance ensemble had come to Düsseldorf for a nearby show and he thought he'd pop in and say hi. He talked euphorically about a few planned gigs in southern Germany and said he was looking for a backing band. Last but not least, he asked whether Bodo and I fancied being part of it. It couldn't be all that difficult to put a band together.

Well, I'd seen his show once before: about twenty dancers with perfect choreography – a really new, red-hot thing. It would definitely be a huge opportunity, one we couldn't let pass us by. So we soon agreed: Sinus will do the gigs.

To seal the deal, Bodo plugged his Gibson Les Paul into the mini-amp and played the wah-wah guitar part from *Shaft*. Lester and Michael loved Isaac Hayes's soundtrack; they seemed to know it by heart. Before long, each of us grabbed an instrument and joined in the groove, and at some point we ended up at Marvin Gaye's 'What's Going On'. What an afternoon! Playing music just for its own sake is a great celebration of its special magic, absolutely sensual and almost impossible to top. When darkness fell we headed out to the old town centre.

Lester called me from Munich at the beginning of March and mentioned almost in passing that the gigs had been confirmed. That meant we only had a couple of days to alert the band, find a van and speed down to the south.

At that moment, it dawned on us that it's almost impossible to play a rhythm & blues set without a piano. I instantly thought of Holger Clausen, who was thrilled with the idea. So we brought Holger and his Fender Rhodes on board.

Lester Wilson had arranged for us to rehearse in the ARD television ballet troupe's space. We set up there and looked at the notes. There were soul numbers like 'Get Ready', 'In the Midnight Hour' and 'Sunny', but we were surprised to find the Burt Bacharach song 'Raindrops Keep Fallin' on My Head', which made Lester come over all sentimental every time we played it. Once we had a handle on the repertoire, we practised the whole thing with the dancers as well. It was pretty cool watching Lester develop the choreography.

And then we launched into our tour around the provincial discos: Augsburg, Nuremberg, Würzburg, Bayreuth. We'd start by warming up the packed clubs with two or three soul tracks, played fairly rough. After the off-stage announcement: 'Ladies and gentlemen, please welcome Lester Wilson and the Extremes!' we'd rock out for about an hour, non-stop.

I don't think Sinus were ever as funky and wild again. If I had a ticket for a time machine, I'd set it to 17 to 26 March 1972, to experience our completely crazy gigs all over again – the first real peak of my career as a musician.

4

LISTENING, FEELING, PLAYING, THINKING

The Percussion Ensemble. The Future of Music. Deutsche Oper am Rhein. Wolfgang and my Black Stage Suit. The Tristan Chord. Prélude à l'après-midi d'un faune. Le Sacre du Printemps. Daphnis et Chloé. Oberkassel Student Digs. Minimal Music. Jazz. Detox.

The Percussion Ensemble

As soon as the 1972 summer semester began, the conservatory had me firmly in its grips. I also took the opportunity to attend a few courses to get myself a school leaving certificate, similar to British O-Levels: art history, German, history, geometry, maths, biology. But of course the focus of my studies was on learning my instrument with Ernst Göbler. He didn't fail to notice how much effort I put in and he became my mentor. It was during this semester that another very important component was added to my training: the percussion ensemble.

In its early days, it was a small group of only five students; no more than that had signed up to study percussion. The title of our first piece, *Sonic Boom* – which Göbler taught us – sounds like a nineties hip-hop track. But it was actually a simple training étude in 5/4 time by Duane Thamm. I was instantly impressed by the transparency of the parts, something that results automatically in a percussion quintet. The sound felt familiar to me from the very beginning, as if it had always been inside me.

One of the best-known works for percussion ensembles, then as now, was the composition *Ionisation* for thirteen percussionists by Edgard Varèse. Percussion instruments are a fundamental element of musical traditions in many world cultures. In classical music, they were constantly developed over the course of the twentieth century but didn't reach the level of other instruments. After *Ionisation* premiered at New York's Carnegie Chapter Hall in 1933, it became clear that the role of a percussionist was changing, that they no longer had to cede centre stage to the other instrument groups, but would be granted a special role in modern music.

Carlos Chávez's 1942 *Toccata* for six percussionists was the first significant composition we performed with the percussion ensemble.

The Future of Music

Exploring the music library, I came across the score for *Construction in Metal* (1939) by an American composer I'd never heard of, a man by the name of John Cage. Over the next few semesters I became more and more familiar with his work.

Cage's technique of preparing a piano reminded me of a percussion ensemble. And then there was his silent super-hit *4'33"* from the year I was born, 1952, in which the performer plays nothing for four minutes and thirty-three seconds, not a single sound. Someone explained to me that Cage defined the noises of the concert hall audible during the performance as the actual composition. When I was young I thought of that as eccentric. His famous 1937 essay 'The Future of Music – Credo' went above my head in the beginning, as well. But I began to find the scope of his groundbreaking ideas more and more inspiring.

At that time, the work of John Cage was part of the Düsseldorf Academy of Art's concert series on twentieth-century music, as you might expect. I loved the performances, and although it was quite an effort to show up there at ten o'clock on Sunday mornings, I became a regular attendee. There weren't many opportunities around to come into contact with avant-garde music, and I really wanted to be an insider in the scene.

Cage's use of record players and radios as instruments in his *Imaginary Landscapes* was a revelation to me in the context of contemporary classical music, like a bridge into the land of pop. On another occasion, I was left open-mouthed when water poured into a metal bucket was instrumentalized in his *Landscape No. 2*. This H_2O performance convinced me once and for all of Cage's musical inventions. I won't claim I understood his work fully in my early 20s – it was more a case of enthusiasm and cautious steps towards the ideas of the avant-garde.

Deutsche Oper am Rhein

Part of Ernst Göbler's job as principal timpanist with the Düsseldorf Symphony Orchestra was putting together the duty rosters for the percussion group. And his training vision included involving me in the orchestra's work. That meant I got to play a considerable cross-section of eighteenth, nineteenth and twentieth-century European orchestral music in the pit and on stage. Whenever interesting works were on the programme but I wasn't playing them, I would simply sit down in the percussion corner and listen. Göbler was right, orchestra rehearsals really were the best lessons. My colleagues didn't let me fall flat on my face, of course; they allowed me to take over certain sections of the percussion part on their behalf until I improved over time.

My bookings in this cultural sector increased rapidly. In 1972 and 1973, I played at more than 200 performances and rehearsals – in the opera orchestra, on stage, at symphony concerts and church services. That included music as varied as *Manon Lescaut* by Giacomo Puccini, Sergei Prokofiev's *Romeo and Juliet*, *Die Soldaten* by Bernd Alois Zimmermann and *Rise and Fall of the City of Mahagonny* by Kurt Weill.

In the conservatory orchestra, we also worked on modern music, performing Prokofiev's *Peter and the Wolf* in the Robert Schumann Hall in early 1973. The piece was composed to familiarize children with the instruments of the symphony orchestra. Each of the characters in the story is represented by one instrument and given its own musical leitmotif: the bird – flute, the duck – oboe, the cat – clarinet, Peter – violins, the wolf – horns, the rifle – timpani, and so on. I saw hundreds of school children react to the musical fairy tale with huge enthusiasm, almost enraptured. Another work we played was Carl Orff's *Carmina Burana*, the version for two pianos and percussion. My appointment calendar was bursting at the seams.

Wolfgang and My Black Stage Suit

Business was booming with the Jokers too, and I started to feel snowed under with work. In the end, the guys started looking around for a kind of long-term stand-in for me. I was really relieved to hear that a certain Wolfgang Flür would take my place now and then.

There was hardly anyone in the Düsseldorf music scene who didn't know Wolfgang. Over the past few years he had played percussion for the Beathovens, Spirits of Sound and Fruit. He cut a fine figure behind his Ludwig drum kit and would easily have passed as an Italian or French actor in a Fellini or Truffaut film. A little later on, he sported a kind of *Three Musketeers* moustache for a while. When a job came up that I couldn't do, he was booked to step in. And that was why Wolfgang came to visit me, to borrow my suit. Lo and behold, it fitted perfectly – because we were both one metre seventy-five tall and weighed a maximum of sixty-five kilos.

Wolfgang made a friendly and approachable impression. We got on right away and didn't have the slightest inkling that we'd be meeting again under very different circumstances. 'Don't drum too hard and fast with the Jokers,' I called after him, and then off he went with my black stage suit over his arm.

The Tristan Chord

Looking back from today's perspective, it's amazing what a broad spectrum of musical knowledge I gained during my degree. Often,

I would deal with music from several different centuries on one day. Johann Sebastian Bach was particularly important. As many of my colleagues would agree, for me the music in our lives began with him. His work is the foundation on which the structure of European music was built. To this day, I have never met a serious musician who does not express sincere admiration for Bach's compositions. In historical terms, the subsequent three centuries of musical evolution are divided into the epochs of baroque, classical, romantic and what is called New Music – a pretty speedy development for a relatively short period, if you ask me.

Experts identify the first traces of twentieth-century music in the overture to Richard Wagner's *Tristan and Isolde*. When the musical drama premiered in 1865, the famous *Tristan* chord cropped up in the very second bar, its harmonic ambiguity anticipating all that was to come. Many theorists describe this chord as the beginning of the long farewell to minor and major. Music was no longer the same after that, they say, and it would be difficult to imagine how the work of Debussy, Bruckner, Strauss, Mahler and Schönberg would have sounded without Wagner.

Prélude à l'après-midi d'un faune

Rainer Sennewald lived just a couple of minutes away from Nordstrasse and I visited him fairly regularly. We would drink tea, munch biscuits and exchange thoughts. One day, he played me Claude Debussy's *Deux Arabesques* for piano from a slightly scratchy old record his girlfriend, Marlis, had brought along. I was immediately a huge fan, and the French composer's music has been a firm part of my life ever since.

The classic Christmas photo – Marietta and me in the town where I was born, Marktschellenberg near Berchtesgaden, in 1953; below: posing in the snow, 1954.

In Düsseldorf's Flora Park, 1956.

My parents, Rosa and Hans-Joachim Bartos, in the early 1960s.

Friedenstrasse in Düsseldorf-Bilk: my entire world in the 1960s.

On holiday with my beloved sister Marietta in Berchtesgaden – in lederhosen, naturally.

1962, with Marietta and my mother.

Christmas 1962 with my grandparents Martha and Alfred Bartos (left).

I had a happy childhood!

1965 – Brits at the Bartos base: Lance Corporal Peter Hornshaw played me my first Beatles record: *A Hard Day's Night*.

Even back in 1966 we knew a press photo was essential. Marietta took the picture in my bedroom – with me are (left to right) Jürgen, Heiko and Karl 2.

My first drum kit, 1967.

The first time I played in front of an audience, on 2 February 1967: The Hotbacks in the Jugendtanzcafe on Bilker Allee. With me on stage: Hans-Joachim (left) and Adolf.

I happened to discover an orchestral work of Debussy's that I didn't yet know on the Düsseldorf Symphony Orchestra concert programme. One cheap student ticket later, I was sitting in the audience at the Rheinhalle. I can't remember the other pieces performed that evening, but eventually the flute played the notes of the introduction and I heard the weightless *Prélude à l'après-midi d'un faune* for the very first time. I thought: all that's up there on stage is woodwind, strings, two harps, and the only percussion is two antique cymbals – how can it be that this music sounds like something from another world?

These days, *L'Après-midi* is part of our musical canon. It is hard to imagine how the audience must have perceived it at its Paris premiere in 1894. I read somewhere that they initially thought the orchestra was still tuning up and the musicians had to repeat their performance.

Le Sacre du Printemps

During my degree, I was most interested in recent symphonic music, such as the work of Igor Stravinsky, a composer who embodies the music of the twentieth century like no other. Paris was the cultural epicentre of Europe around 1900. It was home to some of the most important artists of the time – painters, musicians, novelists and poets. In those days, Sergei Diaghilev – the famous impresario of the Ballets Russes – commissioned Stravinsky to write music for his ensemble. The 28-year-old composer went to Paris for the 1910 premiere of *L'Oiseau de feu* (*The Firebird*) and became a world-famous star overnight. His next commission for the Ballets Russes, *Petrushka*, was also a major success. In his orchestral pieces, Stravinsky makes percussion instruments popular. More than that – he transforms the entire orchestra into a huge percussion machine for long stretches at a time. The premiere of his most groundbreaking work, *Le Sacre du Printemps* (*The Rite of Spring*), in 1913 even caused a scandal, with Stravinsky pulling the acoustic rug out from under his listeners entirely. Why was that?

Up to the end of the nineteenth century, it was general practice in Western music to repeat rhythms in regularly accented patterns known as pulse groups. Time signatures were usually noted in groups of two or three: 2/4, 3/4, 4/4, 6/8, etc. Exactly like in our modern pop music, the schematic repetition of these beats made listeners feel safe. We might describe it these days as 'a groove'. Back then, too, everyone had grown accustomed to hearing harmonies and melodies in equally proportioned chunks of time.

We might compare it to the constitutions on which today's societies are founded, which we tend to forget in daily life when everything is working well. But if they are overruled or suspended, anarchy breaks out. Stravinsky's *Sacre* is not quite anarchy but he did unceremoniously tear out all the pages of the constitution and put them back together in a new order, a new structure. Translated into musical terms, that means: two- and three-part time types are added together without any recognizable pattern, not allowing listeners to find their feet for a single second. He also eschews any predictable repetition.

The composition's most famous section is in the movement 'Les augures printaniers – Danses des adolescentes'. To my ears, the *tempo giusto* sounds like the perfect soundtrack to Fritz Lang's *Metropolis* (1927). Using irregular accents of the quaver chords in the strings, Stravinsky creates a completely unpredictable rhythm. Through the bitonality of his harmonics, a dissonant tension builds but has nowhere to find resolution. Without any recognizable metre, this pounding rhythm moves incessantly forward in irregular periods.

And that is what is really new about *Sacre*: Stravinsky rhythmizes the accent patterns, constantly changing the metre. Applying this trick to an entire piece of music was an incredibly daring idea. The audience at the premiere must have thought his masterpiece was nothing but chaos.

Daphnis et Chloé

It was probably down to a change in the rota that I unexpectedly got to know the music of Maurice Ravel. Ernst Göbler had told me the date of a certain *Daphnis* performance over the phone in March 1973, but hadn't given any more details. Nor did he give me any notes for it. Perhaps he assumed I knew the work? Possibly. I was laid-back about the job. Perhaps a bit too laid-back – I didn't have the slightest idea of what awaited me.

On the day of the performance, I enter the opera house at about 6:30 p.m., through the stage door as usual. The doorman knows my face and waves me through. I take the narrow metal spiral staircase on the left down to the percussion room, where I hang up my duffle coat, fasten my silver tie and then head for the almost empty canteen. Treating myself to a tea and a sandwich for dinner, I read the full title of the evening's piece in a programme that happens to be lying around: *Daphnis et Chloé* by Maurice Ravel. It's a ballet in one act and three scenes for a large orchestra and a vocalizing choir, and is regarded as one of the most significant Impressionist works of music.

The percussion group arrives in dribs and drabs: Ernst Göbler, Hans-Joachim Schacht, Friedbert Haus, Günther Klein, Konni Ries and three more colleagues from the WDR Symphony Orchestra Cologne. Including myself, there are nine of us today; almost a football team. It looks like I'm the youngest again.

It's gradually dawning on me that Ravel's ballet music is a big deal for the percussion group, and my heart sinks to my stomach. In the end, I take Friedbert Haus aside surreptitiously and admit that I don't know *Daphnis* at all. Friedbert – the son of Fritz Haus, incidentally, with whom I first played on the opera stage – doesn't betray the slightest emotion but nudges me slowly towards the exit. In the orchestra pit, he points to the bass drum and says calmly: 'Let's go through your part.'

The score gives me a thorough shock: rapid tempi, compound metres, countless changes of time signature and lots of hand-written additions on every page. Gosh! Perhaps Friedbert sees the panic in my eyes. Whatever the case, he promises he'll help me at the key moments during the performance so that I don't get lost: 'I'll show you how the conductor beats it out. We'll manage somehow today, and for the performance on 23 March we'll take a look at it together, then you'll get it down fine.'

At almost 7:30, I take my place in the orchestra pit with the other musicians. I won't be needed until the finale but I want to understand how it all goes. The auditorium lights begin to dim, leaving only the sheet music illuminated. The conductor comes in, steps up to his platform and is greeted with applause from the audience. Quiet gradually descends. Concentration. Then Ravel's music rises out of the silence.

For me, the most impressive part of the composition is 'Lever du jour', which puts the mood of a magnificent morning landscape in the light of the rising sun into music. Millions of tiny particles add up to an iridescent, constantly changing pattern. The orchestra consolidates this sound more and more until it reaches its crescendo, which breaks like a gigantic wave and then ebbs away again. That moment is of such incredible beauty and intensity that I almost forget to breathe.

I really do only pick up on my cue in the subsequent furioso finale with Friedbert's help. And when I get lost at one point as I'm playing, he brings me back to the 'one' in the metre and even prevents me from beating at the wrong moment by putting his body between me and my drum. I don't know what I'd have done without him.

Ravel referred to *Daphnis et Chloé* as a choreographic symphony; it was another composition for the Ballets Russes commissioned by Sergei Diaghilev. Diaghilev was one of the most important catalysers of art in the early twentieth century. His talent lay in persuading the best dancers, choreographers, painters and musicians to work together, and he had an amazing instinct for successful productions. To this day, *Daphnis et Chloé*, *Le Sacre du Printemps* and *Prélude à l'après-midi d'un faune* are numbered among the most wonderful and influential works of musical history.

Oberkassel Student Digs

In August 1972, Bodo and I decided to move out of our shared flat on Nordstrasse. We were still friends but we felt we needed our independence. I spent a while living in a spare room at Rainer's place. One Friday night, just before midnight, I picked up the freshly printed *Rheinische Post* from the newspaper's offices. The Saturday edition contained small ads and housing vacancies. I was in luck: a place in Oberkassel was advertised, three rooms on an attic floor at number 36, Steffenstrasse. Bright and early on Saturday morning, I picked up the phone and made an appointment to go and see the flat.

Steffenstrasse is a small side street close to Belsenplatz square. Number 36 smelled of coal. The worn steps creaked as I walked up them. On the top floor, I entered a long corridor with three doors. The rooms – perhaps sixty square metres in total – had sloping ceilings but proper windows. Wooden floors. The furthest room from the front door had a washbasin with cold water, then there was an empty room in the middle, and the front room featured shelves and a coal stove. There was a toilet half a flight down.

I took a seat in the room with the adventurous fireplace, closed my eyes and heard . . . nothing. Absolute silence. Good! At the end of the corridor, I discovered a kind of secret door, behind which I found a long room for drying laundry. A ladder led up from there, so I climbed it right away and came out on an unexpected viewing tower; well, more of a platform. I held tight to the railing and enjoyed the 360-degree panorama. Brilliant! The rent for the flat was 188,80 Deutschmarks a month. I was determined to take it, that very day if I could. Presumably no one else applied, so I got the contract and moved in on 1 October 1972.

Three rooms with no central heating and no bathroom – my first flat to myself. I painted the walls, floors, windows and doors and got hold of some cheap furniture. There was a corner shop opposite that sold anything you could possibly need, and I soon became a regular there. On the way to Belsenplatz, I could get my clothes washed and ironed at a dry-cleaners on Sonderburgstrasse. By this point, I had amassed about a dozen white shirts for my opera performances.

Just as my life as a musician was going really well, my first love ended out of the blue. After three years together, Margot finished with me in December. I was pretty shocked when she broke the news gently – I must have been completely blind not to see it coming. I was probably living only in my music, not with my girlfriend. Margot enrolled at the school of applied arts in Krefeld to study ceramic and porcelain design. She was curious about life and open to everything that might come along. It seems she needed someone who understood her better than I did.

The unexpected separation knocked me right off track. I battened down the hatches at home, not going to my classes at the conservatory. All my fuses had blown and it stayed that way for a few days. Then all of a sudden, Ernst Göbler knocked at my door. I opened up in a pretty black mood. Spotting an empty Chianti bottle on the table, he shook his head and told me I mustn't let anything in the world stop me from making music. He said he knew music would play a key role in my life. My talent was a gift; I ought to believe in it and not gamble it away. Things happened in life that you can't control, he said, but the main thing was how you reacted to them – we can all determine that for ourselves. Ernst Göbler told me about his divorce a few years back, and that he'd found peace and stability in music and in God. He took a rosary out of his pocket and held it up to show me. I was grateful for his concern and care, and once he left my flat a little later, my life went on.

I soon felt at home in Oberkassel. I loved living on the left side of the Rhine, which had the charm of a sleepy old-fashioned town, or so it seemed to me.

From the fountain on Barbarossaplatz square, it was only a couple of minutes' walk to one of the most important places in the neighbourhood: Café Muggel on Dominikanerstrasse. It could have been in Paris or Amsterdam, with its mirrored walls above artificial leather benches, round white lamps hanging from the ceiling, a large bar dominating the room with ham and cheese baguettes lined up on its glass counter, an espresso machine and three tall tables with bar stools. I knew no better place for a bistro breakfast before the conservatory. As I ate, I would look at my notes and go through my schedule for the day, usually with an excellent jazz record playing. I remember Miles Davis's *Kind of Blue* and *Virgo Vibes* by Roy Ayers, featuring one of his finest recordings, 'The Ringer'. Music is always a tricky thing in cafés and restaurants. At Café Muggel, however, it felt like you were in a Louis Malle movie – *Elevator to the Gallows*, for instance – and listening to the quiet soundtrack. A small cinema opened up below ground-level in the evenings, with just a few seats.

A very different Oberkassel hotspot was the Vossen brewery pub on Belsenplatz, a former railway station building with big, tall rooms. I would often meet Reinhold Nickel there in the evenings, a fellow conservatory student from the sound engineers' class. We would get a bite to eat and talk about all the 'things that had to be talked about'. Reinhold was studying percussion with Ernst Göbler as his subsidiary subject, which allowed him to join the percussion ensemble. I liked him a lot; we always had a good laugh together, for example, about Manfred the waiter. The longstanding tradition was to treat him to at least one beer – a bit less than half a pint of dark altbier – every time you went there. He would thank you by holding the glass up above his head, yelling 'Zum Wohl,' downing it in one, slamming the empty glass down on his tray, turning on his heel and disappearing as quickly as he'd popped up. The method pushed up his daily turnover to dizzying heights.

Minimal Music

One day, I got a surprising opportunity to see the Steve Reich Ensemble in Düsseldorf's Kunsthalle. The numerous organs, xylorimbas and drums, and the musicians walking between them came across as absolute chaos. It was rather confusing, I thought. But once the characteristic structures of musical building blocks filled the room and transformed into a pattern of sound, Reich's linear approach of seemingly endless loops was perfectly self-explanatory.

The music put me into a kind of hypnosis. Suddenly – like a less dangerous variety of falling asleep for an instant behind the steering wheel – I woke up and noticed that the polyphonic pattern of ornamental figures had changed, though I couldn't say exactly when and how. The music's psychological effect is based on taking familiar-sounding musical material and subjecting it to constant repetition, layering and shifts to turn it into a permanently altering sound ornament. By going without traditional motif and theme developments, this sound, apparently moving on the spot, leads to a new experience of time. If you engage with it, it develops a musical undertow that puts the listener into a trance-like state. This American music seemed to me like a liberating response to the serial techniques that often gave me the impression of the focus being on the concept, with the music merely the end result of a calculated construction.

For the first time, I saw the percussionists' laid-back attitude as they took over each other's instruments as if changing shifts on a production line, not interrupting their part, and drinking Coke during the performance, chatting and laughing like jazz musicians. That concept and the musicians' relaxed performance – technically beyond all doubt – remained in my memory.

Alongside my work in the orchestra pit and on stage at the opera, the concert series and church music, more and more gigs with the Jokers came up in 1973. We played at the Hilton Hotel, the Bochum Press Ball, the Novea trade fair, the Rhine Terraces and for a large Düsseldorf construction company. Over the year, it all added up to about thirty gigs, each earning us 300 to 500 Deutschmarks per head. Sven Jensen – who had a hit with a song that translates as 'Leather Trousers Don't Need Pressing' (he was right!) – a crooner we'd worked with at the end of the sixties, also booked us for a record production. Just back from the USA, he recorded a version of 'Spinning Wheel' with us. This studio job was a real challenge for me; the work was new and exciting. And the fee put me in the fortunate position of being able to pursue my less lucrative musical projects. I didn't have any financial problems during my degree; something always turned up within my cultural network without the slightest effort.

Jazz

Aside from my years at the conservatory, I associate my time in Oberkassel with my growing interest in jazz, the great music of the twentieth century. It was probably to do with the fact that I was focusing my training more and more on the mallet instruments – xylophone and glockenspiel – and on the vibraphone.

After 1945, the vibraphone became very popular among composers of what we call high culture. Before that, though, it first became known through its use in jazz. Looking into the instrument, I immediately came across the recordings of Lionel Hampton, Red Norvo, Milt Jackson, Terry Gibbs, Cal Tjader, Roy Ayers and last but not least, Gary Burton. Burton is without a doubt the most outstanding vibraphonist of our times. The recordings he'd made with Keith Jarrett and Chick Corea were on heavy rotation on my record player. I listened to them over and over, from the first to the last note.

So that I could practise outside of the conservatory, I scraped together every last penny and bought myself a vibraphone, a xylophone and a half-decent piano. At last. I was soon not only immersing myself up to my neck in Bach's *Preludes and Fugues* in my music room, but also diving into what's called the *Real Book*. The book is a collection of all relevant jazz standards produced in the genre, in a simplified notation.

In jazz, the idea is usually to start out by establishing a musical theme and then adapting it in real time. The craftier and cleverer the variations on these themes are in an improvisation, going as far as twisting them to unrecognizability, the cooler it sounds. Although the metre provides the cohesion and all the musicians stick exactly to the chord structure, the song's basic melody is ideally only guessable, at best. When the original theme sounds out again after the instruments' improvisations, it's amazing how they've all found their way back home. The principle has applied since the days of New Orleans jazz or Dixieland. There, every instrument plays its own improvisation after the theme. But none of them go too far away from the opening theme – it's always present in the subtext. Swing music is another form that uses ornaments and formulaic conventions. When a few jazz musicians took the principle to extremes in Bebop, with breakneck tempi, expanded harmonics and crazy improvisations played using acrobatic techniques, things got adventurous.

I would never match the skills of the original modern jazz musicians, that much I knew, but I had a lot of fun improvising on my own level. I spent days transcribing the performances of vibraphonists I admired from records and imitating them until I could play by heart.

Another thing I was developing more and more interest in was harmonics and counterpoint. Inventing and writing down a modulation from one key into another made me forget the whole world around me. I would sit at the piano in my music room for hours, trying out changes and composing.

Alongside my music, I got the feeling my general education could use an upgrade, so in August I started attending a sixth-form college on Mondays, Wednesdays and Fridays, the Franz-Jürgens Fachoberschule. The classes took place in the evenings and fitted more or less into my schedule at the conservatory. I thought I'd squeeze in the opera performances somehow. It turned out I was wrong – I got more and more shifts and it didn't work out in the end. Nonetheless, the year until I left the school again may not have been all that exciting – but it was definitely useful.

Detox

After performances at the opera house, I would occasionally head to the old town centre for a beer or a Coke in the Ratinger Hof to wind down the evening.

One night – I was just on my way from the Kunsthalle to Ratinger Strasse – I heard the sound of live music in the distance. There's a band playing at Creamcheese, I thought. Someone was improvising on the guitar, with an open vibe. The closer I got, the louder the music. It sounded oriental, somehow. I went in. Inside the bar, it was pretty dark aside from a single strip light flickering somewhere. I could make out the musicians' vague outlines. They were the usual suspects who hung out at every jam session in a hundred-kilometre radius. This'll be fun, I thought. And then I spotted a vibraphone in a corner of the room. I went over to the instrument, picked up the mallets lying on the claves and kicked off.

But wait! Something wasn't right. The music rushed past me, making it hard for me to join in. And the guys in the band took no notice of me whatsoever. Or was I just imagining that? No. They'd obviously prepared thoroughly for the session with copious 'shit' or other substances. And without having shared their conscientious prep, I found it really hard to 'keep up'. We simply weren't compatible.

There's a longstanding tradition linking musicians and drugs, not only in jazz or pop. Be it to free themselves from the shackles of reality, to switch into a different, less conscious state in the hope of artistic inspiration – or simply as a mood lifter. Up until then, many of our jam sessions had been minor hedonistic celebrations, the behavioural code including one or two shared joints the way a Martini – shaken, not stirred – belongs to a James Bond film. And I'll admit I even went too far at two or three gigs. So I do know what I'm talking about. That evening, though, was different. I'd just come from the professional surroundings of the opera house, still wearing my suit – the silver tie rolled up in my pocket – and I was in a completely different state to my fellow players. Paradoxically, we would have needed an interpreter to communicate musically.

I asked myself: A joint can't be the prerequisite for an inspired session, can it? With hashish, marijuana, alcohol or whatever in your blood you might be relaxed, it's fun to play, you get that tingling all over your body, you find your way into the music, everything is subjectively great and meaningful – but is it really? Objectively?

Actually, I've never achieved anything sensible in that way, I thought as I walked home across Oberkassel Bridge. It's my sense of judgement that falls by the wayside, above all. My only focus is on experiencing my own altered state and intensifying it even further, if possible. I'm a long way from handing out wise advice, but for me, making music – the combination of listening, feeling, playing and thinking – is a highly complex process involving all the musician's abilities. Meaning there's nothing more important than a clear head. That goes for both making and listening to music, because listening too is related to thinking.

That night above the Rhine, I made the decision that that phase of my life was now over, and I wouldn't let any substance influence me in my musical practice any more. Music is far too important for my existence to experience it with anything less than full awareness. And that's that.

5

A YEAR WITH CONSEQUENCES

Audition in Berlin. Music Student in Düsseldorf. Klaus Röder's Passacaglia. Kling Klang Studio. The Electronic Drum Kit. Golf and the Psychedelic Score. 'The Classic Line-Up'.

Audition in Berlin

When I flew to Berlin on 18 January 1974, the city was still an island surrounded by East Germany, with the Wall dividing Germany into two halves. My generation grew up believing the two German states would continue to coexist unchanged over many years to come.

The Berlin Philharmonic Orchestra – at that time conducted by Herbert von Karajan – had a vacant percussionist position, and my teacher and mentor Ernst Göbler had recommended me for the job. There was no way I could chicken out, so I wrote an application. And lo and behold, I was invited to audition.

So there I was, in the divided city for the first time. I walked nervously up and down Kurfürstendamm before I went to my hotel that evening. To be honest, I didn't get a very good night's sleep. The next morning, I walked into the Philharmonic and was given a friendly reception by a member of the percussion group. The audition was held on the stage, with a few people listening in from the auditorium. My fellow percussionist led me to a snare drum, handed me a pair of very thick drumsticks, and presented me with the score. It wasn't a piece I knew.

'As loud as you can,' I heard someone call out. If you say so – and I beat out as loudly as I could: tam-tatta-tam, tam-tatta-tam . . . 'Good, thanks.'

There followed a few orchestral studies for snare drum and glockenspiel. Then we went over to the xylophone, where the score to *Porgy and Bess* was on the music stand. Right, I thought, of course. There's a notorious part in it that right-handed players in particular practise until they're blue in the face: fast semiquavers with accents that have to sound absolutely light and fluent. 'It has to fizz like champagne,' I heard my teacher saying at the back of my mind. That was one of his favourite metaphors. I was on good form that morning and it really did fizz like champagne. Then came a few orchestral studies for the xylophone and I was done. Handshakes all round, 'Thanks, have a good flight, we'll be in touch,' . . . and back to Tempelhof Airport.

Music Student in Düsseldorf

I didn't get the vacant job with the Berlin Philharmonic in the end, but they did offer me a place at the Karajan Foundation. That meant I could finish my studies at their academy, with a grant that would cover my financial needs. My teacher was conflicted and didn't know what to advise me. On the one hand, Ernst Göbler wanted to teach me up to my examination – and on the other hand, it would be an incredible opportunity, a golden ticket into the orchestra. I had to make the decision for myself, though.

I weighed up the options. On one side of the scales: the Berlin Philharmonic, the Karajan Foundation, a grant – and on the other the Robert Schumann Conservatory, the Deutsche Oper am Rhein, my many musical projects and activities, and all my social contacts. I simply had too good a network in my home town – and I chose Düsseldorf. I went by my gut feeling. From the sixties to the mid-eighties, there was perhaps no city in Germany that was better suited for living, studying and working – at least for me.

Although it might sound strange, with just under 600,000 inhabitants and the uncomplicated size and security of a small city, Düsseldorf offered a wide range of cultural activities. There was (and still is) the world-standard art academy – on the edge of what's called 'the longest bar in the world', the city's old town centre. The renowned fashion trade fair Igedo brought in huge amounts of money – and also a high density of attractive models, as it happened. The carnival season at the end of winter and the marksmen's processions in summer lent their traditional flair to the city just as much as the exclusive discotheques on the legendary Königsallee. In Düsseldorf, all sorts of things were possible at once back then. Anything goes, everything fits together.

You'd see people swaying to cheesy pop hits, drunk on altbier at the bars of the brewery pubs, while next door in the Downtown venue, fans would be applauding trad jazz or out-there musical experiments. And after that they'd all meet up – from Joseph Beuys to fashion models, from musical directors to jazz pianists – for grilled chicken at Hühner-Hugo in the middle of the old town centre.

During those days, I applied for a few more positions as an orchestral musician and was invited to auditions, but in the end the job didn't seem all that attractive. So I went on with my music degree – I was in my ninth semester – and also with my various ventures. I certainly never got bored. Looking through my old calendar, I wonder when I ever slept, because even my weekly lessons added up to many hours. As a rule, I was in the percussion room or the adjacent piano room at Villa Engelhardt by ten at the latest, ready to study and practise. I don't know how many hours I spent in practice spaces and music rooms, alone but never lonely, aiming to master an étude or an orchestral study or find out how I interpreted a certain composition. They were good days, filled with dedicated work and regular happiness. I would usually leave the villa in the evening with the janitor, Herr Riem. If I had a performance I would set off for the opera house at about six. During the 1973/74 and 1974/75 seasons, I worked 150 opera shifts, including Richard Wagner's *Die Meistersinger von Nürnberg*, *La Bohème* by Giacomo Puccini, *Wozzeck* by Alban Berg and Benjamin Britten's *Death in Venice*.

Engagements like these included morning rehearsals and the subsequent premieres and performances. All the stage music and orchestral jobs added up. Things were busy at the conservatory too. The July 1974 programme for the first practice evening of Ernst Göbler's percussion class featured, alongside *Sonic Boom* and other compositions for the percussion ensemble, *Drei kleine Stücke für Stabspiele* by a certain Karlheinz Bartos.

Klaus Röder's Passacaglia

Düsseldorf's Neander Church hosted a forum for New Music, the concert series 3 mal Neu. For young sound artists, an invitation to present their work there was akin to a knighthood. A piece for tape machine and percussion was to be performed at one of these concerts, with the programmatic title of *Passacaglia*. The composer was Klaus Röder. His professor – Klaus was also at the Robert Schumann Conservatory – suggested he talk to me.

> Klaus Röder: 'For the percussion voice, my lecturer told me he knew a good percussionist for me: Karlheinz Bartos. He was just about to take his examination and was a regular in the opera orchestra. So it was a clear-cut thing.'

With his long hair, beard and sandaled feet, Klaus made me think of a strange esoteric type. He could easily have been cast as Jesus at the Oberammergau Passion Plays. His friendly and humorous way of speaking made it very easy for me to communicate with him. Things did get tight, though, because only a single rehearsal was scheduled and we couldn't get through Klaus's rather complicated piece in the short time we had. We did the obvious and improvised: me on percussion and Klaus on his EMS synthesizer.

> Klaus Röder: 'Karl clearly enjoyed himself, as after the concert he said he'd be glad to perform *Passacaglia* again – which made me happy. If I remember rightly, I told him a bit about the band Kraftwerk, which I was playing in at the time.'

He's right. I'd heard the name before but the reality of my life as a musician was very different. The most important thing to me was the regular orchestral shifts and stage performances at the Deutsche Oper am Rhein and my part in symphony concerts. My jobs in the New Music context and the liturgical music of the church year were also a high priority. A sonata by Georg Friedrich Händel on the vibraphone at a Sunday-morning church service, improvised jazz percussion at a reading for the Protestant Church Congress? Why, of course!

The most commercially interesting job offers doubtlessly came from the entertainment world. With the Jokers, I played in large venues and hotels like the Hilton and the Park Hotel that year. We were getting booked more and more often for galas, to accompany prestigious artists like Roberto Blanco, Costa Cordalis and Karel Gott. We wouldn't waste much time rehearsing – someone handed out the scores and off we went. I occasionally drummed for the Horst Stamm Big Band, which had a good reputation in the region, for instance, in Essen's Grugahalle. The repertoire was made up of swing and big band-era classics and was played entirely at sight. I remember a dance competition where classily dressed couples gave it their all with foxtrot, quickstep and Viennese waltzes.

Jobs in the permeable realm between art and entertainment were especially cool, I thought: for instance, an evening with music by Antônio Carlos Jobim or a jazz ensemble and symphony orchestra 'Play Bach Performance' at which I switched back and forth between timpani, percussion and vibraphone. Then there were rehearsals and gigs with Sinus, but also concerts with other bands. And like most music students, I also gave private lessons.

My calendar was really full in 1974 and the diversity of my work was broader than ever. I loved moving in the different musical worlds. Culture is like a conversation on many different levels, they say. And it's true, with the metaphor applying to my everyday life as well. When I switched levels, I also switched languages. Musicians talked differently about music in every setting: at the conservatory, with the symphony orchestra, in the avant-garde New Music circles, with the Jokers, the big band, the jazz ensembles, the soul band and in Sinus. I saw that cultural polyphony as a gift and a great source of wealth. And in basic terms, my undertakings on the different cultural levels also paid my bills.

Kling Klang Studio

In September – about six months after my audition in Berlin – Ernst Göbler had some news for me:

'I got a call from the Kraftwerk group. They're looking for a classical percussionist for their concerts. Have you heard of them? Do you know what kind of thing they do? Anyway, I recommended you.'

'Sure, I've heard of them. They're a . . . hmm, what are they? An avant-garde band? In any case, they're a nationwide success, they make records and they've been on TV. Their music is the theme tune to the *Kennzeichen D* programme.'

There was a lot of talk among musicians about Kraftwerk's expensive sound system, so I was aware they seemed to have plenty of money – but that was about all I knew. I had once spotted a poster of them on the wall of the control room at a studio session. Two musicians facing each other behind all kinds of instruments: organs, cables, technical equipment. 'That's the future of music,' the studio owner said. Ernst Göbler was more interested in the present. 'Give them a call! Here's the number of a chap called "Esleben", I think that was his name. He'll be available at seven. You never know what might come out of it.'

An enquiry like this wasn't particularly special; I often got them. And now Kraftwerk? Alright, why not? I called the number after my classes. 'Hello, this is Karlheinz Bartos from the conservatory,' I introduced myself. 'You spoke to my teacher, Ernst Göbler – what is it you're looking for?'

We arranged to meet up to get to know each other. Until then, I went on with my usual schedule: lectures, lessons, rehearsals, performances, private pupils, practice, studying. I had plenty to do and I thought no more about the appointment.

One Friday less than a week later, at 5:30 p.m. on 4 October 1974, I turned up at number 16, Mintropstrasse. I went into the courtyard through a roller door and up a narrow staircase at the back right, with a sign mounted above the open door saying Elektro Müller. A stairwell, a door, a tiny entrance area and another wooden door. That one was open too, and I stepped into a large, high-ceilinged room: about twelve metres by six metres, with about six-metre ceilings. White brick walls, the obligatory egg cartons. The only window was blocked off with a wooden shutter for sound insulation. A neon tube hung from the ceiling, immersing the space in pallid light. All kinds of stuff was strewn around the room. I spotted an old-fashioned standard lamp, large speakers, a children's drum kit, an organ. But there was no time to inspect it closely. Two guys came to meet me and greeted me formally, restrained but friendly: Ralf Hütter and Florian Schneider. As I later found out, Florian had asked his former private flute teacher Rosemarie Popp – who also taught at the conservatory – for a contact in the percussion class, and she had given him my teacher's number.

After a little small talk, the two of them took me over to a strange device: the console of the electronic drum kit first played by Wolfgang Flür for a performance on the TV show *Aspekte* on 10 October 1973. These days, it would be described as an electronic percussion multipad. On top of the console were several round metal plates, with two metal rods resting on them. On the floor was a kind of light switch, which – they explained – triggered a bass-drum sound. OK, that was easy enough to understand. Without inspecting the contraption any more closely, I kicked off and played a drum pattern that came into my head, switching to another after a few bars. Unfortunately, the rods not only clattered loudly on the metal plates; they also had no weight to them so I couldn't feel exactly when they landed. Then again, percussionists are used to banging out a rhythm with any stick on any object.

Ralf and Florian went to their instruments. Now we were standing just like a chamber music ensemble, facing one another around an imaginary middle point. The two of them logged into my rhythm and played straight away, with no complications. We exchanged glances now and then, laughed and went on playing. Ralf plonked away at the keyboard of a device that looked like a miniature organ. A Minimoog synthesizer, as I later learned. I heard a bass riff that created a strangely pulsating rhythm pattern with the aid of an echo machine. On top of that, Ralf played simple major chords on the Farfisa organ. Florian improvised scales and arpeggios on his flute. The result sounded like a mix of pop and folk music. I experienced our first session as pretty relaxed and easy-going. The music's sound unfurled in the brightest, clearest major keys. Wonderful. After an hour or two, we said polite goodbyes and I set off back to Oberkassel on foot.

The Electronic Drum Kit

It seemed Ralf and Florian could imagine working with me, seeing as Ralf called me to ask if I felt like playing at a couple of Kraftwerk gigs. They didn't have any specific dates lined up, he said, but we could meet up now and then to talk over the arrangements. It sounded good to me. We made a date for 18 October 1974. I suggested to Ralf: 'Why don't you pick me up at the opera house at ten in the evening.' I had a shift doing incidental music for a performance before that.

After my last percussion part, I crept out of the wings, threw on my duffle coat in the changing room, headed up the metal spiral staircase and left the opera house by the stage door. Ralf was waiting in his grey Beetle with the motor running. It was a cold night. When I got in I noticed his black leather gloves. A few minutes later we drove off the 'Millipede'[1] and onto Mintropstrasse. In the studio, the pallid neon light was on again. Florian was standing on the right-hand side of the room behind a metal table, flashing us a charming smile and fiddling with his mixing desk and devices. There was a brief bang. Then another, followed by a hum. Florian leaned forward to his microphone with his flute and suddenly, there it was, the typical sequence of notes he so often played in those days: a rising and falling scale that he sent to a tape echo machine. That echo sequence was his sound signature at that time.

A business-like Ralf went to his Minimoog on the left-hand side of the room. He put his gloves down on the empty spot above the keyboard, pressed a key with his right hand and turned the dials with his left hand. I didn't have the faintest idea what he was doing. But despite being so small, the Moog had a really impressive sound.

I was between the two of them again on the electronic drum kit. According to Florian, he had discovered a drum machine on a trip to New York in the early seventies and bought it on impulse. The machine had a series of buttons on which you could play individual percussion instruments one by one on top of an automatic rhythm pattern. 'Typing' a complete drum beat on these buttons was hard work, though. So the guys had taken the device apart, modified it and put it in a new casing. This time, I took a closer look at the prototype. The rectangular playing console was held by a kind of drum stand. Encased in mother-of-pearl adhesive vinyl, it was reminiscent of a normal acoustic drum kit. My Ludwig set had a similar mother-of-pearl finish.

Beneath the round metal plates on the console were labels giving the names of the percussion instruments: timpani, snare, concert drum, drum roll, cymbal long, cymbal short, bongo, claves, castanets, etc.

Two metal rods were cabled up to the console; they looked rather like knitting needles. When I hit the rods on the metal plates this time, I heard snare drum, cymbal or castanets. Touching the plates worked like an electrical switch that creates a short circuit. Except that it didn't turn on a light bulb, but instead produced a sound.

The switch on the ground for the bass drum was difficult to

116

operate and we never really got the hang of it. Later, we put the bass drum up on the multipad with all the other instruments and played it by hand, which was much more practical. More cables linked the bass-drum switch and the playing board with the electronics, which were contained in a 19-inch box to the left of the console. The construction was a work of genius: this percussion multipad meant the electronic instruments from a drum machine could be played manually.

And then we kicked off again: I drummed a minimalist beat, Ralf played his typical ostinato bass, and Florian trilled joyful cascades of echoes on the flute. And then – as you might expect – the volume knobs were gradually turned up to full. Ralf and Florian's faces betrayed not the slightest emotion or discomfort. I, however, had the misfortune of standing directly in front of the tweeter. Not wanting to look like a complete weakling, I tried to move my right ear inconspicuously out of the danger zone.

I must have totally underestimated the sound of the drum kit on my first visit, as the higher volume gave it definition and power. One major advantage of electronic sound production is being able to change the sound and its dynamic on the mixing desk. The method of sound creation and the limited number of instruments also influences the way musicians play. That meant I could forget all the technique I'd learned over the years – but the timbre and the pressure of the electronic percussion instruments were really astounding.

That second session went on slightly longer. I didn't know the music, but the most important thing was that I created something like a continuous beat with the knitting needles. Everything else would sort itself out over time.

By the by, Ralf and Florian informed me they also worked with the drummer Wolfgang Flür. The description they gave me was something like: great drummer, looks good, fits perfectly into the team, very good at making things. He had been involved in developing the multipad design with them, I was told.

'Sure, I know Wolfgang Flür,' I responded. 'Every musician in Düsseldorf knows him.' We arranged to meet again in eight days' time, and Ralf and Florian foisted two records on me as I left so I could get into their sound. All the relevant titles from their early releases were on them, they told me.

One of them turned out to be a double LP combining the albums *Kraftwerk* and *Kraftwerk 2*. On the black cover, a blue waveform graphic gave an impression of an electronic visualization of sound. The band's name was written in white stencilled lettering. Inside the gatefold sleeve were lots of out-of-focus underground photos. To be precise: thirteen of Ralf, eight of Florian, another eight of instruments – and one photo of Conny Plank, the record's sound engineer and co-producer. Aha, Conny, I thought.

Another thing that stood out was the unusual track names. They seemed like a code to me: 'Ruckzuck', 'Stratovarius', 'Megaherz', 'Vom Himmel hoch', 'Klingklang', 'Atem', 'Strom', 'Spule 4', 'Wellenlänge', 'Harmonika'.

'Ruckzuck' was instantly familiar, as the *Kennzeichen D* theme tune. It really was the perfect jingle for the political magazine programme, and it reminded me of Pink Floyd. The other tracks were slightly reminiscent of them too. The tempo changes leapt out at me – the pieces often sped up over the length of the tracks, increasing their intensity. As I listened, I imagined how I'd play along on the electronic percussion.

The cover of the second record – *Ralf und Florian* – features an old-fashioned-looking black-and-white portrait of the two of them. In the photo on the back, they are sitting at their instruments in the studio. Again, the track list contains a series of interesting song titles: 'Elektrisches Roulette', 'Tongebirge', 'Kristallo', 'Heimatklänge', 'Tanzmusik', 'Ananas Symphonie'.

The A-side begins with a short electronic audio play, after which Ralf and Florian developed a bizarre, extremely lively electro-acoustic space. I can only describe it as a dazzling sound that fragments like sunlight on the surface of water and creates thousands of lightly distorted, glittering reflexes. Against this backdrop, a romantic theme repeats, floating in space like a question. In contrast to the legato melody of the flute and synthesizer, Ralf hammers out an almost mechanical rhythm on the Farfisa piano, animating Florian to his boisterous playing on the children's drum kit. With the sparkling wit of their music, Ralf and Florian manage to convey the dizzy euphoria of a lucky streak.

I recognized 'Tongebirge' as the Taj Mahal-like track Florian had played earlier in the studio. On 'Kristallo' they ramped up the tempo, while the moderate 'Heimatklänge' was very different, almost taking me on a mental trip to Berchtesgaden with its folksy traditions. I also liked 'Tanzmusik' with its strange timing and 'Ananas Symphonie' – which was really made up of several episodes.

Ralf und Florian (the record actually ought to be called 'Florian und Ralf') seemed to me like a development on what came before. The album is made up of instrumental music as well, but it has little to do with the first two records. Florian's part is very confident and Ralf is gradually making the Minimoog his own. I didn't yet know what a vocoder is, so I couldn't identify it on 'Ananas Symphonie' at first. You can really hear on the album how much Ralf and Florian enjoyed playing. Their music – composed only in major keys – progresses through time, joyful and relaxed, and contains the first draft of the band's own musical identity.

The album included a large foldable comic illustrating the six tracks. At the same time, it presents Kraftwerk's geographical, cultural and social environment and determines their musical position, using musical notation, the circle of fifths and a young woman at the piano – Ralf's older sister. But the comic is also a visual ode to the collaboration within the group, depicted by means of their communication, a session in the Kling Klang Studio and a vision of the future. 'You'll soon be hearing new things in Düsseldorf . . .' it says on the last page, as though the lyrics for 'Autobahn' were already on the air.

What I listened to most closely was the drums. Machines didn't have a good reputation with us 'real' drummers. We tended to see them as fun playthings for solo entertainers. Having said that, I had listened to Sly and the Family Stone's 'Family Affair' a thousand times and never realized there was a drum machine playing its loops on the track.

Perhaps it was down to my new personal connection with Ralf and Florian, playing on their electronic drum kit and the atmosphere in the Kling Klang Studio, but in any case, I now heard the drum-machine sound very differently. The more interesting rhythm tracks were on 'Klingklang', 'Tanzmusik' and several of the episodes in the 'Ananas Symphonie'. They weren't at the forefront of the mix, but I did recognize a new quality: the mechanical rhythm gave the metre a light and elegant pulse. The rhythms came across as anonymous, dividing up time systematically like a bar line. Psychologically, my reaction to the machines was affirmative; I got something out of them from the very beginning. They weren't a threat or a challenge, more a great new thing for us to do with music.

So as to keep their arrangements' rhythms flexible if they wanted, Ralf and Florian had developed manual controls for the sounds of their drum machine, in conjunction with Wolfgang. Naturally, the sounds and the performance with the knitting needles on the metal plates encouraged a way of playing that came across as mechanical. As it soon turned out, this was an interesting and important side effect. It makes most sense in pop music when the drums are played in a straightforward way; permanent drum fills are usually counterproductive. It's best for drummers not to fire in all directions in a pop context but to concentrate on the timing, coming up with an appropriate pattern for the music.

Without us ever talking about it, it was clear that the Kraftwerk rhythm section shouldn't take its orientation from rock clichés. Even the hardware made that inevitable. The sound and the later automation of the electronic percussion became an attribute of the group, setting it apart from other bands.

Golf and the Psychedelic Score

On 28 October 1974, a Monday evening, Florian picked me up at my Oberkassel flat. This time, I wanted to take my vibraphone along to the Kling Klang Studio. He turned up at my student digs in his grey leather pilot's jacket and looked around my music room.

It was only about twenty square metres in size, painted white with a wooden floor. The window had a view of the rooftops on the other side of the road, which gave the room a hint of Parisian atmosphere. To the right of the window was my Helmholz piano, piled high as usual with various musical literature and swathes of my notes on sheet music. There was also a metronome – then as now, an essential tool for setting tempo and metre. My xylophone, vibraphone and snare drum were set up to the left of the window. I had hung a large oval mirror exactly opposite so I could keep an eye on my posture while I practised the vibraphone. Next to the mirror was a portrait of Frank Marth, a Düsseldorf guitarist, his eyes closed as he concentrated entirely on his sense of sound.

My music room was the epicentre of the flat. It was where I prepared for my classes and learned new parts for the opera or concerts. Rehearsals were also possible with a few others from Sinus or for chamber music for piano, double bass and vibraphone. Astoundingly enough, the neighbours almost never complained about the noise – even though we practised some pretty atonal compositions for the Sinus repertoire . . .

Discovering twelve-tone music was an extremely exciting adventure at the time. In the early twentieth century, the composers of what is known as the Second Viennese School – most prominently Arnold Schönberg – had abandoned the security of the familiar major and minor tonality and developed a system in which all twelve tones are of equal value.

A series like that seemed a thousand times more abstract to me than a melody with origins in the major-minor-tonality system, which triggers an infinite number of familiar associations for the listener. Particularly some of Anton Webern's pieces, only seconds or minutes long, still seem to me like crystal-clear acoustic creations that float on air, their drastically reduced musical substance demanding that the listener thinks deeply about how they might go on – creating a kind of mental music. Herbert Eimert's twelve-tone textbook *Lehrbuch der Zwölftontechnik* soon became my favourite reading matter, opening up a completely new perspective on composition for me.

Florian flicked through the notes on my piano and music stands, spotted the portrait of Frank Marth next to the mirror, smiled and gave me an appreciative nod. He clearly approved of the student-like atmosphere. Then the two of us lugged the vibraphone down three flights of stairs.

When he opened the boot of his car, I was surprised to see a bag of golf clubs and the matching clothing. Earnest and enthusiastic, Florian explained that he and Ralf had just started playing golf. I interpreted his words to mean that the sport was good for the mind – very meditative. Plus, it took place in the great outdoors and all that . . . But the shoes and the checked trousers looked a little ridiculous to me. I tried to picture what I'd look like in them – but my imagination let me down. Golf? Me? Absurd! Membership of a golf club was very much an upper-class status symbol. It wasn't something I could ever envisage.

We stowed the vibraphone in the boot and headed off. Without exaggeration, I can safely describe Florian's driving as 'sporty', and we turned into the courtyard at Mintropstrasse only shortly later. Ralf was already in the studio. He switched the lights off unexpectedly and a previously unnoticed neon tube on the floor immersed the whole room in ultraviolet light. Incredible. It was the first time I'd seen UV light.

The next song was 'Kometenmelodie', Ralf announced, and put a large sheet of music on the stand in front of my vibraphone. A notation system with a major scale and a few symbolic diatonic arpeggios gave off a psychedelic glow in the UV light. Blimey! It wasn't a standard notation of musical content, but more of a pictogram that said: this piece consists of a scale and arpeggios. Ralf and Florian watched to see how I'd react to their little light show and fluorescent notes. I didn't let them see how impressed I was, though. We soon started up and I played my chords. When Ralf switched into a constantly repeated organ riff, I replied with a Steve Reich-style motif. It worked. Florian fired off a few sound rockets with his synthesizer to go along with it all. Next up was 'Ruckzuck'. One of them switched on a rhythm on the drum machine. Then Ralf quickly showed me the motif on the Farfisa organ for me to play on the vibraphone. That freed him up to concentrate on the bass on the Minimoog. And Florian breathed his familiar flute phrasing over the top. It was fun to repeat the motif for what felt like forever, but my vibraphone didn't stand a chance against the sound of the PA, so I went back to the electronic drum kit, which made more sense.

Ralf's performance sounded convincing. He didn't have a virtuoso playing technique getting in his way, which tripped up many prog rock-era keyboarders. That meant he didn't fall back on blues or jazz clichés when he improvised, but instead took his orientation from minimal music motifs. Once we'd finished, someone turned the lights back on. We blinked at each other. That went well.

Thanks to his glasses and his hair, cut relatively short in an old-fashioned style, Ralf came across as both funny and intelligent.

124

Florian – his hair also short and neatly parted – was lively and had a very winning side to him. The two of them seemed like a good match. They were nice and easy to get along with. Even though we hadn't known each other long, I felt comfortable in this new triangle. I was a few years younger than them, but that felt kind of fitting.

That evening, we also talked about our musical reference points and what we were currently listening to. Ralf started out with American bands. I remember him mentioning the Velvet Underground, the Doors and the Beach Boys, plus the Kinks from England.

Florian mentioned the Beach Boys too – I think we talked about *Pet Sounds*. Stevie Wonder's songs seemed to be important to him as well. The names Roxy Music and Pink Floyd came up – Florian nicknamed them 'Pink Flink', incidentally. Apparently, Kraftwerk had played at an open-air festival in Aachen in 1970, where Pink Floyd were booked too. I didn't find out what Florian thought of them. When he talked about Roxy Music, though, it was to do with the white captain's jacket that Bryan Ferry had worn for a concert in the Rheinhalle in Düsseldorf . . . Dress codes – in general or individually – weren't something we discussed to begin with, but it seemed that Florian and Ralf were very style-conscious and placed a lot of importance on their clothing.

They were never worried about developing technical skills on their instruments. Instead, they made efficient use of their natural instincts as a stylistic device. And although they knew their way around elementary music theory, from the very beginning I saw Ralf and Florian more as fine artists, later designers and above all, entrepreneurs. Their interest lay primarily in

125

music of newer origins. We talked about minimal music, and it wasn't long before we ended up on the subject of Stockhausen's Cologne experiments.

What did surprise me a little was that Florian knew the name Mauricio Kagel, who also taught at Cologne Conservatory. He seemed to like his film *Match for Three Players*. Over the next few minutes, the two of us vied to imitate the players' theatrical gestures. We laughed ourselves silly at our contortions. That was the moment when I first realized we had a lot in common.

At some point – as our conversation went on revolving around electronic music – Ralf pointed at his Minimoog. He and Florian seemed to be convinced synthesizers would give rise to a new species of pop music. A synthesizer, they said, could imitate any musical instrument with ease, and create entirely new sounds. To demonstrate, Ralf played a few bars of a bassline and then, having flicked a few switches and turned a few dials, moved into a register that sounded like a woman's voice. With another two or three quick adjustments, he altered his vox humana setting into white noise. And that was where we ended our third session.

The next time we met, Ralf showed me the new, not-yet-released Kraftwerk album *Autobahn*. He took out the white paper sleeve, stuck a sticker with the German motorway sign on it, and wrote underneath it, in capital letters, the names of a few pieces that were clearly to form the set-list at the coming gigs: 'Ruckzuck', 'Klingklang', 'Atem', 'Autobahn', 'Kometenmelodie 1+2'. After rehearsing, we arranged another session for November, where Wolfgang would play with us too.

At home, I took a closer look at the album's artwork. Especially in the 1970s and 1980s, record covers communicated the artist's identity or the album's concept – or both. With his picture on the cover of the original LP, the Düsseldorf artist Emil Schult certainly managed exactly that. Using a sophisticated device, he puts the listeners inside the band's moving car, looking out through the windscreen. Ahead of us are a few miles of autobahn cutting through a hilly green landscape. A bridge crosses the motorway and disappears behind two fir trees. The sky is blue but for one perfect white cloud, the sun just casting its first rays behind the hills, and a plane is flying in the distance. Parallel to the road, we can see the pylons of an electric power line. The road is almost empty, shared only with a black Mercedes and a grey VW Beetle.

The back cover features a black-and-white photo of the band: Ralf and Florian sitting alongside Klaus Röder and Wolfgang. As I later found out, the original photo was of Emil next to the other three. I don't know why, but Emil then superimposed Wolfgang's head onto his own body. When *Autobahn* was published in the collection *Der Katalog* many decades later, this retouch was reversed. The circumstances had changed and now Emil's head is back on his own body.

Of course, I instantly recognized Klaus Röder, sitting cheerfully between Florian and the morphed Emil-Wolfgang. Klaus had played violin and guitar on the album but was no longer part of the band. I found it hard to put Emil's collage in a stylistic category, but in some ways it reminded me of the style of the cinema posters and advertising drawings of my childhood.

Then I played the record. The piece begins, as we all know now, with a small acoustic audio play – someone opens and closes a car door, starts the engine, revs up, toots the horn twice – as if greeting the listener – and drives out of the imaginary landscape. My first thought was: Great, these real sounds are fun in a way, but not a joke.

After a strange electronic-sounding voice that reminds us of the name of the track, a bassline sets in with an echo effect that I knew from the studio. There's an instrumental verse followed by a chant that called to mind the humourist and poet Wilhelm Busch: 'Wir fah'n, fah'n, fah'n, auf der Autobahn . . .' – 'Driving hey, hey, hey on the motorway'.

Florian had used a vocoder back on *Ralf und Florian*, making him one of the first to do so in the pop world. From 'Autobahn' on, electronically created synthetic language became a fixed element of the Kraftwerk sound. Its effect is like that of an absurd Lewis Carroll story in which animals, plants or objects possess human qualities and can suddenly speak. On 'Autobahn', so it seems, a combustion engine is speaking to us. It's so uncanny when technology talks.

It's almost impossible to imagine it these days, but in the early 1970s, language was only synthesized at universities by an elite circle of academics. The idea comes from the USA. Originally, the North American telecommunications company AT&T wanted to deploy a vocoder to make more efficient use of trans-atlantic underwater cables. During the Second World War, the US military built on that idea and encoded speech via vocoder. The device played a role in secret telecommunications well into the Cold War. Allegedly, John F. Kennedy dealt with the entire Cuban missile crisis via a vocoder.

'Autobahn' fills the record's entire A-side. Three verses alternate with free, improvised-sounding intermediate parts, in which alternative melodies or sound collages are developed. I thought the chords in the song's structure were particularly impressive, along with the unbeatable rhyme and the flute solo. I liked the other tracks on the album a lot too. *Autobahn* – it was impossible to miss – was a consistent continuation of the positive mood on *Ralf und Florian*.

As I perceived it, it was clear that the two of them ignored American blues music and never used blue notes, jazz chords or typical rock chords. Instead, they placed themselves in the tradition of European folk and art music. And yet through its song structure and chanted vocals, the record is doubtlessly pop music. Ralf and Florian had taken the incisive step from instrumental to vocal music. To my understanding, *Autobahn* combined pop music, electro-acoustics and the tone painting of late Romantic programme music into a sound that determines directions like a compass, marking out a new location.

'The Classic Line-Up'

Over the days that followed, I was busy again with lectures, teaching and rehearsals. On the early evening of Friday, 8 November 1974, I arrived at Mintropstrasse after a lecture on the theory of form and a rehearsal with the conservatory orchestra. Ralf, Florian and Wolfgang were gathered around the electronic drum kit at the back of the room, their heads together in concentration. They appeared to be discussing what sounds to put on what pads.

My first encounter with Wolfgang had been a while ago, but we greeted one another as though it was yesterday. One of Wolfgang's most pleasant characteristics is his uncomplicated way of communicating, always generous and open for everything.

Nothing has changed about that, to this day. 'Look what I've made for you,' he said, and drummed on a second percussion multipad with the knitting needles.

The device looked like an oversized cigar box, only it contained not cigars but electronic components. Wolfgang had screwed six round metal plates to the top of the lid, contact surfaces for the round metal rods just like in the prototype. The side facing the player housed the operating equipment – dials and faders, plugs and cables. The lid of the box could be opened to reveal its electronic innards. Like a master instrument-maker, Wolfgang had also decorated this smaller machine with the mother-of-pearl self-adhesive vinyl specific to drum kits. The sounds of my instrument were different to those of the prototype. Through the varying timbres, the drums were easier to differentiate and tell apart.

Then we played 'Autobahn' together for the first time. I would never have dreamed that journalists would one day call our four-man combo 'the classic line-up'. It was an ensemble rehearsal on a Friday night – nothing more than that.

From the percussion section's point of view, the song's arrangement is easy to understand. Almost all the transitions flow naturally or are announced in advance, and it's not difficult to follow the composition's storyboard. Wolfgang and I sat side by side looking over at each other, and as we learned to work better and better with the round metal rods, I watched the natural choreography of our synchronized movement evolve.

At the end of the session we made a date to meet up again in January 1975, about six weeks later. *Autobahn* had only just come out and no one knew at that point how everything would develop.

As Wolfgang and I walked down Mintropstrasse, we talked about the new situation. 'Funny how life is,' I said. 'Now we're bandmates. Who'd have thought that when I lent you my Jokers work outfit a few years ago.' 'I was never much into light entertainment music,' Wolfgang answered. 'Playing 'Tanzmusik' with Ralf and Florian is a whole different ball game, though. Anyway, it's great that you're on board now too – I could use the company. Those two have their own view of the world. I like playing percussion for Kraftwerk and it's a lot of fun together, but we're very different people.'

Strange, I thought; why would Wolfgang mention that? The sessions were going well, weren't they? OK, Ralf and Florian were a few years older than me and very different to my usual social circle. They didn't come from a student setting but seemed to be movers and shakers instead, dynamic types with entrepreneurial energy. Then again, there was the subcultural level that came from the relaxed studio atmosphere, Ralf's grey Volkswagen and their initially unpretentious clothing. Their whole demeanour and the tone of our communication came across as pleasant. It was kind of cool to be with them. Our conversations covered pop music but also classical avant-garde and established high culture. For them, and equally for me, the boundaries between them were permeable, and we moved freely between the different fields. Aside from that, there were also flights of fancy and nonsense involved. I appreciated this precise counterpoint of cultural awareness and kidding around.

What impressed me about Kraftwerk was the autonomy of their sound. Before Kraftwerk, I had always placed myself in an existing musical tradition and made its paradigms my own. That was the case with sixties music, entertainment music, classical music and jazz. I was too young at that point to formulate my own artistic statement. As yet, I had no idea where my musical journey was heading. Ralf and Florian, though, had managed to create a musical concept of their own from the mix of their points of reference. I could identify with the sources of their music; they very much corresponded with my own life, my own sound biography.

The fact that Kraftwerk were releasing records put them a step above all the other bands in the region. As you might imagine, I felt good in that context. Then again, I knew nothing about how the group was organized, internally or externally. That meant it was difficult for me to see a perspective for myself in the band. I didn't think about it at all, though – things couldn't have been going better at the conservatory. The winter of 1974/75 was my tenth semester. Even though I was occupied with music morning, noon and night, I never felt my activities were a burden, only ever a privilege. I felt at home among musicians. It wasn't on the official curriculum, but I learned intuitively from my teachers and fellow students that being a musician is not a profession – it's a way of life.

NOTES

1. 'Tausendfüssler' ('Millipede'), the nickname for a flyover in the centre of Düsseldorf, demolished in April 2013.

132

6

WITH KRAFTWERK TO AMERICA

On the Autobahn into the US Charts. My Polyphonic Life. Three Warm-Up Gigs. Take-Off. New York, New York. On Broadway. Itinerary April, May, June.

On the Autobahn into the US Charts

Work went on uninterrupted for me in 1975: rehearsals for Puccini's *Turandot*, followed by the premiere. Next came *Death in Venice*, after that incidental music for *La Bohème* and the Jokers' annual performance at the Press Ball in Bochum. In comparison to all that, the sixth session in the Kling Klang Studio paled into insignificance at the time. But then Ralf called around the end of January. He said he and Florian would like to talk to Wolfgang and me about something. He clearly didn't want to say much more about it on the phone, so we arranged to meet up that afternoon.

We drove to a nearby café in Ralf's VW Beetle. The tension was ratcheting up . . . Ralf gave an enigmatic smile, cleared his throat and finally asked us if we could imagine playing a couple of gigs in America. *Autobahn* had made the charts over there and was moving inexorably towards the Top Ten. Now they'd received a request for a tour. They didn't know how many concerts we'd be playing but we'd definitely be spending a month in the States. Two or three warm-up gigs before we left, and then in April we'd be off.

This new perspective really relaxed the mood, and we thought about which other artists from Germany had been a success in the USA since the Comedian Harmonists. Someone mentioned Horst Jankowski, whose single 'A Walk Through the Black Forest' got to number 1 on the US charts in 1965. Frank Sinatra sang Bert Kaempfert's 'Strangers in the Night', I remembered. Wolfgang knew from somewhere or other that Klaus Doldinger had toured the States with his band in the sixties. And that was it. We couldn't think of any other German musicians who'd made it there. So *Autobahn*'s success was very unexpected and exciting.

I thought it over. In terms of my studies, I felt pretty secure. Plus, the long break between semesters started on 1 April anyway, so the timing was fine.

Then Ralf and Florian brought up the subject of money. Wolfgang and I would receive a flat fee, no matter how many concerts we were booked for. I was earning my living at the time in the opera and playing background music. Perhaps I'd lose a month or two through the Kraftwerk tour. But I could live with that. The pay wasn't the main thing. In fact, the offer seemed to me like a once-in-a-lifetime chance to get to know the country where the roots of popular music lay. It was unlikely I'd get there any other way in the foreseeable future. 'I'm in,' I heard myself say.

First, though, was a planned spring concert with the conservatory orchestra, where I could make a solo appearance. I absolutely wanted to experience being a soloist. There was also a piece on the programme by the contemporary composer Friedrich Zehm: *Carpriccio für einen Schlagzeuger und Orchester*. After two orchestra rehearsals, we performed the composition in February in the Robert Schumann Hall. For the first time, I read my name in the local press in a cultural context: 'The excellent percussionist Karlheinz Bartos – from the class of Ernst Göbler – sprinted light-footed between the xylophone, bongos and jazz drum kit, and demonstrated his virtuoso skills.' It felt good to be noticed in Düsseldorf's cultural landscape.

My Polyphonic Life

February was also time to have an official picture taken of Kraftwerk in the new line-up. We met up for the occasion at Foto Frank on Blumenstrasse. Herr Frank, an old-school photographer, had previously shot the portrait for the *Ralf und Florian* album, and the group picture of the band's previous incarnation including Klaus Röder was also from his studio.

The four of us ended up standing in front of a grey curtain – the classic pose. Herr Frank stepped behind his huge old-fashioned camera, which was mounted on a wooden tripod, and explained with a friendly smile: 'Now I'm inserting the special film.' What he meant was a glass photo plate. Then his head vanished beneath the cloth attached to the camera, he pressed the button, and – watch the birdie! – took the first ever band photo featuring Ralf, Karl, Wolfgang and Florian.

After that, the next week or so was given over to the Rhineland carnival tradition. I attended a party at the Robert Schumann

Conservatory, played three nights in a row with the Jokers until the early hours at the Düsseldorf Hilton, and on the day before last of the season I met up with two musician friends in the old town centre. We wanted to earn a few drinks in bars as a samba band – in a rather strange combination of two snare drums and a piccolo. I can still remember the beginning of our 'virtuoso' busking performances. Then it all goes blank and I woke up the next afternoon in my attic flat in Oberkassel – with my drum resting on my belly. A perfectly normal episode in the life of a Rhinelander in the epicentre of carnival.

At my seventh Kling Klang session on 18 February, the four of us practised for the warm-up gigs already booked for Leverkusen, Paris and Cologne. What made me nervous was an entirely different event awaiting me at the conservatory the next morning: my piano examination. I had been practising three pieces for it for months.

Sitting at a Steinway grand piano in a large wood-panelled room one morning and playing for a committee was a very odd experience. I felt like the keyboard was made of rubber and was swaying imperceptibly to and fro. Luckily, though, my hands stayed dry and I calmed down slightly. I played the three pieces by heart: Ludwig van Beethoven's *Sonata in G major*, *The Little Negro* by Claude Debussy and Johann Sebastian Bach's *Invention in B minor*. The committee awarded my little recital a *merit*. Phew! The day after that, I sat exams in counterpoint and aural theory.

At the end of February, we met in the early evening for Kraftwerk sessions eight and nine. During the preparations in the studio, Ralf and Florian discussed the poster for the American tour. They wanted it to pick up on the look of Fritz

Lang's film *Metropolis*, I remember – the city of the future, transport, electricity, and the movie's main theme, the coexistence of man and machine. The *Autobahn* tour poster, made to their requirements by a graphic designer in the USA, already featured Ralf and Florian's term 'man-machine'.

Three Warm-Up Gigs

I played my first Kraftwerk gig at the Forum Leverkusen on 27 February 1975. Setting up, we each took care of our own equipment, in my case, my vibraphone and the electric drum kit. Plugging it all in was a new experience for me, with a huge jumble of cables, instruments, microphones and effect devices – a wild live-electronic set-up – slowly taking shape. Then came a terrible surprise at the soundcheck: Florian's synthesizer wasn't working. We were horrified. By chance – or perhaps by clever design – Florian happened to have the phone number of the Bonn Synthesizer Studio in his pocket. He called them up and asked Dirk Matten and Hajo Wiechers to help him out of this tight spot.

Once the new ARP had arrived, we were ready to go. The stage at our first shows looked quite simple. Ralf – on the left – played the Farfisa Professional Piano and the Minimoog. He also had a mixing desk and an echo machine at his disposal, and sang 'Autobahn' through a Sennheiser MD 421 microphone. Opposite him – on the right, in other words – was Florian with his ARP Odyssey. His other instruments were an F-flute, saxophone, microphone, mixing desk and echo machine. With his rolled-up sleeves, he looked pretty cool behind his synth. For the first time, I was the second from left on the vibraphone or electro-drums. Next to me was Wolfgang, drumming on the prototype percussion multipad. At the first shows in the classic line-up, the two of us played sitting down because we were still using the foot switch for the bass drum. The four of us wore dark trousers and pale shirts, T-shirts or sweaters. Our stage set-up was more like a performance of live electronic music than a pop event.

The set-list consisted of 'Ruckzuck', 'Tanzmusik' and 'Tongebirge'. We played the whole of the *Autobahn* album.

Three days later, we met up for session number ten at the Kling Klang Studio. Ralf and Florian had already got their names made up as neon signs for their eponymous 1973 album. They would put the neon names on the stage in front of them when they played live, like illuminated advertising on a shopfront. Now they wanted to get Wolfgang and me our own neon signs, and they asked me very cautiously if I'd be alright with 'Karl'. The nine letters of 'Karlheinz' made it pretty long and rather pricy . . . Karl, though, would only be half as expensive. I agreed without thinking much about it. And so, from then on, I was called Karl.

Our next destination was France. We met up at the Kling Klang Studio on the morning of 11 March and loaded our instruments into two borrowed vans, then drove to Paris in several cars, ready to play at the Bataclan theatre the next day. The venue was to come to tragic fame through the terrorist attack of November 2015.

During the concert – where we were swathed in clouds of marihuana smoke from numerous joints in the audience – a young man clambered on stage and sat down next to Ralf on the organ. The stoned monsieur beamed away in blissful happiness. We had neither a crew nor a security team and certainly not a manager, who would usually sort things like this out. But Ralf took it in his stride and had words with monsieur, who made an understanding exit after a while.

We spent the next day hanging out in Paris together. Relaxed and happy, the four of us were strolling along the Champs-Élysées when Florian spotted a pair of shoes in a shop window. He dashed in, beside himself with joy, and came out with the shoes and a huge grin a few minutes later. It was a bizarre moment, especially because the fancy footwear was extremely expensive, from my point of view at least. Also, they had woven fronts and looked pretty odd. Florian was overjoyed, though, and his enthusiasm was infectious.

It was there on the Champs-Élysées that I first realized I had no idea how much Kraftwerk got paid for a gig. That was different in my other bands. But what good would it do me to find out? In any case, we had a lot of fun together and Ralf and Florian treated Wolfgang and me to an opulent business dinner that evening of champagne, oysters, filet mignon, sauce béarnaise and profiteroles.

The next day we made our way back to Düsseldorf, and on the Sunday I played a gig with the Jokers. Sadly, I had to explain to my bandmate, Franz, that they'd have to do without me at the next few jobs because I'd be touring the USA with Kraftwerk. It was an offer I simply couldn't turn down, I told him. For the likes of me, a trip to the States was an unaffordable luxury in the 1970s. Franz wasn't exactly pleased but he wished me luck.

We used our eleventh session at the Kling Klang Studio to discuss a few musical and logistical issues. Then two days later, we loaded up our equipment again and sped over to nearby Cologne. We played our third and last warm-up gig in the WDR Sendesaal – the broadcasting hall where Karlheinz Stockhausen had premiered his *Gesang der Jünglinge*. A lesson with Ernst Göbler on 25 March and a performance of Donizetti's *L'elisir d'amore* were the last dates in my diary before I left. Off to America!

Take-Off

Düsseldorf Airport, 29 March 1975. When I saw Wolfgang's horribly pale face, I knew straight away there was something wrong. I was right – he'd hurt himself badly while parking his red Opel Kadett. He'd slammed the driver's door against his left thumb as he closed it – ouch! It had swollen up and was starting to turn purple. It must have been hell for Wolfgang but he put on a brave face and kept going. What else could he do? Once we boarded the Pan Am plane, a stewardess brought him cold water and ice cubes to at least lessen the agony. Then we lifted off and headed west. It was my first transatlantic flight – my second flight ever – and I was pretty excited.

On arrival at John F. Kennedy Airport in New York, I noticed the four of us didn't exactly have a standard dress code. At home and at our warm-up gigs, Ralf and Florian had gone for a fairly relaxed look. Now Ralf was wearing a black cotton coat with a fur collar, grey trousers and white shoes. Plus the obligatory leather gloves. He was also carrying a black diplomat's case. His glasses – the ones from the album cover of *Ralf und Florian* – made him stand out from the crowd. Florian was dressed in a beige camel-hair coat, also with a fur collar, and a white scarf. He was clutching a golden Samsonite case. The two of them looked like they'd just fallen out of a Fritz Lang film.

Emil Schult was travelling with us too. His shoulder-length brown curls and soft grey-blue eyes gave him a gentle look, in a positive sense. Emil had studied at the Düsseldorf Art Academy, taught at a grammar school, and made a name for himself at a few Kraftwerk gigs as a roller-skating guitarist. He was credited on *Autobahn* as co-author of the lyrics and the graphic designer for the cover. Unlike Ralf and Florian, he went for a very different style. In his pale trench coat over a suit jacket, white shirt and tie, he could have played a part in a *nouvelle vague* movie.

Wolfgang was the most colourful of us, without a doubt. He had bought a brightly coloured three-quarter-length checked wool jacket for the trip, and wrapped a scarlet scarf around his neck. The lumberjack look earned him the name 'Plaid McTrench' – the first of many nicknames he tolerated patiently over the years. I was walking around in jeans, a sweater and a parka, stylishly accessorized with an old-fashioned neck pouch containing my passport, plane tickets and money – dressing down like a typical student, as always.

Despite these 'little differences' in our travelling party, we got along well – the mood was friendly, relaxed and full of imaginative fun. Even though *Autobahn* was climbing the Billboard charts at a rate of knots, the trip felt like an experiment for all of us. None of us had the slightest idea where it would all lead.

New York, New York

Ira Blacker came to meet us at Arrivals. His management company, Mr I. Mouse Ltd., had organized the tour in advance. He was accompanied by the tour manager, Henry Israel. Henry – a man of around 30, like Ira – had pretty much the same hairstyle as Wolfgang and a neatly trimmed beard to go with it.

A black stretch limousine with tinted windows was awaiting us outside. The chauffeur opened the doors and we got in, sank into the plush seats and were heading for Manhattan. At 22 years of age, I was fairly laid-back, but it felt a hell of a lot like I'd ended up in some kind of movie. As we crossed the 59th Street Bridge over the East River and I recognized the world-famous skyline, that feeling intensified. And yet it was all real. We were cruising along the mean streets of Manhattan to our hotel.

First, Wolfgang and I were dropped off at the Gorham at 136 West 55th Street, not exactly a classy joint at the time. We shared a double room, which was the way it stayed for as long as we were on the road together, incidentally. As we checked in, Henry warned us to be careful and never leave any valuables in the hotel room: 'Always lock the door, guys.' The many locks on our door seemed to confirm his concerns. He advised us to switch on the TV when we left the room so it would sound occupied while we were out. Then he headed off to take care of Ralf and Florian with Ira Blacker. The two of them were staying at the Mayflower Hotel, 15 Central Park West. I can't say now where Emil slept. To be perfectly honest, I didn't think much of it at the time. Everything was new, everything went so fast. But after one or two days, Wolfgang and I moved into the Mayflower as well, to simplify communication and logistics.

Once we were alone in our hotel room, I opened the window. There was a clear view of the surrounding skyscrapers from the 27th floor. We looked down on neon ads, air conditioner ventilation pipes and wooden water tanks on the roofs of the smaller buildings. And, of course, all the metal fire-escape ladders hanging from the facades like scaffolding. None of it looked particularly modern; it was more reminiscent of the 1920s. Down on the streets, the people and cars looked like toytown, and as we leaned out of the window, we first consciously heard the soundtrack of the Big Apple – a rising and falling tide of traffic noise and sirens of all kinds, something I'd only come across in films up to that point. I remember the two of us looking at each other and listening to the sound of the city, fascinated. All that was missing was for someone to turn on a radio in the next room and Gershwin's 'Rhapsody in Blue' to sound out.

What we didn't know then was that New York City had been in a hopeless financial situation since the early 1970s. The city was crumbling and run down, with a very high crime rate. Living there seemed to have its risks, to put it mildly. But there's an unwritten rule that the entertainment industry thrives in exactly those kinds of surroundings. Artists are magically drawn by these conditions and there are even jobs for them! Maybe that magic has something to do with the illegal substances that make up part of the basic set-up in show business. With or without chemical boosts, the feeling of life in a run-down city inevitably colours the art made there. We can track the phenomenon through music's development. In the first half of the 1970s – with the Summer of Love (1967) and Woodstock (1969) still

143

firmly embedded in the collective memory – punk, disco and hip-hop were all invented in New York City.

Henry took Wolfgang to a hospital that evening, where he finally got the medical treatment he needed and was relieved of his pain in the emergency room. We had breakfast together at Café Rumpelmayer, just a few minutes away from us in the Hotel St. Moritz on Central Park – right where Broadway meets Columbus Circle. Large, bright rooms with mirrored walls and palm trees – Florian was in his element. The air conditioning wafted cool air in our direction, creating wintery temperatures. American food was another new experience for me; everything tasted kind of synthetic. American breakfast with eggs, toast and bacon was fine though, if you didn't think too much about it. There was a lot to learn, like new words for ordering a meal: 'How do you like your eggs – scrambled, sunny side up or over easy?' And then the ritual tap water on the rocks . . .

We laughed a lot that Easter Monday, as we quickly grew accustomed to our new surroundings. As the five of us walked down Broadway to Times Square, the city laid itself out at our feet and it all fitted together perfectly. I was impressed by the beauty of the skyscrapers. It was time to look and listen, not think. I couldn't escape the city's fast pace and the traffic's rhythm. People were constantly streaming out of the subway stations. They all looked like they were rushing not to miss their next meeting. Along the way, I bought a pack of chewing gum from one of the street vendors. When he found out where I come from, he called out a cheerful 'Heil Hitler' and raised his right arm in the Nazi salute. I could hear him laughing himself silly over his joke even as I walked away. Wow, that was a shock.

For the first time, I'd been shown in no uncertain terms what it means to have a German passport.

After a while, the general wanderlust faded away and Wolfgang and I were the only ones left. We roamed the streets of Manhattan until after nightfall, going nowhere in particular, with our Super-8 camera always at the ready to capture what we saw. There were thousands of yellow taxicabs on the move. Precisely the same taxis as the ones Martin Scorsese paid homage to in his most famous film *Taxi Driver*, released a year later. New York by night, as Wolfgang and I walked around, looked exactly like in *Taxi Driver*: the porn cinemas, gadget shops and souvenir stalls, the huge ads for musicals and neon signs, the hotdog carts and hamburger restaurants, the swarms of tourists, the vagrants and of course the street musicians . . . The drummer with black hair painted onto his forehead playing Gene Krupa's 'Rudiments and Paradiddles' on Times Square . . . There he stood, live on a traffic island, banging untiringly on his snare drum. When I saw Scorsese's movie later on, I recognized him. And then there were the mysterious clouds of steam that rose from the underworld through the manhole covers by night. Perhaps Robert De Niro, alias Travis Bickle, even drove past us in his yellow taxi as he was filming?

There was a photo session booked for us at the Maurice Seymour Studios the next day. Originally from Chicago, the brothers Maurice and Seymour Zeldman opened their photographic studio in New York City in 1950 and both had gone by the name of Maurice Seymour ever since. They had first begun taking celebrity portraits back in the 1930s and were now among the most famous showbiz photographers in America. I can't say which Zeldman brother really photographed us in New York that day, but the result bears the signature Maurice Seymour. Pictures from the session were later used for the cover design of the album *Trans-Europe Express* and as a promotional tool by the record labels.

Next up was a reception at the Famous Music publishing division, confirming pretty much all the clichés you can possibly have about show-business meetings. My first lesson in business talk. I remember one of the gentlemen turning with a smile to Wolfgang and enthusiastically informing him of how great his sweater was. You couldn't make it up!

What do you do on a free morning in New York? I found the following address in the Yellow Pages: Professional Percussion Center, 832 8th Avenue. Not knowing what awaited me, I headed straight over. Frank Ippolito's store was housed on three floors of a very old building. On the first floor, I wended my way through a smorgasbord of drum sets and percussion instruments that completely filled the room. It all seemed normal and down to earth, a little bit old-fashioned and not snobbish or exclusive at all. The second floor was packed from floor to ceiling with drums, skins, cymbals, components, accessories and cases. And there were two teaching rooms on the third floor, used by the famous jazz drummers Elvin Jones and Jim Chapin. On a poster on the wall, I saw that Billy Cobham and Tony Williams had just held drumming workshops there. A little later, one of the staff told me: 'Back there are Gene Krupa's and Buddy Rich's drum kits and also Lionel Hampton's original Deagan vibraphone.' A shop just for drummers – it was paradise! I felt instantly obliged to buy all kinds of mallets and notes, returning to the hotel with two bags stuffed full of percussionist booty.

146

In the afternoon we headed for a rehearsal studio. A haulage company had delivered our equipment by that point. We didn't yet have flight cases; our instruments travelled in cardboard boxes rigged up with tape. My vibraphone had stayed at home, since Ralf and Florian had rented a Deagan vibraphone with pick-ups for the tour. Later on, two chrome-plated suitcase rests from a Holiday Inn were refunctioned into keyboard stands.

As I arrived in the studio, Ralf and Florian were doing an interview with a television crew. From a distance, I heard Ralf describe Kraftwerk's music as 'romantic realism'. It was astounding how comfortable the two of them felt in front of the camera. They spoke fluent English and they took turns answering the questions, which made for a lively interview. Once the TV crew had left they proudly showed off their new watches, gifts from Famous Music for their outstanding sales figures.

I can't recall our first gig in Rochester, New York. All I remember is the weather – an ice-cold blizzard came out of the blue, as they say, and buried the entire region in snow that evening. The airport was closed and we had to drive back to Manhattan in a rented station wagon – about 500 kilometres south at a snail's pace along the slippery highway. Our two roadies, hired by Ira Blacker, brought the equipment back in a van. We were due to play our second gig in Philadelphia but it was cancelled, so we spent the next day in New York.

On Broadway

And then the big day arrived – our concert on Broadway was lined up for Saturday, 5 April 1975. The Beacon Theatre – 2124

Broadway at West 74th Street – is a historical venue built in the days of the vaudeville shows of the golden twenties.

As opening acts, Ira Blacker had booked Michael Quatro, brother of Suzie, and the band formed around the former Colosseum keyboarder David Greenslade. Their bassist was wearing a skin-tight skeleton costume on stage – even though *Spinal Tap* wouldn't be made for years!

Before our performance, we got up to the usual nonsense backstage. There was no huge responsibility weighing me down. I had nothing to do with *Autobahn*'s success and my part on stage wasn't exactly a major musical challenge. That meant I wasn't particularly nervous. Ralf and Florian seemed rather tense, though. After all, Ralf had the hardest part to play on the keyboards. He shared the lead vocals on 'Autobahn' with Florian.

During this first US tour, I realized that the way Ralf played keyboards reminded me of Richard Wright and Ray Manzarek. Richard Wright's set-up with Pink Floyd was very similar to Ralf's – except he used a Mellotron rather than an Orchestron. Another reason was that Wright had taught himself to play the piano, so he didn't have a marked technique. Ralf wasn't a virtuoso on the keys, like Rick Wakeman or Keith Emerson, for example. Fortunately, I have to say. An echo machine had a major influence on Wright's sound, and he integrated synthe-sizers into his set-up early on. There were also parallels to the keyboarder from the Doors, Ray Manzarek. The Doors found it hard to find a bass player, with the result that Manzarek had to play the bassline with his left hand on his Vox or Farfisa organ. His right hand was free for chords or melodies on his Rhodes Electric Piano.

Essentially, Ralf set himself up in the same way, only using a Minimoog for the bass. To add to that, he wasn't able to coordinate his hands independently. His left hand would usually play a rhythmic pedal point of octaves on each root note. Then an echo machine added a delayed copy of the original. It was these factors that led to Ralf's unmistakable style – easy to hear on 'Autobahn'.

The moment we stepped on stage, the Beacon Theatre fell absolutely silent. Unlike at our previous gigs, we were dressed as if for a classical concert: suits, white shirts and ties. That made the audience expect something fairly conservative, at first glance. Our set-list: 'Kometenmelodie', 'Ananas Symphony', 'Kling Klang', 'Ruckzuck', 'Tongebirge', 'Tanzmusik' and 'Autobahn'. By the time we got to the coda of 'Autobahn' the people out there had relaxed and sang along with the refrain.

Looking back, it's amazing how little effort it took us to make an enormous impression in 1975. Our repertoire was basically made up of more or less improvised instrumentals and the LP version of 'Autobahn'. The instruments we were using weren't much different to those at our European warm-up gigs. All we'd added was my borrowed Deagan vibraphone with pick-ups and the Orchestron we'd bought in the USA.

The Vako Polyphonic Orchestron was a hot prospect, acoustically. What it looked like, though, was a hybrid of a Philicorda home organ, a Minimoog and a 1950s music cabinet. Dave Van Koevering, a former employee at Moog Music, had just launched the device onto the market in 1975. He hoped the Orchestron would be a competitor to the Mellotron – the typical sound of which could be heard in the flutes, choirs and violins on albums by the Beatles, Pink Floyd and King Crimson. The electro-mechanical Mellotron created sound on a tape basis, a number of strips housed in a frame. The sounds recorded there could be played using one or two manual controls. Its disadvantage was that the sounds could only be held for eight seconds and then broke off. When you took your finger off the key, a spring returned the strip of tape to its starting position.

The Orchestron didn't use magnetic tape; it worked on the principle of modulated light. The sounds were stored on thin discs and read photoelectrically. Changing the discs made orchestral instruments or human voices available, and in theory, any sound that could be recorded could be played back on the device – for as long as you liked.

The extremely rare photos of the tour show that our stage set was not exactly complicated: coloured neon tubes in the background, and on the floor in front of us four minimalist Plexiglas boxes containing our names in neon letters. Emil projected a few slides with motifs like the *Autobahn* cover onto a relatively small screen above our heads. The visual aspect had the look of a university seminar.

Bravo magazine, Germany's biggest youth medium for music at the time, reported exclusively and called our NYC concert 'triumphant'. The piece went on: 'The atmosphere is tense at the Beacon Theatre on Broadway. A shock to kick off – the four krautrockers come on stage in dark suits, white shirts, black bow ties and neatly combed hair. Kraftwerk place no value on showy effects, focussing entirely on the music. [. . .] "Many left the Beacon Theatre as reverently as if leaving a church," writes New York's most respected newspaper the *New York Times* the next day. [. . .] The big breakthrough for Ralf, Florian, Karl und Wolfgang.'[1]

150

Itinerary April, May, June

Thanks to the US chart success of *Autobahn* – both LP and single – we received more and more offers for live performances, and Ralf and Florian extended our trip. Of course, we all thought that was great. We started on the East Coast and played in Boston, Massachusetts. Then we set off for the Midwest to cities like South Bend, Louisville, Carbondale, Cincinnati and Pittsburgh. Our gig at the Aragon Ballroom in Chicago on 19 April was a highlight, with around 3000 people in the audience.

We would keep a regular check on *Billboard* magazine. In the issue dated 19 April 1975, *Autobahn* is in the charts for the eleventh week, climbing from number 8 to number 7. As I flicked through, I caught sight of Pink Floyd's *The Dark Side of the Moon* at number 118. The album, released on 1 March 1973 had reached number 1 at the end of April that year but two years later was still going strong. That was great for Pink Floyd, but I wouldn't mention it if the album hadn't featured the relatively short instrumental 'On the Run'. The basis for the sound on that track is the AKS synth made by EMS, which came with a rudimentary sequencer. Both the synthesizer sound and the only eight tones of the modulated loop on the song were groundbreaking. On top of that, the white noise generator created a percussive sound. Other synth sounds are reminiscent of car and plane engines moving from left to right in a panorama – including a doppler effect. Still astounding listening to this day, this track is in my opinion one of the founding sequences of electronic pop music and its derivatives like ambient, synth pop, house and techno. Was it perhaps also an inspiration for the tone-painting part of Kraftwerk's drive on the 'Autobahn'?

We headed further south, playing Atlanta, Birmingham, Kansas City and Memphis. After our Memphis gig we danced like little kids in a nightclub to a top-class cover band. Those southern boys sure do know how to make music.

One day we actually heard 'Autobahn' on the car radio. Even I was excited, despite not having been involved in recording it. Other than that, the radio stations played songs like 'Philadelphia Freedom' by Elton John, Barry White's 'What Am I Gonna Do with You', 'Walking in Rhythm' by the Blackbirds, 'The Hustle' by Van McCoy, and most often 'How Long' by Ace. Then we flew over to the Pacific, first to Vancouver and then down the West Coast: Portland, Seattle, San Francisco, San Diego and Los Angeles, continuing via Salt Lake City to Utah and Denver, Colorado.

During a day off before our San Francisco appearance, Wolfgang and I explored Chinatown, the largest in the United States, as Henry Israel informed us. The ties – one black, one gold – that Wolfgang and I are wearing on the cover of the US edition of the *Trans-Europe Express* album date back to that afternoon stroll around Chinatown. I failed to get a look at the Golden Gate Bridge and didn't make it to Haight-Ashbury either. We didn't have a lot of time on the road.

In LA, where we arrived by car from San Diego, we pulled off a real media coup: our first television appearance together, on *The Midnight Special*. The NBC series was screened after the Friday-night edition of Johnny Carson's *The Tonight Show* – that alone meant people watched it all over the country. The acts didn't mime along to playback as usual; they played live in front of a studio audience. We set up our equipment like for any concert.

152

Then we spent all day in the studio, watching Wolfman Jack, the Temptations and the amazing orchestra, and waiting hours for our on-camera rehearsal. After a long day, we finally played 'Autobahn' live for an audience of millions. You can still watch a recording of the show online – jazzed up with the very latest video effects of the time by NBC. After our gig in Santa Monica, I went to visit Neil Young at his home with our roadie Billy. I couldn't believe it. It turned out Billy had toured with him and wanted to go and say hello. Neil Young and Nils Lofgren were practising with their band and gave us a really friendly reception. There were guitars everywhere, the buffet in one room was huge, and the rehearsal seemed more like a laid-back party to me.

The next stops on the tour were Dallas, Little Rock, New Orleans, Miami and Gainesville. Via Philadelphia on the East Coast, we went back to the Midwest, playing Cleveland and Detroit. When we arrived at the Cleveland Holiday Inn on 31 May – my 23rd birthday – we couldn't believe our eyes. A large board read: 'Welcome Chicago, Beach Boys, Kraftwerk.' The Beach Boys and Chicago were playing a double-feature in a huge football stadium. We absolutely had to go!

I can't say now how many people were in that stadium on the Saturday afternoon. Maybe forty thousand? It was warm and pretty crowded. I walked slowly around in the midst of all the happy people, taking in the fantastic mood. Lots of young women were sitting on their boyfriends' shoulders with a can of Miller Light or Coke in their hands, enjoying the party. All around me I felt nothing but joy and happiness.

Suddenly, something moved on the stage. It hit me straight between the eyes when Mike Love kicked off with a yell of 'Watch it!' and Keith Richards' uber-riff filled the entire stadium – the guys started their set with 'Jumpin' Jack Flash', by the Stones. What a sound! Then Mike Love sang Jagger's lyrics with his trademark voice: 'I was born in a crossfire hurricane / And I howled at my ma in the drivin' rain . . .' The band that embodies the eternal summer and feel of California life like no other bowed down to the London lads, who had called America's attention back to the country's Black musicians and their work. Or that was what it looked like, at least. More hits came firing out of the speakers: 'California Girls', 'Help Me Rhonda', 'In My Room', 'Get Around', 'Good Vibrations' . . . and then 'Fun, Fun, Fun'. I can't say whether that 1964 track – part of the American pop canon – was the blueprint for the 'Autobahn' lyrics, but wouldn't it make sense if Emil had associated his 'Fah'n, Fah'n, Fah'n' with 'Fun, Fun, Fun'? Both songs are about driving cars, after all.

That concert in the summer of 1975 changed my understanding of music. Whatever the Beach Boys had in mind by opening their performance with a Stones song, I was overwhelmed by happiness at that moment. Music connects people. That's its very nature. Right then and there, I really understood what cultural transfer means, how everything is interconnected and music can overcome all barriers. In a football stadium in Cleveland, Ohio, we experienced a perfect demonstration of American youth culture – with Chicago on next after the Beach Boys. The final was the two bands together. That's the way to do it. Everyone in the stadium sang along, everyone was happy. Coca Cola, popcorn, cheerleaders, rock'n'roll – America celebrating itself, and me in its midst, feeling as happy as a pig in shit. At that moment, the Robert Schumann Conservatory was thousands of miles away – and I don't just mean geographically.

From Detroit, we headed back to Canada for three gigs in Toronto, Kitchener and Ottawa. But we were gradually beginning to show signs of exhaustion and were glad to get back to our starting point of New York on 7 June. Only a day later, we boarded a plane for home. Along the way, we kept checking the 'Singles Radio Action' column in *Billboard* to find out what number 'Autobahn' was at in the charts. And if I remember rightly, it was on the flight back that I first heard the word 'Radioactivity' in conjunction with a new Kraftwerk album.

7

RADIO-ACTIVITY

The Pursuit of Happiness. The 'Final Solution' to the Music Problem? Recording Radio-Activity. Radioland. Airwaves. Intermission – News. The Voice of Energy. Antenna. Radio Stars – Uranium – Transistor. Ohm Sweet Ohm. Artwork. My Crash Course. The Silent Treatment? In the Realm of the Schneider-Eslebens. Kraftwerk: The Backstory. Radioactivity – the Film. Counterpoint and Promo Tour. Number 9, Berger Allee. Advanced Performer's Degree. Sinus and Sci-fi. Summer Hit.

The Pursuit of Happiness

When I was finally alone in my attic apartment in Oberkassel after the US tour, jetlag knocked me off my feet. In the middle of the night I came to, and was surprised not to find myself in a king-size Holiday Inn bed. I needed to reflect on our tour, so I spread out everything I'd brought back from across the pond on the floor by my bed, like a collage: mallets and sheet music from Frank Ippolito's Professional Percussion Center in New York, two ties from San Francisco's Chinatown, a couple of Florian's Polaroids, three or four crumpled backstage passes, my pocket calendar and a few notes scribbled on a piece of paper: 'Musser Pro-Vibe, PAS – Percussive Arts Society, *The Catcher in the Rye*, *musique concrète* – Pierre Schaeffer, Pierre Henry, Stax Records'.

156

There wasn't much left of my tour fee but I still felt like life had given me a plethora of gifts. The memories of the past ten weeks, during which we had travelled from coast to coast across North America, were still reverberating in my mind. The richness of the continent's geography and culture had overwhelmed me, along with its apparent material wealth. It was obvious that people there assumed anyone could make it big through their own hard work. Even the Declaration of Independence famously grants Americans the irrevocable, God-given right to the pursuit of happiness – the basic prerequisite for what they call the 'American dream'. I had felt these same ideas of being able to achieve what I wanted for myself, ever since I'd started trying to be a musician. Now I'd found out that show business was valued far more highly by American society than at home in Germany. And, by the by, the United States was the largest music market in the world.

For the band, our gigs there were incredibly important because they meant we got international feedback – a new experience for all of us. The amazing reactions gave us confidence. If I had the opportunity, I'd gladly go to the States with the lads again – that much was clear, and from then on, the idea was part of my pursuit of happiness.

Then again, the present was much more interesting than the future. The summer semester had just started. Lectures, private lessons and my work at the opera dragged me right back into my old life. I didn't meet up with Ralf and Florian for some time, only running into Ralf in a bar in mid-July. I was really pleased to see him again. We talked about the tour, remembered a few highlights together, enjoyed a spot of banter . . . As a bonus for the tour, Ralf said, he and Florian had brought me a Musser vibraphone from America. What a great gesture, I thought. It was a second-hand instrument with an amazing sound.

I didn't know what Ralf had been up to in the meantime, but I could imagine Kraftwerk were planning a follow-up to *Autobahn*. And, in fact, he invited me to work on the next record as a drummer. After our American adventure, the offer didn't come as a complete surprise, of course. This time, Ralf told me, he and Florian wanted to produce the new album themselves. Before that, though, they had to get set up with professional equipment. On the previous albums, Conny Plank had been the man for technical expertise and tools. That meant basically a multichannel tape recorder, the mixing desk to go with it and good microphones.

There was a solution, though – in Florida, we had met Hans-Otto Mertens, the manager of the German comedian Otto Waalkes, and found out their company had an eight-track recorder for live recordings of Otto's stage shows. Ralf and Florian simply borrowed it from them.

We started recording at the Kling Klang Studio in July, when Peter Bollig appeared on the scene. Peter lived in the Eifel region south of Düsseldorf, and studied communications engineering in Cologne. His refreshing sense of humour meant we got on well from the very beginning.

At some point in 1974, Ralf and Florian noticed a Siemens grey phaser at Conny Plank's studio, built by Peter. They obviously liked the signal processor's design and sound, and the two of them started working with Peter. Copying a device or building something similar or improving on it – in those days, the studio was a real adventure playground. When the time came to record *Radio-Activity*, it made sense to ask Peter to help us out. Peter concentrated on recording equipment, kept an eye on the tape levels, made sure all the signals were clean and there was no interference.

The recordings for *Radio-Activity* were made in two sessions. I can barely remember the first one, though, because my other life was a whirl of teaching, lectures and opera at the time. On top of that, the Robert Schumann Conservatory moved premises during the semester break. All of us Göbler students helped to lug timpani, drums, percussion and mallet instruments into the new building.

I had a lot to do, in other words, and also it was a wonderful summer, hot and dry. That meant breakfast in a café, then cycling to an outdoor pool to hang out all day, or alternatively a trip to the funfair. The only interruption to my temporary slacker lifestyle was my hard work as best man at Marlis and Rainer Sennewald's wedding. I can't remember any other summer like that in my life . . .

In the midst of these idyllic salad days, I found out a UK tour was being organized for Kraftwerk to promote with live appearances. Fate meant well for the band, that much was clear. My holidays went on until 6 October, so I had time to spare! We met up again at Düsseldorf Airport on 2 September.

The 'Final Solution' to the Music Problem?

Of course, it's great when the press reports on you releasing a record or going on tour. In the UK, though, we were to find out that an interview can also go completely belly-up.

There had already been a lot of media interest in Kraftwerk

during the US tour. Lester Bangs – the new gonzo journalism star – had done an interview with Ralf and Florian for the respected *Creem* magazine. His Kraftwerk feature[1] is now regarded as the first relevant study of the band's philosophy. Bangs was aware that a new approach to pop music was being formulated in Germany, one that ought to be taken seriously. In his introduction, he answers the question 'Where is rock going?' with 'It's being taken over by the Germans and the machines,'[2] and predicts a new music for the technical age.

Famed and feared for his brilliant rhetorical skills, Bangs wanted to sound Kraftwerk out. Even at the start of the interview, he ironically points out that German scientists invented the drug 'speed', making them part-responsible for the development of American counterculture. Throughout the conversation – and in his choice of the answers printed – he plays on well-known clichés about Germans. And Ralf and Florian play along. Ralf inhaled Bangs' remark '[. . .] the next logical step would be for the machines to play you'[3] and made it part of his own repertoire from then on. Other subjects of the interview are Germany's alleged cultural vacuum after the Second World War,[4] the advantages of electronic instruments[5] 'and that their Wernher von Braun sartorial aspect was part of the German scientific approach'.[6] These topics were to accompany us for years to come.

While we were touring the UK, *New Musical Express* printed the interview in its 6 September issue, with a new headline: 'Kraftwerk: The Final Solution to the Music Problem? Lester Bangs vivisects the German Scientific Approach'.[7] Great, thanks for that. As if that weren't enough, the magazine also illustrated the interview with a photo montage, featuring the group shot of Kraftwerk copied into a historical photo of the Nazi party rally grounds in Nuremberg. Swastikas and Gothic type need no translation. The headline and the buzzwords taken out of context (Germany, science, man-machine, final solution, Kraftwerk) lend the interview a very different tone. Was this the British sense of humour we'd heard so much about?

Whether music fans understood the *NME* dog whistle or not, they stayed at home. We played to empty auditoriums in Newcastle, Hampstead, Bournemouth, Bath, Cardiff, Birmingham, and finally on 11 September in Liverpool. That afternoon, I walked around the city in search of . . . well, what was it I was looking for? If I'd had more time I would have headed to Penny Lane, by bus of course . . . A few years later, I made up for it with a sightseeing tour of Liverpool with Andy McCluskey, who was sitting in row Q, seat 36 in the Liverpool Empire Theatre on that 11 September, and who says to this day that his interest in electronic music was born right there and then.

Next up were Middlesbrough, Edinburgh, Manchester, and a concert on 15 September in Glasgow's Apollo Theatre in front of about 500 people. Our gigs in Southport, Brighton, Yeovil, London and Croydon were also fairly poorly attended and left no lasting impression on me. At the end of the tour, I looked back at our three weeks in Britain. *Autobahn* was actually in the charts, with the single reaching number 11 and the album as high as number 4 in June. But I think audiences at the time found our concerts pretty odd. We simply didn't offer any of the established fixtures of rock performance, like acoustic drums, guitarists or a lead singer screaming his message into the microphone with varying levels of sex appeal. Instead, our stage shows featured four young men in suits. We even got whistles of disapproval at a few gigs on the tour.

161

Despite the mixed audience reception, the atmosphere in the team was excellent. A few below-the-belt punches from the *NME* weren't enough to get us down.

Recording Radio-Activity

By this point, the ambitious concept for the follow-up album to *Autobahn* was in place. Essentially, it was based around the ambiguity of the word 'radio-activity' or 'radioactivity'. Florian put it like this in an interview: 'First of all it's the activity of the radio stations. That's what made us famous. Secondly, it's the atomic energy of bombs and nuclear power stations.'[8] The twelve tracks on the album were put into either one category or the other. We went on with the recordings in October.

Whenever I hear the song 'Radioactivity' somewhere these days, a flood of associations instantly fills my mind: the 'Singles Radio Action' section of *Billboard* magazine, Pink Floyd's 'Astronomy Domine' including the Morse code opening section, and the chord sequence on 'Echoes', nuclear power stations, bombs, Nazi radios for everyday family listening, but also OMD's 'Electricity', New Order's 'Blue Monday' . . . all the way to a text by Pierre Schaeffer, the inventor of the term *musique concrète*, in which he talks about a radioactive isotope in the process of creating a sound structure.[9] I certainly connect a whole lot with this one song. Perhaps that's because I was still very much under the influence of the North American tour during the recording sessions, and constantly thinking about Kraftwerk's music. Apart from that, it was the first album production I was part of.

We didn't have a sequencer for recording 'Radioactivity'. But with the continuous quavers in the bass frequency range on the Minimoog synthesizer, created by an oscillator, Kraftwerk were coming ever closer to the concept of the man-machine. The Morse code, clearly audible in a higher frequency on the spectrum than the bass, stands for telegraphy, which first made it possible to transport coded information long-distance at inconceivable speeds.

Our working method was incredibly simple: Ralf and Florian played me the song and I learned it as I played along. The syllables of the word 'ra-di-o-ac-ti-vi-ty', which Ralf repeated over and over to find the beat with me, led to the now-familiar drum pattern. Over the course of our American gigs, I had got fairly used to the knitting needles and this basic pattern was straightforward to play. The difficultly with such monotonous rhythms is keeping up maximum precision all the way through. Especially when you're playing a duet with a machine.

Recording the percussion tracks separately wasn't a particularly stimulating exercise. But that's the only way to make sure the instruments can be set individually in the mix. Every few bars, the metal beater made insufficient contact with the metal plate, causing an unrhythmic 'flam' or 'thwack'. Using what's called a drop-in/drop-out process – recording again on the same tape track – repairing these spots was not a major issue. Florian had the idea of running the tape more slowly as we recorded. We tested out the variable speed until we found the point at which the sound didn't change too much when we played it back in the normal, fixed-speed mode. And that's how I managed to drum out a more stable rhythm.

It was this slow tempo, this 'floating in the beat', that produced the link in my mind to Nick Mason's drumming style, but the track has more parallels to Pink Floyd; to be precise, to their song 'Astronomy Domine'.[10] It too begins with continuous quavers and Morse code, although that sound model only lasts a few seconds. German public television still uses that brief intro as title music for special news programmes to this day, thanks to its dramatic effect.

It was on 'Radioactivity' that Ralf first used the Vako Orchestron vocal choir sound in the studio. The chord progression is the same one as on Pink Floyd's 'Echoes'[11] – except in C sharp minor instead of A minor. Not that that matters; in my opinion, all the music in the world is interrelated and interconnected. I had understood that much at the Beach Boys concert in the USA.

Production on magnetic tape worked like making a lasagne in several layers. First of all, Peter Bollig recorded the Minimoog bass on the first track. The arrangement was sketched out, and while I counted the bars out loud, Ralf transposed the quaver sequence on the keyboard. The quavers in the bass, which were then on tape, provided a precise metronome, to which I recorded the electronic percussion. Florian hammered out a staccato motif on his ARP synthesizer, which sounded familiar. During our gigs, we sometimes combined the pieces 'Mitternacht' and 'Kristallo'. When Ralf improvised on the Farfisa piano on 'Kristallo', I occasionally heard that same motif. Now we used it as the main motif for 'Radioactivity'. Ralf played the Orchestron choir, and Florian tapped the Morse code onto tape. The accelerating bass drum and the Geiger-counter sound were added to the intro later on.

To this day, I still have my problems with the ambiguity of the album's subject. It refers both to sending and receiving sound

164

through radio waves, and to the emission of radioactive substances. In the title song – sung in German and English – these two perspectives come together and are intermixed. The lines 'Tune into the melody' and 'Strahlt Wellen zum Empfangsgerät' ('Emits waves to the receiver') and the Morse code can be filed under the communication perspective, radio waves. The second perspective – the emission of radioactive substances – is addressed in the rest of the lyrics. Whereas 'Is in the air for you and me' and 'Für dich und mich im All entsteht' ('Created for you and me in space') refer to cosmic radiation and 'Wenn's um unsere Zukunft geht' ('When it comes to our future') sounds like a 1970s advertising slogan for the nuclear power lobby, the part about Marie Curie discovering radioactivity doesn't stand up to closer inspection.[12] The line 'In the air for you and me' could refer both to nuclear radioactivity and radio airplay. But what is it actually about? Years later, the ambivalent lyrics became an anti-nuclear credo and the Third Reich *Volksempfänger* radio on the album cover was replaced by a radioactive pictogram.

Back in 1975, however, the album's main emphasis – as illustrated by the radio design on the cover – was on communication. In my view, the other half of the concept – radioactive emissions – was intended to be absolutely neutral. How else could we have been photographed for the album promotion at a nuclear power station, decked out in white coats and protective shoe covers? I wasn't aware of the anti-nuclear movement until after the album was released, when friends made critical comments about its content and I was embarrassed to find I couldn't explain it.

Radioland

'Radioland' remains one of the most atmospheric Kraftwerk compositions ever written. The rhythm section divides up time as regularly as a metronome. Ralf and Florian take turns singing the lyrics in German and English. I still find Florian's vocals strangely touching. I get a sense that he's revealing the closeness that can come about when singing or speaking, how much we disclose of ourselves. 'Radioland' was to be the last song to feature his voice. Kraftwerk's later records only included sampled fragments.

Ralf plays efficiently on the Orchestron's violins setting, while Florian is in charge of the sound effects, like a Foley artist on an animated film, providing acoustic illustrations of the lyrics on the synthesizer. But it's the refrain that makes 'Radioland' an extraordinary piece of music. A synthetic voice sings 'Elektronenklänge aus dem Radioland' ('Electron sounds from radioland'), with an almost unearthly quality to it. That impression is intensified by the change of harmony on the word 'Radioland' – the moment when the track lifts off.

The Detroit-based French-Canadian computer scientist Richard T. Gagnon had little interest in unearthly phenomena. Instead, he developed a phoneme generator in his basement in 1970, building his research around recordings of his own voice. Under the name Votrax International, Inc., he launched the world's first commercially available speech synthesizer in 1972, the Votrax VS-4. On our US tour, Florian had visited Gagnon in Detroit and bought himself the latest update. Sounds are inputted manually on a special phoneme keyboard.

166

Basically, the Votrax VS-6 was a speaking typewriter. The circuitry was usually top-secret. If you unscrewed the casing, all you saw was an epoxy coating over the circuit boards. But not for Florian. Gagnon had actually sold him an unsealed Votrax. That meant he could input every audio signal via an external jack and modulate it with the phonemes. The inventor himself had revealed the secret to him. And that was how Ralf and Florian created the other-worldly sound in the refrain of 'Radioland'.

Airwaves

Following a classic sci-fi sound effect, Ralf begins the song with his Orchestron riff, with Florian joining him on the ARP synthesizer. Then the rhythm section starts in, Minimoog and electro-drums hammering along like a machine at almost 180 beats per minute.

The track contains another innovation: Florian's electronic flute, which he had commissioned Peter Bollig to make. On *Autobahn*, Florian was still using a normal metal acoustic flute, amplified by microphone like the vocals and then altered using effect devices. The new model consisted of a Plexiglas tube screwed to a microphone stand with a gooseneck. Florian would plant himself motionless in front of it and play the Airwaves melody along with Ralf. He had set the glide effect on the synthesizer, which simulated a smooth glissando between notes, and 'sang' the highest notes on the new electro-flute. Inevitably, the motions evoked a Theremin, one of the first electronic musical instruments.

Intermission – News

The A-side ends with the interlude 'Intermission' followed by the sound collage 'News'. News readings related to nuclear power stations on various radio channels – distinguished by basic signature melodies – fade in and out. None of them reveal any content. The language remains unintelligible, more sound than message.

The Voice of Energy

The album's B-side opens with a vocoder voice telling the listener it is a giant electrical generator. 'The Voice of Energy' reminds us that images and sounds are broadcast and received with the aid of electricity, and finally claims to be both our servant and master. We get one last tip from the voice: 'So take good care of me – me, the genius of energy.'

Antenna

The vocals on 'Antenna' remind me of rock'n'roll aesthetics – it sounds like the tape echo on recordings from the Sun Studio in Memphis. Like on 'Radioland', sung passages alternate with noises from the electro-sound toolbox. As we can easily tell in hindsight, the vocal harmonies on 'Airwaves' and this track didn't have a great future with Kraftwerk.

Radio Stars – Uranium – Transistor

These pieces are faded into each other or linked by a miniature radio play, creating an interconnected sequence.

On 'Radio Stars', the Minimoog synthesizer's third oscillator produces a science-fiction sound effect, over which Ralf intones an almost absent-minded 'Radio stars broadcasting from space'. Like on 'Radioland', Ralf and Florian input a polyphonic audio signal via the Votrax's external jack, modulating the phonemes of the words 'quasars and pulsars', which Florian types on his 'speaking typewriter'.

After about three and a half minutes, a chord of Orchestron choir crossfades into the end of the sci-fi sound. This time, a white-noise signal is put into the Votrax and a text about the emission of radioactive substances from uranium crystal is modulated. There follows an 'ear cleanser' in the form of a miniature audio play, and the subsequent small echo study by the name of 'Transistor' reminds me – as do several other aspects of *Radio-Activity* – of the 1973 album *Ralf und Florian*.

Ohm Sweet Ohm

I've thought a lot about what kind of mood the last track of the album puts me into. I think 'Ohm Sweet Ohm' is an example of a rare musical phenomenon: it is sad and happy at the same time. After the Votrax intro, the instrumental starts off in a solemn tempo, with elements from German folk music that can be traced back to the live version of

'Morning Walk'. Ralf plays his Orchestron with skilful imperfection, and as on earlier Kraftwerk albums, the speed picks up perceptibly after a while.

Artwork

Even today, it's a mystery to me why Emil thought the 'Deutscher Kleinempfänger DKE 38' radio, also called the *Volksempfänger* ('people's radio'), would make an appropriate cover image. He once said he drove around and around with Ralf to get hold of the exact model for the photo on the back cover.[13]

Even though the swastika underneath the speaker was replaced by the album title, and the '1938' on the back, to the right of the words 'Deutscher Kleinempfänger', was removed, it is nonetheless still the radio that Joseph Goebbels commissioned for mass production. Hitler's propaganda minister knew that communication between radio and listeners was key, but it wouldn't happen with political messages alone. People were much easier to reach through emotive songs like 'Ich weiß, es wird einmal ein Wunder geschehen', 'Freunde, das Leben ist lebenswert' or 'Lili Marleen'. The *Volksempfänger* was the main medium for information during the Second World War, but also for entertainment. By coincidence or intention, quite a few things about Kraftwerk seemed loaded with historical symbolism. On *Autobahn*, the not-so-subtle hint at German identity through the title and the Mercedes and VW on the cover had worked well. And now this mysterious reminiscence?

Emil's characteristic signature is clear again in the collage on the back of the inside sleeve: the antenna and his portrait with

170

tools in hand – screwdriver, brush and pencil. That's the real Emil, without a doubt, 'Malermeister Klecksel', as we used to call him, an affectionate nickname meaning something like 'Mister Splott the Painter'.

For the group photo on the front of the inside sleeve, Wolfgang and I were invited along to another session at Foto Frank. Like our first group shot, the autograph card, this one was also to be in black and white, only this time slightly more elegant, in suits and ties. Wolfgang wore the black tie I'd spotted in San Francisco that May, and Florian a classic dark one. Ralf, from now on without glasses, had opted for his favourite tie, sporting a picture of a German shepherd dog. I decided on my silver work tie from the opera. Aside from that, the instruments were at least partly in view, like in a classic band photo: Ralf is depicted with a Sennheiser microphone attached to a 'spider' shock mount, and Wolfgang and I brought along our knitting needles and held them in our hands like conventional drummers would their sticks. Florian presented his electronic flute for the first time in a photo.

My Crash Course

To my mind, this album is an avant-garde audio drama divided into twelve episodes. The pop songs 'Radioactivity' and 'Antenna' were lifted for the A- and B-sides of the single. Three other pieces – 'Radioland', 'Airwaves' and 'Ohm Sweet Ohm' – are linked by interludes made up of experimental electronic sounds and spoken word.

In classical music, the imperative is to perform Beethoven as if you'd never heard Wagner or Mahler. I like to imagine the musical context of 1975 when listening to *Radio-Activity*. For me, it was our recording medium, limited as it was to eight tracks, that led to the transparent arrangements. The most important musical design tool is the creation of original sounds through speech synthesis, in combination with the Orchestron's recorded violins and choir settings and the synthetic sounds of the synthesizers. The drums have a merely ordering function in this context, and yet they meet the definition of electronic music through the sound they create. The only natural sound sources on the album are the human voices and the violins, like in Stockhausen's *Gesang der Jünglinge*, electronic and acoustic signals meld together and form an electro-acoustic sound composition.

By this point, Ralf and Florian were already old hands at record production. And yet I think they were under a fair amount of pressure after the success of *Autobahn*. They didn't let it show, though. The atmosphere was focused but relaxed, and Peter Bollig's expertise and sense of humour helped a great deal to get successful recordings on tape.

The musical ideas for the tracks already existed in the two co-authors' minds by the time I came along to play my parts on the electro-drums. I helped to find the right rhythmic formula for each song. My input was within the usual expectations of a studio musician. Wolfgang discussed his tasks with Ralf and Florian. Filming the footage for 'Radioactivity', the two of us drummed together, in any case. These days I think: the drum tracks are fine, they serve their purpose – and anyone could have played them. I can't judge the extent to which our paraphrasing commentary on the recordings were important for the compositions' development.

172

After the recording sessions, Ralf and Florian drove to the Rüssl Studio in Hamburg – now Gaga Studio – with the tape machine and the multitracks, and mixed the album with the sound engineer Walter Quintus. For me, making the record was an auditive crash course. Interesting. Exciting. New. But I separated my work with Kraftwerk from my studies and my other musical activities.

I would have loved to be there when the gentlemen from the American record company took the master tape and artwork for *Radio-Activity* out of the FedEx envelope. I fear they won't have seen the black Third Reich radio as a particularly 'Fun, Fun, Fun' kind of object. My imagination lacks the scope to picture how they must have listened to the 'Kling Klang audio play'. As a follow-up to *Autobahn*, the *Radio-Activity* album was a relative flop not just in the USA, but worldwide. It scraped into the US charts at a modest number 140 for a couple of weeks. In the UK, it didn't even graze the lower regions of the charts. The record with the radio did make it to number 22 in Germany, though. And in France? The label manager at Pathé Marconi did a great job. I'll come back a few more times to Monsieur Maxime Schmitt, who first proved his special 'radio-activity' that year.

The Silent Treatment?

It was the winter semester of 1975/76, and I immersed myself back into my parallel musical world, meeting up with the Play-Bach ensemble and working on Béla Bartók's *Sonata for Two Pianos and Percussion*. A performance with the conservatory's percussion ensemble was the first opportunity to use my bonus from the American tour: the Musser vibraphone. In the meantime, Kraftwerk had made it to Düsseldorf's local media and people were beginning to associate me with the group.

The *Neue Rhein Zeitung* wrote: 'Of all the performers in the percussion ensemble [. . .], one stood out for his musicality and the innate agility and lightness of his playing: Karlheinz Bartos, who has just returned from a successful American tour with the Düsseldorf pop group Kraftwerk.' And the *Rheinische Post*: 'One of Düsseldorf's most talented percussionists and vibraphonists is Karlheinz Bartos, a student in the class of Ernst Göbler at the Robert Schumann Conservatory and an accomplished rhythm-maker at numerous concerts in and around Düsseldorf. He accompanied Düsseldorf pop band Kraftwerk as a soloist on their very successful US tour – why must America once again notice such talent before we do?'

That kind of press wasn't exactly helpful for maintaining good relations with my fellow students. Slowly and imperceptibly, my social contacts changed. At the conservatory, I was one of the best-known students, but people stopped talking to me much. And I couldn't shake the feeling that my colleagues at the opera had started seeing me differently too. Had they misunderstood my cheerful postcards from New York, Los Angeles, San Francisco and Vancouver? Even my friendship with Marlis and Rainer Sennewald no longer felt as playful and light-hearted. Being a member of Kraftwerk seemed to have marginalized me with my other friends in some way. But it was just a feeling, nothing specific, nothing tangible; more a vague suspicion I was being given the silent treatment. I didn't go into it any further, and set the thought aside.

Then I got a phone call from the Jokers. I should have seen it coming, really – Franz fired me for being away all the time. I didn't protest; he was right. The Jokers were very successful in their field and I hadn't been particularly professional towards them. Essentially, I had mentally left the band while I was in America. I didn't worry at all about losing my regular income. Being a member of an authentic group of artists meant more to me than playing in a cover band. I'd make up for the financial loss somehow, I hoped.

In October 1975, I took my written examinations in aural theory, harmonics, counterpoint and theory of form. There were more sessions going on in the Kling Klang Studio at the same time.

In the Realm of the Schneider-Eslebens

The four of us hadn't seen each other since the end of October, so I was glad when we met up at Florian's parents' house in Golzheim three months later. Golzheim was one of Düsseldorf's posher neighbourhoods. The family had gone on holiday, it seemed, and Florian was keeping an eye on the place. He acted very cool, showing me around the house and explaining the furniture his father had designed, his pictures and *objet d'art*. The high-end stereo played a soundtrack in the background: Brian Wilson's masterpiece *Pet Sounds* or a Stevie Wonder record.

Florian's father, Paul Schneider-Esleben, was a rather famous artist and architect, the designer of several major post-war buildings in Düsseldorf. His projects included the Hanielgarage multi-storey car park, the Mannesmann building, St Rochus' church, and even Cologne Bonn Airport. While Florian was aware of his privileged background, he distanced himself from upper-class rituals. I began to see him as a kind of luxury punk without a home, for whom music was clearly a vehicle to develop his own identity. He started playing the flute as a child; his sister Claudia once told me he was considered very talented. He was taught by Rosemarie Popp – Fräulein Popp, as the Schneider-Esleben family called her. Florian began to run with the Düsseldorf art scene as a teenager, partly through family connections. Long before he met Ralf, he was part of light and cross-over performances by Ferdinand Kriwet, for instance, at the Kunsthalle. Joseph Beuys, the Zero Group and other artists were friends of the family. So art played a major role, and I think Florian was attracted by the dynamic developed by artistic expression in those years. In 1967, Hans Mayer, the owner of the Galerie Denise Renée Hans Mayer, made an appearance. His gallery put on spectacular events that everybody wanted to attend. A contact that proved extremely helpful – later, Hans Mayer booked Ralf and Florian to play in the space.

Kraftwerk: The Backstory

It was at exactly this time that Florian met Eberhard Kranemann, who had enrolled at the Düsseldorf Art Academy in 1965. Eberhard was to accompany him on his first musical excursions. Kranemann experimented with sound, noise and repetition, and founded the band Pissoff in 1968. When he learned that Florian played the flute, the two of them started making music together

176

and began bringing in other musicians. Kranemann had taken part in a jazz course at the Akademie Remscheid[14] and recommended his young flautist should try it out as well.

And that was where 21-year-old Florian Schneider-Esleben met the 22-year-old organist Ralf Hütter, in 1968. They soon found they had a lot in common – they both rejected the clichés of technique-oriented instrumental practice, instead focusing their creativity on finding their own form of musical expression. They quickly bonded. In a long interview with *Mojo* magazine some forty years later, Ralf described it aptly: 'When we first met, we talked the same language,' he said of himself and Florian. 'We were two *einzelgänger* (loners, mavericks), Mr Kling and Mr Klang. Two *einzelgänger* produce a *doppelgänger*.'[15]

In his younger years, Ralf had played the organ in the cover band the Quartermasters, as a photo dating back to 1965 shows. He started studying architecture in Aachen but didn't give up music, switching to the beat group the Phantoms and coming second in the North Rhine-Westphalian beat championships in Düsseldorf's Rheinhalle at the tender age of 20, in February 1967.[16]

After the jazz course, Florian brought Ralf into his Düsseldorf circles and they set up a free music project with frequent changes of personnel. They played a lot of local gigs in 1969, until finally running into Conny Plank. Years later, Conny told the German magazine *Soundcheck* about their first meeting: 'In Düsseldorf, in a basement in the old town centre, I found [. . .] a group called "Organisation", mainly consisting of Ralf Hütter and Florian Schneider. [. . .] The most important thing about the group, though, was that people came together who couldn't play an instrument properly but had a lot of clarity and power in their expression. I discovered that you can express yourself without being able to play an instrument. I found that again with Kraftwerk, who took a very distinct approach to their music.'[17]

Ralf Hütter, Florian Schneider, Butch Hauf, Basil Hammoudi and Alfred Mönicks recorded their first album in the Rhenus-Studio Godorf near the big refineries on the Rhine in December 1969, and it came out on the British RCA label in 1970. The studio was the exact same place where I had a session of my own with Conny a year later, in August 1971.

In the spring of 1970, Ralf and Florian changed the name and the philosophy of their musical project – and Organisation became Kraftwerk.[18] They rented a commercial property in the rear building of number 16, Mintropstrasse, and set up their business headquarters. In the summer of 1970, they produced their first album by the name of *Kraftwerk* with Conny Plank, and it got to number 30 on the German charts. There followed countless live appearances by Ralf, Florian and Klaus Dinger, one of the two drummers on the album; the other was Andreas Hohmann. Occasionally, Emil Schult and Plato Riviera would make up the numbers for a quintet. Klaus Dinger once called this constantly changing version of Kraftwerk 'the floating line-up'. And then Michael Rother turned up.

Michael Rother: 'A guitarist friend invited me to come along to a band called Kraftwerk's studio, early in 1971. When I walked into the spacious room in Mintropstrasse, Florian Schneider and Klaus Dinger were sitting on a couch. Ralf Hütter was playing his Hammond organ, Charly Weiss was on drums. I grabbed a bass and improvised with Ralf. Musically, we got along instantly. We clearly had a similar taste for European harmonies and melody lines, absolutely free from the usual blues structures. We swapped phone numbers and then things went their way.'

According to reports, there were repeated differences of opinion in the line-up at that time, and at the end of 1970 Ralf left Kraftwerk for a few months, with Michael Rother taking over on the guitar. Ralf kept an eye out for other musicians.[19]

Klaus Röder: 'Ralf had just left Kraftwerk and asked me if I fancied playing with him. We were soon rehearsing together: Ralf on keyboards, Charly Weiss on drums and me on guitar. That's not listed anywhere. Ralf was studying architecture and living with his parents in Krefeld. Charly and I would go there for rehearsals, and Ralf would open the door with the words "Hi, girls." We didn't play many gigs but I do remember one concert with Ralf and Charly in the Röhre venue in Moers: Ralf tinkled away on his e-piano and I made weird electronic sounds to go with it. We spent most of the evening improvising. I enjoyed it, but we didn't play in that line-up again afterwards.'

After Ralf left, there were two groups by the name of Kraftwerk for a while, from the end of 1970 until September 1971. On 19 December 1970, Ralf presented his thoughts and ideas about Beethoven, playing with an anonymous fellow musician in Mauricio Kagel's 'Beethoven's Musical Salon'.[20]

Florian's Kraftwerk played the piece 'Rückstoss Gondoliere' on the TV show *Beat-Club* on 22 May 1971, featuring Florian Schneider, Michael Rother and Klaus Dinger. With a variety of musicians, Florian played a whole load of gigs over the next six months to sell the first album.

> Michael Rother: 'When I joined Kraftwerk we were initially a quintet: Florian Schneider, Klaus Dinger, Houschäng Nejadepour, Eberhard Kranemann and me. After two concerts, Florian stopped inviting Houschäng and Eberhard to play live. Florian, Klaus and I were a compact musical team, and we toured as a trio until some point that summer.'

The trio's attempt to record the second Kraftwerk album in Conny Plank's studio failed, however.

> Michael Rother: 'It turned out we weren't capable of taking the unique quality of our live performances – their musical tension – into the studio. Even Conny Plank couldn't do anything about it. After the recordings panned, we all realized we wouldn't stay together. Klaus and I felt our musical goals were more closely related, so we decided to continue as a duo and we founded Neu!. After we left, Florian got back together with Ralf, whose absence over those few months is often swept under the carpet in the official Kraftwerk narrative.'

The success of the first album and all the live appearances garnered more and more attention for Kraftwerk. Then the use of 'Ruckzuck' as the title tune of the *Kennzeichen D* programme from September 1971 increased their popularity even more, making the band a phenomenon in the German pop scene. You could say Kraftwerk had become a prospering business

180

enterprise. After Michael Rother and Klaus Dinger left, Ralf came back to record the second album with Florian and Conny in the Star Studio Hamburg in September/October 1971. Shortly after that, Conny Plank produced Michael Rother and Klaus Dinger's debut album. *Kraftwerk 2* and *NEU!* came out simultaneously in January 1972.

A double LP featuring the first two Kraftwerk albums was released in the UK. That was the record Ralf had given me after our second session. Ralf and Florian played lots of gigs in 1972 and 1973, including at the Festival of German Music in France.

One thing's for sure – 1973 was a very important year for the two of them; it saw a whole lot of changes, including on the business front. Conny Plank had launched them with Organisation's *Tone Float* album. He was regarded as a top man for progressive productions in Germany, had the best contacts to the music industry and offered labels his productions in the name of the bands. It was during this time that Kraftwerk's record contract with Philips came about.

Those days were a kind of dawning of a new era in experimental music. Absolutely independently of each other, several groups were working on a new sound for German music. What distinguished Ralf Hütter and Florian Schneider from the others was their ability to run their operations, in legal and economic terms, like a medium-sized business enterprise. Since the days of *Ralf und Florian*, they had stuck to the principle of maximum control and autonomy in all things Kraftwerk:

1. Production spaces: they had already taken the first step of investing in business premises. Their recordings took place

in their own studio on Mintropstrasse – although the mixing was still done elsewhere.

2. Copyright: they wrote all their own tracks (from *Ralf und Florian* on, without the 'Esleben' in Florian's name), and their newly founded Kling Klang publishing company, a member of the German GEMA collecting society, now controlled their publishing rights. (This was another very important step, as the publishing rights to their previous albums went to external companies, a model often used to compensate for the costs of studio usage.)

3. Personnel: the band's personnel structure and outward appearance changed. A cover with stylistic reminiscences of Warhol, like the pylon had served its purpose, similar to the Velvet Underground's banana, but it was anonymous. The two musicians are pictured on both the front and back cover of *Ralf und Florian*. Plus, of course, the record bears their names. Like the artists Gilbert & George, they were now focusing on themselves.

4. Producer: on *Ralf und Florian*, Conny Plank was no longer credited as co-producer like on the first two albums, but only listed as the sound engineer. It was a visible uncoupling from him, preparing in the medium term for point five, below.

5. Record label: Kraftwerk's record contract with Philips/ Phonogram expired with the *Autobahn* album, which meant Conny Plank was out of the equation. Kling Klang Records, set up in the meantime by Ralf and Florian, took a different direction. After *Autobahn* they made new deals with EMI Electrola for West Germany, Austria and Switzerland, with Capitol for the USA and Canada, and with EMI for the UK and the rest of the world.

182

The third Kraftwerk album, *Ralf und Florian*, came out in Germany and France on the Philips label in October 1973 and in Britain on Vertigo in January 1974. The duo concept seemed to work on the album, but presenting the tracks live called for an expanded line-up. On 10 October 1973, they performed 'Tanzmusik' on the ZDF culture show *Aspekte*, with Wolfgang Flür on the electronic drums.

At their next gigs – for instance at Hessian Broadcasting's large recording auditorium in January or in Hamburg's Ernst Merck Hall in April 1974 – Kraftwerk appeared as a quartet, made up of Ralf, Florian, Wolfgang and Klaus Röder. The four of them then recorded *Autobahn* with Conny Plank. In the summer of 1974, Klaus Röder left the band to devote more time to his own musical ideas.

And it was on 4 October 1974 that I first went through the door at number 16, Mintropstrasse.

Radioactivity – the Film

Even in 1976 – five years before MTV – a film was very important for promoting a record on the international music market, although there weren't yet regular formats for showing promotional material on TV. Ralf and Florian wanted to make a film for 'Radioactivity' in the Kling Klang Studio and use the visuals to shape the group's image at the same time. They took their cues from 1920s German cinema. The Yellow Pages helped them find a cameraman, eventually coming up with Günter Fröhling – who had learned his trade at the East German DEFA film studio in Babelsberg, the heir to Germany's pre-war movie industry.

Fröhling was a physically small cameraman with a large body of skills. On Wednesday, 28 January 1976, he recorded our first music video on his Arriflex camera at the Kling Klang Studio. Even the very first frames recall 1920s cinema: the iris shot at the beginning, the radioactivity symbol – which admittedly didn't yet exist in the twenties – the glowing Kraftwerk lettering, Wolfgang's silver gloves, our group photo from Foto Frank, the Morse code. Then there's the montage of Florian's Morse solo and Wolfgang's glove ballet, in which he rhythmically breaks through a ray of light. Here's one to try at home – if you turn down the colour on your TV, it looks even more like an old Babelsberg production.

Counterpoint and Promo Tour

Regardless of all that, I took my final oral exams in February 1976, again in aural theory, harmonics, counterpoint and theory of forms. One day later, we met up at Mintropstrasse and set off for France in several cars. Emil and Peter were on board again, like in England. We had a number of gigs lined up around France, later followed by more in Denmark and the Netherlands. Ralf dubbed the undertaking a 'promo tour', being very precise about his choice of words. It became an indispensable element of his vocabulary over the years to come. A 'promo tour', as I duly learned, is not about making money, but about advertising a product. In this case, *Radio-Activity*. It made sense to me that I couldn't expect a normal fee for this kind of tour, but only a kind of allowance for travel expenses. At the time me and my fellow students always played in clubs and venues for little money. Nobody had an entrepreneurial mindset. Ralf and Florian came from a different background. They benefitted from our easy-going lifestyle and sailed in the warm social winds of the 1960s. But I imagined that even before *Radio-Activity*'s recording session, they may have had an attorney with an office in Rockefeller Center, New York. Not bad, right?

We played in Lille, Lyon and the famous Olympia in Paris. Not a bad gig, if I remember rightly. Except that my electro-drums broke just before the start of the show and went absolutely silent. Peter Bollig popped up on stage with a soldering iron in his hand and a cigar in his mouth – we didn't yet have a curtain – and soldered the thing back together with his characteristic calm.

Socially, things were very relaxed with Ralf, Florian, Wolfgang and Emil. Florian walked around in his grey flying jacket and threadbare grey trousers, Ralf in a black pleather jacket and jeans, Emil always cut a cool figure in his suit jacket in those days, and Wolfgang looked great all the time anyway.

At our first gig in Lille, we met Monsieur Maxime Schmitt, the manager of the EMI label Pathé Marconi. Only slightly taller than us, he wore his dark hair shoulder length with a centre parting. His trademark was a pair of glasses with red-tinted lenses. Maxime was a big fan of Kraftwerk's music and began to work hard for the group. He saw hit potential in 'Radioactivity'; it was the sound that won him over, rather than the ambiguous concept behind the LP.

We stayed a few days in Paris, where Maxime booked us into the fancy Royal Monceau hotel on Avenue Hoche and took us to La Coupole for the first time. The restaurant on the Boulevard du Montparnasse was to become our regular Paris haunt.

Entering the place, I was blown away by the high ceilings, the Art Deco lamps and the painted cupola in the middle of the room. Artfully designed pillars divided the dining space, where countless tables – complete with white tablecloths, napkins and classic cutlery – conjured up an atmosphere apparently only possible in Paris. The mood over our long weekend in the city was amazing. After a two-week break in Düsseldorf, we continued our tour with gigs in Copenhagen, Aarhus and Rotterdam.

I spent May, June and July attending lectures I had signed up for after my theory exams, and numerous opera performances. The date of 4 June 1976 – at the end of the 1975/1976 opera season – wasn't exactly an outstanding day in my sound biography. It began at 10 a.m. at the Robert Schumann Conservatory with a lesson on free composition. Then I practised for my percussion exam and set off for the opera house in the evening. For some of my English friends, though, that date had a very different significance. They experienced a band that was still relatively unknown, playing Manchester's Lesser Free Trade Hall. Looking back, I note that on the day the Sex Pistols played their famous Manchester gig in front of a handful of people – leading to the creation of Joy Division – I was sitting in the orchestra pit at the Deutsche Oper am Rhein, at a performance of Sergei Prokofiev's *The Tale of the Stone Flower.*

Number 9, Berger Allee

Gradually, a certain collective feeling was developing among us, connecting us outside of work as well as on stage and in the studio. We were spending more and more time together. I would occasionally meet up with Ralf on Düsseldorf's famous 'Kö' boulevard or Mata-Hari-Passage in the old town centre. At some point, we talked about the flat he had rented at number 9, Berger Allee. Its inhabitants at that time were Wolfgang, Emil and Plato Kostic Riviera – an earlier Kraftwerk member and a former fellow student of Ralf's. The ground-floor flat was huge, he told me, with five rooms, a kitchen, hall, bathroom and utility room, plus an extra room at the semi-basement level. If I wanted, he said, I could move in, and then the whole crew would be under one roof. We arranged to meet the next day so I could take a look at the flat.

Berger Allee is just yards away from the Rhine, on the edge of the historic town centre, within eyeshot of the Mannesmann building designed by Florian's father. The whole block was made up of large Art Nouveau houses that had just reached the perfect state, somewhere between functioning and rotted away.

Wolfgang opened the door to us and I noticed even from the hallway how spacious the flat was. The ceilings were very high, decorated with Art Nouveau stucco. There was a faint smell of paint in the air. The first room on the left was Emil's, the parquet floor creaking as we entered. His décor seemed extremely minimalist to me. It consisted essentially of a handmade wooden bed with a foam mattress and a large workbench with a wooden chair by the window, which opened onto the big pond opposite. A couple of swans were just gliding past. Framed by tall old trees, the water looked like a German Romantic painting – I couldn't imagine a better view from a residential space. Emil's paintings covered the walls all the way up to the ceiling, giving the room a gallery atmosphere. Despite their different motifs, his portraits, landscapes and sci-fi cities built underneath huge glass domes had a clear signature style.

A self-portrait of Emil with a Les Paul caught my eye – he looked like a young guitar god.

We passed through a large double door into the huge, almost empty room next door – the flat's central space – which Emil seemed to be using as an art studio. There were gas cylinders and spray guns on the floor, and I noticed a couch covered with a tiger-print blanket, facing an old TV set with an indoor aerial.

At the back end of the studio, a door led into Wolfgang's room, complete with a view of the Rhine. Wolfgang had moved in shortly after the *Aspekte* performance in October 1973. He too was a minimalist in terms of furnishings and fittings.

The large kitchen-cum-living room, bathroom and toilet were accessed via the hallway, as was the semi-basement level. Plato Kostic Riviera occupied two rooms behind the kitchen and bathroom. All in all, the flat must have been about 200 square metres in size.

Ralf, Emil and Wolfgang told me I could move into Emil's studio if I wanted, and when Plato had finished his architecture degree and gone back to Greece, I could move into his rooms. On top of that, the back room in the basement would make a great practice space for me. The rent would be 150 marks a month to start off, and later 230 marks.

So I left my student flat in Oberkassel, which was actually a great place, and moved to Berger Allee. Kraftwerk's gravitational pull was simply too strong. The biggest influence on my decision had been our tour of America, but the recording sessions for *Radio-Activity*, the UK gigs and the 'promo tour' at the beginning of the year were also amazing experiences. The international flair that came into my life through our tours, the authenticity of the music, our group dynamics – all of it really appealed to me. I wanted to be part of the gang, belong to the clique. In the end, Peter Wollek from Sinus helped me transport my belongings in his car, and from 1 July 1976 on, I was an official resident at number 9, Berger Allee.

In contrast to my attic apartment, I now had central heating and a normal bathroom. But the quiet days were over; friends, acquaintances and hangers-on were constantly coming and going. I soon felt at home in our 'company flat'. As in any shared home, its heart was the kitchen. One other point worth mentioning: the three fridges. My flatmates had obviously given up trying to share just one. The three refrigerators did have a down side, though – they weren't lockable, and under some conditions, respect for other people's provisions fell below a certain level and led to 'enemy extractions', which in turn paved the way to a zero-tolerance policy with inevitable revenge attacks. The telephone bill was a similar case. The records we jotted down of our calls were never correct and the respective shares were usually worked out in a typically Rhineland slapdash style.

I often think back to my legendary 'wardrobe': a towering construction of a good dozen cardboard removals boxes. My piano and vibraphone were in the front of my two rooms. I remember playing old jazz standards there like 'Moonlight in Vermont', 'The Shadow of Your Smile' and 'Misty'.

For a while, I'd been meeting up with the outstanding pianist Mario-Ratko Delorko to work on a concert programme together. We planned to play sonatas by Bach, Handel and Francis Poulenc, and also practised Claude Debussy's *Suite Bergamasque* with its famous third movement, 'Clair de Lune'. I have to say that the motorics of baroque music, the counterpoint, the inter-woven voices hugely impressed me. Sometimes my brain practically flew out of my skull as I listened and played! With Debussy's music, though, we developed a joint feel for rubato.[21] That is, the art of making everything seem improvised despite a just about tangible basic timing, creating not only sounds but also a floating atmosphere beyond the notes themselves. Tempo rubato – robbing or stealing time – is a magical formula.

Our flatshare was a mixture of a musician's workshop, an artist's studio and a kids' holiday camp – or that's how it comes across to me now. There was barely any routine; something unexpected was always happening. Now and then, Emil, Wolfgang and I would even go on proper family outings to the Bergisches Land or the Eifel. And alongside our idyllic countryside jaunts, there were also the legendary Berger Allee parties.

Advanced Performer's Degree

The date is 14 July 1976, and I leave the Berger Allee flat early in the morning. The weather is pleasantly warm. I walk along the Rhine to the Robert Schumann Conservatory. Today is my final exam. The night before, I lugged the percussion instruments – timpani, drums, xylophone, vibraphone, glockenspiel – into the hall on the first floor of the new building with the help of the caretaker, and set them up. When I arrive, the examination committee is sitting at a long table, members of the conservatory's senior staff, several lecturers and chamber musicians. Ernst Göbler introduces each piece or orchestral study with a few words of explanation.

I begin with chamber music for timpani and drums, with piano accompaniment by Alexander Tscherepnin and Friedrich

Zehm, and a composition by Gary Burton for solo vibraphone: *The Sunset Bell*.

These are followed by orchestral studies for snare drum, xylophone and timpani by Franz von Suppé, Daniel-François-Esprit Auber, Rimsky-Korsakov, Maurice Ravel, Igor Stravinsky, Paul Hindemith, George Gershwin, Richard Strauss, Ferruccio Busoni, Béla Bartók, Ludwig van Beethoven, Richard Wagner and Peter Tchaikovsky. The whole gamut. It's not exactly a kid's birthday party but neither am I overly nervous. All the members of the examination committee have seen and heard me over the past few days at symphony concerts, opera performances or concerts in various other contexts.

After my audition, I am sent out of the room so the committee can discuss my performance. Only a few minutes later, they call me back in and tell me calmly that I've passed my exam with *summa cum laude*. Not bad, I think. Sure, of course I'm pleased, relieved and happy. But somehow, I also fall into a vacuum. I've spent twelve semesters preparing for this day. And now, after just over an hour, I'm clutching my graduation certificate in my hands at the age of 24. It attests to a high theoretical level – allegedly, I also possess particular interpretation skills and outstanding artistic skills on my instrument. Good to know.

Once I've carried the instruments back down to the percussion room, I roam the city aimlessly. I don't want to go back to the flat; I lead a very different life there. I feel alone, watching the ships on the Rhine but not really seeing them. I cross the river via Oberkassel Bridge, sit down at a table at the brewery pub Vossen in the familiar neighbourhood of my old flat, and order something to eat. When Manfred the waiter brings me another drink, I put the glass back on his tray and set off for home. Now I'm ready for human company again.

Sinus and Sci-fi

The next day was a perfectly normal one: I spent the afternoon tutoring my private students and the evening with a gig by the Peter Weiss Quartet in the Downtown jazz club. The big advantage to performing jazz is definitely that the standards are a reliable method of allowing very different musicians to make music together instantly. We used the *Real Book* as our common reference. As a vibraphonist, I was now getting to know the jazz standards from a new perspective.

Incidentally, for the young Karlheinz Stockhausen, jazz improvisations were clichés learned by rote. Was he right? Yes, perhaps, but then again . . .

Analytically speaking, musical improvisations consist of learned and consciously combined melodies, scales and arpeggios, unconscious actions, coincidences and possibly even mistakes, but I've seen and heard musicians whose allegedly cardboard-cut-out improvisations made me lose all track of time – which, as we all know, is what music is made of.

In my understanding, the spontaneous invention of music is comparable to an unscripted, unplanned conversation. Although we use familiar sentences and figures of speech, our communication creates new senses and contexts over and over again. I think a good conversation is a matter of the participants' vocabulary, eloquence and imagination. Yet the result is never predictable, the outcome is open . . .

192

The idea behind Sinus was also based on improvisation. Oddly enough, it was this unplanned music-making with my friends that brought a consistency into my life. I think we all felt the need to make music together. But our line-up also changed over time. Peter Wollek was now studying e-bass at the conservatory. He and our fellow student Reinhold Nickel on the drums made up the rhythm group. Via Rainer Sennewald, who had started studying photography at the Folkwangschule, we found the young pianist Ralph Rotzoll. Ralph was thinking about studying art but then decided on music in the end. We got plenty of gigs in and around Düsseldorf up to the summer – including one at the Düsseldorf Kunsthalle.

Sinus met up regularly at the conservatory to rehearse for a show with a mime artist, or we would organize musical performances along with Emil Schult at Club Domizil. Emil called them 'sci-fi evenings'. Our sound pieces had names like 'Sun Sounds', 'Mambo Universitario', 'Marimba Polytechnic' and 'Strings Funk'. The poster, designed by Emil of course, featured a space ship with a garden on board, underneath a glass dome. He had also drawn a robot on it. They were pretty strange events, I have to say, with us playing behind a transparent cellophane curtain and sending bizarre electronic sounds to the other side.

Sadly, the sci-fi nights with Emil came to an abrupt end. It was on the Berger Allee grapevine that I first heard that you were either exclusively in Kraftwerk or you did something else – but then you weren't in Kraftwerk. I thought it was odd but I'd soon forgotten it again.

Independently of all that, something changed in my thinking. Although I still love jazz to this day, I lost interest in developing the art of jazz improvisation. Instead, I was much keener on focusing on creating music with its origins in improvisations, but not obliged to the idioms of a particular genre.

Summer Hit

In France, Maxime Schmitt had convinced Jean-Loup Lafont from the radio station Europe n°1 to use the track 'Radioactivity' as the title song for his show. The jingle was astoundingly successful and the single became a summer hit in 1976, reaching number 3 in the charts. In December, the station chose *Radio-Activity* as its LP of the year. In the photos taken when we were awarded the golden records in our label's office, the five of us and Maxime are posing with a model of the famous dog recognizing his master's voice coming out of the gramophone's funnel speaker. There is no doubt that Maxime Schmitt played a key role in the single and album's major sales. His influence on Kraftwerk during his time at Pathé Marconi should not be underestimated. People really bought into the album in the French-speaking countries. And I mean that in both senses – both as a product and as a blueprint for the productions of French and Belgian artists.

That success felt good. In July 1976, Ralf, Florian, Wolfgang, Emil and I went to visit Maxime in Paris for a long weekend. Once again, we stayed at the Royal Monceau. A weekend in Paris tends to fly by, but the Monday was reserved for a session with the celebrated photographer J. Stara, whose studio was very close to the hotel on Rue de Tilsitt. An impressively unreal-looking photograph of Soraya, the former empress of Persia, was on display in the window of his salesroom, making the place feel like a gallery.

J. Stara's special art was limiting his camera settings to only a few angles. He collaged individual portraits together to make group pictures. The lighting in his studio was always the same, the angles standardized; he used them like templates. Colouring the photos subsequently gave them their affected style, his unmistakable signature. When it came to details, Stara was an incredible perfectionist. At the photo session, Wolfgang and I wore our silk ties from Chinatown in San Francisco. Ralf chose to do without his sheepdog version on this occasion. One at a time, we sat on the chair in four different positions and stared into space past the camera, with a look of hope and confidence in the future.

NOTES

1. 'Kraftwerk: The Final Solution to the Music Problem? Lester Bangs Vivisects the German Scientific Approach'. By Lester Bangs, *New Musical Express*, 6 September 1975, pp. 20–21
2. Ibid.
3. Ibid.
4. "After the war," explains Ralf, "German entertainment was destroyed. The German people were robbed of their culture . . .'" Ibid.
5. 'I think it's [the synthesizer] much more sensitive than a traditional instrument like a guitar,' Ralf is quoted. Ibid.
6. 'They then confided that they were going to spend all of the money from this tour on bigger and better equipment, that they work in their lab/studio for recreation, and that their Wernher von Braun sartorial aspect was "part of the German scientific approach."' Ibid.

7. Ibid.

8. 'Bald singt bei uns ein Computer! Aus der Hexenküche von Kraftwerk'. *Bravo*, no. 42/1975

9. Pierre Schaeffer: *In Search of a Concrete Music*. University of California Press: Berkeley 2012, p. 17. (*A la recherche d'une musique concrète*. Éditions du Seuil: Paris 1952)

10. Pink Floyd: *The Piper at the Gates of Dawn*, 1967

11. Pink Floyd: *Meddle*, 1971

12. See David Buckley: *Kraftwerk – Publication. A Biography*. Omnibus Press: London 2012, p. 78. 'Radioactivity was, in fact, discovered in 1896 by the French scientist Henri Becquerel. Marie Curie coined the term radioactivity, developed the theory of radioactivity, and discovered two elements, polonium and radium.'

13. Pascal Bussy: *Neonlicht. Die Kraftwerk-Story*. Bosworth Music: Berlin 2006

14. 'The Akademie der Kulturellen Bildung was founded in 1958 as the Akademie Remscheid and in 2016 officially renamed Cultural Education Academy of the German Federation and North Rhine-Westphalia. It is the central institute for cultural education of children and young adults in Germany and North Rhine-Westphalia. As a further education academy for specialists working with young people, in social, educational and cultural work, it is a recognized institution for the support of children and young adults and provides qualifications across the spectrum of cultural education.' http://kulturellebildung.de

15. In: 'Paranoid Android'. By Simon Witter, *Mojo*, September 2005

16. 'Zum 60. Geburtstag von Ralf Hütter'. By Michael van Uem. *Die Heimat* 77/2006, 20 August 2006

17. 'Alles verkurbeln und verbiegen'. Interview with Conny Plank. *Soundcheck*, 18 December 1986

18. From my perspective, there are two key influences in this period: anonymous and singing sculptures. Between 1969 and 1973, the Düsseldorfer Kunsthalle hosted the experimental exhibition series 'between', applying subjects such as 'democratization' and 'societal relevance' to the art industry. 'between 4' took place on 14 and 15 February 1970, with contributions by Bernd and Hilla Becher, who caused a furore that year with their illustrated book *Anonyme Skulpturen*. In 1976 Bernd Becher took on a professorship at the Düsseldorf Art Academy and founded the 'Becher School' with his wife Hilla. Its most

prominent representative was the photographer Andreas Gursky. Alongside the Bechers, the 1970 exhibition 'between 4' also presented the work 'The Singing Sculpture' by the English artists Gilbert & George. Both these artistic approaches are found later in one form or other in Kraftwerk's products.

19. Interview Ralf Hütter: Kraftwerk. 'Industrial plant for the Production of Electric or Atomic Energy'. *Musik Express*, April 1971

Musik Express: 'Ralf, you have left the group now, why?'

Ralf Hütter: 'On that I would like to say the following, that this departure is incomprehensible for many, but for me it is very natural. You may compare my break with the group with that of an erotic relationship to a woman, which cools down with time. If you have reached such a point, it would be absurd to continue. But it's not that I've isolated myself completely from the group, I am still in good contact with Kraftwerk, as reflected in sessions, personal conversations and other things.'

20. 'Experimente in Beethovens Salon'. By Petra Strenzke, *Aachener Nachrichten*, 21 December 1970

21. *Rubato* or *tempo rubato*: a musical term meaning a flexible interpretation of a piece's tempo

8

TRANS-EUROPE EXPRESS

Germany is in Europe. The Synthanorma Sequencer. Europe Endless. The Hall of Mirrors. Trans-Europe Express (Song). After the Recordings. European Tour. La Bastide Blanche. On the Road Again. The Roundhouse Concert. TEE, Finishing Touches. Metal on Metal – Abzug. Eurodisco. Showroom Dummies. Franz Schubert – Endless Endless. Artwork. On the Orient Express to Reims. Filming in a Pale Trench Coat. Reflection. Fair Play. Zyklus für einen Schlagzeuger. Nightclubbing. Ratinger Hof.

Germany is in Europe

Despite its success in France, *Radio-Activity* didn't do all that well in the rest of Europe. One reason might well have been that we'd manoeuvred ourselves into a dead end with the German symbolism and a rhetoric that addressed technology without thinking deeply enough about it. The perspective for the next album was to be more open. Perhaps it was Lester Bangs, of all people, who laid the first trail in his infamous feature, by describing his impression of a Kraftwerk gig in the USA: ' . . . and the perfect synthesized imitation of a choo-choo train which must certainly be the programmatic follow-up to *Autobahn*.'[1] Was that one of the triggers for the new direction? I don't know; we never talked about it. A more likely influence on the album concept was the

198

French journalist Paul Alessandrini. During one of Ralf and Florian's visits to Paris, they met up with him for lunch at Le Train Bleu – a fancy restaurant on the first floor of the Gare de Lyon. The station – built along with the luxurious restaurant for the World Exhibition in 1900 – links Paris to the Côte d'Azur, Italy and Switzerland. The famous *Orient Express* once used to stop at the Gare de Lyon. Alessandrini recalls saying: 'With the kind of music you do, which is kind of like an electronic blues, railway stations and trains are very important in your universe, you should do a song about the Trans-Europe Express.'[2]

That suggestion may well be the reason why Ralf and Florian thank him and his wife Marjorie on the inside sleeve of *Trans-Europe Express*.

Eight months after the release of *Radio-Activity*, the two of them decided to start on the next album. This time, we wouldn't be driving our car; we'd be taking the train. Europe was the magic word. We still had a German passport, of course, but Germany is in Europe, as everyone knows. In my opinion, this wider focus pointed the way out of the cul-de-sac we'd ended up in. An electro-acoustic European road movie really was a much more positive vehicle than the difficult ambiguity of radio waves, bombs and nuclear power stations, connected by outdated German symbolism.

A fifteen-day window was planned for the production's initial recordings, from the end of June until mid-August 1976. Ralf and Florian had meanwhile invested in studio technology and bought an analogue two-inch sixteen-track tape machine from MCI and a mixing desk from Allen & Heath – worth tens of thousands in Deutschmarks. And Peter Bollig returned to the fold as sound engineer.

The Synthanorma Sequencer

As well as all that recording tech, there was another new appliance in the studio: a veneered wooden box about 80 x 50 x 50 cm, with a black metal plate on the front housing a whole host of dials. In purely visual terms, the box reminded me of the Enigma machine that the German military used to code its intelligence messages during the Second World War. But what Hajo Wiechers from the Synthesizerstudio Bonn had built wasn't a coding machine, it was an analogue step sequencer. The Synthanorma was connected to Ralf's synthesizer and controlled it by applying electrical voltage. The dials could set a certain number of frequencies – a maximum of twelve in those days. When you fired it up, it repeated the sound sequence over and over, as if you'd written repeat marks into a musical score and added 'ad infinitum'.

Automatic musical instruments have been around since ancient Greece.[3] Essentially, the analogue sequencer was a continuation of the glockenspiels, barrel organs and mechanical music-makers of the following epochs. In mid-eighteenth-century Paris, a certain Monsieur Vaucanson built mechanical androids that played the flute and drums. They had a repertoire of numerous melodies, which they performed with 'movements of the lips and the fingers and the same breath of air from the mouth as a living man'[4] while also beating the drum.

The step sequencer continued the principle of mechanical music-makers by electronic means, linking it with the concept of repetition of short sequences of notes. The idea of voltage-controlled manipulation and automation of electronically created

200

sound had been floating around for some time. The American musician and technician Raymond Scott played a key role in developing the technology, experimenting with electronic control of sounds as far back as the 1940s. In about 1953, he dreamed up and created a huge sequencer, and nicknamed it the 'Wall of Sound'. It was at that time that he also met the young physicist Robert Moog, who developed switching circuits for him in the 1960s. The first electronic sequencer Moog ever saw was at Scott's place. Over the next few years he constructed his famous Moog synthesizer, which contained a sequencer module, and launched it in 1964. Moog's opposite number was the synthesizer pioneer Don Buchla. His first modular synthesizer, dating back to 1963, could also be fitted with 8- or 16-step sequencer units. There was no alternative to the analogue sequencers from Moog and Buchla on the market until 1971, when the EMS Synthi-A was launched. The 'AKS' version contained a sequencer, which Pink Floyd used on 'On the Run' in 1973. That device was based on a different technical concept, though. So how did that wooden box, Hajo's sequencer, get into our studio?

Hajo Wiechers: 'Dirk Matten and I met Klaus Schulze at the Frankfurt music trade fair in 1974. He wanted to buy himself a sequencer, and I bravely told him I was capable of making one that was better than the Moog and also much cheaper. Klaus didn't waste time, and ordered the device on the spot – but at that point, it only existed in my mind. We didn't have a shop yet so I put the Synthanorma prototype together on my mother's kitchen table. It took ages, and Klaus was on the phone every day of the last phase. I finally finished and we packed the box into Dirk's

VW and drove it through East Germany to West Berlin. At the border, the GDR officers asked us if it could be used to send radio signals. I said no, which was the truth, and they let us cross unhindered.'

Hajo spent the next two days in Klaus's studio in Schöneberg to integrate the sequencer into its technical environment. That was when he met Edgar Froese from Tangerine Dream, who literally lived next door. Tangerine Dream already had a large modular Moog system with an integrated step sequencer, but Froese was impressed by Hajo's Synthanorma and ordered one for himself.

'Special thanks for the Sequenzer SYNTHANORMA' Klaus Schulze announced on the cover of his 1975 LP *Timewind* – and added the phone number for the source, which led to more orders. In the early seventies, Hajo's sequencers made their way into commercial music production. And that was the beginning of Synthesizerstudio Bonn's success story.

Hajo Wiechers: 'I'd always known Kraftwerk could use a sequencer – their music is made up of repetitions, to a large extent. And those repetitions aren't fixed – they move, they change. Up to that point, it all happened manually. Then one day we went out for a meal in Bonn with Ralf and Florian, and we told them everything you can do with a sequencer. With the Synthanorma, they'd be able to auto-mate a series of notes and modulate them during the process. And that was just the beginning . . . They weren't convinced at first because there was no way they wanted to sound like Tangerine Dream or Klaus Schulze. We talked it over for a while and in the end, they tried the Synthanorma out and soon realized what it was capable of.'

A musical automaton like that fitted perfectly into the man-machine agenda. Florian's playing already sounded very mechanical at times on 'Autobahn', even though the track had been played manually from beginning to end. From the recordings for *Trans-Europe Express* on, the Synthanorma sequencer was a fixed part of the machinery, marking out Kraftwerk's compositions until the mid-1980s.

Europe Endless

As far as I recall, we first used the Synthanorma on the track 'Europe Endless'. Ralf began by setting a tempo, and after the start the machine churned out cyclic repetitions of an empty bar, into which any frequencies could be inserted on mathematically calculated parts of the musical measure (bar), and also removed again. At the same time, we could transpose and modulate the material. This technology opened up the possibility for us to be musicians, composers, listeners and producers all in one. Even the very first time we used it, it was clear that the machine laid the ground for a new playing technique and enabled a kind of improvisation that belonged to no particular genre or category and still offered sufficient space for experiments.

Ralf programmed the bass and we played live to the short sequence. I drummed and Ralf transposed the chords, came up with his melodies and sang along. That was how we determined the song's structure.

203

The Synthanorma didn't yet have a synchronization option for the multi track machine, so we recorded the sequencer track first. It would serve as our guide track and metronome. For these recordings, Peter Bollig took care of the levels while I announced the bars and sections of the arrangements, like a répétiteur at an opera ensemble rehearsal. Ralf probably counted along and transposed the sequence onto the Minimoog keyboard. We basically stuck to this method of recording an arrangement on magnetic tape for the next three years. It worked quickly because we divided up the labour. The percussion was not a technical challenge: a quaver feel, mechanical, straightforward and inconspicuous.

Ralf had come up with a melody that instantly reminded me of Johann Strauss's operetta *The Gypsy Baron*. 'Wer uns getraut' is the name of the duet I was thinking of. Ralf composed the instrumental section ad hoc. In the refrain, he sang the track's title and Florian added an 'endless, endless' with the vocoder.

The Hall of Mirrors

If you don't count the violins and vocal choir on the Orchestron, no acoustic instruments have been used in Kraftwerk's music since *Autobahn*. Guitar, flute or vibraphone no longer fitted into the concept, and so Wolfgang built me an electronic vibraphone. The Vibrolux, as we called it because of its interior lighting, worked in the same way as our percussion multipads, except it controlled not drum sounds but an electronic organ.

Ralf, Florian and Emil wrote the lyrics to 'The Hall of Mirrors' together, and their content determined the music's breathing, so to speak. Like in a film, the soundtrack was intended to render a protagonist's footsteps, leading to a slower tempo of about 95 beats per minute. The footsteps were up to the percussion department, and Ralf developed the now-familiar phrase on the Synthanorma, which again controlled the Minimoog in the bass register.

Along with this sequence, I played a motif in E minor on the Vibrolux. Ralf changed the order of my four notes through repetitions and added a note, but more or less kept the pitch, the position in the bar and the motif's structure. After three verses it was time for an instrumental passage, and I played an impromptu solo. I didn't need many takes; I was in good form. Ralf and Florian clearly liked my performance – my solo has been a fixed element of the song ever since. And Florian's fluctuating, bubbling up, slightly unhinged sounds reflect the protagonist's mental state within the track's narrative.

Trans-Europe Express (Song)

The moment the subject of TEE was on the agenda, a good few train songs came to my mind: 'Marrakesh Express', 'Last Train to Clarksville' or 'Mystery Train', to say nothing of 'Chattanooga Choo Choo', Glenn Miller's classic 1941 swing hit, which I'd played countless times in my earlier bands and dance orchestras. American songwriters looked back on a long tradition of train songs. But Europeans too have written music about the railway since the early nineteenth century. It was, after all, the first symbol of progress visible to everyone; the first machine that inspired composers on the basis of its marked acoustic qualities alone. Acceleration, motion and speed were easily transposed

205

into the timed medium of music. In his famous 1923 sound poem *Pacific 231*, Arthur Honegger translated his perception of a locomotive into music for a symphony orchestra.

And it's here that the notion of futurism comes into play again, as it so often does with Kraftwerk. A whole fourteen years before Honegger's *Pacific 231*, the French newspaper *Figaro* published the 'Manifesto of Futurism' in February 1909. It was written by the eccentric son of an Italian millionaire, Filippo Tommaso Marinetti, a great admirer of scientific discoveries, progress and mass culture. In provocative style, he cast aside traditional values, romanticized the reality of modern work and life, and engaged in the cult of the machine: 'A racing automobile with its bonnet adorned with great tubes like serpents with explosive breath . . . a roaring motor car which seems to run on machine-gun fire, is more beautiful than the Victory of Samothrace.'[5]

Mass culture in an electrical world of technology and the permanently increasing speed of modern modes of transport, which he experienced as ecstatic and which altered the perception of space and time, became the source of inspiration for Marinetti's visions. He was even enthusiastic about war.

The Futurists set themselves the goal of transferring the logic of technology and the essence of the machine into a new form of art aesthetics, which corresponded with the modern feel of life with new technology. Their theory centred around the representation of motion and the simultaneity of seeing and hearing.

The group of Futurists gathered around Marinetti included the musician and painter Luigi Russolo, who called for the emancipation of sounds in his own manifesto *L'arte dei Rumori* (*The Art of Noises*), published on 11 March 1913. Russolo and his disciples were interested in the new sound sources of the metropolis and the factories. They understood the sounds of the modern age as an aesthetic challenge, an inexhaustible resource for the creation of a new type of music. Russolo called it 'bruitism', noise music.

To put it into practice, he constructed noise-making machines, which he called *Intonarumori*. Russolo took his lead from acoustic instruments and formed six families of noises. These included things like roars, whistles, whispers, creaking, crackling, buzzing and scraping. There were noises made by beating metal, wood, leather, stone, pottery and other materials. And there were also the voices of animals and people; in other words screams, shrieks, wails, shouts, hoots, howls, death rattles and sobs.

Russolo anticipated a lot of what later became possible through sound recording. How might music have developed without his revolutionary ideas? Perhaps I'm generalizing, but in my opinion, Futurism is more alive in the sound of our contemporary music than it ever was.

But back to the Kling Klang Studio of the seventies. Working intensively on 'Trans-Europe Express' over the next few days, we didn't have any acoustic references in mind – as far as I remember – just our own imaginations.

So how does a railway train sound? Independent of speed, the double wheels of a train carriage crossing the gaps in the rails create a rhythm that sounds something like this: 'Dadum-dadum . . . dadum-dadum . . . dadum-dadum' and so on and on. Regardless of that, Ralf programmed a continuous rhythm on the Synthanorma. It was not supposed to be a sonic copy of a locomotive, though, more the manifestation of the idea of how wheels sound on tracks. Florian modulated the signal with an effect device, making speed and motion audible – that did the trick!

This rail sequence set up a fairly slow tempo. I think it was Ralf who suggested the pattern for bass drum and snare drum to me. It really did hammer away like the piston strokes of a locomotive. Ralf then positioned the Minimoog bass precisely on the first two beats of the bass drum – and the mechanical beat was done. Finding the right tempo for a piece of music demands a good ear for a pulse. To stick to the metaphor, it depends on how many passengers you want to transport. A small number requires fewer carriages than a large amount. In music, the density of events takes you to the right tempo. For a lot of notes in a bar, you need more space – in other words, more time – to sound them all out than for just a few notes.

What Ralf played along to our rhythm formula on the Vako Orchestron's violins preset didn't sound like the TEE; it was more like the film music for *Murder on the Orient Express*. But that didn't bother us because the short melody was very catchy and convinced us immediately. Aside from which, 'When too perfect, God angry,' as a certain Nam June Paik once explained.

We already had a few lyrics and we talked about the shape we wanted to give the track. There was one thing missing for a solid construction: a second element as a contrast to the *Orient Express* theme. I instantly thought of Stravinsky, who preferred the less tired intervals like seconds, tritones, fourths or fifths in his compositions. So I suggested to Ralf that we could try out fourths, and gave a brief explanation of the tie-in to Stravinsky's music. Whereupon Ralf played two fourth arpeggios using the Orchestron violins. It worked pretty well. While the *Orient Express* theme is a nod to film music, the minimal fourth melody comes across like a sound icon of musical modernism.

After the Recordings

A good two weeks later, my part in the recordings was over. I experienced them as very intensive and stimulating. There was one difference to the sessions for *Radio-Activity*, though – with this new album, the music had only existed before the recordings as a vague idea in Ralf's and Florian's minds. The rhythm, melodies and harmonies and the shapes of the tracks only came about during the recording sessions. My suggestions also flowed into the music's creation – not necessarily to the detriment of the compositions' musical substance, in my opinion. I made a mental note to raise that issue when an opportunity came up. That wouldn't be for a little while, though, because Ralf and Florian headed off to Los Angeles a few days later to mix our recordings at the Record Plant Studio.

Shortly after their return from California, Florian threw a fabulous party at his parents' house in Golzheim. Alongside the Kraftwerk team, a few members of the wider circle were also invited: Ralf's former fellow student Volker Albus, the orthopaedic specialist Dr Willi Klein, Teja the hairdresser and others. We hung out around the pool in the garden and Florian barbecued cutlets for us. While he was at it, the ivy on the outdoor chimney caught fire and nearly burned the house down. Florian had to climb up like Tarzan and suffocate the flames with a blanket before we could go on with the party. It was an awesome night.

European Tour

About a year after our last concerts in the UK, Ralf and Florian started getting dates booked for the next tour. Our agency swiftly lined up gigs for us in Holland, Belgium, France, Switzerland and Britain again. Our last stop, I read on the itinerary, would be London. *Radio-Activity* had been released a while ago, but of course these gigs too were another 'promo tour'.

We kicked off in Utrecht on 8 September 1976. From there we went to Arnheim and then Amsterdam, where we played at Paradiso, a former church, on 11 September. The set-list featured a couple of new songs, but that wasn't the only reason why our performance followed a different dramatic set-up. A few things came together; for example, we now played classical music over the PA before we went on stage, as a kind of overture.

Ralf also went without his Farfisa Professional Piano for the first time. The instrument looked great but the keyboard was a hopeless case. With the equipment ergonomically facing the middle of the stage, the audience now viewed Ralf in profile. The Orchestron and Minimoog were still arranged in front of him, as before. The Sennheiser microphone was mounted on a stand with a boom in the Neumann spider mount. To his left came the new components, the Synthanorma sequencer and a second Minimoog, with which Ralf reproduced automatic rhythms, bass figures and melodic arpeggios on 'Trans-Europe Express', 'Radioactivity' and 'Europe Endless'.

And my set-up? On some songs I played the good old percussion multipad, on others the brand new Vibrolux. I occasionally experimented on it with basslines, while Wolfgang drummed on his multipad. One thing's for sure – I had to be incredibly careful with the thin metal sticks. But it looked far better on stage than another synthesizer.

Wolfgang's new magic trick reminded me of Leonardo da Vinci's ink drawing *The Vitruvian Man*. He climbed bravely into a metal cube to which he had attached photoelectric sensors along the side struts, and then he cut through the light rays rhythmically with his hand to trigger drum sounds. It was an amazing special effect but sadly, no one in the audience got it. It seemed like the time was not yet ripe for that kind of fun and games.

Florian played the electro-flute, which was linked up to one of his two ARP Odysseys. He played the other manually via the keyboard. Aside from that – and this was the highlight of the stage set-up – after the tape intro to 'The Voice of Energy' he would sit unexpectedly on the right edge of the stage and type out 'the sun, the moon, the stars' on his speaking Votrax typewriter. He would modulate sounds that Ralf sent him with the keyboard's phonemes. Florian's interlude had the audience all agog; it was a real show-stopper every time. For the vocal passages, he used a rock'n'roll microphone from Shure, also called the 'Elvis mic'. He was very fond of the vintage design.

Looking back now, our show was reminiscent of theatre staging, with darkness and light playing a key role. Neon strip lights that immersed the stage in a different colour for every song encircled us from behind. Above them, slightly further back, was a large screen for Emil's slide projections. In front of us were our names in neon, as usual. Wolfgang and I wore dark suits, and Ralf and Florian sported their pale grey tailored versions, in which they were beginning to look more and more like Gilbert & George.

From Amsterdam, we went on to Brussels for an appearance on the very well-known *Follies* show on RTB Television, and then back to Düsseldorf.

La Bastide Blanche

We had a few days off before our next gig in Lyon. To pass the time, Florian invited the whole team to his family's country estate near Saint-Tropez. The atmosphere on the road was good and no one felt like hanging out on their own in Düsseldorf. So off we set for the Côte d'Azur. It was a pretty long trip by car.

Once we got to the grounds of La Bastide Blanche, we discovered the main building next to a field of artichokes. But we were billeted in a smaller holiday house not far from the sea – with a separate room for each of us. Having got our bearings, we drove carefully along a sandy track to the road and then to Saint-Tropez to look at the luxury yachts on the waterside promenade. The Mediterranean climate relaxed us and even Ralf seemed suddenly laid-back. We ended up in the famous Restaurant Sénéquier, drinking Orangina, espresso and beer, eating bouillabaisse with baguette, and stayed put until late at night, people-watching and commenting on the scenery. The stars in the sky above the Mediterranean were overwhelming.

On the Road Again

From La Bastide Blanche, we headed north to Lyon. Unfortunately, we got the timing wrong and arrived late for our concert.

We had no other option but to set up in front of the waiting audience, and then the Orchestron went up in a puff of black smoke as well. It was pretty embarrassing all round. Despite that – or maybe because of it – we made the best of it and our French fans forgave us. A few gigs later, we appeared at the Pavillon de Paris, in the north of the French capital, on 30 September. The venue seemed a little over-proportioned in terms of capacity, but just over 2000 people in the audience made for a great atmosphere. Outside of Paris, the concerts weren't well attended. And later, when the album *Trans-Europe Express* got to number 2 in the French charts in 1977, we didn't get any bookings. There was simply no way to sell our live show in France.

In Geneva, we played twice and then moved on via Düsseldorf to Brussels. There, Jean-Marc Lederman[6] was in the audience for our show on 6 October 1976. He still remembers our appearance in the university auditorium.

Jean-Marc Lederman: 'When the band came on stage and stood behind their synthesizers, they were visibly nervous. But they also seemed extremely concentrated. The synthesizer was still a relatively new instrument and many people only knew it as a solo instrument from prog-rock albums or early ambient music. Through songs like 'Autobahn' or 'Radioactivity' with their basslines and singable melodies, I became aware of the huge potential harboured by electronic instruments. Kraftwerk looked at the synthesizer in a whole new way – they used it like an orchestral instrument with changing timbres.'

The Roundhouse Concert

The next day, we crossed the Channel by ferry from Calais to Dover. There was a jukebox somewhere on board, and on close inspection I found Can's 'I Want More' on it. Our Cologne colleagues had presented their hit single a week before on *Top of the Pops*. Respect.

I was keen to see whether things would go better in the UK this time. During that hot summer, Britain's musical climate went through a change. The punk scene was picking up speed and the media were reporting in detail on the new phenomenon and its protagonists: Siouxsie and the Banshees, the Clash, the Damned, the Buzzcocks and of course the Sex Pistols, who signed a deal with EMI on Friday, 8 October 1976. That was the exact same date as our first gig, in Coventry. After that came Sheffield on the Saturday, and on the Sunday we played at the famous London venue, the Roundhouse.

For some reason I missed our opening act, National Health. But I do remember the stage shifts afterwards very clearly. Then it was our turn. The speech synthesizer made its proclamation and we swiftly entered from the wings. Ralf informed the audience 'You are going to see a film,'[7] and then we started in with 'Kometenmelodie'.

I recall the concert well. The place was packed, the audience lively, and things took off pretty quickly. When we left the stage after 'Autobahn', the frenetically applauding crowd demanded an encore. Sure, no problem. At our last recording session in July/August, we had tried out Ralf's 'Showroom Dummies', so it was still fresh in our minds. Ralf counted himself in and we ended the set with a bang.

214

There was absolutely no comparing the atmosphere at the Roundhouse with our gigs around the UK the previous year. I got the feeling our music and performance were now accepted and understood in their context. John Foxx once described Kraftwerk's artistic aesthetics wittily as a Marcel Duchamp version of rock'n'roll.

The timing was good, with the emerging punk movement creating a mood of cultural change, in which Kraftwerk wasn't one of the stiff, established opponents but part of an alternative movement.

TEE, Finishing Touches

After our return, we met up at the Kling Klang Studio for a briefing and a look back at the promo tour. Playing the songs live turned out to be a great boon, as it showed us which arrangements weren't yet working optimally. We had already made changes on the road and tried them out, abandoned them and tested them again. Ralf and Florian weren't afraid of what we called 'open-heart surgery' in those days.

We arranged to work from 10 November to 3 December on the new versions. Florian got hold of a strange home organ from somewhere, with a tone that blended well with the Orchestron violins on 'Trans-Europe Express'. Ralf and Florian carried over our on-tour experiences into the arrangement, for instance a change in the fourth theme. Wolfgang had managed the monotonous drum beat well on stage, so it definitely worked. And last but not least, we added a few percussive elements to our 'train trip'.

215

Metal on Metal – Abzug

I wasn't involved in putting into practice the idea of making the train take an acoustic journey across an imaginary metal bridge. All I did was stumble over a zinc-coated wash basin, pipes and various tools lying around in the room outside the studio.

Luigi Russolo would have loved this sound spectacle: beating on metal objects and throwing mic stands on the floor with a bang. Peter Bollig wasn't quite happy with the recording, though, he told me later: he wished he'd had more time. It was only down to the dynamic compressor that they got the distortion more or less under control.

The 'Metal on Metal' segment consists basically of a white noise sequence, the drum beat and a slightly varying rhythm pattern of metal sounds over the top. The rhythm was played manually with minimal fluctuations and it swings in its very own way. For me, that makes it superior to all later mechanical variations.

In the coda that follows, called 'Abzug', the composition's three key elements – the *Orient Express* melody, the fourths and the vocals – are combined into a polyphonic conclusion. Incidentally, the name 'Abzug' is a term from musician-speak at the time. It means quite literally a train departing. In other words, the band gives it their all and really takes off, full steam ahead.

At the end of 'Abzug' things get concrete again. The recording of a braking train comes across like a reminiscence of Pierre Schaeffer's famous *Étude aux Chemins de Fer* from 1948. Interestingly enough, the aural portrait of the 'solo locomotive' corresponds with the start of 'Autobahn'.

Eurodisco

It was around the middle of the seventies that disco started conquering the nightclubs. Some of the songs even made it to the charts and mainstream radio. Disco spread a positive attitude to life and was glorified into an almost ritualistic leisure activity. Not that we were immune to that glorification . . . The music originated in the New York underground. Now, though, white people could dance to the 'four-on-the-floor disco groove', which multiplied the target audience and the music's commercial potential for the record industry.

After our experiences on tour, we wanted to move 'Europe Endless' slightly more in a disco direction. In search of the perfect tempo, we ended up at 112 beats per minute. Except that I didn't play the bass drum in 4/4 on every beat like in disco, but two half notes per bar.

Showroom Dummies

In the lyrics to 'Showroom Dummies', Ralf sketches out a story about 'us' standing in a shop window, feeling watched, changing poses and finally smashing the glass to break out and go dancing in a club. The first step had been taken towards the 'real' show-room dummies later modelled on us.

We didn't use a sequencer to record it but got the piece on tape live – each instrument separately, with everyone helping out. Like on 'Radioactivity', Ralf used a motif for this song that I knew from his improvisations. Florian was in charge of the bass, doing a great job. A bassline as jagged as that was really unique at the time, and its phrasing gave us a not very constant rhythm pattern. But it was exactly that which created a stomping, slightly dizzy rhythm, to which even a few punks were happy to pogo – as I've seen with my own eyes. On the line 'And we break the glass,' Florian mutated into a foley artist again and recorded the concrete sound.

Franz Schubert – Endless Endless

The first time I heard Ralf's homage to Franz Schubert, which remains in G major for almost five minutes, was on the finished LP. It's a derivation from 'Europe Endless', which makes it seem to me like a reprise, lending the album an air of closure. Ralf's Schubert reduction became a piece of electronic chamber music and flows into the repeated word 'endless' . . .

Artwork

Emil was once again involved in the album's artwork, this time along with Mike Schmidt's Düsseldorf company Ink Studios. As always, Ralf and Florian organized it all. In this kind of situation, Ralf would slip into the role of executive producer, meaning he made the choices, checked the results, critiqued the outcome and gave the final OK. Florian had a right to an opinion but I can't remember there ever being arguments over major decisions.

What I think works really well is the Futura typography in conjunction with the three horizontal strokes per line of text,

218

which reminds me of the style of the Odeon Electric record catalogues of the twenties and thirties. The German front cover features a group shot from the photo session in the Maurice Seymour New York studio on 1 April 1975, with the aforementioned portrait montage by J. Stara of Paris on the back – both in black and white. For the American market, the photos were swapped around and the Stara picture was used on the front, this time in colour.

Emil designed the front of the inside sleeve with one of his typical collages, put together out of one of our group shots – also from the Maurice Seymour studio – and a landscape painted in subdued shades. The four of us are sitting in more or less relaxed poses at a table with a checked tablecloth under a linden tree, looking the observer in the eye with almost friendly expressions. An atmosphere like on an excursion to a countryside restaurant on the Rhine. The photo-painting montage is also included in the package as a large folded poster.

The back side of the inside sleeve looks like a sheet of yellow music paper with the names of the authors and other information added to it. Each piece of music is represented by a little drawing or a Letraset illustration. The interesting thing about the graphic design is the circle of notes symbolically presenting 'Europe Endless' as a loop.

This album cover features the most copious presentation of our line-up, with three pictures of us. It was maximum intensity. Kraftwerk manifested itself with this cover design as a self-contained group of four, a unit – the classic line-up. For Emil, however, there was no visible space in the concept any more and he was absent from the cover art.

On the Orient Express to Reims

Sensational – that was what our French label Pathé Marconi promised our party for the release of *Trans-Europe Express* was going to be. And Maxime Schmitt had a magnificent idea for it. He went ahead and invited the Paris media, celebrities and hangers-on to a ride on the nostalgic *Orient Express* – or rather in a few of the legendary railway line's restored carriages – from Paris's Gare de l'Est to Moët et Chandon in Reims, 130 kilometres away. Who could resist an invitation like that? And so, practically all the media partners he'd invited really did turn up on 9 February to board the train to Reims with us, listening to our new album at full volume on the speakers in their compartments.

Once we got to Reims, we all transferred into waiting buses that took us to the famous champagne makers. And there, we were treated to a classic French dinner in a huge torchlit basement room. The garçons flitted between the tables with monumental magnums of champagne and topped up the glasses as soon as a sip was drunk. I don't think I'm exaggerating when I call it a truly glamorous party. Anyone with a scrap of imagination will have no problem picturing what went on in the torchlit vaults until we were taken back to Paris. And we spent the rest of the night continuing the party in a club . . .

Filming in a Pale Trench Coat

Back home, things went on uninterrupted. Ralf and Florian wanted to make another film for 'Trans-Europe Express', so we met up in the Kling Klang Studio on the afternoon of 14 February 1977 for the shoot. Günter Fröhling was hired as the cameraman again. As well as his Arriflex camera, he brought along the make-up artist Frau Hartkopf, who gave us white faces with eye shadow, lipstick and all the trimmings.

The dress code was inspired by Ralf and Florian's wardrobe on the US tour, building a visual bridge to the Weimar Republic and the thirties and forties: coats with fur collars, smart hats, leather gloves. Frau Hartkopf seemed to take her orientation from UFA films as well. I couldn't afford any suitable vintage clothing, so I just put on my pale trench coat. To my surprise, I later saw Jean-Louis Trintignant running around in a similar coat in the 1966 Franco-Belgian movie *Trans-Europ-Express*.

During filming, Ralf and Florian started 'designing' my hair. They had come up with the idea of giving me the Mephisto character's haircut sported by Gustaf Gründgens in his defining role in *Faust*. Their idea stuck with me for some time. Wolfgang was wearing a black double-breasted blazer that day and had the longest hair out of any of us. Any stylist or costume designer at the Babelsberg film studios would probably have lost their job after our production. And yet the lack of perfection reveals the improvised character of our session. Our dress code and make-up weren't deadly serious. Once we were made up, we went to Düsseldorf station, bought five return tickets to Dortmund and boarded a regional train.

We were soon seated in a first-class smoking compartment. During the fifty minutes of each leg of the journey, Günter Fröhling filmed all possible perspectives of groups of four, groups of two, and close-ups. He even climbed into the luggage rack for one shot. Everything happened in a state of flux, and yet

Fröhling managed to capture at least some of the passing light sources in the window of our compartment. To be honest, I've forgotten whether we brought along a tape player with a recording of the music or not. I don't think we did. But the sound was inside us, anyway.

Alongside our shots on the train, this production was the first to use archived documentary material from old weekly news-reels. Fröhling also filmed shots of a model railway moving through a miniature landscape. Once the footage was organized and all the films were developed, Ralf and Günter Fröhling edited the raw material together in Fröhling's studio on Herzogstrasse. The dramatic arc of the montage resulted automatically from the song structure.

Interestingly, after the obligatory iris shot the film starts with archive recordings of the propeller-driven zeppelin on rails that set a new world speed record in 1931, at 230.2 km/h. A hybrid airship and train, it looked really fantastic but it had nothing to do with the Trans-Europe Express that connected European states from 1957 to 1987 – other than the fact that it travelled on rails. That didn't matter, though. It was important to Ralf to give Kraftwerk's music an unmistakeable visual identity. And although the name 'Trans-Europe Express' is repeated sixteen times on the single, the film's aesthetics are more rooted in the thirties.

Reflection

Mixing some of the tracks for *Trans-Europe Express* at the Record Plant Studio in Los Angeles was an ambitious undertaking.

But the West Coast mix came across as rather alien in the Kling Klang Studio. I call it 'The Eagles' mix! The songs sounded smoothed out, liked they'd been mixed on Valium, with no jagged edges. In the end, Ralf and Florian booked Otto Waalkes' Rüssl Studio in Hamburg again to do the final mix with the brilliant sound engineer Thomas Kuckuck, who had made a name for himself working with Udo Lindenberg, Frumpy, Birth Control, the Rattles, Karthago, Eloy and Novalis. The Record Plant Hollywood was at least mentioned in the album credits, though.

Back in the previous year, the renowned German journalist Ingeborg Schober had been at our gig at the London Roundhouse. Now, she wrote a concert review to coincide with the LP release in March, headlined 'Techno Boogie from Neon Tubes'[8] and described how Kraftwerk 'performs a world of mechanical artificiality in all its perverse beauty.' The picture caption was: ' . . . we'll soon be driving hey, hey, hey on the railway!' In actual fact, *TEE* does pick up on the non-committal nature of the *Autobahn* album's content: our little travel group has further adventures in Paris, Vienna and Düsseldorf. Even Iggy Pop and David Bowie come along for the ride this time.

The common factors on *Trans-Europe Express* and *Autobahn* are obvious. Both compositions line up a series of narrative units and link them to one another in a larger form. Alongside the tonal means of musical expression, sound imitations play a central role. To a minor extent, also concrete noises. The vocals – human and synthetic – remain in the pop idiom. To state the obvious, the content of both albums refers to travel – for me, the songs are acoustic road movies.

If I take a step back and look at the big picture, I recognize the railway and the automobile as former symbols of modernist progress and objects of the cult of the machine, as practised by the Italian Futurists, for example. Aside from the sound imitations of technology, the environment and nature, both compositions also translate the perception of speed, motion and monotony into music, very much in line with the Futurists. This look backwards is mixed with the sound tools of the seventies.

When the album came out in March 1977, the reception from fans and the media was not quite euphoric, but definitely positive on the whole. Glenn O'Brien wrote in *Interview* magazine: 'Fusing classical melodies, advanced electronic music technology and Afro-Aryan rhythms, they have created a new sound that is as intellectually stimulating as it is danceable. In fact Kraftwerk's last album, *Trans-Europe Express*, made an enormous impact on the world of disco in the last year by combining perfect dance beats with graceful, intelligent melodies and fully conceptualized themes.'[9]

In France, Maxime Schmitt did a fantastic job for Pathé Marconi. *Trans-Europe Express* was picked up by the relevant French media, sold particularly well in the country, and made it to number 2 on the album charts. To our surprise, the single 'Trans-Europe Express' – with the rail zeppelin on the cover – went into the Italian Top Ten. In Germany, the album got to number 32, in Britain 49 and in the USA number 119.

The success in France was clear-cut, but compared to the significance many critics later ascribed to the album, the release didn't make huge waves. At this point, Ralf and Florian switched track – to stick to the jargon – and abandoned the familiar concept of supporting record releases with gigs. Although we'd toured in September and October with *Radio-Activity* and had played a few tracks from *TEE* in our set, now the two of them

224

changed their live policy and refrained from promoting sales of *Trans-Europe Express* through concerts. At the time, I didn't think about whether the decision was right or wrong.

Fair Play

As far back as I can remember, Ralf always arrived everywhere late. It was almost a principle, you might say. That's just his nature – he's a notorious latecomer. But when I got to the Kling Klang Studio on Friday, 15 April 1977, I was amazed to find him already there. The sequencer was tootling away and Ralf was playing quietly for himself. A good month before, I had made the cautious point to him that I felt some of the musical ideas I had contributed to the last album went beyond a studio musician's usual input. Now, my motif and the solo had ended up on 'The Hall of Mirrors' and the suggestion of trying out fourths on 'Trans-Europe Express' had gone into the material. And yet I wasn't credited as a co-author on either of the songs.

Opinions often diverge on the value of artistic contributions. For instance, I've heard rumours that at the start of a studio session by a famous jazz pianist, each of the many musicians found on their music stands a blank sheet of music signed by the pianist himself, identifying him in advance as the sole author of the music yet to be composed.

Paul McCartney has also talked about credits in songwriting. For him, to give an example, George Harrison's guitar solo on 'I Saw Her Standing There' is a sixteen-bar improvisation and not part of the composition. Harrison played it once the song was already finished, in fact. I think my musical contribution to 'The Hall of Mirrors' must have been more of an ad lib for Ralf and Florian, as well.

As an author team, the two of them didn't exactly work like the songwriters of New York's Tin Pan Alley or the modern version, the Brill Building. Nor did I know at that time that Florian couldn't be classified as a composer in the traditional sense. He didn't know much about chords, arrangements or song structures. Leaving aside his core skill of artificial language, his talent consisted in creating sounds or noises. Edgard Varèse, called 'the father of electronic music', apparently once said: 'I work with tones, sounds and rhythms – melodies are just the chatter in music.'

Perhaps that applies to Florian as well in a certain way, but I see him more as a sonic Jackson Pollock. He mastered a kind of 'action painting in sound', which occasionally bowled me over. Whenever things were heading in a straight line in one key, Florian would produce an absolutely unexpected sound, tied in to acceptable timing. It was him, after all, who made the most lasting mark on Kraftwerk in the beginning, with his energy and determination.

Back to Mintropstrasse. I had neither the slightest idea of the impact of our conversation, nor could I objectively assess the quality of my contributions to our last production. The question of how copyright is distributed was entirely new to me. And perhaps I was completely wrong. Petty haggling would certainly poison the atmosphere, I thought. I really didn't want to annoy anyone; I wanted to come across as cool, relaxed and a good sport. Aside from which – obviously – countless new Kraftwerk records would be made, and the opportunities in the future were far more interesting than the past sessions.

I think Ralf and Florian must also have thought seriously about my current and probable future contributions. And a change really did come about – I was to help make the next Kraftwerk album as a credited co-author. Well then, I thought with relief and a touch of euphoria. We're going to keep working together.

Zyklus für einen Schlagzeuger

I was gradually preparing for my concert examination and starting to put my programme together. Karlheinz Stockhausen's *Zyklus für einen Schlagzeuger* was at the very top of my list. Years before, I had seen and heard a performance of the ten- to twelve-minute composition written in 1959. I could hardly wait to play it myself. The piece has no defined beginning or end. The percussionist starts with any one of the sixteen spiral-bound pages of music and then plays a cycle. The direction the notes are read in – turning the pages to the left or the right – is also up to the percussionist. Surrounded by percussion instruments – marimba, vibraphone, drums, tam-tam, etc – the soloist turns in a full circle during the performance. What attracted me so much to the piece was the alternation of fixed and free elements – and the choreography created through its performance.

But the cycle alone wouldn't help me much. I spent weeks researching like crazy for suitable literature, searching through catalogues, ordering piles of notes and records. I didn't want to reel off a showpiece to display my virtuosity; I wanted to compile a musically sophisticated programme appropriate to the role of percussion in twentieth-century music. There were certainly plenty of great compositions for percussion ensembles, but I found it hard to track down literature for a lone percussion soloist.

In the end, I explained my unfortunate situation to the dean. I was in my fifteenth semester at the conservatory and thanks to my numerous performances, my work at the opera, my concerts and not least my involvement in a certain electro-combo, he knew me well enough. He advised me to concentrate on the 'tuned percussion instruments' like the vibraphone, marimbaphone and glockenspiel, and gave me the go-ahead for the next two semesters.

Nightclubbing

Since I'd moved in to the flat on Berger Allee, I'd been accompanying Ralf, Florian and Wolfgang to clubs. Music was moving more and more from the stage onto the dance floor, so that was what counted at the time. I didn't really know my way around the nightlife phenomenon, but I wanted to learn. It was closely related to music and also had the side effect – not to be under-estimated – that we could admire good-looking dancers. A very sensible reason to go out clubbing, at least when you're 25 and young, free and single. Our first stop was always Mora's Lovers Club on Schneider-Wibbel-Gasse, about a ten-minute walk from Berger Allee.

The small club was on the first floor. If you managed to get in – we were soon familiar faces, as semi-famous night owls – you took the stairs and came out almost in the middle of the dance floor. Ralf, Florian and Wolfgang danced now and then

– I rarely did. What interested me was how the floor filled up for certain tracks and emptied with others. These were the days when I saw all that for the very first time, and I had a lot of fun. The ladies who were regulars like us soon got aliases like 'the Roman Villa', 'the White Shark', 'the Cherry', 'the Calf', 'the Duchess' or 'Mother Hulda'. And they gave as good as they got, I found out later, with names like 'the Bore', 'the Sex Maniac', 'the Trainer [as in 'training shoe]' or 'Prince Charming'. Fair enough, really. It's hard to imagine these days, but people once used to smoke so much in clubs and restaurants that the air was always dense with nicotine fug. My eyes would start watering almost the instant I arrived and I could barely breathe. But I put up with it. Our justification for our frequent clubbing sessions was the claim that they brought us close to our 'target group'.

We soon found our regular spot in the club, directly to the right of the DJ booth. When I wanted to know the name of the track playing, I could just knock on the glass and ask. The DJ – everyone called him Jimmy because he looked like Jimi Hendrix – played pretty great tunes. Jimmy's spectrum was made up of a mix of rhythm & blues, rock, soul, funk, disco numbers and crossover mainstream songs. Classics like 'I Got You (I Feel Good)' or 'Get Up (I Feel Like Being a) Sex Machine' by James Brown, 'After Midnight' and 'Cocaine' by J. J. Cale, and disco hits like 'Fly Robin Fly' by Silver Convention were an excellent basis for any club night in the second half of the seventies, but songs by the Steve Miller Band like 'Fly Like an Eagle', Lou Reed's 'Walk on the Wild Side' and Marvin Gaye's 'I Heard it Through the Grapevine' were also a perfect fit. And then there were the hits of 1977, such as Santa Esmeralda – 'Don't Let Me

Be Misunderstood', Diana Ross – 'Love Hangover', David Bowie – '"Heroes"', Space – 'Magic Fly', Space Art – 'Onyx', Donna Summer – 'I Feel Love'.

If you fade these tracks into one another, you'll find yourself precisely inside our sonic club environment of the time. This was where we carried out our 'sociocultural studies' and felt close to the music of the day and the audience's reactions. I remember running into Houschäng Nejadepour in the gents' toilets in Mora's for the first time in years, on one of those nights. He recognized me straight away, looked me in the eye and exclaimed: 'Karl, there are no limits any more!' Houschäng was clearly having a good time. It's amazing that I can remember that particular highlight. I too had experienced my own experiments and adventures in all things ecstasy and loss of control, including gaps in my memory.

As well as Mora's Lovers Club, there were a few other night-clubs we would look into. There was the Peppermint Club, which mutated into the Rockin' Eagle. On Königsallee there was Malesh, later renamed Checkers, and Sam's, which was actually on a parallel street but it counted as the same road for us. The club by the name of Sheila transformed at some point into the Match Moore. Another place to meet in the late afternoon or early evening – for messing around, seeing and being seen – was Café Bagel: the laid-back place to be for the city's beautiful people, the models, fashion designers, photographers and advertising execs, the hairdressers, exotic creatures and characters who were simply rich and nothing else.

Of course, all these addresses could be creatively linked and integrated into a daily or nightly itinerary. Some of us were champions at these integrations. I was more of an also-ran on that front, but I was always in the know about what was going on. I have to admit, 'flying through the night' was really great fun for a while.

Over the years, though, Ralf, Florian and Wolfgang shifted their focus to Cologne and dived into the neighbouring city's nightlife more and more often. Although Cologne and Düsseldorf are traditionally 'enemies', the other city seemed somehow cooler, more relaxed, more modern. You'd meet up either in Moroco on Hohenzollernring or later in the Alter Wartesaal right next to the main station and the cathedral.

Ratinger Hof

From Berger Allee, I had a ten or fifteen-minute walk to Ratinger Strasse. Evening visits were unavoidable, especially during the week. To make sure I didn't miss anything or anyone, I had to check in at all three of the main joints on the street – Einhorn, Uel and Hof. Everybody did it. Einhorn and Uel stayed true to their style all the years, to this day. The Ratinger Hof was different, though. Carmen Knoebel and Ingrid Kohlhöfer took over the bar in the mid-seventies and changed the interior, transforming a hippie cavern into an urban punk space with white walls, mirrors and bright neon light. A TV hung from the ceiling, flickering soundlessly. People said Carmen's husband Imi Knoebel, already renowned as an artist, had been involved in the refurbishment. The regulars changed drastically and the Hof became one of *the* places to be over the next few years.

It opened in the morning and operated non-stop until Düsseldorf's mandatory closing time at 1 a.m. Things didn't get interesting until the early evening, though. Anyone who was anyone would pop in. The Hof was *the* artist hangout, what with the art academy being directly around the corner. But the bar also magically attracted creative types from the ad agencies, art directors, graphic designers, photographers, architects, in hairdressers, boutique owners, models, dealers, schoolkids, students, blue-collar workers, white-collar workers, slackers, freaks, scene royalty, and not least musicians and 'amateur geniuses'. In the best days of the Ratinger Hof, there was no bouncer on the door. That was a good thing because it enabled a mixed crowd of all social classes and educational backgrounds.

It was the music from the speakers that built the bar's identity. The people on the turntables were usually expert at mixing everything with anything, and not scared of strong contrasts: the Ramones, the Sex Pistols, the Clash, the Buzzcocks, of course Iggy Pop and, from 1978, Daniel Miller's eternal 'Warm Leatherette', plus Motown, soul, reggae and rock'n'roll. I even heard early Beatles, Stones, Kinks and other first-generation bands there. Incidentally, only a handful of songs, like Bowie's '"Heroes"' or Blondie's 'Heart of Glass' got played everywhere – from the Ratinger Hof to Malesh and Sam's to the traditional corner pub in Flingern.

For years, I went to the Hof in the evening to meet people and see what was going down. I'd usually get myself a beer at the bar and then stand with my back to the wall for a while, taking a surreptitious look around. It wouldn't be long before my Kraftwerk friend Volker Albus, our hairdresser Teja, the drummer Frank Köllges or Wolfgang came along. Ralf and Florian used to come by occasionally but soon started to feel increasingly uncomfortable there.

232

It was better not to stand too close to the dance floor in the Hof; it was occasionally a dangerous place when dancers started pogoing around the room. The toilets were an absolute no-go area. You might think you'd stumbled directly into an open drain. There were days when it wasn't wise to enter without waterproof footwear. What went on there did have a certain surreal quality to it at times. If the slogan 'No future!' ever had any meaning, then it was in the toilets at the Ratinger Hof.

Speaking of 'No future!' – for the music business in England, the punk movement of the seventies had an important palate-cleansing function. It was high time to disrupt the staid structures of the British record companies and try something new, musically and with different business models. That energy had now made it to Düsseldorf and was put into musical practice right there at the Hof. I didn't find out until much later that lots of bands started off there and used the bar as their headquarters, rehearsed in the basement and played gigs upstairs. It was here that Die Toten Hosen launched their sensational music career under the name ZK, out of S.Y.P.H. and Mittagpause grew the band Fehlfarben, and the still active Die Krupps used to call themselves Male. The band DAF – Deutsch Amerikanische Freundschaft – also originated there. Der Plan are a cult phenomenon to this day and the all-female band Östro 430 is another one that occurs to me – it's impossible to count up all the groups and projects, but they all made the Ratinger Hof into a cultural petri dish.

At the end of the seventies, the curators-in-chief Carmen Knoebel and Ingrid Kohlhöfer stepped back from the Ratinger Hof and handed the keys and the beer licence to a successor. Some of the bands from the Hof's practice room and the environs of Ratinger Strasse set out on the road from subculture to mainstream and turned up in the German charts in the 1980s: Fehlfarben – *Monarchie und Alltag* (1980), DAF – *Die Kleinen und die Bösen* (1980), Die Roten Rosen – *Never Mind the Hosen – Here's Die Roten Rosen* (1987). I spent a whole lot of time in the Ratinger Hof. But I had nothing to do with what went on there – my musical path was a different one. And it took me on the straightest route to the next chapter in my sound biography.

NOTES

1. 'Kraftwerk: The Final Solution to the Music Problem? Lester Bangs Vivisects the German Scientific Approach.' By Lester Bangs, in: *New Musical Express*, 6 September 1975, pp. 20–21

2. Pascal Bussy: *Man Machine and Music*. SAF Publishing Ltd., Conway Gardens, England, 1993, p. 86

3. Heron of Alexandria (known as Mechanicus): *Automata* (*Book of Machines*)

4. From the announcement of a performance in Strasbourg, 1746. Quoted in: *Für Augen und Ohren – Von der Spieluhr zum akustischen Environment*. Exhibition catalogue, Akademie der Künste Berlin, 1980, p. 20

5. Filippo Tommaso Marinetti: 'Manifesto of Futurism', text of translation taken from James Joll, *Three Intellectuals in Politics*, sourced from http://bactra.org/T4PM/futurist-manifesto.html ('Manifeste du Futurisme'. *Le Figaro*, Paris, 20 February 1909)

6. Jean-Marc Lederman later made a name for himself as a musician in Fad Gadget and the Weathermen, and as a film composer and music producer.

7. 'Bionic Teutonics'. By Dave Fudger, *Sounds*, 16 October 1977

8. 'Kraftwerk – Techno-Boogie aus der Neonröhre.' By Ingeborg Schober, *Sounds*, March 1977

9. 'Kraftwerk: Deutsche Disko.' By Glenn O'Brien, *Interview*, 1977

The Anthonies' String Group's famous flower-power bus, 1969: Jörg (James), Franz, Brigitte, Günther and me (top to bottom). FRIEDHELM HOLLECZEK/NRZ

Professional: The Jokers at a Social Democratic Party election event, 12 November 1969.

My gigs with The Jokers paid my living expenses as a student: (left to right) me, Reiner, Klaus, Wolfgang and Franz.

Woodstock was still in our collective memory: 1971 with acoustic guitar in our shared flat on Nordstrasse in Düsseldorf-Derendorf.

Sinus 1971: (left to right) Rainer, me, Peter and Bodo – from jazz improvisation to twelve-tone music.
RAINER SENNEWALD

Sinus plus dance ensemble: poster for the theatre concert in December 1972. On the floor (left to right) me, Rainer, Peter. Standing (left to right): Margot, unknown, Frank, Marlis, Conrad, Angelika, unknown, Karin, Georg.

I think this is the only photo of me on timpani: in 1974, the class of Ernst Göbler (back right) performed Carl Orff's *Carmina Burana* in the Robert Schumann Hall.

My first music room of my own in Oberkassel, 1974. RAINER SENNEWALD

Capriccio für Schlagzeug und Orchester by Friedrich Zehm. The conservatory orchestra in the Robert Schumann Hall, 1975. On xylophone and percussion: Karlheinz Bartos.

First gig with the classic lineup: Kraftwerk in the Forum Leverkusen on 27 February 1975. KSTA/HOLGER SCHMITT

'Now I'm inserting the special film!': photo session at Foto Frank on Blumenstrasse in Düsseldorf, 1975.

A performance at Alex Cooley's Electric Ballroom in Atlanta, Georgia, 21 April 1975.
TOM HILL/GETTY IMAGES

Before our gig at the Olympia, Paris, 28 February 1976: (left to right) Angelika Sendner, Maxime Schmitt, Emil Schult, Ralf Hütter, Draga Kuzmanoviç, me, Florian Schneider.

9

THE MAN-MACHINE

Recording The Man-Machine. Metropolis. The Robots. Filming Showroom Dummies. The Model. Manuscripts. Moonstruck. Spacelab. 'Best European Group, Male'. Germany in Autumn. Depressive Phases. New Musick. Neon Lights. Christmas in Paris. The Man-Machine (Song). We Turn into Sculptures. Mixing in the Rudas Studio. Artwork. Copyrights. Premiere: The Robots on TV. Le Ciel de Paris. The Man-Machine in the UK. The Cultural Channel. Filming The Robots and Neon Lights. Hit Parade. Paris – Rome – Venice.

Recording The Man-Machine

As so often at that time, I was sitting in Café Bittner on Düsseldorf's Carlsplatz one late morning in early May of 1977. My mind drifting, I peered over the top of my newspaper at the hustle and bustle of the market outside. The old-fashioned café was only a few paces away from our flat, and I'd made a habit of going there to wake up gradually. Everything had developed extremely well with Kraftwerk over the past three years, and my studies – I was working on *Zyklus* with Ernst Göbler – were going well too. That afternoon, I would be teaching one of my private students on the snare drum, and I was set to meet the boys in the Kling Klang Studio in the evening.

Trans-Europe Express had been released just a few weeks ago – the album was still in the window of some record shops – but we were planning to get to work on our next product as quickly as possible. This time, however, we had to do without the support of a sound engineer. Peter Bollig was too busy with his studies to go on supporting us.

To get the recordings done professionally, Ralf and Florian had what we called an input desk built for them. It was a sturdy black Plexiglas box – about as large as the Synthanorma – with the function of a matrix. The incoming signals from the instruments were adjusted there and routed to the different tracks on the magnetic tape.

In conventional studios, the producers and sound engineers watch from the control room while the musicians play in the recording room, protected by a multiply soundproofed sheet of glass. The acoustics of the recording room are important; microphones pick up not just the instruments, amplifiers and voices, but also the room itself. That's why the room's structure is significant: its size and architecture, the ceiling height, the arrangement of what we call gobos, movable acoustic isolation panels. Is there soundproofing material on the walls and ceilings? Is the floor wooden or carpeted? The right choice of microphone is also enormously important for a recording. Besides that, the sound sources and microphones can be moved around the room until the right place is found for the desired sound. Decisions like that are made in the control room, because from there you only hear the sound put through by the microphone. There are countless myths and legends about the most suitable speakers, with pseudo-religious debates raging in specialist magazines over these devices that use membranes to make the air vibrate. Naturally enough, the prices for speakers reflect that insanity. On top of all that, insurmountable problems arise when several musicians play at the same time in one room, as the various signals can't easily be separated out again.

The Kling Klang Studio was not a conventional recording studio with acoustically isolated recording and control rooms. It was a single rectangular room, twelve by six metres with six-metre-high ceilings. Originally designed as a rehearsal space, musical workshop and writing room, it developed more and more into a control room where electronic instruments were sent directly to sub-mixers, which were then wired up into the aforementioned input desk. There was no need for us to use microphones to record instruments, only for the vocals. But compared to other studios, we didn't pay exaggerated attention to the mics. The advantage of this set-up is obvious: while playing and composing, we had the atmosphere of a live performance. That originated from the instruments scattered around the room, several components of the PA and the large JBL speakers attached to a metal frame on the six-metre back wall of the studio, which made for vivid acoustics. The disadvantage was that the sound spread around the room and bounced between the back wall with the speakers and the parallel wall twelve metres away, where the mixing desk and the tape machine were positioned directly next to the door. The soundproofing pyramid foam attached to the side walls only insulated the middle and high ranges. The actual problem, for us, was in judging the bass frequencies. I can still picture Florian with his head jammed into the corner between the door and the side wall, murmuring something like 'bass trap' over and over. It was certainly hard to get a grip on the bass sounds from the oscillators. As far as I remember, the Auratone near-field monitors installed at the mixing desk at some point didn't yet play a significant role at that time.

Today, I believe it was these unconventional acoustics that brought us pretty workable results. We invented our music under not-quite-perfect acoustic conditions, but on the positive side we had the buzz of a live performance. At least as long as we used mainly analogue equipment and played the music at the same time in the same room.

Alongside the input desk, there were other new purchases awaiting us in the studio. Hajo Wiechers had managed to develop the Synthanorma sequencer further. The machine no longer had the rustic look of the prototype. Fitting in with the studio norm, the electronics were housed in a dark 19-inch casing, making the device look more technical. The new model also had sixteen steps, which made a lot more sense for pop music with its 4/4 time tradition. An added 'Intervallomat' created quantized sound intervals, enabling us to set sound sequences quickly and reproduce them. And there was also a sync-to-tape function for multitrack recordings – just to name the most important features.

Plus, there was one more thing. It was on this production that we first used the Polymoog – a hybrid of an electronic organ and a synthesizer. While the Orchestron was omnipresent on *Radio-Activity* and *Trans-Europe Express*, the Polymoog now opened up a new sound perspective. Physically, it also occupied the Orchestron's position – Ralf could rest the Minimoog neatly on top of the new instrument, too.

Metropolis

Ralf's new keyboard seemed to have been made just for him. He had a real flair for the Polymoog, as they say. At our first session on 5 May 1977, he played a few chords using the pre-set synthetic violin sound, improvising melodies on the Minimoog to go with them. The Polymoog sound reminded me of a conventional string ensemble, but the notes seemed to float around the room, twisting and turning very slightly.

To prepare for the upcoming sessions in the Kling Klang Studio, I tested out a few riffs and motifs on my piano at home. Sometimes my subconscious passes something on to my hands without informing my brain in between. That was the case with this particular riff, which somehow reminded me of traditional Cuban music: rumba, mambo, son and salsa – it all belongs together in some way. Salsa (meaning sauce) is a good name, to my mind. The pianists in Latin American orchestras play fantastic syncopations, and once you log into them they don't let you go until you start perceiving the whole world in that rhythm, like through a filter. My ostinato – basically just one bar – sounded lively, swift-moving, almost boisterous; the more I repeated it, the better I liked it. I took that syncopated motif along to the studio. Played in the bass register, it was a perfect fit for Ralf's Polymoog chords. Ralf entered my sequence into the Synthanorma, put it into a regular basic rhythm and manipulated it slightly, until it became the grid-like bass sequence of 'Metropolis'.

Using the new sync-to-tape function, we could now record one track after another synchronously on magnetic tape.

That meant we could also let the sequencer control the percussion instruments. Hard to imagine these days . . . but at the time, I saw that mechanical precision as a completely new form of musical expression. 'Metropolis' was the first time we used this method.

When Ralf came up with the main melody on his second Minimoog, over the floating sound of the Polymoog, we recorded it on cassette and listened to his improvisation while out on a drive. Ralf and Florian had each bought a Mercedes-Benz with very good stereo systems by that point, and we cultivated our 'sound rides' from that first demo on. These nocturnal drives around town became a fixture of our studio sessions during the production of the next two albums. I think it was that *Taxi Driver* thing, the mood in which Travis Bickle cruises the streets of Manhattan as the credits of Scorsese's film roll. Driving a car slowly around the city and listening to music, while the surrounding buildings, streets and lights glide by like in a movie. It would be ridiculous to compare Düsseldorf to New York, of course, but looking back, that audio-visual aspect was an important part of our decision-making. We brought together a creative process for making our music, made up of one person's suggestions, the others' comments, our group improvisations, the use of technical tricks, our continual playing around with raw material and that final assessment of the results.

We usually drove across the Knie Bridge to Oberkassel and back to the studio via Theodor Heuss Bridge. Our sound rides lasted fifteen minutes, sometimes half an hour. Occasionally, we'd take several drives to compare changes we'd made. Once we'd listened to the new track, we knew it was worth working more on it. The music's atmosphere seemed almost Russian in a way, and we gave the track the working title of 'Don Volga'. That gave our new album a direction from the very beginning: facing East.

One day, we watched Fritz Lang's classic 1927 silent movie *Metropolis* at the Regional Film Archive on Prinz-Georg-Strasse. The rare screening was a sensation, so the auditorium was full. We couldn't get seats and had to watch it standing up, through the door. Our US tour had been advertised with posters using the term 'The Man-Machine', so I imagine Ralf and Florian must have already known the film. All I had seen of it at that time was stills.

Seeing the original models of the 'city of the future' in the cinema made a huge impression on me. I was also struck by the way the anonymous masses of workers were stylized, moving around the underground machine halls in sync, with their heads lowered. It seemed that in their case, the mutation into machine form, as euphorically demanded by F. T. Marinetti in his *Futurist Manifesto*, had already taken place.

I was particularly impressed by the scene in the inventor Rotwang's laboratory, in which his 'Man Machine'[1] is given Maria's face. The insane room full of complicated, confusing devices: switches that make electricity flow through cables, induction coils, resistors, flywheels, transmission tables with mysterious formulae, chemicals simmering in glass bowls, retorts and test tubes, delicate wire links and a series of mysterious objects and phenomena like the circles of electric light encasing the 'man of the future, the machine man'.

The story is set in the year 2027; not so far away from our present day. In the megacity Metropolis, workers toil in machine halls deep below ground, under inhumane conditions. Upper-class magnates live high above them in their skyscrapers. When the oppressed plan a revolution, they find hope in the words of the 'saintly' worker Maria. 'The mediator between the head and the hands must be the heart,' she preaches.

Instructed by capitalist-in-chief Freder, the genius Rotwang goes on to construct a 'Man Machine' intended as a doppelgänger of Maria, to tell the workers they can expect neither a mediator nor a change in their conditions. But Rotwang programmes the android Maria's 'software' to make it incite the workers to rebellion. The artificial Maria agitates the workers so successfully that the situation gets out of control and chaos breaks loose. The incensed masses destroy the machines. Yet at the end of the film, everything is back to the way it was. The message: revolution is pointless.

In its time, *Metropolis* caused more of a sensation than any other film, even during production. Filming went on for over a year at the UFA Studios, with an army of around a thousand extras available for the mass choreography; the production costs allegedly ate up five million Reichsmarks, an incredible sum for the 1920s; and although there have never been so many offcuts, the end result was more than seven hours of film.

The *Metropolis* myth was born, and Fritz Lang too began working on the legend during his own lifetime. He stated, for example, that his trip to America in October of 1924 had inspired the movie, which experts now doubt. The idea of the megacity had been around since the beginning of the modernist era. As early as 1914, Antonio Sant'Elia had published drawings of his *Città Nuova* along with the *Manifesto of Futurist Architecture*, declaring it the ideal of Italian Futurism. It is no coincidence that the design of *Metropolis* recalls these ideas. Paul Citroen's 1923 photo collage '*Metropolis*' was presumably also a fitting model for Lang.

First shown on 10 January 1927, the two-and-a-half-hour premiere version was a flop with both critics and audiences. But the science-fiction fairy tale did have its admirers. The National Socialists seem to have understood the story as a blueprint for their masterplan. Fritz Lang initially came to an arrangement with the Nazi regime, but he had a Jewish grandmother and could anticipate how things were to develop in Germany.

After further unsuccessful productions, Lang made the talking film *M* and then *The Testament of Dr. Mabuse*. The latter was banned by the German propaganda ministry in 1933, however, for 'endangering public order and safety'. Fritz Lang claimed to have had a legendary conversation with Joseph Goebbels at the end of March 1933, although there is no evidence of it actually taking place. In a film interview,[2] the director described his meeting with the 'tremendously gracious' Goebbels in his office at the ministry. He secretly hoped to persuade the Reich propaganda minister to remove the ban on *Mabuse*, but Goebbels told him he'd have to change the film's ending.

Goebbels allegedly informed him 'what he was planning with various actors and actresses, what kind of films ought to be made, and then he returned to the subject of my work, in other words how I should make all these films as suited the Nazis. I told the minister how honoured I was, took my car – I was soaked to the skin with fear – drove home and told my butler to pack my suitcase, saying I had to go to Paris for a week or two. I left Germany that same evening and never came back.'

The story of his escape, told by the monocled Viennese director in his inimitable manner, is simply fabulous. Lang 'delighted in telling the story and embellished on it a little more each time,'[3] according to the film historian Lotte H. Eisner. Visa entries in his passport call the details into question, however. But does that matter? It's certainly true that he emigrated to American via France in 1933.

Metropolis is now rightly acknowledged as a milestone in cinematic history. The legendary director Luis Buñuel analyses the reason: 'What it gives us in the way of story is trivial, turgid, pedantic, and imbued with a stale romanticism. But if we prefer the plastic photographic nature of film to storyline, then *Metropolis* will surpass all expectations; it will astonish us like the most marvellous book of images ever composed.'[4]

And Lang achieves this painting of a film, this designing of perfect surfaces, with incredible mastery. He even draws sound into his picture book, for instance the four columns of steam rising from the factory sirens, which were painted onto the negative after filming. 'In the noisy visual orchestration of *Metropolis* – a silent film – we can almost hear [the machines], like the factory whistle.'[5]

If we look at the architecture of the city and the human masses, the fantastic laboratory and the 'man machine' as abstract elements isolated from the plot, it is easy to see Fritz Lang's *Metropolis* as a not insignificant influence on Kraftwerk's aesthetics and later on the public image we communicated.

Ralf once said Kraftwerk was the band that Fritz Lang might have cast for *Metropolis*.[6] Perhaps that was an attempt to express appreciation of the film's aesthetic. In purely musical terms, the statement makes little sense, especially taking the time factor into account. It was a far better trick, though, to borrow the 'man machine' as a metaphor for our musical concept and as an eponym for the album we were working on.

Back to the Kling Klang Studio. We were building the piece with the working title 'Don Volga'. When Ralf came up with the idea of linking our instrumental music to the film *Metropolis*, we instantly had visual references. The factory sirens calling the workers to their shifts in the movie were our inspiration for the start of the track. These days, I would download the film, let the rhythm and melody of the images take effect on me, and compose the music as I watched. There was no film projector in the Kling Klang Studio, though. Aside from that, we had no way to access the film. As a result, that visual reference was not present in the moment; we composed from our collective memory.

After kicking off the album production with 'Metropolis', we embarked on a long weekend of clubbing and all met up the following Monday for an Eagles concert. That's right; we went to see the American country rock giants. The band effortlessly transformed the stage of the Düsseldorf Philipshalle into a 'Hotel California' for the length of their gig, impressing me with their music's consistency, sensational sound quality and a performance as smooth as silk. Sounds from another world.

The Robots

By the time *Star Wars* premiered in American cinemas on 25 May 1977, no one believed it would be a hit. Filming had proved extremely difficult, it was over budget and 20th Century Fox was no longer expecting to make up the originally agreed three-million-dollar production costs at the box office. And yet, even though science-fiction movies had gone out of fashion somewhat during the seventies, *Star Wars* hit the right note for the zeitgeist. The worldwide success surpassed all expectations by far. Considering the gross takings of the subsequent *Star Wars* episodes and the spin-off products, the franchise is one of the most successful undertakings in film history.

For the music, though, George Lucas did not follow a futuristic concept. Instead, the composer John Williams created a contrast to the science-fiction world on the screen. The traditional sound of classical music was intended to take viewers (and listeners) into familiar, 'non-futuristic' acoustic surroundings. With a few exceptions, incidentally, this is a common approach.

What did make *Star Wars* acoustically exceptional, however, was the film's soundscape: loud jets roar above the audience's heads, lightsabers slice through the air, and robots speak a hitherto unheard language. It was the sound designer Ben Burtt who made C-3PO and R2-D2 speak. He created their electronic voices and the mechanical sounds of their movements. Burtt spent a year recording sounds and using every trick in the book to manipulate them, making Lucas's film come alive. This was the first time the world came across the job title of 'sound designer'. Ben Burtt revolutionized cinema sound with *Star Wars*.

Although Lucas's film wasn't shown in German cinemas until 1978, no one could escape the media promotion. What was significant for us, to my mind, was the two robots. C-3PO was clearly recognizable as the male version of the machine woman from Fritz Lang's *Metropolis*, while the smaller R2-D2 was a likeably goofy model from a different product line. The two of them derived from the tradition of the American comic duo Laurel and Hardy, and were the movie's secret heroes.

Even before *Star Wars*, there were numerous associations with robots for Kraftwerk. On our *Autobahn* tour of the States, we were announced on posters and ads modelled on the Art Deco style of *Metropolis* as 'The Man-Machine'. The press too referred to us as human machines, robots, androids or mannequins. These comparisons were by no means intended positively, however. In a review of one of our gigs, a critic complained: 'Unfortunately, in order to achieve their synthetic product, Kraftwerk has dehumanized its musicians into robots.'[7] Another article wrote of 'robot-like detachment'.[8] A German journalist, exhausted from listening to *Trans-Europe Express*, declared: 'After two sides of Kraftwerk, I feel more like a robot myself.'[9]

Star Wars and particularly C-3PO and R2-D2 changed that negative view. The mystical machine men had developed into friendly droids and had arrived in the pop-cultural mainstream, just like the sound aesthetic of music machines.

That May of 1977, we had heard of *Star Wars* but not yet seen the film. At that time, though, we loved dancing in clubs and discos even more than going to the cinema. It's not hard for me to call up my memories of Mora's Lovers Club. They would regularly play the new funk track by Johnny 'Guitar' Watson: 'A Real Mother For Ya'. I had no idea what the song was about; the key words I picked up sounded good but I didn't find out about the trick with the disguised 'motherfucker' ('Mother For Ya') until much later. The song's guitar riff loops in syncopated circles around the minor seventh, sixth and fifth. 'A Real Mother For Ya' worked perfectly on the dancefloor.

One evening in May – our last clubbing session still reverberating – we got together in the studio again for a spot of jamming. Ralf tinkered around on the Synthanorma and the Minimoog until he came up with the two-bar phrase that later became famous as the riff from 'The Robots'. With its 116 beats per minute, it sounds astoundingly rhythmic despite its straight semiquavers. The unique sound comes about by altering the timbre on the Minimoog. Ralf's manual manipulation made the mechanical aesthetic of the music machine come to life, gave it a human touch. By opening and closing the filters at a rhythmic pace, Ralf created a similar effect to a guitar put through a wah-wah pedal. I immediately thought of Isaac Hayes's 'Theme from Shaft' and Jimi Hendix's 'Voodoo Child'.

In any case, the riff was an instant hit when we listened to it on the big JBL speakers in the studio. The sounds seemed to bounce around the room like invisible ping-pong balls, encased in a wafer-thin layer of rubber, like a drop of water has a membrane enclosing it and holding it together.

Aside from the periodicity of their riffs, 'A Real Mother For Ya' and 'The Robots' don't have much in common. But for my feeling, they do belong together, because we all danced our feet off to that track in Mora's club.

We'd been compared to robots ourselves, and in *Stars Wars* the machines were given human characteristics and conquered viewers' hearts. So in 1977, there were several prompts for us to compose a song about robots. And the synthesizer riff was the first step in that direction. It sounded like the translation of mechanical motion into music.

But we wanted to acoustically depict our machine men more clearly, and we invented a robot portrait in sound. It consists of electronically imitated sounds of electric engines, mechanics and sonification, which we arranged in a miniature sound collage. The three of us practised the rhythmic pattern together – "Ui Ui Ui Ui – boom, clang, braaat, dididoing" – until we had it down pat, and then we recorded it.

The earliest example of cinematic narrative audio art is Walter Ruttmann's *Weekend*, which premiered in Berlin in 1930. In the 1920s, the new optical sound process for motion pictures had enabled sound montages. For his eleven-minute audio-drama-like piece, Ruttmann made a film about life in Berlin. However, he refrained from using images, recording only 'found' sounds via a microphone onto the celluloid's sound track. He cut and pasted this sound track, consisting of tones, sounds, snatches of language and silences, until the acoustic raw material became a movie without pictures: the first sound montage in music history. Ruttmann himself understood *Weekend* as 'jazz of labour' and 'photographic audio art'.

During the session, our polyglot Ralf remembered his basic Russian and pointed out to us that the word robot[10] – *rabota* – originally has a Slavic root, meaning work. Then he had the idea of having the robot add a line of Russian to our sound collage: 'Ya tvoi sluga, ya tvoi rabotnik' – 'I am your servant, I am your worker.' That expanded on the link to Russia. Ralf and Florian then brought a number of Russian visual artists into play, the association to constructivism being an obvious one. I think it was the very next day that we ended up poring over a book about the work of El Lissitzky, which Ralf had opened up on our mixing desk. And really: Lissitzky's dynamic constructions seemed to me programmatic for the form of our music.

Our mental arrangement developed with our minds on Lissitzky's abstract geometrical use of forms, and we used our usual method to record it onto magnetic tape. For the drums, I suggested a march rhythm, which changes its pattern during the sound-rabotnik collages. Ralf had the idea of using a tuned snare drum as well, which follows the chord scheme – like the guitar in numerous rhythm & blues or soul tracks from the James Brown and Motown era.

We sensed that this song wasn't the worst song of all time, and we worked with extreme precision and concentration. Absolutely everything we did worked out and led us to our goal. It looked very much like 'The Robots' would become the title track of our album.

But we weren't the only people who had noticed robots were on the up. In June, the new Alan Parsons Project album came out, *I Robot*, named after Isaac Asimov's science-fiction short stories *I, Robot*. I remember us listening to it for the first time on the studio system and talking about it. The music, the different singers, the title, the cover – it was all very consciously produced and excellently designed. There was absolutely no doubt that this album would be a huge success. A Kraftwerk album called *The Robots* would have looked like plagiarism.

That didn't affect the song itself, though. We spent a few more weeks working on it. What I particularly like about the lyrics is their deliberate lack of pathos, the lines coming across like texts in comic speech bubbles. Florian voiced the lyrics with his vocoder. After some fifty sessions between May and September, we finally had 'The Robots' wrapped up. Even back then, Ralf predicted we'd forever be linked to the image of robots.

250

Filming Showroom Dummies

Trans-Europe Express and the single of the same name had been on the market since March. To push the album a little more, 'Showroom Dummies' was to be released as a second single in August. Another film was produced for marketing purposes, for which we all met at Günter Fröhling's studio at the end of July. Frau Hartkopf, the make-up artist, came over again with her case full of tricks and skilfully applied our familiar make-up. The procedure reminded me of the opera house. The fluffy powder brush was pleasant but the eye make-up killed me.

The storyboard follows the song's lyrics, cropped to single-length for the media. Using shop dummies seemed an obvious choice. I think Ralf and Florian had the thought even before filming that the dummies ought to have our faces. But where were we to get four modelled heads so quickly? We couldn't put the idea into practice with so little time, so someone got hold of a few industrial showroom dummies. In the film, they take up our positions on the instruments and are marked out as our representatives in neon letters.

The kicker comes at the line 'We start to move, and we break the glass,' when the four of us move towards the camera in pretend slow-motion, our faces expressionless, and a pane of glass copied over the picture smashes to match the sound effect.

'We step out and take a walk through the city' was sacrificed for timing purposes, leaving a little scar in the edit, but by then the lyrics had taken us to the club and we started dancing. And how. Florian – the master of pirouettes and shaken bar mixer hands – remained deadly serious. Incredible but true: Ralf and

Wolfgang are smiling just as the invisible 'screenplay' dictates. And me . . . well, never mind. Those were the disco days and I gave everything I had . . .

I hadn't seen the video for years and I was pretty surprised when I watched it carefully again recently. Of course, the camera shots are very long by today's standards and the cuts could be better timed. But it's still very entertaining, in this age of smartphone film editing.

Maxime Schmitt encouraged us to make a version of the song for the Francophone market, 'Les Mannequins'. He wrote French lyrics and was listed as a co-author. And that was another premiere: with German, English and French versions, this was the first trilingual Kraftwerk song. I love the design of the 7-inch single by Pathé Marconi with 'The Hall of Mirrors' on the B-side: the cover is a group shot by J. Stara, and the back features a photo taken by Fröhling at Düsseldorf's main station, in the style of a 1920s expressionist film. In the UK, to my knowledge, 'Showroom Dummies' did not chart in 1977 but was re-released in 1982 and reached number 25. The song wasn't a huge hit, but it still plays an important role in the Kraftwerk discography for those who know our repertoire.

The Model

In the summer of 1977, synthetic wave forms were flooding out of all the speakers in our environment. In France, too, the electro scene was gaining acceptance and carving out a place for itself. The band Space Art were everywhere with their hit 'Onyx', and Jean-Michel Jarre had his big breakthrough that year with the album *Oxygene*. But it was 'Magic Fly', the French band Space's summer hit, that captured my attention the most. The instrumental was well produced, like all the electro hits of the time, and sounded like it came from a French branch of Kling Klang. 'Magic Fly' got to number 2 in Britain that summer and number 1 in the German charts in July. The song was on heavy rotation on the radio. Like most electro products, Space hung their visual communication on the science-fiction peg hyped up by *Star Wars*. From today's point of view, their reflective space traveller helmets make them look like an early version of Daft Punk, purely optically.

We were curious, and took a look at the frequencies of 'Magic Fly' in the spectrum analyser. I found it interesting that the bass drum also showed up in the upper middle range. It sounded like a 'nick'. The pulsing bass and the sound sequence of the melody reminded me of 'Radioactivity'.

Emil had always published booklets of his work, which he had printed in small numbers. For the songbook *10 Lieder*, which he produced in 1977, I helped him to transcribe the music. One of his songs had the title 'Sie ist ein Model'. Somehow, a copy of the songbook ended up on the mixing desk at the Kling Klang Studio. Ralf and Florian liked his lyrics as well. Düsseldorf is a fashion city, so we were always coming across models: at Mora's, at Rockin' Eagle, in Café Bagel or Mata-Harie-Passage. Alongside the futuristic tracks, 'The Model' also fits in well with *The Man-Machine* because it essentially continues the story of 'Showroom Dummies' from *Trans-Europe Express*: we go to the club and there we meet . . . the model.

The chart hits that summer had their fair share of electronic instrumentals. Up to that point, no other artists had brought out electronic pop music with a song structure and vocals; there were no international references for an electropop song. A good thing for us, because it gave us plenty of scope for our imagination. 'Radioactivity', 'Trans-Europe Express' and 'Showroom Dummies' were already heading in that direction, but another two years were to pass until the release of OMD's 'Electricity', Gary Numan's 'Are 'Friends' Electric?' and *Reproduction* by Human League. The most important elements and inspirations for the third song on our album were spread out before us: Emil's unfinished lines and the electronic pop music – mainly instrumental – of that summer. And yet it was not at all easy to invent German pop music that didn't sound like blues or try to imitate the jazz of the twenties to forties.

Things usually worked differently for us, but on this song Ralf designed the melody around Emil's lyrics, which he completed like a seasoned singer-songwriter. He wrote the A section and the baroque Polymoog solo, and I wrote the B section and a few additional notes of the melody – hardly worth mentioning. And – it goes without saying – the beat. The two of us put the song structure together jointly.

I think we pretty much ticked off everything on the to-do list for writing a pop song from this perspective. Everything except composing a chorus. 'Oh man, if we just had a singalong chorus this track would be a dead-cert hit!' I exclaimed to the guys, exasperated. I was to be proved wrong. Perhaps it's the lack of a chorus that makes the song unusual.

One possible explanation of why the song works is that a lot of people can relate to its glamorous subject. We were lucky, too, of course – the elements of the music fit together organically, and in the late seventies and early eighties our model reference sounded strangely familiar yet modern, plus its continuous vocals made it great for radio.

Manuscripts

By early August, all we needed was a few more songs for the album. With 'Metropolis', 'The Robots' and 'The Model' recorded, there was no reason to get nervous.

I sometimes prefer putting down rhythms, melodies and chords in musical notation to recording them acoustically. Even without hearing the recording in real time, the graphic representation of music lets you see all the relevant 'data' in one glance. And aside from the practical use, notation has always made me reflect on music. For example, about the antagonism at the base of music. Music itself is dramatic; its essence consists of contradictions, and we can see that clearly when it's noted down on paper. Musical expression draws its effect from the juxtaposition of differing realities: short–long, high–low, soft–hard, light–dark, loud–quiet, fast–slow . . . Music can be by turns hesitant, then determined, can condense from a lyrical expression to strong rhythmic accents, and much more. The contrast that this change engenders makes listeners feel emotions like expectation and resolution. I think the strongest contrast that occurs in music is that between sound and silence. A clear case, you might think; either someone's playing the piano, or not. Yet a glance at the sheet music reveals that for every note value representing a sound, an equivalent of silence exists; except that silence in music is called a rest. To be precise, music is thus composed of sound and silence. Whatever the case, for me it was always an advantage not only to listen to our music, but also to see it in its written form to help me 'grasp' it. And so I began to keep a musical sketchbook.

One of the things I kept in there was a list of keywords that I noticed in the media, for instance, which I saw as linked to our work in the Kling Klang Studio. At home and also at our sessions, I always had a music notebook or a few pages of blank score sheets at hand to note down rhythms, tones or chords. I chose the titles spontaneously, just to give a reference to the stylistic context. In conjunction with my music cassettes, pocket calendars and other notes, the result is a kind of sound diary, which provided me with a useful timeline for writing this book.

It was around this time that I first came across the Voyager Golden Records. These famous recordings are on board the NASA spaceships *Voyager I* and *II*, which were shot into space from Cape Canaveral in August and September 1977 to study the outer planetary system and interstellar space. The spaceships each carry a 30-centimetre record made of gold-plated copper, storing sounds and images of the diversity of life on earth and its culture. The record includes greetings from the then-US president, Jimmy Carter, and a selection of nature sounds: waves, wind, thunder, birdsong, whale calls and other animal noises. There are also examples of music from various cultures and epochs, including Peruvian pan pipes, Navajo night chants, pieces by Johann Sebastian Bach, Wolfgang Amadeus Mozart, Ludwig van Beethoven, Igor Stravinsky, and 'Johnny B. Goode' by Chuck Berry. *Voyager I* is still in space, sending data back to Earth.

Moonstruck

On 16 June 1977, the legendary space pioneer Wernher von Braun died.[11] He had led a breathtaking life with a career reminiscent of a rocket take-off. The future scientist's childhood and youth would set any biographer's pulse racing. His musical talent emerged at an early age; he played the cello and composed his own music. But young Wernher was also interested in the sciences, and began tinkering with cars at the age of 12. He was intelligent but also a restless spirit who often played with fireworks. When his marks at school took a turn for the worse, his parents sent him to boarding school in Weimar.

His mother's confirmation gift to him was an astronomical telescope, which he used to observe the planets at night. Reading the space-travel pioneer Hermann Oberth's book *By Rocket into Planetary Space*, with its mathematical and physics-based suggestions for rocket technology, launched his lifelong obsession with space. He was firmly convinced man would one day land on the moon. In 1929 – two years after *Metropolis* – Fritz Lang's film *Woman in the Moon* was released and the 17-year-old Wernher managed to introduce himself to Lang's scientific adviser – that very same Hermann Oberth – eventually becoming his assistant.

Braun graduated in engineering from the technical university in Berlin in 1932. The young idealist was still obsessed with the idea of reaching space. He hoped the military would provide him with the necessary resources for his experiments and made contact with the Army Weapons Office. By this point, his father was agriculture minister in the Reich government and his aristocratic name opened plenty of doors for him. Wernher von Braun had a confident manner, aided by a gift for convincing others of his abilities. He was indeed made an offer. He became a civilian employee of the Reichswehr and was allowed to experiment on the testing grounds of the Army Research Centre. The idea was to perhaps circumvent the Treaty of Versailles using a 'flying canonball' not fired by the artillery.

By the time Adolf Hitler was appointed chancellor in 1933, Wernher von Braun was already working on his dissertation. He gained his PhD in physics aged 22 in 1934. His work on the liquid-fuelled rocket was declared classified information by the military, and word of the young physician's extraordinary talent got around among the Nazis.

Dr Wernher Magnus Maximilian Freiherr von Braun was only 25 years old in 1937 – the same age as me during the production of *The Man-Machine* – when the German army and air force set up a modern rocket city especially for him in Peenemünde on the Baltic coast, spending hundreds of millions of Reichsmarks. An enclosure with its own harbour, station, airfield, research institutions, test stands, launch bases, factories, power plants and accommodation for staff was built from scratch. There had never been a secret military project like it. Braun was made technical director of the Army Research Centre (HVA) Peenemünde, and was not only a very good engineer but also a brilliant manager. His enthusiasm was infectious, soon gathering the most capable scientists, technicians and engineers around him. And the SS provided them with a huge contingent of forced labourers. Wernher von Braun imbued his rocket science with a military objective and forged a stellar career, joining the Nazi party and the SS, where he climbed to the rank of Sturmbannführer, comparable to a major.

In 1939 the Germans began the Second World War by attacking Poland. Wernher von Braun, however, was the archetype of the unpolitical scientist; for him, science and politics were separate realities. And after five years of intensive work, the day finally came. On 3 October 1942, a rocket was successfully launched in Peenemünde. The 'Aggregat 4' – a 14-metre-long rocket weighing 13.5 tonnes with a diameter of 3.5 metres – reached a height of 84.5 kilometres and became the first man-made object to enter the boundaries of outer space.

The Red Army offensive at Stalingrad in November 1942 is regarded as the turning point of the Second World War. The Germans began to retreat. Armaments minister Albert Speer promised an 'arms miracle' and 'wonder weapons' for the anticipated 'final victory'.

In July of 1943, Braun flew to the Wolf's Lair Führer's Headquarters in East Prussia to convince Hitler to go on investing in his rocket programme. A master of self-marketing, he even commissioned an animated film about rockets. Hitler was thrilled, not just by this dynamic young man but also by his explosive product, and he assigned the highest priority to the 'miracle weapon'. The projectiles were to be deployed in large numbers. As mental stimulation, the Führer personally bestowed him with a professorship. Wernher von Braun was 31 years old at the time.

After the Allied invasion of Normandy in 1944, the German artillery fired more than 3000 rockets, mainly on London and Antwerp. The Nazi propaganda machine dubbed the rockets *Vergeltungswaffe 2*, meaning 'retaliation weapon' or V2 for short.

They killed thousands of people. Yet the terrible death toll was higher than first thought. After the Royal Air Force bombed Peenemünde in 1943, production was relocated to Kohnstein, a mountain range in the Harz region northwest of Nordhausen. In the underground Mittelbau-Dora Factory, a concentration camp, many thousands of forced labourers died assembling V2 rockets.[12]

Wernher von Braun had long been aware that Germany would lose the war, and was already planning for his post-Hitler future. He knew the Germans had a headstart of at least ten years on rocket technology, and the Americans, British, French and Russians would stake a claim to the results of their research. But he was also certain that only the Americans had the necessary financial means to grant rocket science a future. On 2 May 1945 – a few days after Hitler's death – Braun and his closest colleagues defected to the US forces. The nuclear physicists, rocket constructors, aviation engineers, electronics and missile-guiding specialists were not put into prisoner-of-war camps, instead helping to organize the removal of uranium supplies, rocket parts, jets and tonnes of construction drawings before they fell into Soviet hands. The Americans were immensely interested in the German specialists' knowledge. Wernher von Braun's expertise was of inestimable value to them. Being an astute businessman, he made a deal. He would be neither indicted nor called as a witness to the Nuremberg trials, but instead transferred into the service of the USA. The V2 constructor and former Nazi party member landed in the States as early as September 1945. Over a hundred members of his staff were also taken to the USA, with more to follow.

Over the next few years, Wernher von Braun improved on the V2 on behalf of the US military and designed a mid-range rocket for nuclear warheads. He envisioned space stations from which nuclear rockets could be fired. However, he also published journal articles about manned space flight. An American citizen from 1955 on, he continued to indulge this passion. In 1957, he advised Walt Disney for the film *Mars and Beyond*. He made space travel popular and came to unexpected fame. 'Missileman von Braun', *Time* magazine named him on its cover in February 1958. The ex-SS man was regarded as a luminary in the USA and joined NASA, the National Aeronautics and Space Administration body founded in 1958.

After the shock of the Russians launching Sputnik in the 1950s, the Americans experienced another unpleasant surprise. On 12 April 1961, the Soviet cosmonaut Yuri Gagarin was the first man in space. The race for dominance over space was well underway. And when President John F. Kennedy announced the American manned moon landing following the Cuba crisis at the height of the Cold War, Wernher von Braun was prepared to give his all. Having once convinced Hitler in person of the V2 'miracle weapon', he now got on wonderfully with the Democrat JFK. On 16 July 1969, his vision of manned space travel became reality with the *Apollo 11* mission. A million spectators gathered on the coast of Florida, while more than half a billion television viewers around the world watched as his Saturn rocket lifted off from Cape Canaveral and took three astronauts to the moon.

After the moon landing, Wernher von Braun was an American national hero, the shining star of the rocket industry. Five more manned moon landings took place in the subsequent three years of the Apollo programme but the focus gradually returned to Earth, where the Vietnam War was becoming an increasingly important influence over public discourse in the USA. Fame fades, and Wernher von Braun was removed from operative service at NASA, apparently no longer useful. From 1970 to 1972, he was made Deputy Associate Administrator for Planning at NASA Headquarters, which concentrated on the future of American space travel. He made failed attempts to promote a manned mission to Mars; there was no budget for such ambitious ideas. He was successful, however, in suggesting simplifying the technical concept of the reusable Space Shuttle. The plan was signed off by President Nixon in 1972 – the only time he gave an OK on space travel. Wernher von Braun left NASA that same year. 'One of those rare engineers with charisma,' wrote the *New York Times*. In July 1975, he was elected onto the supervisory board of Daimler-Benz in Stuttgart. He never had to answer for his Nazi past, distancing himself from the crimes of National Socialism and denying any personal culpability. Science, it seems, did not have a moral dimension necessary to deal with him and his funders.

Spacelab

Depending on how one views it, the story of that dynamic German physicist plays a role in our song. 'In a way we feel related to Werner von Braun; German scientific research is related to our music. We make acoustic rockets,'[13] Ralf explained to *Interview* magazine, rather bluntly.

On 12 August 1977, the *Enterprise* – a prototype for NASA's Space Shuttle programme – took its first untethered flight in the atmosphere. The name refers back to the science-fiction series *Star Trek*. The *Enterprise* was launched using a modified Boeing 747 and released at altitude. The shuttle then flew unpropelled to its landing strip, just like after space travel. The aim was to transport a reusable space lab into orbit, so as to carry out experiments under weightless conditions. The piggyback film footage was all over the global media. The project hit a nerve and we too reacted to the event in the Kling Klang Studio, thinking about how to put the subject of space travel into music for the fourth track on our album.

The title is built on the back of a rudimentary disco beat, and is correspondingly straightforward. Ralf's relay of sequencer and Minimoog produced a percussive sound that he used for the first time, though it was to decisively influence the sound of the electronic drum kit on our next album, *Computer World*. On top of that, Ralf composed a melody that seems to come from a different century. A drawn-out Minimoog bass rounds off the spectrum in the low-frequency segment. I added, among other things, the typical brass chords E flat major and C major, which make up the vocoder refrain. Although not intended, the chords have a certain Wagnerian *Star Wars* feel to them, or at least it seems that way to me now. The second voice of the melody and the break in the middle developed organically as we worked on the arrangement. I also had the idea of painting an audio picture of a take-off using an accelerating whole-tone scale, which went well with the brass chords with their plaintive synthesizer motif. We put together an intro made of the shuttle start, and repeated it at the end of the track. Apart from Florian's vocoder, the song was orchestrated entirely on Moog synthesizers.

Without me noticing, after several postponements the first Space Shuttle was deployed on 12 April 1981, the virgin flight of the *Columbia*. A total of 22 Spacelab missions were flown between 1983 and 1998.

And now we'll come back down to Earth.

'Best European Group, Male'

The recordings we were working on were great. I couldn't imagine a better way to spend our time together or better subjects to talk about. A kind of team spirit had come about on our tours, during film and photo shoots and in the studio. We were spending more and more time together outside of work too, at cinemas, cafés and restaurants. The shared flat on Berger Allee and our nightclubbing and parties helped foster that feeling. It was in this atmosphere of close bonds that we came up with our music.

One particularly positive influence on the team spirit was the nocturnal swimming sessions to which Florian invited us, our first joint sport activities. He was living at the time in an exclusive penthouse with a sensational view over Düsseldorf. The apartment building had a private pool and it was perfectly fine to use it at three in the morning. Now and then, a few friends came along with us. Admittedly, it was a little decadent to drive our girlfriends straight from a disco in Florian's Mercedes into the underground garage, for a lounge around the pool. The whole thing happened very much in the spirit of the sixties, and had something innocent to it despite the permissive atmosphere. When people came close during these fun 'sports parties' it had an absolutely positive effect on the group feeling in our small circle – how could it be any other way? After a few lengths of

264

crawl, breaststroke, backstroke or butterfly – always far removed from athletic prowess – we took the lift up to Florian's penthouse and four or six or more of us would empty one or two bottles of champagne. During the *Man-Machine* sessions, of course, we switched to Crimean sparkling wine for that authentic Soviet feel.

While researching this book, I came across a full-page ad in *Billboard* from 22 October 1977, with the headline 'Kraftwerk Story . . .' The ad refers to us receiving an award at the Beacon Theatre on Broadway. Kraftwerk had been picked as 'Best European Group, Male' at the Popular Music Disco Awards. Underneath our press photo – taken at Düsseldorf main station – I read the caption: 'Kraftwerk members Florian Schneider, Ralf Hütter, Karl Bartos, and Wolfgang Flür. They are surprised at their success in the disco scene!'[14]

During the production process, it had emerged that our new album might be called *The Man-Machine*. The term, which had been with us since our 1975 US tour, seemed to be a good alternative to The Robots, as picked up by Alan Parsons with his *I, Robot* album. The next job on the list was group photos. On 29 September, we shot the cover photo in Günter Fröhling's stairwell at number 46, Herzogstrasse. Dress code: red shirt, black tie, grey trousers. The make-up artist was once again Frau Hartkopf. The photo session went quickly, and I remember Wolfgang and I driving back to Berger Allee in full make-up afterwards. We were still excited from the shoot and were messing around in the kitchen. I had lost track of time and was surprised when the doorbell rang and Bettina showed up. She stared in amazement at the white-faced guy in a red shirt who opened the door for her. Bettina Michael had just turned 18 and was in her last year of high school in Kaiserswerth. We had met a few weeks before at the Peppermint Club and had seen each other several times . . .

The next day, Klaus Schulze was playing in the Robert Schumann Hall, something we didn't want to miss. We took Florian's Mercedes 600 directly from Berger Allee to the main entrance and out we got: Ralf and Florian with their girlfriends, Bettina and me – the girls dolled up to the nines. I tried to view our turning up in the 'cauldron', as we called the Mercedes, as a kind of parody. It was funny. But Bettina told me later that people she knew who were queuing outside thought our showbiz antics were pretty embarrassing . . .

Inside, Klaus Schulze was sitting cross-legged on his Flokati rug, between numerous keyboards in front of a giant Moog modular wall. He gave off an air of deep relaxation. There was a mirror attached above him so he could see the audience even when he turned his back. Schulze played a chord – for the experts, I should probably say 'a synthesizer pad' – with a string ensemble. His hand weighed heavy on the keys. And then: a sequencer faded in slowly! 'As soon as the sequences rattled off, people would flip out,'[15] Klaus Schulze once said; it was sequencers that made classic electronic music famous in the first place. That was followed by an improvisation that lasted several minutes – as you'd expect from a cosmic courier. I must say, Klaus had done his homework.

Germany in Autumn

We worked at a constant pace. But while we were busy behind the shutters of the air-conditioned Kling Klang Studio, Germany was being shaken by the second generation of the terrorist Red Army Faction. On 5 September, the RAF kidnapped the president of the Employers' Association, Hanns Martin Schleyer, intending to exchange him for the release of leading members of their group from behind bars in the Stuttgart-Stammheim high-security prison. As a consequence, the Federal Criminal Police (BKA) deployed state-of-the-art investigation methods that we now know as computer-aided dragnet searches.

News blackouts, a law banning communication for prisoners and the establishment of a crisis committee that made decisions on behalf of the German government – these key measures shook the foundations of German democracy. Like all over West Germany, there were RAF wanted posters plastered everywhere in Düsseldorf and Cologne for years. The police clamped down hard, regularly checking IDs in the student cafeteria at the Robert Schumann Conservatory. And we Kraftwerkers also came into contact with the effects of terrorism and anti-terrorism measures in our everyday lives.

Autumn 1977. We were coming back from one of our sound rides in the middle of the night. Ralf's Mercedes cruised down Mintropstrasse and stopped outside number 16. Before Florian could get out of the car to open the gate, an unmarked car overtook us and parked in our way. Two men in jeans and leather jackets got out and cautiously approached our car. A bunch of men driving the empty streets at night was a perfect match for what the police were looking for.

Mintropstrasse is close to Düsseldorf's main station, in the middle of the red-light district. The neighbouring buildings housed a series of strip clubs, private clubs, gambling halls and poker bars, attracting plenty of dodgy characters by night. We'd never had any problems with the neighbours, though. And now? One of the men positioned himself a few feet behind our car, one hand concealed strangely in his pocket, while the other leaned down to Ralf in the driving seat: 'Vehicle spot-check. Let's see your ID, please!'

In our own interest, we refrained from dumb remarks or jokes. The police were too nervous in those days, having become a target for the terrorists themselves. Ralf had a good strategy for avoiding unwanted reactions: he immediately switched on the interior light and put his hands clearly on the steering wheel, with the rest of us also making sure the officers could see our hands.

We ended up telling them we were working in our studio and that we were the band Kraftwerk. The two plainclothes officers had heard of us and were pleased when we invited them in to take a quick look at the studio. So we marched them across the backyard and up the stairs – and still the men were nervous. One walked ahead with Ralf while the other brought up the rear. They didn't calm down until they saw the flashing instruments and coloured neon lights in the studio, then looked at it all for a few minutes and said their goodbyes. I think the police were as relieved as we were.

That was how it was in those days. Not exactly relaxed. The Red Army Faction announced its disbanding in the spring of 1998.

Depressive Phases

Early one morning a few days later, I was in the waiting room of the local army recruitment office. At that time, men still had to do a year of military service in Germany, and that threat had been dangling over my head like the sword of Damocles since my first semester at the Robert Schumann Conservatory. I hadn't attended any of the army physicals I'd been summoned to so far, postponing the agony by sending university enrolment certificates. After my final exam, though, the army got very tough – I was summoned to a physical only days later.

The waiting room was packed with young men, all around 18. Some of them were considering signing up for a few years as professional soldiers. I was not. I had frantically gone over what to do so as not to get drafted. Determined to try anything necessary, I went to a psychiatrist and neurologist and told him about my experiments with drugs and the turmoil I sometimes felt. After a thorough interrogation, he wrote in his evaluation that I suffered from sporadic depressive moods. And he added: during these phases of depression, the patient frequently abuses drugs. The patient – I in other words – also described conflict situations arising from homosexual attraction. His finding: a long course of psychiatric or psychotherapeutic treatment was presumably essential. Homosexuality was still a big no-no in the German army.

When I was called up to face the physical examination committee – a row of men in uniforms and white coats – I was quite nervous. I had dressed up smart and didn't feel comfortable with the way I looked. One of the doctors read my evaluation but didn't look particularly impressed by my 'depressive phases' and 'homosexual conflicts'. I tried to read his thoughts: musician, drugs, gay, depression sounds logical – this one's no good! The doc smiled at me – yes, he really smiled – and asked me to take a seat back in the waiting room. I hadn't said a word other than 'Hello' and 'Thanks'. A few minutes later, a secretary handed me an envelope containing my exemption from military service. A huge weight fell from my shoulders. I'd never been so overjoyed by a rejection.

New Musick

'Hey Karl, are you still in Kraftwerk?' Bettina asked me on the telephone. 'Why, what do you mean?' I answered her question with another question, confused. 'I just saw the new issue of *Sounds*[16] and it has Ralf and Florian on the cover, but there's no sign of you and Wolfgang!' I headed straight to the station and got myself a copy of the magazine at the international press kiosk.

It's probably hard to imagine how important the British music press was at that time. But *NME, Sounds, Melody Maker, Record Mirror, Smash Hits* – and from 1980 *The Face* – were *the* most influential print media for music and pop culture in the UK, which meant they were relevant all across Europe. I don't know how many times I accompanied Ralf to the station to buy an impressive pile of foreign music magazines. He kept himself regularly informed on the state of play in the British Isles.

Unbeknown to me, the new term 'New Musick' had been making the rounds of the British scene in the autumn of 1977, as it began to liberate itself from the punk movement. *Sounds* published a long article on the subject, divided between two issues.

For the title page of the 26 November *Sounds*, Caroline Coon had photographed Ralf and Florian on the banks of the Rhine in Düsseldorf, with the fog-veiled North Bridge in the background.

The two of them looked confident and relaxed, even making friendly faces at Caroline's camera. Like *NME*, the magazine was printed in a newspaper format. The cover design could be described as extremely minimalist: only the magazine's title, date, price and at the bottom of the page the headline: 'New Musick – The Cold Wave'. In microscopic letters, outside the frame of the photo on the far left: 'Kraftwerk's Ralf Hütter & Florian Schneider'. Inside, another photo of the two of them and two press photos from the 'Showroom Dummies' film.

In the interview itself, Ralf talks about his favourite subjects: the cultural vacuum he perceived in post-war Germany, the backwardness of classical music and above all of classically oriented musicians, Kraftwerk as a man-machine system ('Also we have cassette recorders built into our heads. This is called tape consciousness'[17]) – and the subject of the acoustic environment: 'Walk in the streets and you have a concert. Cars playing symphonies. [. . .] The source of sound is what matters today. It's a new awareness of the sources of sound that we bring about in our music.'[18]

The article clearly fitted into the zeitgeist. When I met up with Andy McCluskey and Paul Humphreys recently in Hamburg, Andy recalled:

'Karl, you have to remember that I saw you in September 1975 two years before this article. I was already converted. The whole article was very much the Ralf and Florian manifesto and reinforced my adherence to the Kraftwerk ethos. And I swallowed all of it hook, line and sinker. Paul and I tried so hard to adopt Kraftwerk attitudes because it was a celebration of the new and an avoidance of Anglo-American rock'n'roll clichés. We tried to recreate the sounds of a telephone kiosk, wrote songs about aeroplanes, warfare, and oil refineries using concrete sounds. We learned to do this from adopting the Kraftwerk theory. And we consciously tried to avoid rock cliché lyrics, especially the word "love", for five years in lyrics.'

Neon Lights

At that time, we were constantly creating new musical content through the use of innovative technology. And when that led to an unusual way of playing and phrasing and an unknown sound filled the room, it was always a great moment.

One example: while we were improvising to a relatively slow rhythm of 108 BPM, Florian had a flash of inspiration. He plugged the audio output of the Polymoog into the external input of the Minimoog. And suddenly we heard this brand new, exciting rhythmic pattern. What had happened? Because the Minimoog was controlled by the Synthanorma sequencer and Florian had synced it with the Polymoog, we could now also rhythmically manipulate the sounds from the Polymoog and synchronize them with precise timing into a multitrack.

The triggered Polymoog created an electrically charged atmosphere – almost like a synthetic Impressionist landscape. I couldn't remember ever having heard anything like it. That flickering sound seemed to have no past. And so Florian's trick grew into the first impression of the song, which we expanded on bit by bit.

Our track was untitled for a long time, but at some point, Ralf came into the studio with the well-known lyric. That was it. A second verse might have led to more cover versions, but 'Neon Lights' was still covered by OMD on their 1991 album *Sugar Tax*. Simple Minds recorded the song in 2001 and even named their album after it. In 2004, U2 added a version of 'Neon Lights' to several releases of their single 'Vertigo'.

Christmas in Paris

By 23 December 1977, we had over 100 album sessions on the meter and 'Neon Lights' was half-finished. The composition's mood carries with it the atmosphere of Düsseldorf by night, which glided past us on our sound rides like a film: brightly lit shop windows, neon letters, other cars' headlamps . . .

The way I see it, the imagery in 'Neon Lights' matches our mood in the Kling Klang Studio at the time. Without being aware of it, we were doing everything right – in musical and interpersonal terms. And so we arranged to spend Christmas together in Paris. Maxime, we were told, would invite us to the Hotel Le Royal Monceau in the name of Pathé Marconi – and the rest would sort itself out.

Wolfgang wanted to do something else that day, so we were a fairly small group: Ralf and his girlfriend, Florian, Bettina and me. It wasn't easy for Bettina's parents to let her go to Paris with her new boyfriend on Christmas Eve. They hadn't met me yet, so stress was inevitable. But the way girls do at 18, she got her own way and turned up at Berger Allee on the afternoon of the 24th, looking very pretty and kitted out with a small backpack and a huge smile. I beamed back at her – we were very much in love.

When Florian drove up at seven in the anthracite-grey Mercedes Coupé he'd got himself as well as the 600, we cheerfully leapt into the car. Just like us, Florian was very excited and looking forward to the trip. Then Ralf plus one joined us. He waved at us as they drove past in his Mercedes, and we all set off. We managed the 500-kilometre drive in less than four hours, arriving at the hotel before midnight to find Maxime waiting for us at the bar. Not losing any time, we took two taxis to our favourite dining spot, the Brasserie La Coupole.

I was floored all over again by the place's magnificent atmosphere. As we entered the room, the air was saturated by the sound of countless voices. In short: it was the ideal spot for our Christmas dinner. Florian confidently ordered champagne for all of us and two tiered plates of oysters.

That evening – although it may have been another evening, but it fits in so well here – the Ramones from New York were sitting in a large group a few tables along. They'd obviously recognized us, and out of the corner of my eye I saw Joey Ramone making his way towards us, as always leaning forward slightly. He said hello like a perfect gentleman and passed on the respects of the Ramones. Ralf thanked him politely and the tall, spindly singer turned on his heel and went back to his table. For La Coupole, that was probably absolutely normal, but for me it was a very special encounter.

The mood at our little Christmas celebration couldn't have been better, not least due to Monsieur Schmitt. No one would ever deny that he'd played a key role in the success of the two past Kraftwerk albums in France. But aside from that, I felt

Maxime had a great sense of authority and human warmth. We laughed a lot that evening. Shortly before midnight, a few garçons ganged up somewhere in the room and headed for a table, loaded down with a cake and sparklers – and the next moment, an opera singer burst into an Italian aria. The whole of La Coupole applauded: bravissimo!!!

Back at the Royal Monceau later, Bettina and I rounded off our Christmas Eve with a miniature bottle of champagne from the minibar and soon retired to bed. We spent the Saturday and Sunday on the classics: exploring the Champs-Élysées and sitting in cafés, before we met up with the others to do things all together. Time flew while we had fun. On 27 December we circled the Arc de Triomphe twice and then sped down the autobahn back to Düsseldorf.

At home, I somehow obtained a copy of the Christmas issue of *NME*, featuring an interview with Ralf and Florian. They'd obviously given the interview in New York when they'd received the Disco Award in September. 'For Kraftwerk the world began in the 1920s, with Fritz Lang's utopian cinematic visions of machine-land,' Toby Goldstein explains to his readers. Ralf adds, 'Where the scientists and artists are working hand in hand.' He continues: 'We are the children of Wernher von Braun and Fritz Lang. We start from the 20s and jump to the 70s and 80s. We're not concerned with history lessons, we are concerned with today. I think that's one of the basic faults of society, to look backward and all this fool stuff. It's like, if you are driving a fast car and you look too much in the back mirror you might crash in front. We'd rather watch what we're doing right now, what we could do today or tomorrow.'[19]

Between Christmas and New Year, we went back to the Kling Klang Studio to fine-tune a few tracks, and then met up with our girlfriends on 31 December in Florian's penthouse, to see in the year 1978 the only appropriate way – with Crimean red sparkling wine and a symbolic portion of caviar.

The Man-Machine (Song)

On my nights out at the clubs, one song had caught my attention. In fact, it wasn't a song at all, more of a rhythm track, but it was certainly cool. I remember noting down the drum pattern on a napkin on the edge of the dancefloor at the Rockin' Eagle. At home, I messed around with the offbeats, and in the end the complementary rhythm took on a mechanical quality. The pattern, with its 120 beats per minute, seemed ideal for the sixth and last track on the album: 'The Man-Machine'.

A key element of the composition is the minimalist synth motif in the high range. Ralf developed the sequence tone by tone on the Synthanorma to the running rhythm track. The melody was easy to transpose and took on a flowing quality through the electronic echo. All the music's other components were more or less oriented along this F minor motif and the rhythm formula.

While we were working on the track, I naturally thought of *Metropolis*. 'Come! It is time to give the Machine-Man your face!' the inventor Rotwang declaims as he attacks Maria. We then witness the mad scientist creating a robot in human form in his laboratory. That takes place, as we recall, on the orders of Joh Fredersen, the powerful capitalist. Strangely reminiscent of Wernher von Braun, to my mind.

Kraftwerk's musical concept was not complicated in those days. We musicians, humans in other words, hook ourselves up to the complex machine – the electronic music studio – and form an interactive man-machine system. It's clear and comprehensible, in my opinion.

It wasn't until much later that I learned about the origins of the theoretical concept of viewing the world as a machine. With the advent of mechanization came the beginning of thinking about interconnections. In the 17th and 18th centuries, philosophers placed man, machine and God in interrelation. René Descartes, for instance, in his posthumously published *Traité de l'homme* (*Treatise of Man*, 1662),[20] explores the idea that man is like a machine created by God. For the German polymath Gottfried Wilhelm Leibniz, even 'the organic body of each living being is a kind of divine machine or natural automaton, which infinitely surpasses all artificial automata.'[21] And the French doctor and philosopher Julien Offray de La Mettrie came to the provocative conclusion, as the title of his 1748 treatise *L'Homme Machine* (*Man a Machine*) suggests, that man was a machine,[22] thus carving out a spot for himself in the pantheon of philosophy.

Please go easy on me; the scholars' thoughts on the machine paradigm are no doubt very wise, but for me they're only approaching comprehensible. And today's engineers' and futurologists' understanding of living beings as kind of protein-based computers[23] is equally puzzling to me. I can't make much out of it. Thankfully, I'm a music man and not a machines expert. But I have been wondering more and more often recently whether modern efforts to change the cycle of nature – in which all elements are organically linked – into a gigantic growth machine that exploits the earth's resources and transforms them into consumer goods, money and rubbish, shouldn't be called arrogant, or even completely insane.

Incidentally, in the twentieth century the 'mechanical man with replacement parts' was something the Futurist Marinetti was able to imagine as early as 1912.[24] And in 1914 he declared in 'Multiplied Man and the Realm of Machines'[25] that he was preparing the imminent identification of man with the machine. Marinetti was so high on the myth of the machine that he dreamed of fusing into it personally.

He was no doubt familiar with Mary Shelley's 1818 *Frankenstein*, now considered one of the most significant British novels. Experiments with electricity on corpses' muscles and nerves, a subject of much interest at the time, had stimulated the writer's imagination. In a science-based work of fiction, she invented an artificial man: the 'creature'. The pseudo-religious belief in progress, in the prototype of the man-machine capable of being randomly multiplied and hence immortal, anticipated much of what is gaining a new dimension in the digital age: 'transhumanism'. I will return to Silicon Valley's experts on the future and computer science later in the book. But first, let's get back to the analogue technology of the Kling Klang Studio and our 'Man-Machine'.

In absolute concentration, Ralf recorded the soprano part in the song's chorus with the new vocoder from Japan. Florian had a large collection of vocoders, for instance from EMS or Sennheiser, which were quite valuable and sounded outstanding. But the Japanese device was the best one for the refrain. The idea came up to compose a counterpoint with a second, lower vocoder part. We hadn't used the vocoder for this kind of part writing up to that point. At the almost ritual lines 'Man machine / semi-human being,' I couldn't help thinking of hymns from the early phase of polyphony, with

278

their endless 'Hallelujah' melismas. In my view, through its functioning principle – the human voice and electronics – the vocoder is the ideal representation of the interaction of man and machine.

We Turn into Sculptures

Ralf and Florian had set their minds on creating an artificial doppelgänger for each of us. They would give us new options for presenting our public image, that was obvious. So we had to find a sculptor who could make models of our faces. Florian took on the job of researching it, eventually making a contact in Munich. Heinrich Obermaier was a living legend in the world of mannequins and seemed to be exactly the right man for the job. Back in December 1977, we had taken the *Rheingold* train from Düsseldorf to Munich to get our heads modelled in clay by the master. It was, though a little late, our first and only joint trip on a Trans-Europe Express.

A cheerful Heinrich Obermaier welcomed us to his home. He was a friendly man in his 60s, or perhaps he was even 70, with a loveable face and an unmistakable Bavarian accent. And of course he was well prepared, soon taking us up to his attic studio. Although the room was bright, it was still rather eerie, like a strange mix of the sculpture pavilion at the Düsseldorf Art Academy, Dr Frankenstein's laboratory and a workshop for medical prostheses. Shelves were piled high with arms, legs and heads from bygone decades, made out of all kinds of materials. Cupboards and tables held countless heads made of clay, wood or plastic, their eyes or eye sockets staring in all directions.

279

Boxes of glass eyes, arranged by colour, were piled on a sideboard. The remarkable thing about Obermaier's dummy collection was that he based the faces on real people. To this day, his mannequins are classics, with originals traded on the internet as rare treasures. And now we were to model for him over the next few days.

At last it was my turn. Herr Obermaier had already prepared a clay blank on a revolving stand. I stood next to it while he measured my skull with large wooden callipers and then transferred the measurement to the unworked clay, shaping and working the material until the proportions were correct. Layer by layer, spatula by spatula, the lump of clay slowly became my image. It was fascinating to watch.

Herr Obermaier preferred not to talk while he worked. But the radio played quietly in the background and prevented the atmosphere from becoming too magical. I heard the Munich traffic report jingle and then the news that there was a tailback forming around Karlsplatz. Everyday life. At the end of the first session in December, he picked out the right glass eyes – blue, in my case. Herr Obermaier explained he would finish off the clay models and then make silicone moulds.

At the beginning of January 1978, the four of us made another trip to Munich, this time in Ralf's Mercedes. Heinrich Obermaier had finished modelling the clay heads, made the silicone moulds and cast positives. Theoretically, that meant we could make thousands of plastic heads. Now he needed us to model for him again so he could choose the precise colour of the glass eyes and the tone of our faces, mouths, eyebrows and hair. Hair was unusual for Obermaier's mannequins at that time. In our case, the dummies weren't simply given wigs, as was standard; instead, he modelled the hairstyles like classic 1920s mannequins and painted them in the original shades.

That Sunday evening, we returned to the Rhineland and worked every day of the next four weeks to complete the album.

Mixing at the Rudas Studio

February 1978. Ralf and Florian had booked the Düsseldorf Rudas Studio for our mixing session. It was fairly centrally located, near the stock exchange. It also had an MCI multitrack machine, although it only had 24 tracks, the technical standard at the time.

Multitrack? OK, do you know the name Lester Polsfuss? No? That's alright; he's far better known under the name Les Paul. The famous US musician was not only a brilliant guitarist, but also had a great affinity for technology. From the very beginning, he was convinced that music and electronics weren't opposites, that they could enter into a positive collaboration. Fascinated by the possibility of recording his music, he eventually came up with an inspired idea. By adding a fourth recording head to his Ampex tape machine, he invented what he called 'sound-on-sound tape recording'. That was the introduction of what we understood many years later as record production. Another recording could be added to an existing tape track. That combined track then formed the basis for a new recording – and so on. The version of 'How High the Moon' recorded in his home studio got to number 1 on the Billboard charts. An absolute sensation!

Before Les Paul's invention, music recording was merely a matter of reproducing an acoustic event unaltered; a passive transmission that offered little scope for intervention. The sound on 'How High the Moon', however, was not natural but synthetic. Mary Ford's vocals, recorded on multiple tracks, had an artificial quality that no one had ever heard before. Plenty of musicians recognized the potential in the creative use of electronics.

Up to the mid-sixties, three-track recorders were in use, for example on Phil Spector's Wall of Sound productions or some of the early Motown hits – but once the concept broke ground it went further. From the four tracks on which *Sgt. Pepper's* was produced, for example, the development led via eight to sixteen tracks, doubling the width of the tape at every stage.[26]

Multitrack technology had a major influence on the development of pop music. Many people even regard the events of those years as an art form in their own right. In any case, this machine managed to trick time: a duplicated section of time ran clockwise from one reel to the other. Simultaneously or at any random moment, signals could be recorded on one or more tracks. If something worked well, you kept it, and if not, you had another try. To enable synchronous recording of even more tracks, you put up with a loss of sound quality and squeezed up to twenty-four tracks into the conventional two-inch tape width.

Because the sound of sixteen-track recordings was much better on two-inch tape, however, Ralf and Florian had decided on a sixteen-track machine when they bought their recording equipment. Fortunately, it was no problem to add a sixteen-track recording head to the MCI in the Rudas Studio. Mind you, we could only use fifteen tracks for instruments and vocals – one track was always reserved for the sync signal from the Synthanorma sequencer.

Joschko Rudas, the studio manager and sound engineer, was a funny fellow with long dark hair, who liked wearing snake-skin boots. He made his money out of productions for Düsseldorf's prospering advertising industry, which generated a constantly increasing turnover. That meant Joschko didn't rely on pop groups like us; he just enjoyed working with us. His studio could have been anywhere in the world: windowless recording and control rooms, the usual brown-beige wood-and-fabric soundproofing on the walls. Plus dimmable light, air conditioning, the equipment and a small lounge with a bowl of fruit.

Thanks to their long-term international record deal, Ralf and Florian were now in the top league of the music industry. Even then, certain status symbols were part of the business, for instance, mixing sessions in a prestigious studio like Record Plant in Los Angeles. Ralf and Florian chose a different route this time: their finishing touch was to fly in a renowned sound engineer to mix our album. The Detroit engineer Leonard Jackson from the disco label Whitfield Records arrived in snowy Düsseldorf during carnival week in early February.

Our arrangements started off fairly straightforward. We usually managed with the available fifteen tracks, only occasionally recording two different instruments or vocals on one track. At the mixing stage, the tracks on the multitrack tape were routed through the mixing desk's channel strips and mixed onto a stereo track. The first thing was to use a pan control to set the position for every track in the stereo spectrum. Underneath these dials were the faders, used to regulate the tracks' volume in relation to each other. Equalizers for filtering the frequencies were above them. Every channel strip also had other controls for adding signal effects like reverb and echo. In fact, though, the setting of the sound spectrum with an equalizer and the use of effect devices like echo, reverb and phasing had often already been part of the writing process in the Kling Klang Studio, and become an integral element of the composition.

The most important aspect of mixing pop music is to work out a song's 'storyboard', the narrative thread and dramatic structure running through the composition and to reproduce the various elements – rhythm group, melody instruments, sound effects, vocals – in audible quality, if necessary using the faders to adjust the volume of the various tracks during the mixing process. It's often the nuances that make a difference. Of course, there are plenty more factors to take care of – it's really a very complex procedure. But the details are hard to explain in theory. In any case, working in a recording studio in the seventies was a fascinating experience.

Compared to the dynamic mixing of our next album, for which three pairs of hands were at work on the mixing desk, the *Man-Machine* mix was relatively static. Things took off with 'Metropolis' though. While Joschko mixed the track onto the one-inch machine, I manually added a filter sweep for every beat of the snare drum.

A few guests also dropped in during the mixing sessions. Rupert Perry, the head of A&R at Capitol, had appointed a new man, John Dixon, as International Director of A&R. One of his jobs was checking on the 'European product' for the label and filtering it. So John Dixon turned up in the middle of carnival chaos in the Rudas Studio to check and filter. Wolfgang came along and Maxime Schmitt also came over from Paris for constructive support.

Alongside the mix, Ralf's vocal parts for 'Neon Lights' and 'The Model' were also recorded in German and English at the Rudas Studio. Incidentally, he sang the vocals in only one or two takes just before the mixdown.

The Rudas Studio had a reverb plate made of gold foil, which the signals were sent through. When we mixed 'Spacelab', Joschko had forgotten to switch on the reverb and he righted the situation after the speakers were turned on. Click! And that's why the song starts with that sound.

Ralf and Florian are credited as producers of the end product, with Leonard Jackson and Joschka Rudas mentioned in the credits as sound engineers and introduced under 'mixed by' in the English version. I sat in the control room, listened and added my opinions to the mix. And occasionally, when necessary, I lent a helping hand. By the time we'd finished mixing the album after eleven days in the Rudas Studio, I had clocked up a total of around 150 sessions for *The Man-Machine*.

On the morning of 17 February 1978, I wrote in my pocket diary: '*Man-Machine* finished – up working all night – breakfast in Café Bagel, Ralf taking master to courier.'

Artwork

For the artwork, Ralf and Florian followed Günter Fröhling's recommendation and signed up the film artist Karl Klefisch, who had specialized in animated films for fifteen years at UFA productions. When Ralf and I visited Klefisch in his home graphic design studio early in 1978, he showed us his draft for the front and back covers. At that time, graphics were done manually on a plotting board with foil, paper-cutters and glue. Graphic programs with an 'undo' option weren't even in the realm of our imagination.

The photographs shot in September 1977 were the basis of the cover artwork. I think Ralf chose the photo where we looked the best as a group. It wasn't important that I was at the front, although I do remember someone saying I looked kind of Russian. Perhaps that was partly due to my Mephisto haircut, done by our Düsseldorf hairdresser friend Teja. Keeping the crop in shape soon proved hard work, though, and I dropped the look. I don't think anyone had the direction in mind while we were shooting for the cover, but we are all looking east. Our bodies cut out against a red background – wearing red shirts, black ties and grey trousers – and the custom-made multilingual typography, meeting at right angles supported by parallel lines, all add up to an impression of a photo graphic in the tradition of 1920s and 1930s poster art.

On the back cover, Klefisch uses a clever trick for the typography. He sequences the word 'Machine' vertically, transferring – deliberately or unconsciously – our minimalism-influenced music into visual communication. Underneath the names of the six tracks and the credits is a section from a graphic taken from the 1922 children's book *About Two Squares: A Suprematist Tale of Two Squares in Six Constructions* by the Russian constructivist El Lissitzky. The artist once commented that it was a suggestion for a game for children, and for adults it was a play: 'The plot takes place on a film-like basis. The words move in the force fields of the acting characters: – squares.'[27]

The Cyrillic Я твой слуга, Я твой работник – 'I am your servant, I am your worker,' part of the lyrics from the track 'The Robots' – is printed beneath the sound engineers' credits, another direct reference to Soviet Russia.

On the record's inside sleeve, the four of us are posing on the front in our 'uniform' in Fröhling's stairwell. The stairs with their grey and red banisters and the shadows cast by our bodies lend the photo depth and space. There's a definite hint of the Bauhaus aesthetic.

As at the end of a film, the credits show who worked in what position on the album. Just like on the last album, the tracks and their authors are listed at the top. Below the photo, we see the personnel with their functions and the names of the two men in charge of conception and production, the studios and the sound engineers. The photographer and graphic designer are credited on the sides, as is the source of visual 'inspiration', El Lissitzky. On the back of the inner sleeve is the same photo of the four of us, only in a zoomed-in cut-out.

One might think the use of the photos of us living individuals was a mere stopgap solution; Heinrich Obermaier's showroom dummies weren't yet finished at that point.

Copyrights

Many years after its release, a journalist once asked me about my part in creating the song 'The Man-Machine'. 'Funky drum pattern' – he said, or something like that, nodding his recognition and drumming away at an imaginary kit. He clearly thought I was responsible for the beat. And it does indeed say 'Karl Bartos electronic percussion' on the album. My feel for rhythm is certainly not underdeveloped. At the same time, however, I never perceive rhythm separately from the other elements of music. It's not possible to separate the elements from one another – rhythm, melody, harmony, timbre, volume, tempo. So it will come as no surprise that I consider playing or programming percussion patterns an important contribution, but not my key role in Kraftwerk's music.

On closer inspection, the label 'electronic percussion' does denote a distinction from the record's musical content elements, but I never thought the credits were particularly important. I regarded the generalization of my various contributions as 'electronic percussion' as a fairly incidental matter. Seeing as my co-authorship was documented from *The Man-Machine* on, I didn't think much more about it. When I listen to the album today, I notice its clearly outlined structure. And that is precisely what I feel part-responsible for, for developing the musical elements into a well-rounded form.

Once the six tracks were produced, we had a straightforward conversation about how to divide up the rights to the compositions. This was a new situation for Ralf and Florian too – at least when it came to music. They had shared authorship for all the previous Kraftwerk records. Now I was also admitted into the circle of Kraftwerk authors, with credits for all six compositions.

Regarding the division of musical copyright, Florian made the decision that he wanted to be listed as co-author for 'The Robots', 'Metropolis' and 'Neon Lights' on this album. Ralf's name is listed as music and lyrics author for all tracks. On 'Metropolis' and 'Spacelab', he claimed the full right to the lyrics for naming the songs, even though the lyrics consisted only of a single word – the song title.

The Kling Klang publishing arm was not at all on my radar. At that point, I didn't know what a music publishing company is, what it does, what rights and obligations it has and what relationship it has to the authors. I relied entirely on Ralf and Florian's experience in the business. In the meantime, I had learned from them – the co-owners of Kraftwerk GbR – that GEMA is a German organization that represents the rights of composers, lyricists and music publishers, assesses them and calculates income due from those rights for its members. So in March 1978 I applied to join GEMA. Since then, my rights contract has featured the membership number 80852.

But there's another important organization for musicians in Germany: the Gesellschaft zur Verwertung von Leistungs-schutzrechten, or Collecting Society for Ancillary Rights. The GVL asserts the performing rights for practising artists, music-makers, video producers and filmmakers for all kinds of media. A musician friend advised me to register my freelance work for Kraftwerk with them.

As owners of their Kling Klang label and practising artists, Ralf and Florian already participated in the assertion of their rights by the GVL. When Wolfgang and I informed them we also intended to join the GVL, the mood became businesslike. Even though we didn't need their OK to join, the conversation turned tough. But after a few days, they agreed.

Premiere: The Robots on TV

Kraftwerk's last TV appearance in Germany was five years ago by now. Since then, the band's line-up had changed, as had its musical concept and the way it presented itself.

Just in time for the release of *The Man-Machine*, EMI Electrola had managed to acquire a slot on the relatively new TV show

Rockpop, on West Germany's second public channel. We were to perform our first single taken from the album, 'The Robots'. The people in charge had promised us a red backdrop and a complete blocking and camera rehearsal. We were also promised the very latest video effects, to make the performance a real mind-blower. There was no better way to promote a record in Germany at that time. Simultaneously, our performance on *Rockpop* was to be the premiere for Heinrich Obermaier's mannequins – now promoted to robot status.

On Monday, 20 March 1978, we set out for Munich with our four alter egos. That was the day I met Günter Spachtholz, who was transporting our duplicates. Günter was in his early 20s, cool and good-looking. And a very nice person. He did – and still does – various jobs for Kraftwerk. In another context, he would probably have been called our studio manager.

Our performance on the show was announced as follows: 'Back in a German TV studio for the first time in five years: Kraftwerk and 'Robots'. Hello – [shakes hands with Robot-Ralf] – I hope you're well. It's a little difficult to categorize these excellent gentlemen's music. Classical and rock elements definitely have an influence, but that doesn't fit the music a hundred percent. Perhaps we ought to say "science-fiction music" or even better: "electronic rock".'

Our set-up would in fact have fitted in very well in a 1960s or 1970s science-fiction film. The props department had gone to great lengths to erect metal scaffolding in front of a red background, casting a shadow that lent the scene a three-dimensional look. The element linking up with our live performances was the order – Ralf, Karl, Wolfgang, Florian from left to right – and the neon names in front of us. The new sci-fi aspect was manifested in the medium long shots of the real us, our robot replicas in close-ups, and our uniforms: red shirts, black ties, grey trousers.

We're standing behind our technical devices in the TV studio – the electronic drum kit, Florian's electro-flute and the synthesizers, which looked more like science fiction than traditional musical instruments even in close-ups – moving mechanically to the playback, although for viewers in 1978, it didn't necessarily sound like that. Electronic music was far from an everyday occurrence on television. Ralf couldn't bring himself to leave the vocals to Florian alone, so the camera shows either Ralf or Florian sideways on in close-up, lip-syncing to the vocoder voice on the record. There are also close-ups of 'Herr Karl', with digital numbers on his forehead, and Wolfgang's robot. At the line 'Ya tvoi sluga, ya tvoi rabotnik', the TV technicians managed to 'morph' Ralf's real lip movements into the plastic head of Ralf's robot using a video effect. I was pretty impressed. The height of video technology, though, is our dance moves in medium long shot in front of a projection of the Lissitzky building blocks.

A series of close-ups and part-shots of the humans and the robots, video reflections and above all close-ups of Ralf and Florian turning sideways out of shot to reveal the face of their respective robot create a sense that man and machine are interchangeable. The mannequins' modelled hair clearly marks them out as plastic dummies, but the striking similarity has an astonishing effect. The film ends after 4 minutes and 30 seconds with the words 'Wir sind die Roboter' gradually filling the screen multiple times over.

This now-legendary TV appearance was very well received by the viewers. In the seventies, people still believed in progress.

Our performance and the modern-sounding music tapped into the zeitgeist. A lot of people told me they bought the record directly after the show. Another reason for the success is no doubt also the consistency between our music and its visual presentation. Aside from that – and this is my firm conviction – our man–machine balance was still at the right level.

Le Ciel de Paris

The second promotional date in our calendar was in America. Ralf and Florian set out for New York again to present the album *The Man-Machine* at a release party organized by Capitol on 6 April 1978. In retrospect, the timing wasn't ideal. The whole of America was in the throes of a mass *Saturday Night Fever*. The Bee Gees' soundtrack to the John Travolta movie outshone everything else. It was also the last Kraftwerk album with Capitol in America; perhaps the record company wasn't all that interested in the product at that point. Ralf and Florian didn't stay in the States for long. Interestingly enough, *Der Spiegel* featured a rather impressive robot on its cover on the day of their return, throwing a motionless construction worker in the trash with its metal arm. 'The unmanned factory – happiness for everyone', the text quotes a Japanese advert.[28] Not much later, we boarded a plane to Paris.

Terminal 1 of Charles de Gaulle Airport resembles a giant concrete flying saucer, with a central round opening in the middle – like in a vinyl record – through which a number of Plexiglas and metal transport tubes link various storeys of the saucer. The electronic sounds coming over the loudspeakers to herald announcements reminded me of the soundtrack to *Forbidden Planet*. The airport was like a perfect science-fiction backdrop to our arrival. How fitting.

For the release of *Trans-Europe Express* in France a year before, Maxime had come up with the legendary champagne-fuelled press trip by train to Reims, helping the album to hit the media with a splash and sell 350,000 copies. The location of the release party for *The Man-Machine* was no less sensational. The invitation, as red as our album cover, had gone out to the most important media people in France and the UK. And it promised unusual experiences: 'Soirée Rouge Invitation 2 Personnes, Ligne Generale, Vodka, Cinema, Caviar – Tour de Montparnasse 56th Floor.' An offer no journalist could refuse. Anybody who wasn't there wasn't anybody. People still talk about the event to this day; it has become a legend, at least in France.

There was no building more futuristic in all of Paris at the time, not even the Eiffel Tower. The Tour Montparnasse shoots up into the sky like a mushroom of glass and metal, emerging from between the old residential buildings above the Métro station of the same name. It was the highest building in France until 2011. The state-of-the-art elevator – the fastest in Europe in its time – takes only 38 seconds to reach the penthouse club, Le Ciel de Paris (The Sky of Paris) on the 56th floor. The lift felt hermetically sealed, almost like a space capsule shooting soundlessly up. It was a place of superlatives.

When the four of us arrived at the penthouse at around 9:30 in the evening of 13 April 1978, the lift doors opened with a slight hum. We exchanged brief glances and then walked out of the capsule. Maxime showed us around the absolutely packed club. The first thing I noticed up there was the sound of our album and dozens of red spotlights, moving in time with our music and beaming their light around the room. The music was loud – small talk was difficult. Wherever I looked, one of the red spotlights shone right in my eyes.

We continued towards the home-cinema screen at the back end of the club, where a film projector was showing *Metropolis*. The transformation of the protagonist Maria into the robot, with magical energy rings running around her body like laser beams, was a visual sensation and clearly showed the album's context. That evening – fifty years after the film's Berlin premiere – the six tracks of our new album became the soundtrack to the legendary silent movie: 'The Robots', 'Spacelab', 'Metropolis', 'The Model', 'Neon Lights' and 'The Man-Machine'. From time to time, a video installation showed a recording of our performance on *Rockpop*. The video's impressive contrast of mannequins and men was a perfect match for the evening.

In fact, we saw ourselves only as visitors to this *soirée rouge*. The real attraction was on the stage right next to the screen. Dressed in red shirts, dark trousers and black ties, our showroom dummies – sorry, robots – stood by their instruments, fronted by our neon names as usual. The plastic performers looked uncannily like us.

The guests at the *soirée rouge* were the usual mix at press events around the world: media people, record company people and hardcore blaggers. They wore mainly black, the men sporting intellectual glasses and the women bright-red lipstick. Some of them posed in the fashionable punk look, and of course there were plenty of Kraftwerk clones walking around in red shirts and black ties. They stood there like at a cocktail party, glass in one hand, obligatory Gauloise in the other, a few of them dancing.

The journalists, already in a good mood thanks to the vodka and caviar, left us to our own devices. After a while someone handed us a glass of champagne. We simply stood around and got stared at. That evening, we were wearing black shirts and trousers, red ties and black V-necks, in contrast to our doppel-gängers. When we got to the stage we posed in front of the robo-band with Maxime and Rupert Perry from Capitol Records.

As the vodka ran out, the evening lost its dynamic. After the end of *Metropolis*, the operator continued the movie programme with a Russian silent film and things gradually came to a stand-still, so we left the Sky of Paris with Maxime. In the reports later on, we read about the Germans who didn't even say hello. Others were disappointed that we really had appeared in person, commenting laconically that a purely artificial presentation – dummies, film, tape – would have worked better with the futuristic concept. As I later found out, our mannequins were treated rather disrespectfully after we left. Ralf's doppelgänger was left with his flies undone, and Florian's double somehow dropped his trousers to his ankles. The salon punks had exacted their merciless revenge. Florian was upset. Ralf was uptight, like always.

We rounded off the evening in the Brasserie La Coupole again. By the time we boarded the plane back to Düsseldorf on Friday, we knew the visit to Paris had been a complete success. The robots, ex-showroom dummies, lifted us to a new level – and we were sure to go even further.

The Man-Machine in the UK

The British print media reacted mainly positively to us and the new album. *Sounds* magazine ran a snappy 'travel report' on our *soirée rouge* titled 'We ARE Showroom Dummies'. And the influential music journalist Jon Savage reviewed *The Man-Machine*: 'So – funsters – der *zher* fab Ubermensch extend the humanoid boogie in what is probably the most completely, clearly realised conception, packaging and presentation of a particular mood since the first Ramones album. [. . .] This is fine as an antidote, not as a diet. The conception, production, technique and execution are all impeccable and near brilliant.'[29]

NME ran the cover headline 'Kraftwerk the Music Machine'. Alongside a report on the release party, there was a lengthy album review, referring to our work as an 'extraordinary unification of science and art, turning on its head the commonly accepted Kantian split between the classical and the romantic [. . .]. This is a bitch of a dance record; but its complexity of construction [. . .] makes it just as enjoyable for those with broken legs.'[30]

The Cultural Channel

By the spring of 1978, our circle had established a certain lifestyle alongside our work at the Kling Klang Studio. We would meet early in the evening to see and be seen at Café Bagel, go to a gig together and then go out to eat. In those days, we watched acts as varied as Tangerine Dream, the Commodores,

Jonathan Richman, Patti Smith and the Ondekoza Drummers from Japan. We would often round off the night in a disco. They were untroubled times.

After *Autobahn*, *Radio-Activity* and *Trans-Europe Express*, our group was working well, the 'man-machine' was running smoothly. Ralf and Florian got on well and formed the writing team along with Emil and my humble self. Wolfgang was involved in developing the hardware for the electronic drum kits and other devices and in presenting the band outwardly: concerts, covers, films, production. For me, it was important to be part of a group with its own identity and to be able to contribute my musical ideas. The international attention lavished on Kraftwerk had a powerful pull on me, intensifying my enthusiasm even more.

My income from my work in Kraftwerk at that time was less than what I'd been earning before with my many different jobs. But I had no obligations to weigh me down. Our tours, record productions, film shoots, the communication with all the details of the time we spent together, the holidays in Saint-Tropez and also the first-rate fun of sharing a flat with Wolfgang and Emil – the life I was leading was absolutely engrossing. Our artistic group appeared to switch effortlessly between high culture and pop. In that atmosphere of open exchange of ideas, perceived sympathy and not least of trust, a dynamic came about in which creativity developed. I saw our community as a medium, a cultural channel, a band for which it was worth composing. Without question, the sound of our music opened up a central perspective for my future.

There was something else that I didn't want to go on with, however. At the end of the 1978 winter semester, I deregistered from university. I lacked the mental space and energy to practise a musical programme designed to prove my virtuosity in a concert examination. It bored me to death. Composing music a grown more important to me than interpreting other composers' music.

Perhaps it would have made sense for promotional purposes to do some live shows after the album release. We did talk about it several times. I came up with a concept inspired by Erwin Piscator's Simultaneous Theater. We looked at metal scaffolding and wanted to slide down from bars, like the firefighters in François Truffaut's *Fahrenheit 451*. In my opinion a tour with the red shirts and a Bauhaus-Piscator stage would have been fantastic. But for the time being, Ralf and Florian just didn't want to go on tour, sadly, and so we arranged to meet up from 22 June 1978 for our first writing session after 'The Man-Machine'. It might have been a capital mistake that we didn't go on with that. The red shirts-robots aesthetics was given away, thrown away and it got absorbed by 'Computer World'.

Filming the Robots and Neon Lights

In June, *The Man-Machine* climbed to number 53 on the British album charts. Almost three months after the release, Ralf and Florian decided to make two more promotional films for 'The Robots' and 'Neon Lights'. On 1 July, a Monday, we met up with Günter Fröhling in the Kling Klang Studio for the first shoot for 'The Robots'. Like a respectable German promo video, the clip starts with the single's cover and the rhythmized Lissitzky drawing to the robot sounds at the beginning of the song. We used our performance on *Rockpop* in March as a rough storyboard model for the video. Yet the shoot in the Kling Klang didn't use an artificial backdrop; we were in our workplace. We handled our means of production accordingly, Wolfgang inserting a patch cable to the plugboard, me moving a group fader on the mixer, Florian starting the tape machine and Ralf playing around with the input desk.

We slotted the filming for 'Neon Lights' into a Tuesday evening on the roof terrace of Florian's penthouse in Golzheim. Our faces were made up in white, lit up and shot against the contrasting night sky. While Frau Hartkopf was powdering us once again, we took a few photos with Florian's Polaroid camera. It was a warm summer night and we could see the bridges across the Rhine and the illuminated city from Florian's terrace – a view that's hard to top. Günter Fröhling filmed footage of Düsseldorf neon ads to impose over our faces as a second layer. The illuminated words '4711', 'Klosterfrau', 'UFA Universum', 'Optik Ziem', 'Restaurant Stockheim', 'Park Hotel' were familiar to everyone in the city at the time. The same goes for the dancer in the red-light district. As you might imagine, the UFA logo is a reference to the 1920s film industry. And of course Mercedes Benz and Deutsche Bank had to be in the mix as well.

I have no idea whether and if so, when, the film was broadcast. The single 'Neon Lights' got to number 53 in the British charts on 28 October 1978, then disappeared without a trace after three weeks . . .

Hit Parade

That August, Florian invited us to La Bastide Blanche again. We spent the next few days listening to music non-stop. I remember the debut album *Suicide* by the New York band of the same name, 'Rock Lobster' by the B-52's, the Modern Lovers' 'Pablo Picasso', Greta Keller's 'Eine blaue Stunde' – and a whole lot of Isley Brothers.

I couldn't say how many times I listened to the first Suicide LP. Somehow, the New York duo seemed to be related to us, a few times removed. Their music wasn't comparable to what came out of our workshop and they came across as wild and expressionist, but I felt an instant rapport with their music. I liked the combination of Alan Vega's voice and electronics. The keyboarder Martin Rev seemed like an uncontrolled mutation of a 'solo entertainer' playing organ and rhythm machines at tea dances. The album stayed by my side for some time, and I got hold of everything they released for a while. Rev's fragmented melodies really appealed to me. He doesn't vary his motifs, or not noticeably; he repeats them. And then comes the next one.

Barely had we got home than we watched the *ZDF-Hitparade* presenter Dieter Thomas Heck playing 'The Robots' on 21 August 1978. It can't have been easy for Heck, who was a genuine fan of schmaltzy German *schlager* music, but the single was in the Top Ten so he had to play it. As you can probably imagine, Ralf and Florian had turned down an invitation to appear on the show, so Heck simply held the album cover up to the camera while the song was played. I would never have

300

envisaged being on *Hitparade* – one of Germany's most successful TV formats with an average of 27 million viewers. The show stuck close to the hideous formulaic German pop that ruled the charts in those days, with a promotional song for the Smurfs at number 1 when 'The Robots' was first played. Merciless competition, but our single remained on the show until December. EMI Electrola's German promotion for *The Man-Machine* couldn't have been better. Our robot performance on *Rockpop* and the plays on *Hitparade* helped us to reach a large audience. The album got to number 12 in September and stayed in the charts for eight weeks. In France, the LP reached number 14, and in the UK it got to number 53 in May, although it re-entered the chart in 1982, about which more later. In the USA, the highest the album climbed was 130.

Reports in the German print media were few and far between but at least mainly positive. The robot image seemed to be great journalist fodder, with frequent references to *Star Wars* as well. German *Sounds* called the album 'R2-D2's favourite record' and identified 'The Robots' as its best song and an 'electronic earworm', while dismissing 'The Model' as a flimsy 'disco tune'.[31] In the very popular teen magazine *Bravo*, Ralf marked out a few cornerstones of the Kraftwerk image and commented on the mannequins and the role of musicians as 'scientists': 'We humans are completely unimportant, interchangeable. That's what we want to demonstrate with our dummies. [. . .] We say what's interesting about us through our music. We don't consider ourselves rock stars just because we sell a lot of records. We're scientists. We experiment with our machines every day. We research and then we deliver the results – music.'[32]

Paris – Rome – Venice

In mid-September, Maxime got us a slot on a French TV show, so we went to Paris for another weekend to record 'Radioactivity' and 'The Robots' in an empty theatre. After the shoot, we spent the day in the city together: staying at the Royal Monceau, strolling along the Champs-Élysées, dining in the Brasserie La Coupole, dancing in the hip nightclubs Le Palace and Les Bains Douches.

The promotional activities for *The Man-Machine* also took us to Italy. EMI Italiana acquired interviews and TV appearances in Rome and offered a chance to take part in the live show 'Club Lido' from the Palazzo del Cinema in Venice, alongside many well-known artists. The line-up was a wild mix of international acts like Julio Iglesias, Ian Dury and the fantastic Average White Band with their megahit 'Pick up the Pieces'. We had brought along our mini-set again, consisting of instruments, studio machines and neon names.

After the show, everyone met up in the Grand Hotel's basement discotheque. We partied until dawn, keeping the barkeepers very busy. The Bellinis flowed like water, the fruity mix of champagne and puréed peach getting most of us drunk at the drop of a hat. Ian Dury turned up late, headed straight for the bar and downed a few Scotches. He recognized Wolfgang and I saw them start dancing together. All of a sudden, Ian Dury stood on Wolfgang's feet like a puppet, gripped him firmly and let Wolfgang do the dancing. Last but not least, the gentlemen from the Average White Band put in an appearance on the dancefloor with unscrewed toilet seats around their necks. Not bad.

The rest of the night is lost in the mists of time, or perhaps in the infinity of Bellinis. Next morning, I found myself on a taxi boat to the airport with the others, not having got a wink of sleep, and was surprised to note I had a terrible headache. I also felt sick, not helped by the waves in the lagoon. Ralf was the same as ever. At that moment, I envied him for never losing control – but only at that moment. From a safe distance, what I say now is: what a night, what incredible fun! How dull and boring my memories would be without moments like this.

NOTES

1. In an intertitle (01:18:45), Rotwang says: 'Come! It is time to give the Machine-Man your face!'
2. *Zum Beispiel Fritz Lang.* Bayerischer Rundfunk documentary, 1968. (Film interview with Erwin Leiser)
3. Lotte H. Eisner: *Die dämonische Leinwand.* Fischer: Frankfurt a. M. 1955, p. 127
4. Luis Buñuel: *An Unspeakable Betrayal: Selected Writings of Luis Buñuel.* University of California Press, 2002. Translated from the Spanish and French by Garrett White, p. 99
5. Lotte H. Eisner: *Die dämonische Leinwand.* Fischer: Frankfurt a. M. 1955, p. 228
6. 'Germany's music machines march on.' *Future Magazine*, No. 5, October 1978
7. 'Kraftwerk in den USA – Die deutschen Tonroboter?' By Hans Pfitzinger, *Sounds* No. 6/1975 (including a quote from the *San Francisco Examiner*, 'The German Sound Robots')
8. 'robot-like detachment', cf. 'Bionic Teutonics'. By Dave Fudger, *Sounds*, 16 October 1976
9. Album review by Jürgen Frey, *Sounds*, No. 5/1975
10. The word 'robot' makes its first appearance in the play R.U.R. *(Rossums Universal Robots)* by the Czech writer Karel Čapek in 1921.

11. Michael J. Neufeld: *Wernher von Braun. Visionär des Weltraums – Ingenieur des Krieges.* Siedler Verlag, 2009
12. Jens-Christian Wagner: *Produktion des Todes: Das KZ Mittelbau-Dora,* ed. Stiftung Gedenkstätten Buchenwald und Mittelbau-Dora, Göttingen 2001 – https://www.buchenwald.de/320/
13. 'Kraftwerk: Deutsche Disko.' By Glenn O'Brien, *Interview,* 1977
14. 'Kraftwerk Story . . . Disco discovers Kraftwerk!' Ad in *Billboard,* 22 October 1977
15. 'Der Synthanorma SQ 312'. By Manfred Mirsch, *Keyboards,* No. 10/2004
16. 'New Musick – The Cold Wave'. By Hal Synthetic, *Sounds,* 26 November 1977
17. Ralf Hütter, ibid.
18. Ralf Hütter, ibid.
19. 'Better living through chemistry'. By Toby Goldstein, *New Musical Express,* 24 December 1977
20. René Descartes: *Traité de l'homme (Treatise of Man),* 1662
21. Gottfried Wilhelm Leibniz: *Monadologie und andere metaphysische Schriften* (1714). Meiner, Hamburg 2002
22. Julien Offray de La Mettrie: *L'Homme Machine (Man a Machine).* French/ German edition, Reclam: Stuttgart 2015
23. Quote from the Singularity University in: *Welt ohne Menschen,* film by Philippe Borrel, Arte.tv/welt-ohne-menschen, 2012
24. Filippo Tommaso Marinetti: 'Die futuristische Literatur. Technisches Manifest'. In: *Der Sturm 3* (1912/13), No. 33, October 1912, pp. 194–195
25. Quoted from Hansgeorg Schmidt-Bergmann: *Futurismus. Geschichte, Ästhetik, Dokumente.* Rowohlt: Reinbek bei Hamburg 1993 (Filippo Tommaso Marinetti: 'L'uomo moltiplicato e il Regno della macchina', 1914. From the collection *Guerra solo igiene del mondo.* In: idem: *Teoria e invenzione futurista,* p. 298)
26. 1/4-inch = 2, 1/2-inch = 4, 1-inch = 8, 2-inch = 16 and 24 tracks
27. Quoted from Sophie Lissitzky-Küppers: *El Lissitzky – Maler Architekt Typograf Fotograf.* VEB Verlag der Kunst: Dresden 1967, pp. 80–91
28. *Der Spiegel:* 'Fortschritt macht arbeitslos. Die Computer-Revolution', issue 16/1978, 17 April 1978
29. 'Kraftwerk: The Man-Machine'. Review by Jon Savage, *Sounds,* 29 April 1978
30. 'Kraftwerk: Mind Machine Music'. By Andy Gill, *New Musical Express,* 29 April 1978, pp. 39–41

31. 'Kraftwerk: Die Mensch-Maschine'. Review by Ingeborg Schober, *Sounds*, May 1978, p. 50
32. 'Plastik-Menschen vertreten die echten Musiker: Bei KRAFTWERK rocken die Roboter'. *Bravo*, No. 36/1978, 4 September 1978

10

COMPUTER WORLD

Conversations. Kling Klang Writing Sessions 1978–80. Changes. The Cycling Group. Designing the Control Centre. Teaching at the Music School. EDP Workplaces. Rheingold. Electronic Every Day. Drum Machines. The Flying Living Room. The Triggersumme. The Kling Klang Recordings of 1980. Computer World (Song). Computer Love. Pocket Calculator. Home Computer. It's More Fun to Compute. Numbers. Computer World 2. Mix with Six Ears and Six Hands. Artwork. Reflection.

Conversations

The turn of the year from 1978 to 1979 went almost unnoticed. Alongside our promotion activities, we started meeting up at the studio regularly after our stay in Saint-Tropez in August 1978. Saturdays were usually our day off but we would get together for a few hours on Sunday evenings before diving head first into Düsseldorf's nightlife at Malesh on Königsallee. We used to go out to eat together a lot at that time, sometimes before our sessions, sometimes after working for two or three hours. We usually went to an Italian place. Our dinners together became a ritual.

If we disregard social backgrounds, we humans have very similar basic needs. Like in any other company where colleagues meet up every day, one of the things we talked about was our private lives. But our over-dinner conversations covered a wide range of subjects, which made them all the more stimulating.

Alongside debates in the newspapers and magazines, we would often talk about interior design and furniture, for example. Our girlfriends were another never-ending topic of conversation, of course. Ralf's girlfriend had just started an apprenticeship, Bettina had enrolled at university – we talked about that kind of thing.

Occasionally, Wolfgang would come to the studio and we'd have a jam session. There were always plenty of laughs when we sat down together afterwards. And although I personally think cars are a really boring subject, I loved the atmosphere so much I was happy to put up with the other three's endless waffle about their latest motors. We were so wonderfully carefree in those moments.

Florian's taste for unusual clothes occasionally prompted rambling discussions on style, whether he turned up in a Klepper raincoat, wore a strange suit, brought along a new flat cap or joyfully regaled us with tales of tracking down the last pair of winkle-pickers in a long-forgotten shoe shop.

Like workmates the world over, we talked about our health problems, such as an upcoming dentist's appointment, new contact lenses or a long-ago slipped disc on the part of poor Wolfgang, which always made me laugh despite how bad it had originally been, because he could only walk leaning forwards.

We would often play at film critics, praising or damning recent movie releases. A small selection? *Close Encounters of the Third Kind*, *Nosferatu the Vampyre*, *Manhattan*, *The Marriage of Maria*

Braun, Apocalypse Now, The Shining, The Blues Brothers, Cruising and *The Fog*. I remember there were 3D nights at Düsseldorf cinemas, which we went along to. Ralf had been into 3D technology for a while. He was particularly taken by the 'ghost train effect' – that moment of shock when a random object suddenly popped up in the middle of the auditorium. We would often meet up with our girlfriends at the weekend and all go to the cinema together, followed by ice-cream parlours with the inescapable 'Coupe Megalo' sundae.

At the same time – and we were always aware of it – we were the band Kraftwerk. And of course, we chatted about new songs in the charts or bizarre stuff, strange music, unknown sounds that had come onto our radar and might be worth a closer listen. Yes, we did talk a lot about music.

Kling Klang Writing Sessions 1978–80

Looking back, the culture of our writing sessions feels to me like the most valuable thing we achieved during my time in Kraftwerk. Essentially, our collaboration was a permanent conversation, translating our thoughts into the sounds of our music.

My notebook was usually open somewhere in the studio, and I kept a record of our work in a kind of shorthand. Over time, Ralf also wrote a few fun notes and working titles in the book. Even a few first drafts for his lyrics ended up in there. Putting ideas down in writing was absolutely normal at that time. This productive phase of almost four hundred Kling Klang sessions lasted from June 1978 up to the mixing of *Computer World* in

March 1981. We taped many of our sessions. While we were at it, we also added to our machine park. Florian bought himself the polyphonic synthesizer Prophet-5 from Sequential Circuits, and I got myself a polyphonic Korg PS-3100 synthesizer, for which Wolfgang built an additional set of keys I could play using mallets, like a vibraphone.

We didn't pursue a particular concept, didn't have a plan or a goal other than inventing music we might be able to use for our next album. During that time, we came up with a lot of motifs for the songs on *Computer World*, but also for tracks that came out later on *Electric Cafe/Techno Pop*. My sequence with the working title 'The World of Work' became the basis for 'Home Computer'. The 'Megalo' subject turned into a verse for 'Computer World'. Other tracks, for example, were called 'Technicolor' (later renamed 'Tour de France') and – believe it or not – 'Trinidad'. A drum pattern I played, over which Ralf added his E minor motif from 'Computer World', was given the working title 'Dom' – meaning cathedral – and eventually became known under the name of 'Numbers'. What was the story?

One afternoon in 1978, we met up at Café Bagel on Ratinger Strasse. After our usual coffee and banter, we drove to the studio on fine form. Ralf went straight to his Polymoog, I headed to the drums and we both started up. Florian had the presence of mind to tape us. This is how it was: for years, I'd had a mild obsession with one of my sister's 7-inch singles – 'Do You Wanna Dance' by Cliff Richard and the Shadows, from 1962. It's a great song by Bobby Freeman (1958), covered countless times by bands like the Beach Boys, John Lennon, T. Rex and the Ramones. The thing that fascinated me about the recording, even as a teenager, was Brian Bennett's four-bar drum intro. What stuck in my mind, though, wasn't an acoustic photo of those beats. It was the impression, the mood they triggered in me. That meant my subconscious didn't create a copy, but a new pattern. The result turned out rather funky and felt good to play. I have the feeling the advent of sampling has made us largely forget exactly this kind of process.

This is just a small selection, of course, of more than fifty recordings from our sessions. Admittedly, the technical quality isn't particularly good, and the music too – played by hand apart from the drums and sequencers – occasionally contains a few inadvertent wrong notes, but these tapes remind me once again of music's astounding ability to preserve time. When I listen to them, I am re-immersed in the atmosphere of the Kling Klang Studio and feel the sheer joy we got out of playing. And although I've listened to a great deal of music over the years, I find it difficult to place ours in any specific context. Only now am I gradually realizing how valuable those hours of making music together really were. Our improvisations, in which we created polyphonic music in the moment, the act of composing as a group, the invention of these countless musical *tableaux vivants* . . .

Changes

That spring of 1979, Florian started turning up at the studio on a shiny chrome racing bike. It looked incredibly cool. It was very delicate, extremely light, and almost reminded me of the body of a dragonfly. Florian explained that the hairdresser Teja – who cut all our hair and had a group photo of us by J. Stara of Paris hanging in his salon on Stresemannstrasse – rode a racing bike. Florian thought it was great and bought one for himself. Teja was the first racing bike owner in the Kraftwerk cosmos, and Florian was the second. Then on 21 April, I got myself my first racing bike from Willi Müller's cycle shop: a Koga Miyata for 875 Deutschmarks. That was a lot of money for a bike at that time!

Ralf couldn't resist the hype either, and bought himself a Koga Miyata as well. Even Emil suddenly got hold of a racing bike from somewhere or other. We cycled the first short stretches together. In the early phase of our cycling enthusiasm, everything was easy and our new pastime felt like a bonding activity. Ralf was especially enthusiastic about cycle racing. By mid-June, he had read all about it and started training for races. He and I went to the shop run by the ex-professional racer and Tour de France stage winner Rolf Wolfshohl in Cologne, to buy tyres and sprockets. But it wasn't long before the Koga Miyata was not enough for Ralf, and he switched to a super-light professional racing bike.

By this point, I had been sharing a flat with Wolfgang and Emil for three years. Group days out with our girlfriends to the Grafenberg Forest or the nearby Eifel region had brought us closer together, making us feel almost like a family. We talked and laughed a lot; I felt very comfortable around them. And our concert tours meant we also had a shared history.

But I'd been with Bettina for a while, and when she came over I'd rather have lived alone than in a flatshare. To cut it short: I wanted to be independent again and not constantly available for the others. It wasn't hard to find a place to live in Düsseldorf at that time. And only a little later – on 1 June 1979 – I moved into an apartment in Niederkassel, very close to the Theodor

Heuss Bridge. Sadly, I couldn't take my piano with me and had to sell it. The location wasn't bad, the building rather anonymous, perhaps, but I knew my new place wouldn't be a long-term solution. A birch tree grew outside my window on the second floor and I parked my red VW Beetle on the street, a bargain buy thanks to Peter Bollig.

At the end of July, we lads went back to La Bastide Blanche in Saint-Tropez for another two weeks, this time with our racing bikes. I'd rather not think back to our breakneck tours on the narrow roads. Apart from the four usual suspects, Emil and Günter Spachtholz came along too, as did Volker Albus, a former fellow student of Ralf's from the RWTH[1] Aachen.

I think it was this trip where I experienced the incredible effect of the wine the Schneider-Esleben family produced there. I remember losing my bearings in our chalet, in a rather altered state due to a dinner served with La Croix Cru Classé, and ending up in Ralf's room. He wasn't particularly shocked, staying calm and directing me to my own bed. On one of those laid-back days, Volker made lobster and we discussed the ethics of eating animals, at Emil's prompting. Several of us went vegetarian after the trip. I went entirely without meat for the next five years.

We celebrated vegetarianism exhaustively. We read cook-books, looked into organic farming and anthroposophical ideas, frequented rather unusual culinary establishments. I'll never forget the way Wolfgang's face dropped when we recommended a spacy Cologne restaurant, a mixture of a sanatorium, youth hostel and sect headquarters. Our advice was to treat himself to their steamed fennel with béchamel sauce and a glass of mineral water from the Fachinger healing spring – which he presumably thought was totally crazy.

The Cycling Group

After that holiday, a new era began in many ways. Ralf and Florian set up what they called the 'cycling group' – some people called it the 'cycling group north' or came up with other, much more curious names. Florian got hold of a windowless room in an underground garage, where racing bikes were soon hanging from the ceiling on chains, to enable maintenance at eye-level. He put a few benches in too, the kind you see in the changing rooms of sports halls or swimming pools. We would meet there to go cycling together. The newly opened Galaxy ice-cream parlour on the opposite side of the Rhine became a popular stopping point for Ralf and Florian and a few other cycling enthusiasts. My flat in Niederkassel was only a few minutes away, so I popped into Galaxy now and then as well. It was a good starting point for short tours through the typical Lower Rhine countryside.

Our cycling trips were most enjoyable for me when Emil was still coming along. When he was there, everything was more poetic, more relaxed, and our conversations covered more than just professional cycling techniques. Racing bikes were fun for me but I had no ambition to become a better cyclist, practise round pedalling or study the ideal gear ratio for each terrain type. A few lads from Düsseldorf soon joined Ralf's cycling group. I would go along on a tour across the fields now and then in the early days – about sixty kilometres, perhaps. But their plans quickly became too ambitious for me, and too highly charged with cycling ideology.

I preferred to cycle on my own. Wolfgang was the only one of us who never became a convinced cyclist. But there was no pressure on us to be part of the cycling group. For the time being, it remained a side project. Our centre and headquarters at the time were firmly rooted in the Kling Klang Studio.

Designing the Control Centre

The sessions were going really well. We were looking ahead. The last mix at the Rudas Studio had been great, absolutely, but we were determined to mix our next record in the Kling Klang Studio. In the large room, originally sixty square metres, the equipment was set up like on stage. That was how we practised for gigs, like all bands since time immemorial. The concept had proved itself for our recordings as well.

But how should we go on now? Ralf and Florian were used to thinking like entrepreneurs and making their decisions in that spirit. Their strategy was to invest in state-of-the-art machines so as to use sounds that weren't clichéd in their productions. They followed the paradigm: 'With better machines, you will be able to do better work.'[2] That included going to quite some lengths over the years for the development of new instruments and software, all the way to registering patents – electronic drum kit, electronic flute, speech synthesis. The two of them thought on a grander scale than others, in many ways, and decided to invest in a mobile studio, rather like Conny Plank had. The difference, of course, was that the Kling Klang Studio only had one client. The core of the idea was that this mobile studio would also enable us to put on live performances at any time.

The scientist image Ralf built up rhetorically in interviews set the direction, and not much later the first Knürr brochures

314

turned up in the studio. To this day, the company builds basic furniture units for technical labs, control rooms, electronic work-places and so on. The laboratory atmosphere of the mobile studio would carry over to our new live show. But the requirements for our four workplaces were clearly very specific, and the indus-trially made Knürr technical furniture wasn't suitable. And so it was down to Wolfgang again, in August 1979.

Wolfgang Flür: 'Sure, the Knürr work desks gave us the first inspiration for the system's design. We basically took on their slanted ergonomic user surface with 16 height units in a 19-inch format. That was what all the other measure-ments were based on, if we wanted to operate the devices standing up.

Over the next few months, I used the workshop in the basement at Berger Allee to construct the hardware. First, I glued the plywood boxes together and painted them grey. Then I mounted specially made aluminium swivel lamps, which lit up the devices from above. All the lab desks rested on wheeled metal frames. The four of us would stand behind the desks at instrument boards. Every keyboard was cabled up to the electronics behind us. The cables ran through a low platform, on which we could move left to right across the whole stage. I also integrated pedals into the platform to adjust the volume. Then there was an acoustic monitor system for the stage, and I now overhauled the neon light system, which I'd built some time earlier.'

The studio reconstruction would take a while. That meant we had to interrupt our writing sessions, because working in parallel didn't fit with Ralf and Florian's modus operandi. Where else could we have gone? So it was all about the studio rebuild for the time being, a project to which all involved devoted themselves with enthusiasm. I couldn't do much myself, sadly. Music aside, I have to admit I'm not great with my hands. Wolfgang and the others had much more to offer on the construction site.

To be honest, I didn't know exactly how things would go from there. I didn't have much going on at the time, apart from cycling tours, my couple of private students and occasional night-time studio visits, in the hope of running into the lads and going to a disco with them. Well, sometimes I did have things to do. Something other than music had become very important in my life: being with Bettina. We would drive my red VW Beetle to Domberg on the North Sea coast of Holland for a few days of seaside walks, gazing out at the horizon, forgetting all about vegetarianism and enjoying 'schol met frieten' – plaice and chips – in the evenings.

When it came to Kraftwerk, I was certain everything was on the right track to take us into an exciting future. After all, we had come up with plenty of new material in our writing sessions. And yet I didn't want to be on permanent standby mode. I wanted to do something useful.

Teaching at the Music School

Ernst Göbler hadn't got me any more jobs at the opera since I'd left university. It was like when a capo leaves the family in the mafia. Admittedly, I didn't end up at the bottom of the Rhine with cement shoes, and no one sent Bettina a fish wrapped in newspaper. But of course, I accepted that my teacher and mentor didn't understand my decision to work on electronic music with Kraftwerk. I think he was disappointed in me. I'm still grateful to him for his unprecedented support, though. Classical music meant a great deal to me, but at the time I really couldn't imagine a career in an orchestra any more. Equally, I didn't consider working in another classical context, an ensemble, for instance. My work at the Kling Klang Studio was more important to me.

As a student, I'd given drumming lessons. Almost all my university classmates taught; it was part of the system somehow. Now, in autumn 1979, I had the idea of applying to a municipal music school for a part-time job as a music teacher, as my advanced performer's degree qualified me to teach. The symphony orchestra percussionists taught at the Clara Schumann Music School in Düsseldorf, so I tried other nearby schools. I got plenty of positive responses to my applications and decided to teach two afternoons a week.

In Meerbusch, the lessons took place in the unspectacular setting of a normal high school. In contrast, the Krefeld municipal music school is based in Haus Sollbrüggen, an impressive stately home set in huge grounds in the style of an English landscape garden. The percussion room was housed outside the main building, in a pavilion. The windows granted a view of lawns, bushes and beautiful old trees. That was where I gave my lessons. On the snare drum, I ventured an experiment by getting my students to keep their own notebooks from the very first class, and write down their practice pieces. I watched with fascination as they learned to translate the notes on the page into time. I could virtually hear the moment the penny dropped. I taught some of the beginner percussionists the basics of the

317

drum kit. And I also started a percussion ensemble, for which I composed simple pieces in the various standard dance rhythms. To my delight, there was a wonderful Steinway piano in the pavilion, so I could while away my breaks tinkling on it, occasionally even turning up early to play with a view of the grounds.

Not much later, I was offered a full-time teaching job in Krefeld, but I turned it down because I couldn't imagine working full time. I stuck to the original schedule: teaching in Meerbusch on Wednesdays, private students on Thursdays, and Krefeld on Fridays. As Ralf and Florian preferred to work nights – to get more out of the daytime hours, I assume – our sessions in the Kling Klang Studio wouldn't get in the way of my music-school jobs.

EDP Workplaces

The control centre was becoming more of a reality every day. In the Kling Klang Studio, the available space determined the arrangements. On the stage, the desks were to be arranged symmetrically in the shape of a right-angled triangle, open at the front. The left and right lines were each made up of four double and two single desks, both lines ten metres long. According to good old Pythagoras, that meant the imaginary line facing the audience was about fourteen metres long.

The four workplaces had to be self-contained but electronically connected. All of it suitable for transporting, of course. Robust wiring was essential. So now we faced the question of technical competence. Who could make this set-up for us? While talking about it with Ralf and Florian in the studio, I mentioned my contact with the sound engineers at the University of Applied

Sciences. I offered to find us a technical whizz. Reinhold Nickel recommended Joachim Dehmann to me, and at the end of October he paid his first visit to the Kling Klang Studio.

Joachim was in his late 20s, slim and half a head taller than us, with mid-length dark blond hair combed over his ears. He wore a large pair of slightly tinted glasses, like Peter Fonda. Clothing: faded jeans, red T-shirt, denim jacket. 'Before I started studying sound engineering I worked in the service sector for sound and electronic instruments – now all I need is my final diploma,' he told us in a slight Ruhr Valley accent as he looked around the studio.

Joachim Dehmann: 'I found Ralf, Florian and Karl in a rear building. The room was full of electronic instruments, mixing desks and several 19-inch flight cases containing effect devices. All the machines were cabled up to each other across the room, and Ralf and Florian explained their masterplan. It would be my job to make the devices compatible with each other, build interfaces, make the system suitable for transport and wire it up professionally. The Kling Klang Studio had a great working atmosphere. There was a kind of euphoric anticipation in the air, as if to say: the cardboard box days are over at last. We want to set up our equipment professionally and conquer the world!'

Joachim Dehmann completed the Mintropstrasse team. Over the next few months, Wolfgang built the system at Berger Allee and transported the finished components to the workshop at Mintropstrasse, where Joachim started installing the parts and wiring them up in parallel.

The setting-up brought plenty of life into the place. We would often meet in the studio in the afternoon or evening, but at some point, I started getting the impression someone had switched the points and my carriage had ended up on a siding. I had plenty of time to myself to think. The past four years with Kraftwerk had been eventful ones. The atmosphere in the band was still great. And yet I felt useless, because we hadn't made any music since mid-June. In the end, I got myself a Fender Rhodes so I could at least go on composing at home.

Rheingold

Bodo Staiger and I had been friends since our first musical experiments. We hadn't been in touch much over the past few years but we'd never lost contact. After he graduated, he worked as a guitar teacher at a music school and also played with Joe Stick, Peter Wollek and Nappes Napiersky in a pop-rock band obliquely named after the Neu! track 'Lila Engel'. The Lilac Angels got plenty of press; they were real local heroes. Their first record was produced by Conny Plank and Klaus Dinger. Now, Bodo was planning a solo project called Rheingold. We talked a lot on the phone and in November I went to visit him.

Bodo was veritably boiling over with energy. 'I'm kicking off the eighties at 30,' he announced with a laugh. Then he played me his demos and asked me straight out if I wanted to work on his project with him. He badly needed a co-writer and drummer, he said. He already had Conny Plank's OK to produce an album. Great, I thought. The starting conditions couldn't be much better.

Sure, I'd recorded two albums with Kraftwerk, and a third as a co-writer. That was definitely the core of my work. But why should the lads mind if I did an album with Bodo and Conny? So I told Ralf about the offer. His reaction caught me totally off guard. He responded laconically that he expected me to be available exclusively to Kraftwerk. I was on the record covers, after all. It was inconceivable for me to work on other pop projects, he told me.

Aha, so that was how it was. Looking back, it's strange how little I thought about my future. Words like 'building a financial basis', 'moving forward' and 'career' were a foreign language to me. In any case, it would have been fantastic to work with Bodo and Conny, but the new Kraftwerk album was already in the pipeline. And there was no denying that product's market value – although I'd never have put it like that at the time. What else could I do but accept Ralf's demand? After that, we listened to the first cover version of 'The Model', recently released on the Residents' label Ralph Records. The artist was called Snakefinger.

Rather sadly, I explained to Bodo that I couldn't take his offer, as much as I'd like to. But I did give him Lothar Manteuffel's phone number. Lothar was a former student of Emil Schult, I told him, back when Emil had worked as an art teacher at a Düsseldorf high school. He had just started writing lyrics. So maybe they might be able to work together, and he could also connect him with Emil.

On my way back home, I couldn't get the guitar riff out of my head that Bodo had just played me. As it turned out, 'Dreiklangs-Dimensionen' – produced by Conny Plank and Bodo – became one of the first big hits of the Neue Deutsche Welle in the summer of 1981: da-di-da-dumm . . .

Bodo brought out three successful LPs under the project name of Rheingold between 1980 and 1984. And Lothar Manteuffel did end up writing the lyrics. Emil was also part of the writing team on songs like 'Rendezvous', 'Fan Fan Fanatisch', 'Augenblick' and 'Via Satellit'.

Electronic Every Day

Following the now traditional New Year's Eve party at Berger Allee, the 1980s began with cycling trips in the Lower Rhine countryside, occasional meet-ups at Kling Klang and my music teaching. All good. But then one morning, I was woken by a hellish din outside my flat – they were digging up the ground. Unbeknown to me, a contractor had obviously decided to build more apartment houses. Unfortunately, the building site was right outside my bedroom window. There was no getting round it: I had to get out of there! I wouldn't be able to stand it for long, that much was clear. Amazingly enough, I found someone to take over my rent contract with no difficulty at all. I spent a couple of weeks with Bettina in her parents' house in Unterrath. And then I read an ad in the *Rheinische Post*:

'Pempelfort, near Hofgarten: 2-bed apt, approx. 100 sqm, central heating, 2 balconies, 4th floor with lift, 1104 DM, deposit 3 months' rent, from 1 May 1980.'

I hesitated because the 1000 Deutschmarks rent on Taubenstrasse was well above my usual level. Then again, I'd had more than enough of all the recent to-ing and fro-ing. My music school jobs and private students secured me a modest but steady income and kept me in touch with my earlier life. That was one kind of security. On top of that, my collaboration in the Düsseldorf electronic combo was creating a new dynamic in my bank account as we gained international recognition. I'd find the money somehow.

The flat was bright and quiet with a classic layout. One large and one small room facing the front and one bedroom at the back. Plus kitchen and bathroom, as you might expect. One balcony was accessed from the bedroom. Covered in ivy, it was the perfect spot for whiling away the hours. Bettina and I polished off many a plate of spaghetti Napoli out there. With its white walls, newly laid grey industrial carpeting and blinds, the flat was reminiscent of Bauhaus design. I emphasized that with my sparse furnishings, including two tubular steel chairs, a table and a typical spherical lamp that I'd picked up in a Bauhaus flash – probably triggered by hours of conversation in the studio about art, design and architecture.

I declared the fifty-square-metre living room my first home studio. Pure electronic sounds were beginning to fascinate me more and more. I borrowed the programmes and reports of the Darmstadt Summer Courses on New Music from the conservatory library and read in amazement about what had been explored there, way back in the early 1950s. For instance, in his lecture series on 'the acoustic world of electronic music', Robert Beyer covered the topic of Space as a formative moment of acoustic photography – its significance for electronic music.

I didn't differentiate academically between electronic music and *musique concrète*. Noises from sound library records, which I used as atmosphere, for example, for my own music, also became electronic sounds to me. I found these recordings in dusty corners of record shops. They were a bit of a specialist item. It wasn't long before I had a collection of sound library records, which incidentally had the world's most incredible covers. Polydor had brought out *Die HiFi Stereo-Kulisse*, for example, consisting of '98 Sounds for Film and Tape Enthusiasts'. 98! As I listened to the record, I happened to notice that the recording '1 Car Engine Starting and Driving Off from Left to Right 23' in the category 'Traffic Sounds II' sounded suspiciously like the beginning of 'Autobahn'.

I got hold of recordings not just of real sounds, but also sound effect records, for instance *Holiday, Disasters, Death & Horror* and of course *More Death and Horror*. Sometimes I simply let one of them play for hours as a soundtrack to life, on low volume. Even though I now have digital sound libraries containing never-ending sounds, noises and sound effects, these 1970s vinyl records are still in my archive. Romantic? A hopeless case? Maybe. But perhaps it's like with the old photos in this book, which still depict the time when they were taken even in digitalized form. Aside from that, I spent 19,90 Deutschmarks on '98 Geräusche für den Film- und Tonbandfreund' and made it part of my record collection. That's reason enough to keep it, surely.

What fascinated me about electronic music was the creation of a closed system. Analogue to an animated film in which the whole world consists of paper cut-outs, plasticine or drawings, the aim was to create an acoustic spectrum made up solely of electronic sound sources. Stockhausen formulated it similarly. When I composed, I wanted to avoid associations with familiar musical instruments so as to enable a new way to access music. Let's take the electronic drum kit. In my imagination, there wasn't a drummer sitting behind his set. I could disregard the traditional way of playing the drums. That meant there were no role models any more, only my thoughts and the sounds of the music.

It seems odd from today's point of view, but I didn't have a tape recorder while I was a student. It never occurred to me to record my work. Neither practices nor rehearsals nor concerts – nothing. There was no obvious reason for me to record music. Not to check my playing, not even to archive it. It simply wasn't part of my work – just as it wasn't for my fellow students and professors, incidentally. The music we wrote and performed was transitory. If we wanted to 'store' it we could write down the notes. In my university world, music was always tied to the occasions when it was played, an ephemeral phenomenon.

In the meantime, my attitude to recording had changed. I wanted to record my ideas so I could listen to them without playing at the same time. So I got myself a fair amount of electronic equipment for the purpose. Originally, my modest apparatus was limited to a cassette deck, a four-track cassette recorder, amp, pre-amp, record player, speakers, Minimoog, drum machines, ARP analogue sequencer, Space Echo, microphone and the Farfisa Professional Piano I'd bought from Ralf for 100 Deutschmarks. Oh yes, and then there was my Musser Pro-Vibe, which I still used for playing classical music.

I learned to work with sound equipment. I had picked up a few things from Peter Bollig and Florian during our recording sessions, and I was good at bombarding Joachim Dehmann with questions. On top of that, I subscribed to German, British and US magazines on electronic music and studio equipment. They were certainly high on the nerd scale, but if you were interested in technical developments, you couldn't afford to ignore the specialist press. I think Florian also had a few subscriptions of his own.

My electronic everyday consisted of turning on my drum machine and analogue sequencer and switching to autopilot.

They did the playing. Of course, there was always something humming, crackling or buzzing. White noise is just part of the music, I told myself.

Working with automatic music machines is fundamentally different from human music-making, simply because machines reproduce set parameters and aren't capable of listening and reacting. Different instruments offer different forms of expression and produce different results on the basis of their unique characteristics. An improvisation on the piano, for example, leads to very different music to a guitar improvisation, even though they both enable different types of polyphony. String or wind instruments, in turn, favour a different way of playing, and using electronic sound-makers also naturally leads to a unique quality of musical expression.

The new aspect to my electro set-up at the time was that the machines provided me with a type of surface or foundation, to which I could add acoustic shapes. I would listen to the sequence, change it, play a chord, a melody, leave the room, talk on the phone, read the paper, go back and come up with something, for instance, a change of key. I could even watch TV while I played. I usually turned the sound off, though, and improvised a soundtrack to match the images. And occasionally I pressed the red 'record' button. My life took place in the set-up, in the key and tempo of a loop.

Working with the sequencer and drum machines added a new quality to my perception of music. It liberated me from my role as an instrumentalist, so I could devote myself exclusively to creating the music. I considered it a privilege to be able to compose and record a complete piece of music all alone. The sequencer's automatic sound sequences and the drum machine's loops hypnotized me. These black boxes brought the trance quality of African, Indian and Asian musical cultures into pop music, a quality that had been the starting point for the minimalist concept. But where did these electronic drum kits come from?

Drum Machines

During the silent movie era, cinemas used theatre organs. These huge electric machines were intended to imitate an orchestra, and therefore possessed a whole arsenal of percussion instruments, which were operated mechanically. They also added a generous portion of realism to the screenings by means of everyday noises. Special organ stops produced sound effects like thunder, horses' hooves, gunshots or train sounds, intensifying the illusion of reality. Thus, organists became the first noise-makers in film history. When talking films set a new standard in 1927, these live performances were relocated onto the celluloid sound track. The great theatre organs and percussion, however, had forged a connection that survived. Over the next few years, mechanical percussion became electronic. The technical evolution of the drum machine progressed through analogue sound production, digital sampling and microprocessor control.

The first autonomous rhythm machine, in my view, was the Chamberlin Rhythmate, built in 1949 by Harry Chamberlin in the USA, using drum patterns recorded on one-inch magnetic tape loops. The inventor went on thinking, however, and developed an electromechanical, polyphonic keyboard instrument, launched in 1951 under the name Chamberlin 200, with about 100 of them on the market. In the 1960s, Streetly Electronics

327

from Birmingham, England, took over the concept and developed it into the Mellotron. It became instantly popular when the Beatles used it on several of their songs.

The US-based Wurlitzer company introduced the first commercially available rhythm machine in 1959, the Wurlitzer Side Man. 'You play it sweet, Side Man gives the beat' was their fantastic advertising slogan. The machine had the look of a Leslie cabinet. Along with numerous pre-set rhythms, it also had a panel of buttons for playing percussion instruments manually, and an integrated 11-watt amp plus three speakers. Price: $395.

The British company Vox followed up in 1967 with their Percussion King model. The machine looked like the company's bass amp top box as used by Paul McCartney. Again, it offered pre-set rhythms and manual percussion options: castanet, clave, block, bongo I, bongo II, drum roll, snare drum, bass drum, brush cymbal, crash cymbal. The creators had also taken inspiration from the ergonomics of acoustic drum kits and added foot pedals for bass drum and hi-hat.

Via an ad in a specialist magazine, I got myself a Maestro Rhythm King MRK-2, built in 1971 with the serial number 15015. Like with its two forerunners, man-machine advocates could press buttons to trigger sounds, while running a rhythm loop at the same time.

After 1972's Farfisa Rhythm 10, the Korg Mini Pops 7 came onto the market in 1976. Are you familiar with Jean-Michel Jarre's 'Oxygène'? Right, that's a Korg. And the Roland CR-78 from 1978 brings us up to date, or at least up to the date I'm writing about here. The LinnDrum, Roland TR-808 and TR-909 all came later. Of course, there were plenty of other drum machines available at the same time.[3]

I have to confess I developed a slight obsession with the machines: small wood-veneered or plastic boxes from Hohner, Farfisa, Maestro, Ace, Korg and Roland with dials and buttons on the front. Below, above or on these operating elements were the names of the rhythms you could summon up: bossa nova, samba, bolero, rumba, cha cha cha, mambo, tango, slow fox, rock, swing, go-go, waltz, march, western, etc. You could regulate the volume, balance and speed for more flexibility. The cherry on top was that the early models all had their own methods of subdividing time. Naturally, that led to individual timing and distinguished between their sound.

The first target group for these drum machines was amateurs and solo entertainers who played music for dances and couldn't afford a drummer, or didn't want one. Eventually, though, a whole stable of musicians dusted off the machines and used their mechanical aesthetic as a musical means of creation, which broadened the percussion family and enriched it enormously. That was precisely the reason why I now began collecting and working with drum machines.

The early phase of my own electro career was indescribably inspiring. The ostinato from the sequencer and drum machine provided me with a foundation, upon which I invented and developed ever new sonic shapes. It seems I wasn't the only one.

In a wonderful film by Peter Schamoni,[4] the great visual artist Max Ernst talks about having had a problem filling a blank canvas. In his inimitable way, he called it his 'virginity complex'. It was simply impossible for him to apply the first dab of paint to the surface. Until one day, coincidence helped him overcome his inhibitions. Sitting in a small inn on the French Atlantic coast on a rainy day in 1925, his eyes alighted on the wooden floor. The boards were faded from being scrubbed clean, and he noticed the grain of the wood moving before his mind's eye, turning into a kind of animation. To hold onto the moment, he dropped pieces of paper on the floor and traced the grain with a soft pencil, like rubbing brass. To his surprise, he found his vision sharpening as he looked at the lines on the paper. Max Ernst refers it as to 'questioning the material'. These traced basic patterns then went through a series of transmutations in the process of his work, losing their original character and taking on – as Max Ernst describes it – the appearance of incredibly precise figures.

I think my work with analogue music machines in the time between *Man-Machine* and *Computer World* had a similar effect on me as the copied wood grains on Max Ernst's imagination.

While I was 'questioning the material', my open notebook was always at arm's reach. I took some of the resulting ideas along to Mintropstrasse, and some of them were used in our productions and became known over time as Kraftwerk titles.

Others were released later, under my name, for instance, '15 Minutes of Fame', 'International Velvet', 'Without a Trace of Emotion', 'Hausmusik' and 'Kissing the Machine' or by other artists, such as 'How Long' by Electronic.

The Flying Living Room

Wolfgang had been beavering away on the new studio furniture in Berger Allee since August 1979. He then transported it to Mintropstrasse, where Joachim took charge of it. In the meantime, he had set up a professional workshop in the studio's two office rooms. A few worktops housed the unscrewed devices he was working on: racks, synthesizers, pedals, outboard equipment, patch panels, tape recorders, cable drums. It looked pretty darn complicated at times. Flight cases with never-ending drawers and compartments were stuffed full of screws, nuts, fuses, solder and other bits and bobs – you never knew quite what it all might be used for. On top of all that: drills, soldering irons, clamps, flashlights, felt-tip pens, toolboxes.

The metal shelves along the walls were overflowing with catalogues, instruction manuals, handbooks, ring binders, light bulbs, spray cans, oil, zip ties and other studio stuff. Bright office lamps dangled a metre above the tables. Ralf and Florian had got hold of everything needed for the technical work. Joachim Dehmann stood in the midst of it all, clutching a soldering iron, staring at an oscilloscope and muttering to himself: 'Why is the power supply still making that noise?'

After the slanting consoles were wired up, they were fixed to their mobile lower sections. For reasons of space, they were positioned in more of a U-shape than the triangle we set up later on stage. Beneath the consoles were the neon tube lights – in front of them, walking platforms about ten centimetres high, with chrome surfaces on which we could 'glide' perfectly to our keyboards.

The rear wall of the room was unchanged, with its steel framework holding the monitor speakers. Two towers on either side and a two-and-a-half-metre traverse housed parts of the live PA and large JBL speakers. That enabled us to switch between live and studio sound as we chose.

The system looked amazing, all in grey, but it wasn't really ergonomic. The concept was developed mainly for live appearances and was designed along visual lines. For our everyday

331

work, a table and chair might not have been all that avant-garde, but they would have been more comfortable, at least for me. A key design factor for a studio, as I've mentioned before, is the spatial acoustics and the position of the speakers. Even after the refurbishing, nothing had changed in that respect – visual factors were the focus. Ralf called the mobile studio 'the flying living room', a reference to a 1933 children's book by Erich Kästner.

The Triggersumme

Visits to the Synthesizerstudio Bonn always swallowed up whole afternoons. Ralf would usually pick me up from my place and we'd speed over to Bonn together. He and Florian had commissioned two new devices for the current production: an additional Synthanorma sequencer to program 32 steps, and a prototype Hajo called his 'Triggersumme': a music machine triggered by audio signals, in this case by electronic percussion instruments.

Wolfgang and I played the drums live, using our knitting needles on our percussion multipads. Compared to the precision of a sequencer, that was an inexact science, of course – merely human. We were beginning to see that as ever more of a disadvantage in those days. No one ever wrote down any guidelines for our creative work; they were in our heads. For example, the aestheticization of technology. Synthetic sounds played an elemental role, and mathematical subdivision of time was no less important to us. Thus, the essence of the machine was manifested in the order of the motion – the rhythm, in other words. When we recorded, we could control the percussion sounds via the Synthanorma, but only one instrument at a time.

With a synchronous entry matrix, from now on we could create complementary rhythms with different instruments in one take.

The electronics were housed in a chrome-plated box, around 1 metre long, 25 centimetres wide and 15 centimetres high. On the surface there were five different-coloured rows of switches with 16 positions per beat, so one flip switch for every sixteenth note (semiquaver) or rest. Now, when I flipped up one of these switches, it produced a control voltage. This was really new because now we could manipulate the rhythms in a running loop by hand. At the front, the diodes ran through the 16 steps. From today's point of view, Hajo's Triggersumme was a magical piece of equipment!

The Kling Klang Recordings of 1980

We finally returned to our sessions in the Kling Klang Studio on 14 May 1980. The new equipment opened up new possibilities, but it also brought along plenty of new difficulties and sources of errors. It was extremely helpful to have an in-house sound engineer working with us again.

Joachim Dehmann: 'During the album production phase, my job was to maintain the equipment, program sounds and, just like a classic sound engineer, to make sure the signals were recorded perfectly on the MCI sixteen-track machine. The lads had to get used to the new studio concept – thanks to the wiring and above all the patch panels, all the devices could now communicate, which opened up a lot of possibilities. I helped them to set up the signalling pathways, usually until late at night. Florian and Ralf weren't the kind of guys who turned up for work at eight or nine in the morning. They really didn't have that kind of nine-to-five mentality, they were more unconventional. During this production, they were highly motivated and sometimes turned up at the studio at noon or shortly afterwards. Over the years, their working hours shifted back to the night time.'

Computer World (Song)

In his 1932 novel *Brave New World*, Aldous Huxley came up with a terrifying scenario of a technically modified and drone-like mankind, while George Orwell also described a totalitarian surveillance state in *1984*, published in 1949. By 1973, Rainer Werner Fassbinder was focusing in his two-part TV drama *World on a Wire* on a world programmed by a computer, in which the inhabitants do possess consciousness but don't realize they owe their existence merely to computer software. Nonetheless, I couldn't have predicted back then how computers really would change our world. Just for orientation: Ridley Scott's *Blade Runner*[5] was still two years in the future, and William Gibson's debut novel *Neuromancer*[6] was a whole four years away.

Then again, the future had already begun; computer technology had become an established part of our everyday lives and work. Microprocessor-controlled appliances, like those made by the New York company Eventide, occupied a place in music production during the 1970s. At the Kling Klang Studio, for instance, we used an Instant Phaser, Digital Delays and many more of their products, but they weren't computer terminals. Florian had the SWTPC 6800 computer system from the South West Technical Products Corporation, because he needed it for his speech synthesis experiments. Aside from that, though, there was still no 'real' computer in the studio at that point.

The philosopher I mentioned in the previous chapter, Gottfried Wilhelm Leibniz, was not on our agenda at this time either. In actual fact, it was him who had the idea of coding the entire world in a system of ones and zeros. His article 'Explication de l'Arithmétique Binaire' was published in 1703 in the journal of the Paris Academy. He also came up with the idea of a mechanical calculator for numbers, using a binary system. All this in the early eighteenth century.

Once we started looking into the subject in more detail, we went to a Düsseldorf branch of IBM to see first-hand how these computers worked. One thing was for sure: analogue signals processing – as we had known it for a long time – would soon be taken over by its digital equivalent.

For some time, German society had been discussing the Federal Data Protection Act, as a consequence of increasing electronic data processing. A TV series by the name of 'Computers Never Forget' helped form public opinion. The police force had been using computer technology in their manhunts since the 'German Autumn' of 1977. The dominant critical opinion at the time was that collecting and storing personal data presented a threat to a liberal society. Control by the state was not acceptable under any circumstances, doubtlessly down to experiences in German history. The end of Helmut Schmidt's term as chancellor and his liberal social policy was clearly approaching. Resistance was organized against the NATO

Double-Track Decision. Hundreds of thousands of demonstrators took to the streets in the early 1980s. It was the peak of the peace and environmental movement, anti-nuclear campaigners and squatters. I don't think anyone would have thought it possible that people would one day voluntarily provide their private data to electronic social networks.

The four syllables of the phrase 'computer world' were easy to sing along to an organ theme from the first phase of our writing sessions. It sounded instantly convincing when Florian intoned it with his vocoder. No doubt about it – this is what a refrain sounds like. In the German lyrics, the phrase meaning 'time is money' rhymes with the title: 'Computerwelt – denn Zeit ist Geld'. That was a gift; we couldn't have expressed the business world's efficiency model and the capitalist logic of exploitation any better. As we can see these days, profit maximization is also the basic principle of the digital economy. Its business model is based on the fascination prompted by progress and technical innovations. The future is always flickering tantalizingly on the horizon. Against their promises, the global corporation's future experts, sales managers and computer scientists don't actually attempt to improve people's lives, as one might expect. On the contrary, 'MP3 capitalism', as the American sociologist Richard Sennett labels the new intermingled world of work and leisure, forces many people to work around the clock. That is how the future looks in the present. Regardless, we can assume the global digital corporations will continue to make rising profits.

While looking for a verse for the song, we remembered the fragment by the name of 'Megalo'. We spent a while fiddling with it and then Ralf played and sang the melody in unison.

Recited in a newsreader's tone, the first verse of the German lyrics recalls the mood at the time:

'Interpol und Deutsche Bank, FBI und Scotland Yard, Flensburg und das BKA, haben unsere Daten da'.[7]

The English lyrics are cut down to just:

'Interpol and Deutsche Bank, FBI and Scotland Yard'.

As well as the writers named on the record, a Pocket Language Translator from Texas Instruments contributed another, not unimportant, part of the lyrics. Why? Well, it had categories such as: 'Business, Numbers, Money, People, Time, Travel, Communication, Entertainment'.[8]

That was pretty illuminating, making it starkly clear to us how life is organized in modern society.

The arrangement and instrumentation are fairly self-explanatory when you listen to the song. One thing is worth noting, though: Ralf built on the characteristic percussive sound from 'Spacelab' for 'Computer World'. The result was what we called the electro-snare, which later became generally known as the 'zap' sound. With a milliseconds-delayed repeat, this was the second time we used this sound in our music.

Computer Love

An early evening in the studio. I was standing at the Triggersumme and switched on a rhythm, a mix of rumba, bossa nova and twist – something like that. Later, we added an electro-snare. Suddenly an idea came to me. I walked the two paces to Florian's keyboard and played a small theme in G minor in a glockenspiel sound. Not hesitating for a second, Ralf responded with a bass

337

figure on the Minimoog and hit a sustained chord on the Polymoog to go with it. The variation I'd thought up went perfectly. I had come up with the melodies while improvising on the piano at the music school.

On the one hand, we worked organically during our writing sessions – we threw musical balls in each other's direction and responded to the others' suggestions. On the other hand, the process was also synthetic – because we combined elements of different recordings to form a new composition. I had always had a talent for this kind of musical handicraft. And the communication between Ralf and me worked in both directions.

We looked for a second idea, and remembered a session about a year previously. Ralf had come up with a theme and given it the working title 'Ravel'. We now combined that theme with my melodies. Ralf soon thought up the first lyrics and we developed the music's structure as we played it.

As far as I remember, 'Computer Love' almost wrote itself. In the end, Florian added an electronic 'high flyer' to the spectrum as a pointer to the world of computers. By 'high flyer' I mean the electronic equivalent to brightly coloured balloons – in this case data streams – which rise at strategically important points of the music. Florian plucked one of those sounds out of his electronic toolbox at the click of a finger.

Pocket Calculator

The idea of the pocket calculator sound originated from Florian's curiosity, which essentially fuelled his creativity. He would roam the nearby music shops and department stores in search of acoustic objects and audio treasures. On one of these tours, he discovered more models of the Pocket Language Translator we had used on 'Computer World'. He also found a portable children's computer called Speak & Spell. Both of these Texas Instruments appliances could speak. Alongside their synthetic voices, the operations on these pocket computers were supported by electronic sounds.

One day, Florian turned up at the studio with a plastic bag full of gadgets. Joachim Dehmann opened up their casings, found the spots where we could pick up the audio signal, and connected them up to our audio system. Listening to them that way, they sounded both trashy and impressive. They gave us the ideal sounds for an acoustic portrait. From there, we developed a plan to stage a kind of circus act with mini-instruments for the next show. Florian set out to look for suitable sound-producing appliances. And soon enough, a children's piano – Mattel Bee Gees Rhythm Machine – and a Stylophone turned up. They were both hand-sized and portable and completed our set of miniature instruments.

Ralf focused on the Bee Gees Rhythm Machine, and I got stuck into the Stylophone, a miniature keyboard invented by a certain Brian Jarvis in 1967, a worldwide sales hit in the 1970s. In Germany, the pop singer Bill Ramsey endorsed the 'Electronic pocket organ with the super sound'. So the starting point for the composition was the lo-tech sounds of these tiny computers and gimmick instruments. In search of a suitable motif or riff to go with a pocket calculator ensemble, we ended up with a theme Ralf had invented some time previously in its primal form, and built on it.

Then we had the nursery-rhyme-like line 'I'm the operator with my pocket calculator'. And Florian took on the task of complementing the lyrics with the key notes of one of the pocket computers, to illustrate them. As an electro-response, we developed a small rhythm pattern. I feel the pocket computer speaks along with the lyrics at that point. The continuation lists all the things the operator can do with his pocket calculator: 'I am adding and subtracting / I'm controlling and composing.'

At that time, we developed our musical motifs and themes simultaneously. In this part, I switched to hand-played glissandi on the Stylophone, and Ralf also came up with his second theme in parallel. It was presumably this method that prompted the polyphonic character of our music. 'Pocket Calculator' is a good example of how the lively polyphony of our writing sessions felt – we improvised together to invent the phrasing of the musical building blocks, using the mini-instruments and our music machines.

Home Computer

In August, Ralf and Florian spent another two weeks cycling through the heat of the Côte d'Azur. They loved it. I stayed at home because of my work at the music school. After this brief interruption, we went straight back to work. On one of the following days, Florian came into the studio with a line of English lyrics that sounded like something right out of *Star Trek*: 'I program my home computer to beam myself into the future.' Ralf helped translate it into German and came up with the following line: 'Am Heimcomputer sitz' ich hier und programmier die Zukunft mir.'

I can't say any more whether we were already working on the music when Florian presented us with his aphorism. In any case, a conjunction came about with my musical fragment from early 1978, which has the working title in my notebook of 'World of Work'.

Musically, we wanted to go in the direction of 'machine funk'. Ralf started up the Synthanorma. We chose timing of approximately 120 beats per minute. The Triggersumme was in sync with the sequencer. We had programmed the white-noise instruments on the top rows of red, orange and yellow switches with the functions cymbal, open and closed hi-hat. Below them in white, the snare drum, and at the bottom in blue came the bass drum. Gradually, the basic pattern of our automatic rhythm group came about, and the foundation for the song was laid. Like on 'Computer World', we used Ralf's new electro-snare for 'Home Computer' as well. This type of Moog percussion brought a unique new quality into the music. Apart from its function in the rhythm section, nothing about it recalled acoustic percussion, or even the electronic imitations of drum machines.

Once we'd worked on the track and let it rest for a while, we got a surprise. When Ralf started up the Synthanorma at one of our next sessions, we didn't believe our ears. There it was, the sequence of rising notes so characteristic for the title 'Home Computer'. Ralf selected the sinus wave on the oscillator, adjusted the envelope and transposed the sequence through the octaves. We were amazed. They're sixteen tones, but the sequence instantly reminded me of a twelve-tone row. Like Alban Berg's rows, this too sounded not bizarre, but familiar and accessible through the use of well-known arpeggios. What had happened? Sometimes we find something we've never even looked for. Possibly, Ralf had programmed tones in his last sequencer settings, reduced the playback area, enlarged it again, reprogrammed a few sounds, interrupted the process, forgotten what he'd set before, started something new again, abandoned parts of that material, and so on. There are many possibilities for how the sequence may have come about. I think Ralf was unconsciously functioning as a random generator.

So as to exploit the scale's potential to the full, we set up another multitrack. The new tempo was 128 beats per minute, to which we invented a new rhythm track, and Ralf and Florian started a series of experiments to electronically manipulate our tripping scale. We made a mix of this 'sound piece'. It was Ralf's idea to stick the two quarter-inch tapes together at 4 minutes and 19 seconds. The odds didn't look good but the cut worked like a change of scene in a film. Through the tempo difference of 120 versus 128 BPM, I perceived the subsequent two-minute experimental sound sequence as if in fast-motion.

It's More Fun to Compute

One day, we stumbled upon the following phrase on the user interface of Gottlieb pinball machines: 'It's more fun to compete!' These machines were very popular in the 1970s, in practically every pub. Now and then, I caved in to peer pressure and took part in 'pinball competitions', even though I have absolutely no interest in games of any kind. By replacing the slogan's 'e' with a 'u', we changed the last word into 'compute' – and the phrase fitted our album perfectly.

After the two different elements of 'Home Computer' we added a closing part to the piece, known as a coda, introduced with a pretty hard Moog bass and a slightly dissonant synthesizer

342

response, over which Florian intoned the pinball lyric with the vocoder. There follows the reprise of the Minimoog sequencer riff from 'Home Computer', to which Ralf lends a unique intensity with variations and echoes. In my view, the organ motif he developed into a theme is one of the most other-worldly moments on the album.

Numbers

One evening, I switched on the 'Numbers' beat on the Triggersumme, which had the working title of 'Dom' in my notes. Florian was testing out a new effect gadget, the Bode Frequency Shifter. What could we do with this thing? What kind of signal was it best at processing? He routed the percussion signal through it and turned the 19-inch appliance's central dial. All at once, we pricked up our ears. The beat wasn't bad as a starting point, but routed through the Bode Shifter and manipulated manually, the results were amazing. Florian could change the sound spectrum and add to the original. Astounding – what a sound! We went on messing around on the basis of that setting. What's perhaps most interesting about this track is the floating rhythmic sound object at the beginning, for which I can't think of any other description than 'bizarre psycho-sequence'.

I remember Florian putting numbers into his Pocket Language Translator, which were then translated into another language. That resulted in the basic idea for a multilingual composition with lyrics made up of numbers. It was a metaphor for computers' significance and their complex calculations.

The hard part was developing the languages into patterns that worked. We used the vocoder and the Votrax speech synthesizer as further sound sources, and intuitively found beats that sounded convincing to us. The key factor here was that we worked together and developed the complementary patterns according to musical aspects, rather than following the algorithm of a computer program.

Computer World 2

It made sense to us to follow 'Numbers' with a repeat of the E minor motif of the opening track 'Computer World', to round off the first side of the LP.

I think we achieved a moment of clarity in this reprise that is unique for the music we made together. And when Florian's Votrax counts into the fading chords in the last bars, the album's musical thoughts intensify in a way that has lost nothing of its atmosphere to this day.

Mix with Six Ears and Six Hands

I wouldn't describe the final mixing of Kraftwerk's music as a simple matter. It's more of a constant learning process. Mixing *Computer World* in the Kling Klang Studio was no exception.

Florian knew his way around studio equipment the best of us by far. But he wasn't properly trained in recording and mixing, and lacked professional experience as a sound engineer. Nonetheless, his unorthodox approach did lead to some astounding results at times. The Kling Klang Studio was equipped with the best equalizers, compressors, phasers, flangers, digital delays, spectrum analysers and other magic boxes, which he was constantly fiddling with and trying out.

We could use these effects to process the signals and then record them on the multitrack. But we could also use them in our mix and loop them into the signal path at any time. However, the connection via the consoles' patch panels made ergonomic working more difficult because the effects were metres away from the mixing desk. Whenever we didn't know what to do, it was usually a case for Joachim Dehmann, who would then come rushing over in his white lab coat, like a mad scientist.

There were usually three of us at the mixing desk. The division of labour went something like this: Ralf did the necessary hand work on the console, while Florian took care of the signal processing with effects and I gave my comments on the sound of the music. We took turns as tape operator, depending who was needed.

But there were also tracks where each of us had his fingers on two or three faders and the job of running them; in other words, switching them on and off, adjusting the relative volumes, dialling effects up or down, or whatever else was called for.

Fortunately, we had orchestrated the album very sparingly, which helped us to mix the signals as transparently as possible. In purely technical terms, the sixteen tracks of the multitrack recorder are put onto the mixing desk's sixteen channels, processed there and the result – the mix – is recorded on another tape machine in stereo. If you wanted to change the music's sequence at this stage, the only possibility was to physically cut this tape. Ralf had mastered the delicate art of making these edits on the quarter-inch machine. I can see him now, feeding the two spools of the tape machine past the playback head with his hands – back and forth, back and forth – until he'd found the right spot for the edit, marked it with a white pen and cut it with a razor blade to insert another piece of tape – which he'd previously removed from another place and kept looped around his neck – and stick it together. The only other time I saw a similar look on his face was when he repaired his racing bike.

In those days, Ralf and Florian were absolutely motivated and working with them was genuinely exciting. When we met in the early evening to finish a mix in the upcoming session, you could bet on one of us saying our standard slogan: 'Here comes the night of the long knives!' We kept trying until we finally managed a usable mix. Sometimes our arms would cross over, like in a piano duet. We reinvigorated our sound rides to help form opinions on the music.

Considering the way things developed later, our *Computer World* mix is very important to me. Like on no other record, the spirit of our writing sessions shines through, and the album represents our most productive musical phase.

Artwork

Heinrich Obermaier's showroom dummies hadn't made it onto the cover of the *Man-Machine* album, but clad in red shirts and black ties they helped us with promotion. Job-sharing, you might say. In the cover design for *Computer World*, they formed a visual counterpoint to the computer terminal pictured on the front.

Vibraphone solo at a Sinus gig in Kunsthalle Düsseldorf, May 1976. RAINER SENNEWALD

All smiles on the sofa in Rotterdam, 1976. GIJSBERT HANEKROOT/REDFERNS

Second from left: September 1976, rehearsing for the Belgian TV show Follies. ERIK MACHIELSEN

December 1977 in Munich: the legendary showroom dummy artist Heinrich Obermaier modelling 'Herr Karl'.

Bettina as Salome.

13 April 1978 – album presentation for *The Man-Machine*: invitation
to our Soiree Rouge on the 56th floor of the Tour Montparnasse.

The Mephisto experiment: test polaroid during filming for 'Neon Light'.

1980: In my first studio on Taubenstrasse by the Hofgarten park. BETTINA MICHAEL

In the writing sessions days in the Kling Klang Studio. JOACHIM DEHMANN

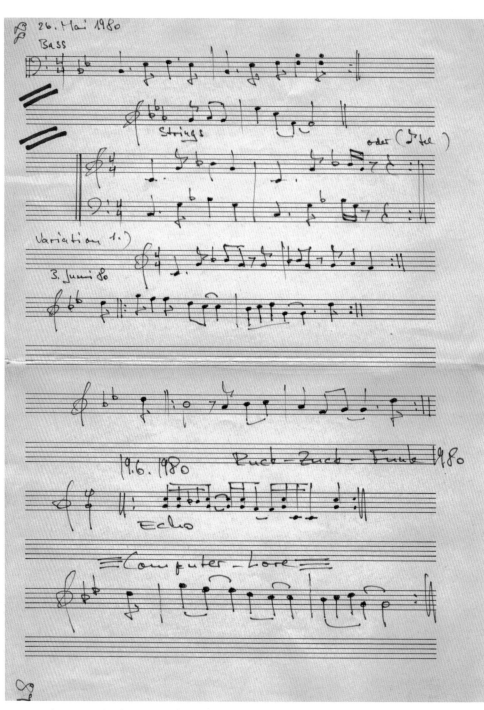

Two pages from my notebook...

'I'm the operator with my pocket calculator': 1981 in The Ritz, NYC. LAURA LEVINE/CORBIS VIA GETTY IMAGES

'Red shirt, black tie': 'Pocket Calculator' with Wolfgang 1981. BOB KING/REDFERNS

The Alps or Paris-Roubaix weren't my thing – I was happy with the left bank of the Lower Rhine. I trained regularly in 1985. BETTINA MICHAEL

While Joachim Dehmann was rebuilding the Kling Klang Studio between 1987 and 1989, the equipment was kept in Studio B. Front right: my midi vibraphone.

Yellow was the new red. Yellow is the background colour on which the freely floating pale grey terminal is imposed, its black screen depicting the inverted graphic portraits of the mannequin heads, like negatives. The back cover is a straightforward section of the front view of the control centre, with the heavy multi-plugs connecting the modules. Our mute stand-ins – Ralf, Karl, Wolfgang and Florian – are standing behind the consoles, facing the camera. There are circuit boards attached to the dummies' shirts to control the LEDs in their ties. Ralf's dummy is the only one holding a plug.

Beneath the photo by Günter Fröhling, the first verse of the title song 'Computer World' is quoted in capitals. This sets the tone for understanding the album, wherein the words' meaning results from subjective interpretation – depending where one stands on the political spectrum. The names of the seven tracks are listed under the lyric.

On the front side of the inside sleeve, the plastic dummies are posed once again in our standard line-up with the mini-instruments we used to record 'Pocket Calculator'. The credits are listed along the bottom. The listing of personnel in three categories – hardware, software and Kling Klang Studio – reflects our emerging digital worldview. I perceived that new perspective as an original artistic concept. The man-machine system clearly resonated within it.

What the credits don't include, however, is who contributed what to the product. In classic terms: drummer, singer, producer, etc. That's not entirely irrelevant, as collecting societies don't give two hoots about art concepts. And they can't do much with the term 'software' in this context.

Back to the artwork: on the back of the inside sleeve, the mannequins are standing by the consoles in front of the left-hand studio wall with the pyramid foam. The metal scaffolding is visible on the right, where the speakers were attached. While we were working on our mix for *Computer World*, the first colour copiers were installed in copy shops. Ralf got rather into them and thought about how to give the photos a different look. For some reason, he loved the way colour copiers transformed the photographs. It's not a bad idea, one might think. It was only years later that the true quality of Fröhling's work came to the fore in a revised new edition.

Reflection

We started our writing sessions for *Computer World* on 22 June 1978. The studio conversion to the mobile control centre took from 1 November 1979 to 13 May 1980. We picked up our sessions again on 14 May 1980. And on 15 March 1981 we finished the album production, after just under three years and almost 400 sessions of writing, recording and mixing.

I regard the consecutive concept albums *The Man-Machine* and *Computer World* as interlinked in many aspects, whereby *The Man-Machine* stands as a metaphor for the band's musical concept and *Computer World* describes the world of 1981.

The showroom dummies are obviously one link. They weren't finished in time to visualize us on the cover of *The Man-Machine*. But they wore our 'uniforms' during the promotion campaign. Alongside graphic elements, the artwork for *Computer World* includes black-and-white photos. You can test my theory by imagining the dummies on the sleeve in red shirts . . . I think the reference to the previous album is clear.

There's no question that the production processes and values were different in certain ways, but we recorded both albums with analogue synthesizers, Vocoders and electronic percussion. If I was to emphasize one instrument that influenced our music most, it would be the Synthanorma sequencer, to which the Triggersumme was added on *Computer World*. Astoundingly enough, neither of them makes a noise.

Not insignificant: the music's poetics. Both albums were written by the same authors – Hütter, Schneider, Bartos, Schult – which may have led to comparable thought processes and outcomes.

The release of the double A-side 'Computer Love'/'The Model' in the UK emphasizes this musical link. 'The Model' got to number 1 in the charts in 1982 – the song was taken from the previous album *The Man-Machine* and was already four years old at the time. Isn't it cool that I co-wrote both songs? This is my 'Day Tripper'/'We Can Work It Out' moment!

Once the production of *Computer World* was done, we recorded a few demos during more sessions. We must have enjoyed improvising together. Wolfgang often came to the studio as well, to drum a few beats and bars with us. When I listen to the tapes from our writing sessions and the finished album these days, I feel transported back to the brilliant productive atmosphere of the Kling Klang Studio at the time. Perhaps *Computer World* was our most successful attempt at translating the dialectics of the man-machine metaphor, as I understand it, into music.

NOTES

1. Aachen Technical University
2. See: 'Kraftwerk: The Final Solution to the Music Problem? Lester Bangs Vivisects the German Scientific Approach'. By Lester Bangs, *New Musical Express*, 6 September 1975
3. If you want to know more, I recommend Joe Mansfield's *Beat Box – A Drum Machine Obsession*, Ginko Press, Hamburg, 2013.
4. Peter Schamoni: *Max Ernst: Mein Vagabundieren – Meine Unruhe*, 1991
5. Based on the novel by Philip K. Dick: *Do Androids Dream of Electric Sheep?* Doubleday: New York 1968
6. William Gibson: *Neuromancer*. Ace Science Fiction Special: New York 1984
7. Translation: 'Interpol and Deutsche Bank, FBI and Scotland Yard, Flensburg and the BKA, they all have our data there'
   Flensburg is the seat of the Federal Motor Transport Authority (KBA), a subsection of the Federal Transport Ministry responsible for road transport. The BKA is the Federal Criminal Police Office, with the task of coordinating crime fighting across Germany, in close cooperation with the regional criminal police offices, and investigating in certain major crime areas involving non-German factors. (Wikipedia)
8. The German lyrics are slightly different: 'Nummern, Zahlen, Handel, Leute, Reisen, Zeit, Medizin, Unterhaltung.' Translation: 'Numbers, figures, business, people, travel, time, medicine, entertainment.'

11

AROUND THE WORLD IN 80 CONCERTS

Preparing the Live Show. Off We Go Again! On the Beach with Chris Bohn and Anton Corbijn. Three Gigs in Germany. A Concert from My Perspective. Sound Exchange with the UK. London. Paris. Back in Canada and the USA. Kling Klang at the Ritz. Behind the Iron Curtain. Japan. Down Under. Bombay in Monsoon Season. Back to Normal. Musique Concrète. Between Kiel and Passau.

Preparing the Live Show

The question that came up now was: How do we reproduce our music live, especially the past two albums? Florian came up with the right idea. For the basic playback, we used the Portastudio, a 4-channel cassette recorder that had come onto the market in 1979. We could record four tracks on it – or actually only three, because one track was needed to synchronize the Synthanorma and the Triggersumme.

The tracks for our playback were allocated according to a fixed plan: On 'The Robots' for example, track 1 – like on all songs – was for the sync-signal, track 2 was Ralf's recorded Minimoog bass sequence, track 3 was for Florian's vocoder, and the basic drum pattern was on track 4. As in our TV appearances, Ralf sang along to this semi-playback on stage in parallel with Florian's vocoder, spoke the Russian part and played the staccato melody live on his Minimoog. I provided the organ live on my synthesizer, Wolfgang switched on a few drum fills on the Triggersumme, and Florian added live vocoder on top. In the Russian part, he shared the sounds of the electric motors with Ralf. By the way, on our 1981 tour, I only played electronic percussion on 'Autobahn'.

The Portastudio technology was only semi-professional, without a doubt, but we took a lot of care recording our playbacks. And the additional live signals made the overall quality acceptable. When the percussion on some songs came entirely from the Triggersumme or was played manually, it added the necessary presence.

For every song there was one cassette and one back-up in case it got broken – eaten up by the player and turned into tape spaghetti, for instance. Florian was the cassette monitor and operator on stage, actually a kind proto-DJ. He took it very seriously and always kept the box of cassettes close at hand.

With regard to the tour, I had to rearrange my life. I talked to the directors of the music schools in Krefeld and Meerbusch about my presumably long absence and suggested someone to stand in for me. No one was overjoyed about it, but they agreed in the end.

It was just at this time that I came across Michael Mertens. He had taken a percussionist job at the Deutsche Oper am Rhein after Konni Ries, my first lecturer at the Robert Schumann Conservatory, had gone into retirement. We met at the conservatory and got on well from the very beginning. Michael had clearly heard from his colleagues what orchestra I was currently playing in.

He told me he wrote songs himself and was interested in electronic pop music. Listeners got a first taste of just how interested he was in 1983. But more about that later. At the time, anyway, it was a rare occurrence to meet a fellow musician with one leg in classical and one leg in pop music, just like me. Sadly, our tour preparations didn't leave me any time to visit him at the opera, but we stayed in touch over the years – to this day, in fact.

At the end of April 1981, we Kraftwerkers spent just under a week in Kaunitz, a small village in Westphalia, where we set up the equipment and tested it in the Ostwestfalenhalle venue with Rock-Sound, the company we'd be touring with. The PA had meanwhile been painted grey, as befitted a mobile version of the Kling Klang Studio, creating an unmistakeable corporate identity together with the neon tube lights and our name signs. Our old outfits didn't match the new look, though, so we agreed to wear black shirts and trousers on stage.

One of the key tracks on the new album was 'Pocket Calculator'. We wanted to make sure we presented it in an unconventional way, so we planned a kind of ballet on the edge of the stage at the end of the gig, each of us holding a mini-instrument. The small devices were attached to the sound system by cables – there were no wireless connections in those days. Florian would hold his Pocket Language Translator, Ralf his mini-keyboard, I'd have the Stylophone. And Wolfgang?

Wolfgang Flür: 'A miniature drum kit didn't exist at the time – so I had to make one. I screwed three insulated steel plates onto an aluminium box and linked them up with a long cable to my drum machine. I held the box in my left hand and a metal rod in the right, using it to play three different percussion sounds. That meant I could move around the stage fairly freely.'

Next, we planned to play 'The Robots' after the first curtain, with the plastic dummies in red shirts.

Eventually, we set off for Italy on Friday, 23 May 1981. We were to start our world tour there to coincide with the release of *Computer World*. This time, we got the coordination right. We could do it, after all! Our tour actually started at the same time as the album's release. Throughout our career we were habitually late with every release, or timed things badly. Ralf himself was often late both in his private and professional life. But this time, it all clicked. Our equipment weighed an impressive seven tonnes and was trucked into Italy. Ralf and Florian couldn't resist driving us the 1200 kilometres in their private cars, though. We met up at Berger Allee and headed due south . . .

Off We Go Again!

The order of the first four gigs – Florence, Rome, Milan, Bologna – wasn't exactly optimal in terms of logistics, which immediately made Florian doubt the planning had been done properly. Herr Schneider always enjoyed going into the processes, distances and arrangements of a tour. Especially once the planning was already in place . . . Ralf seemed deeply relaxed. He behaved like he was aware of his responsibility for our undertaking. Wolfgang had kitted himself out for the trip and was wearing a laid-back outfit. I felt pretty easy-going myself, or at least it seems that way to me now, looking back. Music was the medium that tied our lives to one another, and we thought it was great to be on the road again. Thinking back to the gang at the beginning of the 1981 tour, the thought comes to me that I saw the whole thing almost as a musical family outing.

Along with the four usual suspects, we also had Emil, Günter Spachtholz, Joachim Dehmann and Hajo Wiechers on the team. Emil's calm character enriched our group's conversational culture, as always. He often got terrible cabin fever – travelling was key to his quality of life.

Günter Spachtholz was in charge of the transport crates and kept an eye on the local stagehands and the roadies. He also played VHS cassettes during the show, projecting computer graphics or our own 16mm films onto four screens. The complex technology was provided by Sony. Joachim Dehmann and Hajo Wiechers were travelling with us for the first time; Joachim was there to guarantee the system's security and the PA's sound, while Hajo took care of the analogue devices' electronics.

During the organization phase, Ralf and Florian had made it a condition that we'd be accommodated in classic hotels, prime examples of 'old Europe', as a later American president put it. They were better than any other option, in our view.

The Italian agency made a determined effort to get things under control but not everything went smoothly, especially at the start of the tour. Luckily, there's a long tradition of improvisation in Italy. I think I remember Joachim once even breaking into a high-voltage public junction box outside one venue and re-routing the electricity we needed for our concert into the hall. That certainly didn't spoil the good mood in our little travelling party.

In Rome, Wolfgang had a memorable encounter with the actor Helmut Berger, which he told me about in great detail a day later: their first contact in a local disco, Wolfgang's visit to Helmut's apartment; the advances Helmut made in the bedroom, all the way to a pair of shiny Italian ankle boots that he gave Wolfgang with the words, 'Here, take these, you've earned them, honey.' Followed by Wolfgang's refusal to a disappointed Helmut, who listened on the brink of tears. One thing's for sure: I wasn't there and all I can do is sum up the story I was told. Only Wolfgang can tell it with the appropriate eloquence, which he still does when the mood takes him.

All in all, the first four gigs in front of audiences of 800, 1000, 1400 and 2500 didn't go badly. Much more importantly, though, the crew got the hang of the logistics and we 'stage workers' got the hang of the show. Our technical manager Joachim took care of the sound, mainly.

Joachim Dehmann: 'A central mixing desk in the middle of the auditorium wasn't yet standard, unfortunately. So I would stand on one side of the stage with a small mixer, usually near the curtain. The acoustics on stage were always different to in the audience, of course. I had to get used to that and it took me a few events to get it right. At the soundcheck, I set up the PA as best I could in the empty space. On the first few days of the tour, I often joined the audience during the concerts to check on the sound. But then I could only correct the ratios of the three mixing desks on stage. After a while, I didn't need to do that any more and I did all the mixing from the stage.'

In Bologna, we played an open-air concert in a stadium that almost ended in disaster. The stage construction was pretty high and rather wobbly, and a storm had brought parts of it to the brink of collapse. The front rows of the audience were in serious danger. The roadies managed to pool their strength and prevent the stage from falling on anyone by holding it up – and we could go on with our performance.

On the Beach with Chris Bohn and Anton Corbijn

From Italy, we moved on to Marseille, then Toulouse and from there to Barcelona. We were booked into the fancy Regency Hotel, just the kind of old place we loved: a typical grand hotel with a pristine white facade, plush fittings and furnishings, lots of velvet and gold. That cheered us up. And our show at the Palau Blaugrana was well-attended with an audience of around 2000 – a great concert!

The media was very interested, so EMI had set up a press conference in a function room at our hotel. Independently of that, the journalist Chris Bohn had come from England to interview Ralf for the *NME*. He had booked the photographer Anton Corbijn to take shots of us and our plastic lookalikes. Chris Bohn turned out to be an expert on Kraftwerk references and traced a long multi-thematic line from the Italian Futurists to Bauhaus to the German Federal Criminal Police Office (Bundeskriminalamt – 'BKA'). This time, we got positive reports in the *NME* for our gigs in the UK. We could use them, as they supported our upcoming tour there. Consulting an old copy, I note that *Computer World* had just shot up the *NME* Hit Parade from 21 to 15, after entering the album charts four weeks previously. Ahead of us was *Hotter*

Than July by Stevie Wonder – and one spot behind us was the Moody Blues's *Long Distance Voyager*.

The Dutch photographer Anton Corbijn was in great demand at the time. To me, he came across as very quiet and modest, not at all pushy or transgressive like some of his fellow photographers tend to be, for professional reasons. He wanted to do the shoot at a public beach. His idea was for the four of us to pose in street clothing in the midst of crowds of people in swimsuits. We turned the plan down straight away, though; it felt rather disrespectful to use scantily dressed strangers as unpaid extras. Corbijn didn't insist on it. Looking at the photo of us in between the little changing huts on the beach always makes me grin. I'm wearing white plastic sandals with my tasteful black outfit. I'd bought them for a few pesetas somewhere on the beach and simply left them on, not thinking about it. A typical case of underdressing . . . Incidentally, Corbijn also photographed our showroom dummy heads waiting for their cue backstage, at some point. Their portraits are often on show in exhibitions of the renowned director and photographer's work to this day.

We were now cruising around Europe on a bus hired from a professional travel company. Not a gigantic nightliner with all mod-cons like bands use nowadays, though; it was fairly well equipped but not luxurious. There were comfortable seats at the front and a sofa and armchairs at the back with a table at the centre, where we could hold 'editorial conferences'. The most impressive thing was the bunkbeds in the middle, which meant we could lie down for a snooze whenever we liked. I soon got used to the pale pink sunshades. And the rest of the fittings – fridge, chemical toilet and air conditioning – were fine. As a little money-maker on the side, our driver Erwin had installed a coffee machine and sold it to us by the cup. Other than that, he drove the bus with a cool hand. Erwin was a professional.

From Barcelona, we went on to Lyon, Zürich and Brussels – where 400, 1000 and 900 people attended our gigs. Nothing out of the ordinary happened at any of them, but our three concerts in Hamburg, Berlin and Munich where much more exciting – our first performances in Germany since March 1975 in the WDR Sendesaal.

Three Gigs in Germany

Computer World hit the German charts on 8 June. Even the weekly news magazine *Der Spiegel* ran an article on Kraftwerk, which felt remarkable. A piece in *Der Spiegel* meant a lot, then as now. Or sometimes, at least. To sum it up: for the anonymous reviewer, our new LP was brainless and uncritical 'hot air from the database'. Kraftwerk were allegedly celebrating a 'brave new computer world, unsullied by negative utopias', were making 'robot rubbish', were soulless 'dial turners' who produced 'simple bubble-and-squeak rhythms' and 'artless tunes for fast consumption in lifts and discos'. The journalist seemed to prefer musicians who worked up a sweat on stage. His prognosis for the live experience: 'For the listener who has not yet raised his awareness and sensation to the technological state of the art, it won't be without frustration and boredom.'[1] Obviously, an introduction like that didn't exactly crank up the ticket sales for our German tour. But still, the gigs in the three cities were well attended. About 1600 people came to the Musikhalle Hamburg (now called Laeiszhalle). Once again, we met the comedian Otto's manager,

Hans-Otto Mertens, who this time filmed our show with his team. His company had just invested in modern video technology, and Hans-Otto's crew turned up with four cameras to document the concert. Ralf later used the footage to make the video for our hit single 'The Model'.

The Hamburgers are known for their reserve, but there was no sign of that at our gig that evening. People were dancing in the aisles, cheering and having a real party. Our show concept certainly seemed to work in Germany.

The next day, we drove one of the transit routes through East Germany to West Berlin. It was the first time I crossed the socialist state by road. At some point, Erwin pulled up at a service station. While he took care of petrol for the bus, we entered the state-owned Mitropa refreshments outlet to sample a selection of GDR foodstuffs. That was when I learned a German word that had previously passed me by: *Sättigungsbeilage* – literally, an additional element of a meal intended to ensure satiety; in practice a serving of carbs. Pronounced in a Saxon accent, the six syllables sounded like a magic spell. After that, crossing the border to West Berlin was less spectacular than I'd imagined. The border guards didn't seem particularly interested in us. Without further incident, we re-entered the Federal Republic of Germany singing a few genuine Berlin songs, and soon reached the centre of West Berlin.

A Concert from My Perspective

The famous Metropol Theatre is sold out on this Wednesday, 10 June 1981 – despite the tickets costing an incredible 24

Deutschmarks. The almost overcrowded auditorium is pretty oppressive; the air is as thick as soup and heats up the atmosphere in general. The temperature keeps rising and rising as the tightly packed people start to get impatient. It's after 8 p.m. and everyone hopes it'll start soon. We've never performed in this line-up in Berlin. No one in the audience knows what will happen. And yes, it's really hot.

Shortly before the concert begins, we're sorting things out on stage as we always do. Up here, the climate is subtropical too. Unnoticed by the audience behind the grey curtain, we can tune our synthesizers using headphones, set up the sounds for the first track and discuss a couple of things in advance. But it's also the perfect time for a bit of nonsense to calm our nerves. Emil leaps around and then disappears soundlessly into the dressing room. Günter Spachtholz makes sure his tapes are lined up correctly and Joachim, standing at the mixing desk on the left edge of the stage, gives us his OK: 'Everything's ready, lads!'

There's a little window in the curtain and we take a curious peek into the auditorium. 'Look, Karl, on the left in the front row – doesn't that lady with the huge beehive look kind of familiar? Is it the woman from the B-52's, maybe?' The nervous tension in the audience reaches us too, of course, and we're at least as excited as the 1500 or so people waiting for us tonight. The question is: how will the Berliners react to our performance?

A few minutes before the beginning of the show, as ever, a bizarre sound sequence plays from tape to set the mood. Then Florian fades it out slowly and switches on our electronic announcer.

'Meine Damen und Herren, Ladies and Gentlemen, from Germany: the man-machine, Kraftwerk,' the Votrax speech synthesizer pronounces in a creaky voice. The first applause and shouts echo back to us, and Florian starts the cassette. We hear the 'Numbers' beat and are relieved to note that the sequencer and the Triggersumme are in sync – excellent! Now we quickly leave the stage and position ourselves out of sight in the wings on the right.

The curtain opens, neon tubes flicker on, and to frenetic applause we enter the stage – dressed all in black as always – one after another: Ralf, Karl, Wolfgang and Florian. We take up our places with our backs to the audience.

'One – two – three – four – five – six – seven – eight,' the English speaker counts. A lot of fans now recognize the track from the *Computer World* LP. Even with my back to the audience, I can sense how surprised people are by our stage set-up. The V-shaped control centre, about fourteen metres long and illuminated, takes everyone's breath away at first glance. On closer inspection, you can make out the machines integrated into the consoles: synthesizers, mixing desks, electronic drums, sequencers, televisions, telephones, measuring gauges, the lighting above the 19-inch inserts. It isn't a fake – almost the entire Kling Klang Studio is on stage; all we left behind in Düsseldorf is the walls and the doors. No wonder the media often compare our stage set-up to the bridge of the *Starship Enterprise*.

It's not us that plays 'Numbers' but the system, automatically, and after the countdown of Japanese and Russian numbers, 'ichi – ni – san – shi – adin – dwa – tri', a short break cuts off the flow. We turn to face the audience and Ralf plays the intro to the next track on his Polymoog: 'Computer World'.

The lighting changes at exactly the right moment. It's a simple but incredibly impressive effect, amplified by the flickers of the neon tubes as they make the switch. Behind us, underneath the slanting consoles, there are several rows of neon tubes that bathe the stage in a different coloured light for every song. About two or three metres above us, large video screens are installed for the projections.

We stand behind chrome-plated cases with our instruments: Ralf's Minimoog, Polymoog and Orchestron, Florian's synthesizers and an electronic flute to one side of him, Wolfgang at the Triggersumme and me at my keyboard for the synthesizer housed behind me in the rack.

Wolfgang is solely responsible for the live percussion and controlling the Triggersumme. The only time I help out on drums is in the late passages of driving-sound music on 'Autobahn'. The two of us then stand facing each other in the middle of the stage, hammering at the multipads with our knitting needles. I have to be careful not to burst out laughing when we look each other in the eye. Other than that, I play the basslines on 'Computer World', 'Home Computer', 'The Model', 'Trans-Europe Express' and the encore – the melody for 'Computer Love', 'Radioactivity' and 'The Hall of Mirrors' – and chords and bass on 'Neon Light', 'Autobahn' and 'The Robots'. I'm really glad to be the bass man for 'Computer World'. Thanks to the reduced 'Numbers' beat and the synthetic steel-string bass, the live track has got pretty darn funky.

With his combined headphones and microphone, Florian looks like a helicopter pilot. Normally, he doesn't move much on stage and concentrates on playing. Today, though, the Berliners have managed to relax him. He gives Ralf laid-back hand signals to tell him to play a bit quieter and even breaks into a smile now and then. In actual fact, Florian enjoys the limelight. But for some reason he usually holds back. Ralf is more relaxed tonight as well, even bending his knees occasionally and singing into his headset with a Rhineland accent: 'Interpol and Deutsche Bank . . .' Incidentally, headsets were pretty rare in pop and rock at that time, so they really stood out.

I do cringe looking back at my performance but I do look free and unselfconscious. Each of us has found his own body language in a miniature choreography and is entirely in the music. Today is a good day – we've hit the spot. The first part of the concert consists of the new tracks from the album: 'Numbers', 'Computer World', 'Home Computer' with the coda 'It's More Fun to Compute' and 'Computer Love'. When we then play 'The Model', 'Neon Light' and 'Radioactivity', the audience gets more enthusiastic as they recognize more songs. And with 'Autobahn', 'Trans-Europe Express', 'The Hall of Mirrors' and 'Showroom Dummies' we tip over to almost a nine on the Richter scale. Between the tracks, Ralf makes a few remarks to the audience, like 'Pretty hot in here . . .' or 'I don't know what to say.' People like that. The atmosphere couldn't be better.

At the end, we grab our mini-instruments and walk up to the front edge of the stage. The neon lettering spelling out our names flickers on, another dramatic moment. We play 'Pocket Calculator', supported by the audience. To go with the line 'by pressing down a special key it plays a little melody,' Ralf and Florian hold the mini-keyboard and the pocket calculator out into the audience and invite them to play along. All I can see now is laughing faces. Yes! This is why I became a musician! Man, it feels good. We're celebrating the moment; people love our music. In this instant, everyone around me is happy. I am too. And exactly that is the point of music. We're the best damn band in the world!

After 'Pocket Calculator', the curtain goes down. The last song on the set-list is 'The Robots'. Our four plastic lookalikes are placed alongside us at our keyboards. They're wearing red shirts and black ties with flashing diodes.

Florian goes to his keyboard and starts playing the intro with the robot sounds, laughing out loud. He dissembles the acoustic portrait into its individual parts and streches them as if they were made of rubber. Ralf joins in, taking over part of the sound components. The audience on the other side of the curtain cheers, euphoric now. Florian reacts to their approval and can't stop laughing, repeating the pattern of robot sounds several times with Ralf. The audience is on fire. Florian is in his element and Ralf has also discovered his inner child, somewhere deep inside. The game with the audience feedback turns into an electro-comedy. When the tension finally gets too much for Florian, he starts the cassette in the Portadeck. We'd recorded the sequence with the robot riff slowly and programmed an accelerando – the music begins slow and gets faster and faster as it goes on, until it reaches 116 beats per minute. We give them 'The Robots'. The track always works live; it's a sure-fire hit. Once we finish and while we're still playing the coda, the curtain closes to tumultuous applause.

After that, we improvise another encore with each of us performing a few tricks on his instrument. Eventually, we leave the stage after about two hours, exiting in reverse order: Florian, Wolfgang, Karl and Ralf. Done. What a riot!

I think I can say without exaggeration that this performance at the Metropol was one of the best we did in this line-up under the name of Kraftwerk. Sure, we didn't play the tracks exactly as we'd recorded them on our albums. Instead, our show was reminiscent of the atmosphere and spirit of our writing sessions. There was a palpable but positive tension between the four of us on stage, we maintained eye contact, we touched each other, talked to each other, gave each other signals, laughed, operated our music machines and devices and played our instruments live. The sound that filled the auditorium from the speakers was vibrant music.

I can't remember what happened backstage after the gig. Later that night, though, we put in an appearance at Dschungel on Nürnberger Strasse – the famous nightclub where David Bowie and Iggy Pop and the Berlin scene hung out. We simply had to go and see it for ourselves. What we did there, whether we danced or just stood around – no idea. Mental blackout!

My memories of the following gig in Munich, at Zirkus Krone, are patchy. It had the exact same dramatic structure, of course. But it was a different day, a different audience, and music can never be repeated – if you exclude recordings, at least. I do remember our feast with Fritz Rau. Our legendary concert agent invited us to the Käfer Restaurant after the gig and told one story after another from the live music biz. The best of many: Keith Richards goes to the dentist during a Rolling Stones tour. The German dentist is flabbergasted because the anaesthetic has no effect . . . It was a long evening of listening, eating, drinking and laughing. That night in the Hotel Bayerischer Hof, I checked my itinerary to be on the safe side. The next leg was across the channel to the UK.

Sound Exchange with the UK

Saturday and Sunday were set aside for the journey. The equipment was taken by ferry on a truck, and our travelling party flew from Munich to Manchester. We began the tour on 15 June in front of 2400 people in the sold-out Free Trade Hall, at that time *the* venue in Manchester, a Victorian monster of a building. Then we headed further north to play the obligatory two gigs in Scotland: in Glasgow at the Apollo, in Edinburgh in the Playhouse Theatre.

In an interview with *Sounds* magazine that he did while on this tour, Ralf talked about one of his favourite subjects: the advantages of mechanical music over manually played music. One sentence is a prime example of Kraftwerk's frequently stated blind faith in progress: 'I think if Bach had a computer in his time, he would definitely have used it. I think now it's better to use your own mind and activate certain cells, rather than impose a written score on other people and say, you play that note at that point and you play this note at that point.'[2]

Johann Sebastian Bach's music has a magical power of attraction over us, to this day. But it went over the heads of his peers. He wrote his works as cantor at St Thomas' Church in Leipzig, unnoticed by the rest of the world, pieces that are now canonical – we know over a thousand compositions written by him! Bach was undervalued – not because he was ahead of his time, but because he ignored the musical tastes of the day. He took his orientation from the composers of the Middle Ages and the Renaissance and brought polyphony to a perfection that still astounds us. His masterful skill lies in the artful combination

367

of harmonic movement and counterpoint. But his extremely complex fugues were outmoded even during his lifetime. It's something like if someone were to compose twelve-tone music in the style of Arnold Schönberg today. Bach made no attempt to adapt his work to the zeitgeist. For his audience at the time, he embodied a yearning for the past. Bach was probably the greatest ever non-conformist in music, a convincing example of integrity and independence of thought.

He lived in the Age of Enlightenment, when reason was declared the yardstick for every action. Yet Bach was not a man of science or philosophy but a deeply religious Protestant. 'S.D.G.', *Soli Deo Gloria*, glory to God alone, he wrote under most of his compositions.

Now it came to pass that during his lifetime, the instrument-makers made pianos on which all the timbres and keys of the circle of fifths could be played. Tempered tuning – dividing the octave into twelve mathematically equal parts – brought an extreme expansion of possibilities for musical expression. Bach's *Well-Tempered Clavier* – two collections, each of 24 preludes and fugues in all major and minor keys (1722 and 1742) – played an essential part in the historical establishment of tempered tuning, invented by Andreas Werkmeister in 1681, four years before Bach was born.

We don't know what Bach would have thought of a 1981-model computer. Perhaps he would have used it on his *St Matthew Passion*? If so, what would he have got the computer to do? Even thinking about Bach's life, virtuoso talent and art of composition for just a moment, such a hypothesis seems absolutely absurd. But in truth, Ralf's interview is not about music at all; it's about the magical feeling of progress.

368

Over the course of our *Computer World* tour, that faith in the unstoppable progress of technology developed into a veritable ideology of the machine. It almost seems as if Ralf's rhetoric was anticipating the soundbites currently put about by Silicon Valley's friends of the machine – I'll come back to the digital giants' so-called platform capitalism later on. The technocratic ideas and rhetoric of our PR was tied (presumably out of ignorance of the material) to a notorious rejection of traditional musical performance practice, essentially of any tradition that didn't fit into the modern worldview. I considered that just as out of touch as the Futurist fantasies of Filippo Tommaso Marinetti, who wished he could throw everything that was old into the dustbin of history.

To my mind, though, our little pop song 'Computer Love' and the monumental *Well-Tempered Clavier* aren't mutually exclusive. Why should they be? It really ought to be up to every individual to decide what kind of music appeals to them. Playing or listening to Bach, on whatever level, is one of the most wonderful experiences one can have in life. By the way, I'm convinced that Bach's works will still be played all over our planet in the distant future – by people, entirely without computers. So the only objective can be – as Pierre Schaeffer recommends – to look ahead and at the same time find a harmonious relationship with musical traditions.[3]

The next stop on our concert tour was Newcastle City Hall. The press was waiting for us there, too, and the *NME*'s gig review was positive: 'It's a perfect imperfect mix of POP FUN and crafted work.'[4] We were definitely moving in the right direction. By this point, we had a bit of a routine going. The crew worked well together and everyone knew what to do. *Computer World* had come out in the UK in May as well, climbing to number 15 in the album charts, and earning us a silver record. The single 'Pocket Calculator' got to number 39.

After the success of *The Man-Machine*, the British media were in two minds about *Computer World*, as I saw it. The *NME* noted a certain musical subtlety but called it 'often overlooked' and complained that the lyrics were less serious than on our previous records.[5] *Melody Maker* found our music 'cold but elegant, stark but poignant,'[6] and they also ran a review of 'Pocket Calculator.'[7]

Our itinerary took us on to Sheffield and the Northwest, where we came across a late form of Beatlemania: Kraftwerkmania in Liverpool. I couldn't help thinking about the escape scenes in *A Hard Day's Night*. As we left the Royal Court Theatre after the concert, we were awaited at the stage door by a determined group of fans. They pushed and shoved, laughed and screamed at us. There was plenty of hands-on contact as well. A whole new experience for us. We responded with friendly smiles and tried to stay out of the way of the well-meaning pushing and shoving. Then a few people rushed out of the auditorium and hustled us into the waiting limousine. That's all, folks!

The thing is: every fan is a nice person – but when lots of them get together and 'embrace' us, it's not always pleasant. Who wants to be touched by complete strangers? And even though it might not be meant that way, the people on the receiving end of the attention are under a lot of pressure and sometimes get scared. We all felt like that and we wanted to avoid similar situations in the future, so we changed the way we ended the subsequent gigs. While the last number was still playing, we jumped directly off the stage into a car and drove straight to our hotel – before the fans had time to gather outside the stage door. That worked perfectly for the rest of our concerts in England, and we decided to stick to the routine from then on.

The next day, another enthusiastic audience awaited us at the Odeon Theatre in Birmingham, giving us great support. We were having a really good run.

London

I can't say why it was that we played our four London concerts in three different venues. Maybe the Hammersmith Odeon was booked up, or maybe it was deliberate. Whatever the reason, we appeared once at the Lyceum, once at the Hammersmith Palais, and did two nights at the Hammersmith Odeon. That was a pretty big deal for an electro-band from Düsseldorf. Our concerts got us noticed, at least in the print media and on the radio. It was on this tour that Kraftwerk's multimedia approach developed, and it was understood and celebrated by the press and our fans. It made perfect sense that it had a knock-on effect in other countries.

The British pop scene felt different in 1981 than it had in the mid-seventies, the last time we'd been on a major tour of the UK. Electropop was becoming increasingly respected, with a change clearly on the horizon: 'Fade to Grey', 'Vienna' and 'New Life' were on heavy rotation on the radio and starting to enter the mainstream. But the hype around British electro or New Wave bands like Simple Minds, OMD, Spandau Ballet, Visage, Ultravox, Depeche Mode, Duran Duran, Soft Cell, Heaven 17, The Human League and New Order hadn't yet reached its peak.

371

As we know now, some of these bands were only at the start of their impressive careers.

The success of the punk movement inspired confidence in people making music without fully learning an instrument, and was easily applied to electronic equipment. Machines made all sorts of things possible. But the newcomers weren't interested in the Futurist cult of the machine; they saw synthesizers and electronic instruments as tools, and focused on the art of song-writing. That placed them in a long tradition that first flourished in the 1960s. This approach made the new bands – labelled 'New Wave', 'New Romantic' or 'Synth Pop' by the industry – very successful.

The electro-sound had left its avant-garde experimental niche and was hitting the mainstream. More and more music producers turned up, managing to get their songs into the Top Ten in Europe and the USA at the same time. Even established artists like Steve Winwood and Phil Collins discovered synthesizers and drum machines, scoring international hits with their albums *Arc of a Diver* and *Face Value* in 1980 and 1981. Collins' ballad 'In the Air Tonight' sold millions. Soon enough, teams formed – like in the sports world – working efficiently towards their goal through division of labour and by integrating professional sales teams, managers, sound engineers and other music industry people. That was approximately the atmosphere we came across in Britain in the summer of 1981, when we plugged our lively three-dimensional stage show into London's sold-out concert halls.

At the Lyceum on 28 June, the fans hailed the 'return of their heroes',[8] as the *Guardian* reported. Not even the *Times* could pass us by. Our stage set in the Hammersmith Palais was described – prompted by references Ralf and Florian had once made – as looking 'like something von Braun might have designed in a spare moment for Lang to use on the set of a sci-fi B-movie in the futuristic Fifties.'[9]

We were booked into a London hotel from the Lyceum gig on, resulting in an astronomical room-service bill due to my consumption of countless club sandwiches and all kinds of snacks. We also made two trips to Bristol and Oxford to perform there. Ever since we'd got to the UK, we'd been promising ourselves 'No Sleep 'til Hammersmith', as in the title of Motörhead's first live LP, and finally the big day came. We played the Hammersmith Odeon on 2 and 3 July.

At the last gig, Ralf's mini-keyboard broke down during 'Pocket Calculator'. By this point, though, we had such a routine down that we could deal with technical hitches just fine. I pointed at Ralf's Minimoog behind him and he immediately understood, went over to the synth and played his keyboard part there instead. I focused on him, but I did spot David Byrne in the front row, out of the corner of my eye.

When it came to music, all of Europe looked to England. It had been that way since the early sixties, when the Beatles reinvented the music business. And now we'd just finished an almost three-week successful tour of the UK – it was incredible. For the first time, I felt the meaningful sense of playing a part in music that I had created – partly – myself. It meant a lot to me to be a member of a band whose unmistakable identity was widely perceived.

The atmosphere between us was good, sometimes even euphoric. We were united by our firm belief in what we considered our goals, independently of one another, otherwise it wouldn't have worked. Up to now, we had been on the way up!

Paris

We left the UK and skimmed back to the Continent on the *Princess Anne*, a new-fangled hovercraft. Then it was on to Paris, where Ian Floogs's agency had made a booking for us at Captain Video. Only about 200 to 400 people had come to our concerts in Marseille, Toulouse and Lyon at the start of the tour; we appeared to have fallen out of favour in France over the past three years. Our absence meant Maxime Schmitt's years of clever hard work hit a brick wall. In 1981, at any rate, we didn't manage to get *Computer World* into the higher realms of the charts or get a sensible tour off the ground. So the Paris gig was an important stop to reach the print media, at least.

After the one-off in Paris, Florian invited the whole gang back to La Bastide Blanche, a really nice gesture. This time, though, Wolfgang and I said thanks but turned down the invitation. We preferred to spend the next fortnight in Düsseldorf. Aside from that, I didn't fancy cycling the life-threatening curves around Saint-Tropez and Ramatuelle. Even reading the racing cyclist Rudi Altig's book *Die goldenen Speichen* (*Golden Spokes*) couldn't bring me closer to bike racing. The whole professional cycling culture and the ideology of performance sport just wasn't my thing.

Back in Canada and the USA

On 22 July 1981 we set off across the Atlantic. We had ten gigs lined up in North America over the next fortnight. As you might guess by the low number of bookings, the summer of 1981 wasn't a huge success for us in the USA. It was no comparison to our first tour there. Back in 1975, we'd had a hit single in the charts and travelled around the States with a small crew and not much equipment. On the *Computer World* tour, our luggage weighed seven to ten tonnes, a huge logistical challenge that came at a high price. And the team was twice the size as the last time. That meant our fees were presumably calculated much higher – and it looked like not many event organizers wanted to spend that much on us.

In my view, Kraftwerk were seen in the USA as innovative and influential with a style of our very own, but we weren't considered commercially viable. Things have stayed that way to this day, more or less. And that meant our ticket sales were on the modest side. What we needed but didn't have was a hit single on the radio. At that time, records were promoted centrally via the medium of radio stations. MTV didn't launch until 1 August 1981.

All in all, we managed just over a week in the Midwest and on the West and East Coasts in Detroit, Chicago, Cleveland, Los Angeles, Philadelphia, Washington, D. C., and New York City.

Kling Klang at the Ritz

And yet we played perhaps the most important concerts on the tour – possibly the most important Kraftwerk concerts out of all our gigs – on 3 and 4 August in New York's Ritz. The venue's actual name was Webster Hall. It was a large ballroom in the East Village, the kind that flourished all over the States in the late 19th century. In 1980, the Ritz opened its doors there as a live club and dancefloor. As far as I can judge, it was the hippest club in New York at the time.

We imagined it would be mainly people from the music industry in the audience: producers, musicians, label bosses, managers, A&R men, press and PR people and celebrities. That made me much more nervous than a few years before at the Beacon Theatre. But the crowd was on our side on both nights – we were borne aloft on a wave of affection and enthusiasm that went beyond mere respect. The New Yorkers understood our offbeats, our electronic sound collages, European melodies and the subtle humour of our lyrics. The *New York Post* celebrated our gig as one of *the* music events of the year: 'Monday, the band actually brought Kling Klang to the Ritz. In a setting straight out of *Star Trek*, Kraftwerk took to the stage. [. . .] Kraftwerk designed a truly awesome futuristic audio-visual treat for all its metallic minions.'[10]

After the show, Emil and I walked all the way from the East Village up Park Avenue to the Hotel St. Moritz, including a short stretch through Central Park at the end. Once we got to the lobby, I almost choked when Emil mentioned in passing that he just had to deposit that evening's takings in the hotel safe. If I'd known he had all the cash on him I certainly wouldn't have strolled through the park so cool and collected.

The America of 1981 didn't fascinate me in the same way as it had in 1975. But we were only there for a few days – far too short. I do wonder why we didn't make it onto one of the national TV shows with our *Star Trek*-style setting. Even now, several decades later, it seems to me like a missed opportunity that we didn't establish Kraftwerk in any lasting way in the USA.

376

For our line-up, at least, further success in the States was to remain out of reach. We flew back to Germany on 5 August.

Behind the Iron Curtain

The next lap of our tour took us to Eastern Europe: Hungary and Poland, to be precise. We would have liked to play in the Soviet Union, of course, and in East Germany or other Warsaw Pact countries, but presumably the necessary formalities called for a whole lot of bureaucracy, and there was another not insignificant question: how would we be paid? We'd heard hair-raising stories about artists' fees converted into a currency of sable coats, Beluga caviar or Crimean wine to be taken back to the West. So it was surely no walk in the park getting permission to play there in the first place.

In Hungary, apparently the most liberal and Western-oriented country in the Eastern Bloc, we lodged directly on the bank of the Danube in Budapest's famous Hotel Gellért. The hotel's thermal baths were a real highlight, we were told. Sadly not for us, as they were closed for renovation. It was quite warm in Budapest, and I remember the atmosphere of those days well. During the soundcheck in Kisstadion, several people spoke to me in Hungarian, assuming I understood the language because of my surname. They soon realized they were wrong about that, though.

Our two open-air concerts were lively gigs with 13,000-strong audiences on both nights – our record at that point. From the stage, the crowd looked like a swarm of people. I find it much more of a challenge appearing in a club in front of only a few faces. The applause in Kisstadion was frenetic, giving me a great feeling in my belly and my heart. The two shows were a major success!

On our off day, we went on a cycling tour along the Danube for several hours, ending up soaked in sweat, slurping cold Hungarian cucumber soup in a tavern. Out of the corner of my eye, I saw Ralf's shaved and oiled cyclist legs glinting in the sunshine.

And on we went to Poland. I started to get a strange feeling that I couldn't shake off. From my point of view, the Poles had no reason to be positive about a German band. Weren't the crimes of the Second World War and the suffering caused to them by Germans reason enough to be suspicious? And they might not find it all that funny that we'd brought out a record inspired by Russian art, featuring snippets of Russian and showing us in red shirts and black ties on the cover, either.

As we drove around Poland in our tour bus in August 1981, the political atmosphere in the country was tense due to the catastrophic economic situation and the resulting workers' strikes. A young woman boarded the bus with us and accompanied us from then on. She was wearing civilian clothing but I think she – I'll just call her Olga – held the rank of political officer, and her job was clearly to keep a keen eye on us. Olga didn't speak a word of German and only rudimentary English – or so she said – so we barely communicated with her. Of course, we didn't believe a word she said, so we kept our usual rude comments to ourselves on the bus, speaking in a rather more educated tone. She was nice enough but we gave her what we thought was the hilarious nickname of 'Koteletta Keulova', meaning something like 'Cutlet Knuckle-ova'. Sorry, Olga!

378

Our route took us to Katowice, Wrocław, Gdansk, Warsaw and Opole. The halls or stadiums were full, with an average audience of 6000. Not wanting to upset or provoke anyone, we asked whether it would be a problem to recite the line 'Ya tvoi sluga, ya tvoi rabotnik' in 'The Robots'. Not at all, we were told, people would take it the right way. And they really did – the audiences reacted very positively, and aside from the soldiers shouldering machine guns in front of the stage, I enjoyed the shows too.

I think it was in Warsaw that a group of fellow Germans from the GDR approached us at the hotel. They had come specially to see our concert. Talking to them, I thought I was hearing German from a totally different era. I understood every word but it sounded utterly unfamiliar. And I don't mean their dialect; it really was the language of a different country, even further away than Austria or Switzerland.

Without a doubt, my starkest memory of this section of the tour was visiting Auschwitz-Birkenau concentration camp. We cycled through the camp in silence – the impression over-whelmed me. I looked around the grounds mechanically, as if under anaesthetic, incapable of thought. Knowing about the events of the past and living with inherited guilt is one thing. Actually being inside a former concentration camp is very diffi-cult to cope with, however.

After the Opole concert, we set off for home on 27 August 1981. Our agency had the brilliant idea of getting us paid not in sable coats, caviar or Crimean wine, but in the form of plane tickets. Polish Airlines cooperated with Swissair, which meant we got flights to Japan and Australia – the next stops on our tour.

Back at our Düsseldorf base camp, we had a five-day inter-mission during the last throes of summer. Apart from hanging out, playing the organ and getting vaccinated against tropical diseases, I didn't manage a thing. Then again, it was the best time in the world to relax with Bettina on the balcony until late at night, eating spaghetti, drinking red wine and talking. Mentally, though, I was still on the road; it was just a short break and we'd soon be off again.

Japan

The tour kicked off again on 2 September. We started with a flight from Düsseldorf to Zürich, then switched planes and landed in Bombay twelve hours later. After an endless stopover, we boarded a third plane and finally reached the then-British crown colony of Hong Kong on 4 September, not quite fresh as daisies after another nine-hour flight. To cap it all, we had to wait two days there for our next flight to Japan. Wolfgang and I hung out in our hotel room, channel-surfing. I suspect our ridiculously long journey was down to limited options with the tickets we'd 'earned' in Poland and Hungary.

Back in 1981, Japan was far away in every respect. I had not the slightest idea what awaited us there. My head was buzzing with generalized ideas of politeness, suppressed emotions, sense of duty, control, Shintō and Buddhism, Zen, samurai, judo, hara-kiri, kamikaze, futon, Fujiyama, cherry blossoms, koto, kimonos, chopsticks, sushi, rice, sake, manga, kitsch, consumer electronics, robots and computers. But in fact, I knew nothing about the country on the other side of the world.

In Tokyo, we started our stay at the Keio Plaza, a steel skyscraper of enormous proportions. Even the various hotel restaurants seemed supersized to me. Everything in this metropolis of more than eight million looked so huge that I felt like a grain of sand in the desert. Public spaces were clean as a whistle, even the manhole covers were chrome-plated, and no one littered the streets with dropped cigarettes or tissues. Order and discipline were king, as I saw, heard, smelled and felt everywhere. I was also overwhelmed by the millions of written characters and neon ads. To my perception, the flood of characters and pictograms came across like a Kandinsky painting, but one that moved and changed unceasingly over time, like an abstract animated movie. Especially after our trip to Poland, Tokyo seemed like a city on another planet.

The jetlag made me feel like I was sleepwalking. I lost my orientation somewhat, and that got worse when we were standing by the gigantic world clock in the Keio Plaza lobby, wearing our red shirts and black ties for a photo session and looking up at the names of the cities and the times there. Never before had I seen the world like that; I imagined us playing concerts in every place. Who was to say we couldn't?

Our first two shows were at Nakano Sun Plaza Hall on 7 and 8 September. As at all our concerts in Japan, the auditorium was seated. We were more than happy with 6000 tickets sold.

Two days later, a TV crew was waiting for us at the Shibuya Koukai Do Hall. The show went on air even though we got there late. I had no idea of either the channel nor the programme, nor what it was about – we just went along with it as best we could. One sound memory from our gigs in Japan has stayed fresh in my mind to this day. I can hear the audience applauding perfectly in sync, for a very long time. There were no individual whoops or cheers, something we weren't used to. Later, our record label, EMI, invited us to dinner. We really liked the plastic models of food in the restaurant windows. After that we dived into the city's nightlife.

Tokyo's entertainment district seemed huge and bizarre to me. Everything glowed, glinted and glittered – I was almost dazzled by the millions of light sources. There were clubs and discos in the skyscrapers – a different one on every storey, each playing the right music for a specific scene. Surprised, we stood on the edge of a packed dancefloor, seeing not one single other European. Ralf and Wolfgang weaved their way onto the floor and immersed themselves in their mechanical dancing. In one of the clubs, we met the guys from Yellow Magic Orchestra – a very friendly but reserved close encounter of the third kind made up of polite exchanges, a bit of banter and a few embarrassed looks. We weren't capable of anything more than that, under the circumstances.

For our fourth gig, in Osaka, we took the bullet train. We didn't have high-speed trains back in Europe at that time, with the TGV not darting across France until the beginning of 1982. After the concert at the Festival Hall we moved on straight to Kyoto, where we had a free day on 12 September and viewed the former royal court. The fifth Japanese concert in Nagoya was also well attended, with 2600 in the audience. And despite their traditionally reserved upbringing, the Japanese fans – genuine experts on electronic pop music – gave our *Computer World* concerts an enthusiastic reception.

In Nagoya, I finally took the opportunity to get myself a Walkman. It was an amazing invention, making it possible to listen to music anywhere at all. Launched by Sony in 1979, the Walkman mutated into a real status symbol during the eighties, representing a new mobile auditive lifestyle. I paid about 220 Deutschmarks for mine, which was pretty cheap. I hoped I could use it do something useful during our bus rides and flights. Scouting out a record shop, I discovered classical Japanese music and the albums of Kitarō,[11] a star of the emerging New Age scene. Listening to music helped me to pass the time in airports, planes and hotels.

Here in Japan, we got the best technical support of the tour – and the audience reaction was huge and incomparable. Our music suited the country. But now our travelling party set off for Australia. During the flight, Wolfgang programmed like mad on the TR-606 Drumatix Beatbox he'd bought in Japan, and if I remember rightly I heard from one of my bandmates, on the plane high above the Pacific Ocean, that the next Kraftwerk album might be called *Techno Pop*.

Down Under

Having landed in Sydney, we weren't allowed to leave the plane and spent ages waiting on board. Then officers turned up in white rubber gloves and breathing masks and started spraying the cabin with disinfectant, and I had a panic attack and could only just control myself. Down Under's starting really well, I thought, very chemical! We went out to eat that evening with the local promoter and a few EMI people. Tired and wired at the same time, I shovelled down everything on my plate mechanically and listened to the music-business conversations as though through a bank of fog: 'Love the album, what's gonna be the next single?' Ralf was the master of small talk; I really admired him for it. And Florian? Well, he could rabbit on like the best of them – but you couldn't always rely on it.

There was nothing work-related for us to do the next day, so Ralf, Emil and I rode our racing bikes along the beach. When my chain broke after a couple of hours, I wasn't surprised – who else would that happen to? Luckily, we came across a ferry and chugged merrily past the Sydney Opera House back to the harbour. Wolfgang had spent the day on the beach. 'Just like on holiday: swimming, sunbathing and reading,' he told me later in the hotel lobby.

We had four shows lined up in Australia. Our two concerts at Sydney's Capitol Theatre were sold out, with 2100 tickets each, while the two at the Princess Theatre, Melbourne, were less impressive with about 1200 tickets sold on average. The audience liked the show and the gigs went fine – no more and no less.

The advantage of playing two or more nights at one venue is obvious. On the second day, there's no need to travel and set up, so you can get used to the acoustics and spend the time doing something else. The same applied in Melbourne. On the afternoon of the second day, we met up again at the Princess Theatre, played a little and then hung out at the hotel. Florian went out on his own, as he often did; there was nothing unusual about that. After dinner, we entered the venue by the stage door and went to the dressing rooms to our mobile wardrobe. It contained all our outfits: four red shirts and four black shirts, ties, trousers and shoes. Each of us also had our own private drawer for personal items and the tools and notes we needed: Wolfgang's and my brass knitting needles, the miniature torches, lyrics and synth settings, that kind of thing. Our showroom dummies were set up directly next to the stage for their appearance on 'The Robots'.

Shortly before the show, we checked our instruments as ever behind the closed curtain. But there was something missing after all. Where was Florian? We couldn't find him anywhere. A desperate Emil searched the area, to no avail. Our starting time had already passed and the auditorium was getting restless. One or other of us kept peeping through the curtain to assess the situation. And suddenly, there he was: Florian – in the middle of the audience. Wolfgang whispered at me: 'He's sitting back there all calm and collected in his full stage outfit. What on earth has he got in mind?' Emil ran straight into the hall, with us watching from behind the curtain. He worked his way back to Florian, leaned down and spoke to him. Then we saw him turn around and come back to us. Our eyes were on stalks. Emil explained in a completely neutral tone that Florian wanted to see the show from the audience perspective tonight, and had told us to start without him. We had no idea how to react. But Ralf kept a cool head, as always. No, we won't start without Florian, he decided. It was Florian who started the playback cassettes throughout the entire show. Once again, Emil made his way through the audience to our bandmate. I don't have a clue how he convinced him, but eventually he brought Florian backstage and we could get started at last.

Over the course of the tour, I got used to Florian's strange moods. He was already rather infamous for upsetting journalists, running off, slamming doors or being absent or grumpy at times. But it was mainly directed at others, rarely inside the group.

Bombay in Monsoon Season

On 21 September 1981 we left the fifth continent and flew to Bombay – entering a completely different world. It was raining cats and dogs. When the rain did stop, I had trouble coping with the humidity. And what a noise on the streets! Utter chaos: engines rattling and banging, never-ending car horns. People were constantly shouting, everything whirled into one. I was shocked by the incredible numbers of very young beggars; whenever we got stuck in traffic our car would be surrounded by children. They showed us their maimed limbs and begged for a few rupees, a matter of life or death for them. It never stopped, and I'll never forget it, my whole life long.

We ourselves were staying at the Holiday Inn on Bombay's west coast. What a contrast. Once we got there, the staff explained it was currently the rainy season, monsoon time – possibly the worst time to visit India. Thanks for telling us. And what were we to do until our gigs on Friday? We had three days to kill! Some of the crew felt unwell and everyone retired to their own rooms. But even there, it wasn't really a pleasant climate – muggy, humid, the sheets damp even though they were changed every day. On one occasion, Emil and I went exploring despite the weather, and ended up in a covered shopping passage. Everything in there looked just like at Harrods in London. The biggest surprise: in one of the neatly decorated shop windows, we spotted a couple of Kraftwerk LPs.

The room Wolfgang and I shared was on one of the hotel's top floors. When the low-hanging clouds unexpectedly parted

386

on one of those endless days, the rain stopped and the sun flooded the surroundings. We suddenly had a marvellous view of the Indian Ocean – plus the slums verging directly onto the hotel grounds. People had built their makeshift shacks directly up against the hotel walls down there. The inhabitants, now emerging from beneath plastic sheets as the rain took a break, were a picture of hunger and misery. Children ran around between the hovels, splashing in huge puddles; dog dirt was piled everywhere from the masses of strays, most of them clearly sick. And we were sitting pretty in our hotel room, looking down on them like from a theatre box. I've rarely felt as bad as that in my life.

On the Thursday evening – rather worn down by this point – I accompanied Florian to a concert of Indian classical music. We'd been told it would be worth the effort. We took a short and adventurous taxi ride, walked a few metres and suddenly found ourselves in the midst of provisional shacks and wooden shelters outside a small but very sophisticated-looking administrative building. It looked to me like a UFO that had landed right there in Bombay, for some unknown reason. We bought tickets and entered the air-conditioned concert hall, both very curious. Up in the circle, we had an excellent view. Seated on the stage were musicians with traditional Indian instruments like sitar, sarangi, tanpura, santur, harmonium and tabla, ready to accompany the star of the show, Ustad Munawar Ali Khan. 'The Indian Supremes' – a small and cheerful female choir – had positioned themselves behind the singer. Aside from the impressive music, the communication between Ustad Munawar Ali Khan and the audience was extremely interesting. The people in their seats were part of the performance, talking to the artist in a constant conversation, their comments exerting a major influence over the show. Marvellous! I was really enthusiastic, and recorded the concert on my Walkman.

On the Friday, we were taken to our venue at last, an old concert hall. Our equipment was on stage as always, but it had got wet. As it turned out, the roof had a number of leaks, and our crew did their best to protect our sound system with plastic sheeting. The soundcheck revealed the extent of the water damage. The Synthanorma sequencer was the worst hit; a very sensitive appliance, it now kept changing tempo. We couldn't possibly perform normally with our equipment in this state, so we switched off our autopilot. Now it was down to Wolfgang and me to play the rhythms manually, and we got through the two concerts as best we could.

It was clear that people here read the British press, and Bombay's young elite had turned up to experience our show for themselves. Many of the people in the front rows looked like they'd studied at Oxford or Cambridge. I don't think anyone cottoned on to our technical problems. The concerts were very special, incomparable to any others on the tour. Even the sight of all the turbans in the audience – perhaps two to three thousand – was sensational. The crowd was absolutely silent during our performance, but the moment we finished, a storm of applause set in. At the second show at 10 p.m., it was the same pattern all over again. Most of the audience seemed to have bought two tickets and simply stayed in their seats.

Back to Normal

Arriving back in Düsseldorf felt great after our long trip. At last my clothes were no longer plastered to my body. Living in Europe's not bad at all, I thought in a taxi into the town centre. In my home studio, I sat down at the Farfisa organ and started the drum machine. As if playing automatically, my hands created Indian-style melodies.

On one of the next few days, I made my way to the Synthesizerstudio Bonn to buy a Polymoog from the guys. I really liked the analogue appliance's sound-forming possibilities – and I still do, by the way. One of my favourite pastimes instantly became floating multi-voiced chords on the air with an extremely long sustain – tempo rubato, naturally. Everyday life gradually returned. I even started teaching again.

Ever since we'd been back, my mind had been on the same subject. Things couldn't keep on the way they had been. I'd been working with Ralf and Florian for years now. Our musical development was going great, but then again, I was financially dependent on the two of them. Another thing I didn't like was that I had nothing to rely on other than our spoken agreements, which only ever related to the next upcoming project.

So one evening, I met up with Ralf at Kling Klang. Not beating about the bush, I spoke to him about the perspective of producing a solo record – or alternatively, a possible share of the Kraftwerk record sales. Ralf listened to my ideas. He thought the idea of recording a 'solo album' was absurd – after all, it would never occur to him. When it came to a royalty share, he gave me the feeling he took the matter seriously and would think it over.

Computer World had sold more than 100,000 copies in Germany by this point, even climbing to number 7 in the album charts on 21 October. The single of the same name had about 30,000 domestic sales. Not bad at all. But the media and above all the consumers were more focused on other artists' output that year. Kraftwerk were in the game but our album certainly wasn't the year's biggest hype.

Alongside established names like ABBA, AC/DC, the Police, Dire Straits, Pink Floyd and Supertramp, the Germans were going crazy for their own version of New Wave: Neue Deutsche Welle, NDW for short. The bands called themselves things like Ideal, Deutsch Amerikanische Freundschaft, Fehlfarben or Rheingold. The most famous NDW numbers included 'Goldener Reiter' by Joachim Witt, Bodo Staiger's 'Dreiklangs-Dimensionen', 'Da Da Da' by Trio and Fehlfarben's *Monarchie und Alltag* album, featuring the hit 'Ein Jahr (Es geht voran)'. The music fitted in with the times and reflected a new sense of confidence and awareness among German musicians. All at once, singing in German was in. And the magazines – which were still pretty key for promoting pop music in the early eighties – featured wall-to-wall NDW. Rightly so; a lot of that first 'wave' had a really good basis.

This new music had evolved underground out of the German version of punk music, some of it at Düsseldorf's Ratinger Hof venue. The artists and writers had great ideas, often with surprisingly fresh results. At the same time, independent labels were forming and producing tracks for this new scene. Once the established record companies realized that their products were not only creative but also had commercial potential, they bought independent labels out of the underground. EMI Electrola, for instance, took over the band Fehlfarben's Welt-Rekord label and added it to their roster to sell their own NDW products.

Untouched by all that, we simply went on as before. Joachim Dehmann reinstalled the equipment in the Kling Klang Studio at the end of October. We had itchy fingers. Eager not to lose time, we started the recording sessions for our next album. Ralf's *Techno Pop* slogan set the direction. We didn't know what direction it would be yet, but we were sure to find one.

Musique Concrète

Florian had tracked down a new machine: a sampler. It might be difficult to imagine these days, but at the beginning of the 1980s, the ability to record any audio material digitally was a really hot prospect. The Emulator from E-MU Systems looked like it had been designed by the makers of the Soviet T-34 tank, emigrated to the USA. The grey-and-blue colossus weighed in at about 30 kilos, like a 10-year-old child. It was so bulky that you'd think you could use it to jack up a car to change the tyres. The sample archiving function meant a new quality in dealing with sound recordings – they were stored on floppy disks. Florian's Emulator was the first sampler I ever saw. It cost about 10,000 dollars, a bargain considering the competition's Fairlight CMI came with a 35,000-dollar price tag.

Logically enough, sampling technology is closely linked to the development of sound recording. In the information era, sound recording is as normal as using the internet. No one expends a thought on the fact that sounds were originally linked to the time and place of their creation. Through the invention of electro-acoustic devices for recording, storing and playing back sound, it became possible to separate sound from its source. Telephones, radios and phonographs made sound independent of space and time.

The Emulator's effectiveness made a lasting impression on me. Like a magnetic tape recorder, it could transpose, reverse, cut, splice and endlessly repeat samples – except without razor blades and sticky tape, and in a fraction of the time. And that was just the beginning. It was incredible how recordings of apparently unrelated noises and sounds could be interconnected.

We knew, of course, that we were treading in the footsteps of Pierre Schaeffer, who had experimented with sounds at a French radio broadcaster in Paris after the Second World War. One of his many inventions was the trick with the closed groove – 'le sillon fermé' – on a record, which meant the content of that groove was repeated. These days, we call a technically produced ostinato a loop.

Schaeffer's work and his diary, published in 1952 under the title *A la recherche d'une musique concrète*, became a starting point for experimental sound design, until it arrived in pop music studios in the sixties and changed recording technology and the sound of music – although without Schaeffer's theories going along.

The rhythmic use of samples of varying lengths with differing content influenced not only our music, but the entire pop lexicon of the eighties and nineties.

Over the subsequent three weeks, we worked almost every day on new music. There was one riff, for example, that we'd first played at a soundcheck in London, and we put together a track from the writing sessions for *Computer World* by the name of 'Technicolor', which later became 'Tour de France'.

Between Kiel and Passau

After our overall rather successful tour of the globe, Fritz Rau's agency had booked us for a small follow-up tour of Germany, Austria, Holland and Luxembourg. We kicked off in mid-November. At the start of the tour I wrote down the audience sizes at every stop: Passau – 350, Salzburg – 300, Vienna – 750, Regensburg – 450, Mannheim – 1400, Dortmund – 700. From Braunschweig on, I stopped noting down the figures; it was too depressing. The audience seemed to crumble away from one city to the next: Kassel, Würzburg, Roth near Nuremberg, Mainz, Karlsruhe, Stuttgart, Bremen, Münster, Kiel, Hannover and Luxembourg. Only in a handful of cities like Cologne, Düsseldorf, Frankfurt and Utrecht did we still sell an average of 800 tickets per gig.

After the preceding concerts around Europe, the USA, Japan, Australia and India, the gigs in wintry Germany felt like a crash-landing. Small audiences, not much of an atmosphere. I had the feeling we were driving with the handbrake on. I'd simply run out of steam, and the monotony and modalities of travelling began to be a burden.

The two concerts in the Rhineland were an exception, though. To be honest, Cologne audiences made every one of our gigs there an event. And we played the Düsseldorf Philipshalle in front of around 1800 people. I recognized a few faces in the front row from the Ratinger Hof, watching the show with earnest expressions. We didn't seem to have a gigantic fan base in our home town. Some time later, an eye witness told me with an ironic wink that our stage set had reminded her of a fitted kitchen. And then there was a technical hitch in the middle of the show. The Synthanorma got out of sync with the playback and we had to stop mid-track and start it again. What can you do? These things happen. Somehow, the sparks didn't quite fly that evening. I could even understand it.

Over the past few years, a lively Düsseldorf music scene had developed, with its roots in the punk movement and no interest in Kraftwerk's geometric Bauhaus aesthetics in both sound and image. What the younger community formulated was a new, wild and often intelligent antithesis. They saw our audio-visual communication – I imagine – as too formulaic, stiff and sterile. We lacked subcultural credibility – while the mainstream was out of our reach. We were caught between two stools. The scale went from 'grudgingly admired' to 'infinitely despised'. Kraftwerk's strange success outside of Germany seemed to motivate some people from this scene, though, as if they thought: 'If they can do that out of Düsseldorf, then so can we.' Perhaps that was our most important contribution to the city's music community.

The next day, we went on to Münster, Kiel and Hannover, finally arriving at the Alte Oper Frankfurt – a home game for Fritz Rau. There were rows of chairs set up in the hall when we got there. 'The contract says it's not seated,' Rau murmured, 'so I guess we'll have to resort to salami tactics.' Without much ado, he took off his jacket and started clearing the chairs away himself. Following a brief trip to the Netherlands, we gave our last concert in the 'classic line-up' of Ralf, Karl, Wolfgang and Florian in Luxembourg – playing to about 350 people. If someone had told me at the time that the next gig with Kraftwerk wouldn't be until nine years later, in 1990, I'd have thought they were completely out of their mind, and called a doctor.

NOTES

1. *Der Spiegel*: 'Blubber von der Datenbank', issue 24/1981, 8 June 1981
2. 'Return of the Kling Klang Gang. John Gill meets Kraftwerk at Edinburgh Playhouse 17. 06. 1981', *Sounds*, 27 June 1981
3. 'To develop without rejecting, break away without destroying, contribute something undeniably new to music, yet without making people stop listening to the language that we quite rightly consider to be the language of civilized people.' Pierre Schaeffer: *In Search of a Concrete Music*, University of California Press: Berkeley 2012, p. 121 (*A la recherche d'une musique concrète*, Éditions du Seuil: Paris 1952)
4. 'A Sleeper at the Controls' (Newcastle City Hall 18 June 1981) By Ian Penman, *New Musical Express*, 27 June 1981
5. '*Computer World* is the first Kraftwerk LP for over three years [...] This time around, the concerns are less serious – simply the celebration of the computerised society we actually live in – and the political overtones of conspiracy and totalitarianism consequently less evident although the title track does refer rather coyly in passing to "Interpol and Deutsche Bank, FBI and Scotland Yard", hinting at international databank link-ups in the service of high (tech) capitalism. Other than that, *Computer World* deals mainly with the more innocuous leisure-time activities of Pocket Calculator, Homecomputer, computer dating ("Computer Love") and the like, rounding it all off with a straight statement of belief ("It's More Fun to Compute") whose chilling, hard-edge treatment belies the title. Musically, too, Kraftwerk's subtlety is often overlooked: they seem so straightforward, so logical, it's easy to miss the tonal subtlety of their compositions.' Review by Andy Gill. In: *New Musical Express* 16 May 1981, pp. 36–37
6. 'Their approach is so devious, so subtle. Superficially they purvey a frightening barren landscape as bleak as their song titles but their humanity finds expression in the tight dynamics and controlled rhythms of each piece which is invariably

blessed by a hypnotically haunting melody. Consequently Kraftwerk can be cold but elegant, stark but poignant. Their medium is ruthlessly mechanical, their spirit is warm and glowing. They make the modern world seem empty yet beautiful – no mean task. [. . .] This is Kraftwerk's first pop album. Didn't you always guess that beneath those showroom dummy exteriors was a bunch of whacky Germans looking for a party. Well it looks like they found one.' Ian Pye: 'Kraftwerk: Computerworld'. Review in *Melody Maker*, 9 June 1981

7. 'The great Granddaddies of teutonic technopop return from their retirement, their reputation unexpectedly enhanced in their absence, and deliver one humdinger of a dance-track destined not to be bettered in eons. Blip and beep perfect for nouveau robot manoeuvres currently in vogue at the discos, it takes mechanical minimalism one step nearer nonexistence with deadpan vocals, meaningless lyrics, and a sparse, basic beat.' Review in *Melody Maker*, 9 June 1981

8. 'Lyceum: Kraftwerk'. Concert review by Mary Harron, *The Guardian*, 29 June 1981

9. 'Kraftwerk. Hammersmith Palais'. Concert review by Richard Williams, *The Times*, 30 June 1981

10. 'Kraftwerk's wunderbar.' By Ed Naha, *New York Post*, 4 August 1981

11. Kitarō, real name Masanori Takahashi (高橋　正則, *Takahashi Masanori*)

12

TOUR DE FRANCE – TECHNO POP – ELECTRIC CAFE

Life Goes On. Number 1 Hit Single. Andy and Paul. Techno Pop. Sex Object. Interlude: The Model on TV. Emil's Exit. Planet Rock. Resetting Kling Klang. The Telephone Call. Artificial Voice. Tour de France. Track List. Kling Klang 1C 064–65087. Tour de France (Single). Britannia Row Studios, London. Power Station Mix. The Reinvention of Techno Pop. Boing Boom Tschak. Filming by the Rhine. Rebecca Allen and her Virtual Creations. Flüela Pass – 2383 m. Musique Non-Stop. The Downward Spiral. Electric Cafe. The Plan. Mixing in New York City. Düsseldorf Layover. Remix: The Telephone Call. UFA Again. Reviews of Electric Cafe. 1981–1986: A Techno Pop Odyssey.

Life Goes On

My white-cube apartment by the Hofgarten was great, but it had one major drawback: I could only make music very quietly there. If I wanted to take my own musical experiments further, I'd have to find another space. Bettina was living in her parents' building in the north of Düsseldorf. It wasn't a particularly hip part of town, but when the possibility of living in a ground-floor flat opened up I moved in. We'd been together for five years by this time, after all. Bettina's uncle Manfred lived on the first floor with his hard-of-hearing mother – the perfect neighbour for a musician. Manfred didn't get home from work until the evening and Bettina was still studying at the Heinrich Heine University, so I could make as much music as I liked and not bother anyone. I set up my studio in the largest room of my new flat.

Over the next few days, I went back to teaching at the Krefeld and Meerbusch music schools. The director and my colleagues gave me a friendly welcome, not making me feel the slightest bit guilty about my long absence. Driving my Volkswagen home after class, I was struck by a thought I had never had in this form: what does my life plan look like? My 30th birthday was looming on the horizon but I had no idea. I toyed with the image of how my life would be as a music teacher, teaching every day, perhaps organizing a trip with my class, running an ensemble and growing old gracefully before going a little gaga. Wearing cords and cardigans, of course, with leather elbow patches. Not bad at all, eh?

But my work with Kraftwerk was taking up more and more time. While the *Autobahn* tour back in 1975 had fitted neatly into the summer holidays, our last concert tour had gone on for six months. I assumed things would continue that way; gigs are important, a fixed part of the musician's life. We had at least laid down the groundwork for a truly self-sufficient stage show, which we could build upon. The staging was like an open tool box, all the instruments ordered by size and available at any time. From my point of view, it was just a question of time as to when we'd reach the next stage of our development with another album. The idea of spending my future life as part of

398

the group felt perfectly natural. Working as a music teacher in parallel wouldn't be sustainable, though, that much was clear. But it was hard for me to let go. I hesitated long and hard before finally terminating my contracts with the music schools.

There was no contract between me and Kraftwerk, the Kling Klang publishing house or the label of the same name, however; not even a handwritten agreement. Up to this point, we'd agreed everything in person. But we never talked about conditions or defined my activities precisely. Basically, our business relationship was pretty precarious.

I wasn't reckoning with a regular monthly income. But I did assume we'd be embarking on frequent international tours in the near future. The concerts were one potential income source, and the other was the copyrights to the songs. My rights to *The Man-Machine* and *Computer World* would cover my outgoings for a while, and *Techno Pop* existed, albeit sketchily, in our minds. When it came to the music, I had no reason to complain. Quite the opposite, in fact. Our work was inspiring for me, gave me direction. I rather liked the freelance artist's existence.

On paper, however, my occupation was that of a freelancer with only one client: Kraftwerk. Although I declared my taxes as self-employed, I found it hard to regard Ralf and Florian as my customers; that was too abstract. After all, I worked almost every day with them in the studio and we spent a lot of time together outside of work as well. I think it was a mixture of creative spirit and enthusiasm that gave me a romantic feeling of belonging, and made the group the focal point of my life. But now I decided it was time to put our business relationship on a more professional standing, bring it up to the level of our artistic dialogue.

399

Over the past few months, I'd talked a few times to Ralf about a possible share in the turnover from record sales. Licences like that would be a third income source. Now, in January, the three of us met up to discuss the situation briefly. Ralf started off the conversation and explained to Florian in a few words what we wanted to talk about. It appeared the two of them had already discussed the matter, and our conversation went rather like the previous one about co-authorship. We found an appropriate allocation formula for licences, and when their lawyer, Marvin Katz, arrived at the Kling Klang Studio from New York a few days later, we informed him of our agreement.

Number 1 Hit Single

Then came 3 February 1982 – to all appearances, a perfectly normal Wednesday. I had spent the whole afternoon wiring up the instruments in my studio room, testing out settings and trying to get something done. Evening came and I was just about to make a recording when the phone rang. It was Ralf. Without much ado, he cleared his throat and said some words that sounded like: 'Karl, "The Model" is at number 1 in England.'

That past summer, EMI had put out the double A-side single 'Computer Love'/'The Model' to coincide with our UK gigs reaching the Top 40. Just before Christmas, 'The Model' started to be played on radio and the single began to really take off. Soon we'd sold 300,000 singles, I was told. Four years after its release, *The Man-Machine* also re-entered the album charts and was set to go gold, which in the UK meant 100,000 copies sold.

Ralf didn't quite know what else to say and nor could I think of anything much. It was a very strange phone call. Sure, we were pleased, but not euphoric over our success. Ralf had a dispassionate tendency anyway, and I didn't want to get carried away either. To be honest, I'd been much more excited in the past about smaller things. But still, it was pretty damn cool.

At the end of the conversation, Ralf suggested we could go to Bochum that Friday for the OMD concert. 'OK, let's do that. I'd like to see what the Brits have to offer,' I replied. I remember exactly what I thought after I hung up the phone: It's all well and good, but what does a number 1 mean for us? And how will it go from here?

Andy and Paul

Since 'Electricity', there had been no ignoring Orchestral Manoeuvres in the Dark. The Liverpool band was now one of the most respected groups in Europe. Over the past few years, the British synth scene had been through a huge development. There were artists all over the country producing electronic pop music, and more and more of their tracks sounded like potential hits. The new OMD album, *Architecture & Morality*, would go on to sell 4 million copies, and a single from the LP, 'Maid of Orleans (The Waltz Joan Of Arc)', went to number 1 in the German charts and hit the UK Top Ten. Yes indeed, OMD were much more commercially successful than Kraftwerk back then, in early 1982.

Ralf and I watched the concert at Zeche Bochum from the circle, and I mulled over the show. While we set up a physical

Metropolis control centre for the Kraftwerk gigs and provided an audio-visual media art performance, OMD found it perfectly natural to present themselves in the tradition of a British rock band, with Malcolm Holmes' drum kit at the centre of the stage. Paul Humphreys' and Martin Cooper's keyboards were set up on either side, and Andy played a Fender bass, giving the set-up even more of a traditional rock look. Andy McCluskey's heroic tenor filled the space from the very beginning, but when Paul sang 'Souvenir' it made the whole venue happy in a very special way. His voice was simply the ideal match for the song. It does have advantages when more than one person in a band sings.

Pop music tells stories of all different kinds, and once again I realized that live concerts rely above all on vocal performance and communication with the audience. Aside from that – in contrast to our press spokesman's rhetoric – it doesn't matter, to my mind, whether music is created by vibrating strings or sound generators. When we got to 'Maid of Orleans', the show's big number, I first saw Andy's very own type of body language. He danced like a dervish. The OMD boys certainly knew how to make efficient use of their means.

After the gig, we stayed behind in the venue and eventually did run into Andy and Paul. My memories of our conversation are vague – but oddly enough, I remember exactly what they were both wearing: trousers, V-neck jumpers, shirts and ties. They looked like two gentlemen partaking of tea and cucumber sandwiches at the cricket club. Over the years, I got to know Paul and particularly Andy much better. In real life, they're warm-hearted northern lads with a great sense of humour. We became friends.

Techno Pop

In February, we started the recording sessions for our next album. Once again, a new chapter of my work with Ralf and Florian began; from that point on, I received royalties not just from the music copyrights, but also from the record licences. In the studio, though, it felt exactly the same as before. The atmosphere was not much different from the spirit of our past writing sessions. We leapt back and forth between the instruments and mixing desk, tried out alternative motifs, modulated sounds, improvised to the music scheme, made recordings – there was a vivid sense of excitement in the air.

Chords are the building blocks of pop music. As a first step into the new phase, I came up with a chord sequence inspired by the compositions of Claude Debussy. Of the twentieth-century composers, he was always one of my greatest role models. His idiosyncratic, unlinked chords abandon the realms of traditional harmonics, more or less playing havoc with them. Ralf was instantly on board. The music sounded like Kraftwerk to my ears, and Florian liked it too. In other words, the basis for the album's title track was laid: 'Techno Pop'.

Back in the mid-seventies, we had developed a method for presenting various sound perspectives on a single idea. For me, this approach was similar to the principle in classical composition technique of processing a theme freely. In the early phase, we also made several different versions of 'Techno Pop': an instrumental pop version, a percussion mixdown, a floating version without drums and one in which numerous Florian-esque sound UFOs played a role. The recordings are between two and ten minutes long. We varied, commented and added to the song's basic idea. That was the right way to do it.

Sex Object

One of the standard settings on my synthesizer was an unmistakeable twang sound. On the UK tour, I'd started experimenting with it until a riff fell out of my fingers, which could be built on using everything a pop song needs. Ralf added an organ sound, played his melody and sang along straight off. For a brief moment, we sounded like the Doors (presumably more to do with the organ than the vocals). The song was instantly there. When it comes to music, we had a direct connection, an intuitive link. It seemed as though pop songs were floating on the air for us and all we needed to do was reel them in. And when Florian then joined in with our 'conversation', a pretty usable idea often came out of it. The music resulting from our improvisations was impossible to predict, though. Rarely was any one impression repeated. We always chose a different tempo, a different key, concept, context. There were no rules, not even rules we'd made for ourselves.

Working on the song again in the studio, we arrived at a tempo of about 132 BPM as we played. Over the course of the session, we recorded percussion, bass, synthesizer, organ and guide vocals.

Ralf wrote the lyrics in the first-person singular, the classic singer-songwriter perspective. He even tells someone to show their feelings. And then the title: 'Sex Object'. I was speechless.

Interlude: The Model on TV

Life didn't get dull. Thanks to the UK charts, 'The Model' had a moment in the rest of Europe, so EMI Electrola set up a TV slot for us in Germany. We all went down to Munich, where we appeared on the first episode of Thomas Gottschalk's show *Na sowas* on 29 March.

The four of us stand in front of our instruments against a black backdrop – Ralf on the Polymoog, me on the Minimoog, Wolfgang on my brand-new TR-808 drum machine, Florian on the second Minimoog – and mime to the playback, dressed all in black. Even now, I think it was a pretty good performance. Only Ralf took a few seconds at the beginning to drop his Buster Keaton impression. Wolfgang was reminiscent of Bela Lugosi and Florian managed an expressionless glare at the camera towards the end.

The rest of the show's line-up was also interesting, it featured Klaus Nomi, Johnny Hallyday, the band Dschinghis Khan and the designer Wolfgang Joop. On the way to the dressing rooms, we ended up in a photo session for *Bravo* magazine. We slung a few cameras around our necks and posed like a sixties pop band. Our promo trip took effect. Once the show aired, 'Das Model' climbed to number 7 on the German hit parade before the spring was out.

Emil's Exit

Emil has been travelling the world for as long as I've known him. Even back in the seventies, he would disappear for a few weeks occasionally. Then the letterbox at Berger Allee would fill up with postcards from all over the globe. From an Amazonian expedition in the South American rain forest, for example, or the Caribbean. Emil had been to the Bahamas several times. Before our world tour, he had gone to ground there for a while. And on our return, he set off straight back to the islands. Emil had a strong sense of wanderlust, which kept him moving. It seemed he had now found a place he really liked, and he spent the most part of the year there. He didn't give up his room at Berger Allee, though.

In April, Emil put in another appearance in Düsseldorf and visited us at the Kling Klang Studio. We played him our rudimentary versions of 'Tour de France', 'Sex Object' and 'Techno Pop'. I remember his reaction to that last song very well: he thought our music had something ritual about it. Emil spent the next few days in Düsseldorf and we wrote the first version of the 'Techno Pop' lyrics together. On 2 May he left Germany for the Bahamas again.

Planet Rock

We rarely see disaster approaching. When Florian called me at home one Sunday, the news hit me out of the blue. The first thing he told me was that Ralf had had an accident. He had fallen on a cycling tour and been severely injured. 'Now what?' I asked. Florian explained that we'd have to wait and see. Later, I heard that Ralf had crashed into the cyclist in front of him while riding in his slipstream, when the other man suddenly cut his speed or braked. During the unavoidable fall, Ralf hit

406

the ground head first. Unfortunately, he wasn't wearing a helmet that day, so it was good luck that the impact wasn't harder, the accident happened near a hospital, and his fellow cyclists had the presence of mind to do the right thing. After all the medical examinations, we found out his life was not at risk; Ralf would soon make a full recovery.

Florian suddenly seemed much less worried and when I spoke to Ralf's sister a week later, she seemed very relieved. It would only be a few days before her brother was back home. We all got away with no more than a fright, that time.

When I talked to Ralf on the phone he was back to his old self, warning me never to cycle without a helmet. After he came out of hospital we met up at Rolf Wolfshohl's professional bike shop in the second week of June and bought ourselves the best models he had.

At the end of the month, Ralf and I took a trip to Cologne. It was about time we showed our faces at Moroco again. We stood around, glass in hand, enjoying the barrage of drum machines: the amazing 'The Message' by Grandmaster Flash and the Furious Five, ABC's Trevor Horn-produced pop hit 'The Look of Love' and the dynamic Human League single 'Don't You Want Me'. And then all at once, we heard the extremely spartan production values of 'Planet Rock' by Afrika Bambaataa and the Soulsonic Force. We stared at each other dumbfounded as the dancefloor filled up more and more. Although I worked with the TR-808 Rhythm Composer every day in my home studio, I was pretty surprised at how sensational the machine sounded over the club's PA.

Aside from that, though, the track interested us mainly because its musical structure consisted of the beat from 'Numbers'

407

and it quoted the melody of 'Trans-Europe Express'. Bambaataa rapped over the rhythm. There were also synthesizer and vocoder sounds and a whole lot more. I suspect the readers of this book are probably familiar with the song. Later, I found out that the producer and mixer Arthur Baker and the keyboardist John Robie had rented an 808 machine via an ad in the *Village Voice*, especially for the two-day recording session.

As you can imagine, Marvin Katz contacted the label Tommy Boy Records on Ralf and Florian's behalf. When I talked to Ralf about it during the negotiations, he told me there'd be a financial arrangement any day now. The authors of 'Trans-Europe Express' were well known and the US publishing rights to the title were held by Kling Klang publishing's American subsidiary No Hassle Music Inc. Rhythm patterns weren't part of the songwriting, however, he told me, and were exempt from copyright. Although the entire 'Planet Rock' track was built on the beat of 'Numbers', that meant the deal was based only on the melody of 'TEE'. Tough luck for a percussion artist. A drum pattern is in the public domain – even one as unmistakeable as the 'Numbers' beat. Kling Klang publishing's hands were tied in this case, it seemed, and they couldn't get me any form of royalties. There was apparently absolutely nothing they could do . . .

I didn't hear any more about the deal with Tommy Boy after that. But the rhythm has been very popular ever since. Years later, I once met Arthur Baker in London, and he told me the label had simply put the price of the record up to cover the compensation losses. That's what I call creative.

In July, we headed off to La Bastide Blanche in Saint-Tropez again. The drive there is the last sound ride I remember. We listened to our demo cassettes of the 'Techno Pop' variations countless times along the way. Volker Albus came along with us, and Maxime zoomed over from Paris soon after in his black Mini Cooper.

Ralf and Florian went on long cycling tours on an almost daily basis. I went with them at the start, but the narrow roads in the glaring summer heat of the Côte d'Azur weren't my thing, so I spent the next couple of weeks by the sea. Volker and Maxime took a relaxed approach too and we hung out together. We'd all meet up back at the house in the late afternoon and make spaghetti or some other meal. While doing nothing on the beach, I also contemplated our strategy and tactics. Ralf and Florian were very obviously ignoring our number 1 hit single. Perhaps they thought reacting to it was too trivial. I think they saw themselves as cool-hand strategists, wanted to project an image of not being hungry for success, and acted like nothing had happened. Hit single? Easy now, better not show any excitement.

One episode from this stay remains unforgettable: the screening of the football World Cup semi-final between Germany and France, won by the Germans 5:4 in a penalty shoot-out during extra time. The German goalkeeper Toni Schumacher's infamous 'defensive action', after which France's Patrick Battiston ended up unconscious on the ground with a damaged third vertebra, caused a major sensation in front of our TV. Maxime kept yelling: 'Schu-ma-sche! Schu-ma-sche!' The shot went wide, the referee didn't give a foul, Battison was carried off on a stretcher, and in the end, the result was simply the award of a goal kick rather than a red card. The incident became known inter-nationally as 'The Night of Seville'. *L'Équipe* – Ralf's favourite sports magazine – wrote: 'Toni Schumacher, profession: monster.' Luckily, Patrick Battiston recovered and continued his career.

409

Resetting Kling Klang

On 9 August, we all met up again at the Kling Klang Studio. The electronics and acoustics company R. Barth KG had delivered a new MCI JH-600 recording console and installed it with Joachim Dehmann – not without giving it a special coat of grey paint beforehand, of course. Far too heavy for its dimensions, the console had a mere 16 channels, a useful patch panel, automation and – most importantly – it met professional quality standards.

More rooms had been rented in the meantime, helpful extensions to the studio. A door led off left from the stairwell, which took you up to Elektro Müller on the second floor, into the Kling Klang Studio and the basement room beneath it. Down there, Ralf and Florian installed several closed metal shelving units for archiving the multitracks, and one large open shelving system for all the instruments not currently in use, like synthesizers, glockenspiels, a child-size drum kit and other stuff. Through the door on the right in the stairwell, you got straight to the workshop and behind it the toilet and a small kitchen, its most important piece of equipment being the fridge. Another corridor from there led to the common room, carpeted in dark grey. One of the Sony screens was connected up in there so we could watch TV. Florian donated a huge leather sofa and a few seats, which enabled a completely new quality of hanging out. The blinds at the windows to the backyards usually stayed down, their slats adjusted according to requirements. Behind the TV room were two more small rooms with windows onto Mintropstrasse. At the front, in what we called the office, was a telephone with an answering machine, an electric typewriter and a large set of deep wooden shelves, where old posters and concert ads gathered dust. In the back room, Florian set up the 'language lab', which he used to test the various machines with his computer and prepare word sequences for the recordings. Synthesizers and analogue sequencers piled up on the worktops affixed to the wall. The front door in the corridor led to the front stairwell, and from there straight onto Mintropstrasse.

Florian's latest hobby consisted of copying photos from books about electronic music, framing them and hanging or propping them up everywhere. His favoured motifs were from the early days of electronic studios: rooms with sound generators and reel-to-reel tape machines, composers staring earnestly at measuring devices or clutching reels of tape. Notations on graph paper rounded off the pictures. All that made for a good atmosphere in the new rooms.

The Telephone Call

My melody with the working title 'Italo-Disco' had existed since back in 1980, or so my notebook says. After that, I recorded several variations on the theme in my home studio, and in the late summer of 1982, Ralf and I did some more work on elements of the music. The result was our track 'The Telephone Call.' As well as the main theme, this time the lyrics were also my work. I had been collecting ideas for song lyrics for a while and typed them out on my travel typewriter every day, not spending a long time thinking about them. The words that flew in my direction simply ended up on paper. It was fun, and I thought the typewriter's sound, feel and look were pretty cool. One draft was about telephones, another contained the fragment 'Zuneigung und Zeit' – affection and time.

In the studio, we linked the two ideas together and I tried to synchronize the rhythm of the words with the music. And that's how I came to sing. Ralf encouraged me, hoping to establish a new vocal style, different to his type of chanting. During the recording, Florian kept scurrying about me, joking around. His comments were meant to be funny but they weren't really helpful in getting good results. At the same time, I didn't yet have any experience controlling my voice's articulation and intonation, and I relied on feedback. I can say one thing for sure: Ralf and Florian did help me in their own ways on my vocal debut, but I wouldn't exactly call them didactic geniuses.

Presumably, in search of material in the old days, we would have had the idea of using the sounds of a telephone and recorded them on magnetic tape. The sampler was a tad faster, though. The Emulator proved to be the ideal instrument for experimenting with telephone noises without restriction. Florian sampled the recorded message 'Beep beep beep – the number you have reached has been disconnected,' and as you might expect, there followed dials, dialling tones, calling signals, ring tones and other automatic messages and sounds. These attractive telephone sounds may well be the reason why no conversation gets off the ground in the song. All the protagonist's hard work turns out to be nothing more than a vain attempt to make a call.

Autumn came and John Bagnell – who worked for EMI London – visited us in Mintropstrasse. We played him everything that sounded vaguely like a song. After the audition, he reported on our remarkable reputation in the UK and the countless enquiries he'd received. Even Elton John wanted to work with us, he said. Not bad, but I couldn't imagine a collaboration like that. Ralf and Florian had many outstanding qualities; empathetic interaction with other artists wasn't one of them, though. Their key concern was maintaining autonomy and control over their product.

Artificial Voice

Change of scene: Ruhr University Bochum. During our writing sessions for *Techno Pop*, the engineer Wolfgang Kulas was a research fellow at the Faculty of General Electrotechnology and Acoustics. Together with a colleague and a student, he developed a program capable of translating continuous text into audible language. Just like Florian, the young researcher worked with a Votrax speech synthesizer. The program with which they controlled the Votrax ran on a 68000 computer from South West Technical Products (SWTPC). This exact same make, which Florian also used, had already modelled for the cover of *Computer World*.

At that point in time, Florian was definitely the most clued-up musician on the subject of speech synthesis in Germany, or even in Europe. It was terra incognita, and he put a lot of energy into the whole area. And yet he never made a big deal out of it; he kept it close to his chest, as they say. I think he was interested not only in its possible uses for artistic expression, but also in the commercial aspect that opened up through this pioneering process. Alongside the Votrax, Florian had bought other speech

413

synthesizers: for example, the huge modern US-developed DECtalk, which was delivered complete with several impressive handbooks. He also had all the versions of the Swedish Infovox, with all the circuit boards for different languages. However, getting all these machines up and running was quite a task.

Word of the Bochum project's activities soon got around in the speech synthesis community, and Florian also found out about it. The perfect fit! He didn't beat about the bush and contacted the uni to make an appointment. Not much later, he visited the text-to-speech pioneers and persuaded them to work with him. From my point of view, both parties benefited: the research group got access to Florian's valuable machines and documentation; and Florian profited from their engineering skills.

Tour de France

At the end of 1982, we wanted to have our photos taken with racing bikes for the cover of the new album. But we got so cold at the photo session by the Rhine a week before Christmas that we had to break off the shoot and postpone it to a later date. In the spring of 1983, we tackled the song 'Tour de France'.

Recording real-life bicycle sounds was a no-brainer. Ralf brought one of his extremely light bikes into the studio and we tried to make its mechanical parts speak. A bicycle bell, the most recognizable bike sound, doesn't come into play with racing bikes, of course, so we left that out of the equation. But there are other mechanical noises, for instance, freewheeling. Ralf lifted the back wheel off the floor and 'pedalled' with his right hand. When he stopped the motion, Florian recorded the whirr as the wheel revolved. There were also the abrasive sounds made by the piston of an air pump when filling up an inner tube, and the hiss of a valve being removed: pfff! The freewheeling whirr was attractive but Ralf's bike didn't make many more characteristic noises. At least not for a slice of pop music. The breathing sounds made by a cyclist were much more interesting. In the end, we had breathing, pumping and freewheeling sounds on the keyboard of Florian's sampler.

We used our familiar method for the arrangement. For this song, I had come up with a simple chord structure some time previously, which served as a basic scheme to which we added the *musique concrète* building blocks. As I understand it, the piece consists of only a few elements: the rhythm, which represents the dynamics of the race, the narrative voice of a reporter informing the listener, the acoustic close-ups of the athletes on their bikes, and finally the 'film music', which conjures up a projection of an Alpine panorama in Technicolor in my imagination.

When Maxime visited us in the Kling Klang Studio, he and Ralf wrote the French lyrics together. Ralf had the idea of repeating the title as a response to the lines in the lyrics. That made the verses into a refrain at the same time.

Track List

In the meantime, we had recorded four titles on multitrack tape: 'Techno Pop', 'Tour de France', 'Sex Object' and 'The Telephone Call'. When we wanted to work on a different song, we put another tape on the machine. However, using magnetic tape meant we were tied to the fixed structure of the pieces, which was to prove a major disadvantage.

For the first time, I began thinking about the number and combination of pieces of music on our records. Of course, the number of tracks says nothing about the diversity, complexity and quality of an album, but for some curious reason we had fewer and fewer of them as time went on. There are six tracks on *The Man Machine* and only five distinct songs on *Computer World*. It would be only logical if *Techno Pop* had just four titles, but I couldn't shake the feeling that we might be overdoing the reduction idea.

This was also the time of my first business trip with Ralf; we flew to London to visit our British label. In those days, the Parlophone HQ was in the legendary EMI building on Manchester Square. We were there to talk about the album release, for which the label suggested a deadline in the spring – but they didn't put any pressure on us. That more than corresponded with our internal planning; but ultimately, everything remained vague.

Kling Klang 1C 064–65087

One evening on a walk around Düsseldorf, Ralf suddenly stopped stock still outside a specialist philately shop on Graf-Adolf-Strasse. He had spotted a Hungarian 20-forint stamp from 1953 in passing, and he was clearly transfixed. The motif was a drawing of two racing cyclists, wheeling diagonally through the frame from top right to bottom left, looking very dynamic.

The next day, he went back to buy the stamp and immediately sketched out an image for the planned album cover by doubling the number of cyclists to four and adding the words *Techno Pop* in a font reminiscent of Art Deco. The next step was getting the four of us photographed in profile, then having these portraits reproduced by a professional graphic artist and added into the stamp motif. The order of the cyclists is the same as our stage line-up: Ralf, Karl, Wolfgang and Florian. The back cover featured our four individual sketched portraits. The inside sleeve boasted another group photo, taken during a performance of 'Pocket Calculator' on Italian TV, with four portrait photographs of us on the other side. Ralf had a four-page print made of the cover artwork in the original size, which hung on the studio wall near the door for the next few years. It was always in our sightline when we stood at our instruments. These days, that first *Techno Pop* cover is also doing the rounds on the internet.

The photos and drawings reflect the way we worked at the time. The photographs represent the sampling, and the sketches stand for the electronic sounds. Cycling is also effortlessly integrated into the design, as a symbol of the man-machine concept.

On 10 March we moved to the Rudas Studio. Once we got there, though, despite having mixed *The Man-Machine* successfully in the same place with Joschko in February 1978, we couldn't find our feet. We spent more than a week trying to mix the telephone track. Sadly, without success – it sounded awful. As a consequence, we decided to produce a few mixes in the Kling Klang Studio to test for danceability. During this phase, we made regular trips to the Moroco disco in Cologne. The resident DJ, Carrol Martin, played the cassettes we brought along with our latest mixes, and we listened to our music under dance-floor conditions with a full house. Düsseldorf's fancy Malesh on Königsallee was another venue for our tests. At this stage, we made several edits to the rhythm groups on 'The Telephone Call' and 'Sex Object' to give the music the right drive.

Despite the setback in the Rudas Studio, Ralf and Florian obviously assumed we'd be releasing the album that same year. In May, they placed an ad in the then-hip Düsseldorf magazine *Select*, featuring the cover of *Techno Pop* in white with the red Art Deco lettering and the four cyclists. It wasn't a normal advert; there was not yet any clue to what it was about. It was a kind of guerrilla move to draw attention to our product without advertising it directly. These days, that kind of thing is a standard tool in professional marketing, especially with viral placement in social networks.

Meanwhile, our A&R man at EMI Electrola, Heinz-Gerd Lütticke, placed a more official advert: a full page in the German industry magazine *Der Musikmarkt*. He had visited us in the studio in February and taken the cover art with him. Alongside the cover, the slogan 'Es wird immer weitergeh'n – Musik als Träger von Ideen'[1] and the catalogue number 'Kling Klang 1C 064–65087' advertised the new record specifically. The tension was rising! Now the cat was out of the bag; as it turned out, too soon – Ralf later told the press the ad hadn't been approved by the band.[2] Really? But if there'd been no mention of an advert, what else was the A&R man going to do with the cover artwork?

Tour de France (Single)

We kept on working on 'Tour de France'. One day Maxime suggested offering the song as a signature tune for media reporting to the Amaury Sport Organisation (A.S.O.), which organizes cycling races, including the Tour de France, and also published the newspapers *L'Équipe* and *Le Parisien*. On his suggestion, the idea came up to pre-release a single from what we thought was the foreseeable album publication. So we mixed the recordings from 7 to 15 June in the Kling Klang Studio. In parallel, Ralf designed the cover by integrating the colours of the French flag – blue, white and red – into the cyclist drawing.

On 16 June 1983, Ralf couriered our mix to Pathé Marconi in Paris. Three days later, he told me one evening in the Kling Klang Studio that everything had gone smoothly in France and the tapes were on their way to the other EMI branches. In Germany, EMI Electrola announced the product like this: 'TOUR DE FRANCE '83 – WITH GERMAN PARTICIPANTS. Four gentlemen in black from Düsseldorf are the only active German participants in this year's race. The new title from the Kraftwerk music-workers has been chosen as the official signature tune of this most significant cycling event. All reporting on France's many TV and radio stations will be indicated by Kraftwerk's 'Tour de France'.

In France, Pathé Marconi placed ads with a similar message: 'The anthem of the summer, this year the official theme-tune of the tour . . .'[3] That sounded not bad at all, but sadly the single wasn't released to sync with the tour, after all. Timing production and marketing wasn't one of our greatest strengths. After all this fuss, there was a four-week silence in the Kling Klang Studio. The Tour de France, however, started punctually on 1 July, and after the 22nd stage, the French cyclist Laurent Fignon took the laurels.

At the end of July, Florian picked me up at home and we went on a jaunt on our racing bikes. I can't remember ever having a more open conversation with him. We did some straight-talking about the current production. The strange thing was, although we had released the 'Tour de France' single in the end, something seemed not to be right about our mixes. We felt we couldn't keep up with the latest production values. But we didn't understand why that might be.

Barely had Ralf returned from his holiday, when EMI London informed us they'd arranged an appearance on *Top of the Pops*. Normally, bands performed on the show to playback. We'd done the same a year before with 'The Model' on ZDF in Munich. In this case, though, Ralf and Florian were dead-set against a playback performance. They wanted to produce a video instead. We didn't have much time, so we came up with the idea of using archive recordings again. Ralf and I took an early-morning flight to Hamburg to view *Deutsche Wochenschau* newsreel material about the Tour de France. Ralf picked a couple of sequences and bought the usage rights. We had to get a move on; Ralf spent Friday to Sunday editing the footage into a promo video at the Rudas Studio. The process took about thirty hours. I stayed in the studio as long as I could stand it. The result was a compilation of black-and-white sequences from historical cycling races. Was it suitable for promoting the record? Who knew, but Ralf certainly loved it when the sportsmen cycled into a bank of fog. On the Monday, we sent the 'director's cut' to London.

For the press photos, we posed with our bikes by the Rhine, wearing black cycling jerseys. Wolfgang came along too. He looked like he'd done nothing else over the past ten years but practise cycling. An impressive phenomenon.

420

Britannia Row Studios, London

The 'Tour de France' single was already out but we still went on working on the song, searching for the perfect sound. We tried it in the EMI Studio in Cologne – to no avail. So we went back to Kling Klang and tried out our mixes at Moroco. This was the time when Madonna first came out, and 'Holiday' sounded amazing. I really liked that New York sound. Another hit was Herbie Hancock's 'Rockit', which had a video full of automatic machines and apparatus, creating a funny mechanical atmosphere. And then we heard 'Blue Monday' by New Order. What an incredible musical magnet! The combined drums/sequencer groove and the passive vocals were practically a command to report instantly to the dancefloor. I got the impression the track was something like a basic lesson in pop music. We cast a glance at the 12-inch maxi-single and found out the sound engineer: Michael Johnson. If the man can make a sound like that, we thought, we need to meet him. We did a bit of research, packed our sixteen-track tape and set off to mix 'Tour de France' in the place where 'Blue Monday' had been produced: Britannia Row Studios in London. The renowned studios were set up in 1975 by Pink Floyd after their *Wish You Were Here* album. They recorded *Animals* and parts of *The Wall* there once it was built.

On 24 August, Ralf, Florian and I showed up at the Britannia Row Studios to meet the pretty young, pretty cool sound engineer Michael Johnson. The most important machine in the studio, he told us, was a new three-band compressor. Apart from that, he pointed out the Oberheim DMX drum machine used on 'Blue Monday'. Michael was a really good sound engineer. He spent a

421

day and a night, from 12:30 to 6:30 in the morning, mixing our 'Tour de France' professionally and efficiently. By the time we left the studio we were completely wiped out. Back at the hotel, I fell asleep with the track's ever quieter breathing sounds revolving in my head.

That evening, we met the London producer and DJ Rusty Egan at the Camden Palace nightclub (now known as KOKO), which he ran along with Steve Strange. Rusty was the former drummer in the British New Wave band Rich Kids. Over the past few years, he'd made a name for himself with his DJ sets at the Blitz club and was regarded as a key figure in London's nightlife. I think he really was one of the main promoters of electronic pop music and the New Romantic movement in particular. While he showed me and Ralf around the empty club, he wanted to persuade us to do a live appearance. I found it interesting to be thinking about gigs again, but we were still looking for the perfect sound for our next album and that took priority. Before we left for Düsseldorf the next Friday, Ralf got a vinyl test pressing of our mix made while Florian and I went to Turnkey, a specialist shop for studio music equipment, to admire the amazing Synclavier. The trip to London was quite hard work. And yet in the end, we didn't use the Britannia Row mix after all. Why not? I can't remember.

Power Station Mix

Although 'Tour de France' had climbed to number 22 in the British single charts in early August 1983, selling about 70,000 copies, and made it to number 47 in Germany at the end of the month, we were still working on the track's sound spectrum and the individual instruments like the bass drum. We were going around in circles. Over the course of that September, we made a total of four trips to Cologne to listen to our latest mixes at Moroco.

We'd done more than 280 album sessions since the world tour, by the time the new copies of 'Tour de France' were taped in the Rudas Studio at the end of September and sent out to Germany, the UK, France and the USA. It was unlikely we'd get the whole album finished that year, but a 'Tour de France' maxi-single for the American Christmas season might still be possible.

But how were things to go on with our mixes now? In November 1983, our studio work ran aground. In search of a solution, Ralf suggested New York. He would mix our four tracks there, he said. By way of research, he looked up the engineers on records that sounded good in the clubs, and he came across the name François Kevorkian in the credits.

At the beginning of November 1983, Ralf flew to New York with our multitrack tapes on board to work with Monsieur Kevorkian. The planned fourteen days turned into three and then four weeks.

By the time we listened to the tracks together at the Kling Klang Studio, we were in a strangely melancholy mood. Perhaps we'd spent too long mixing the new songs already by that point. Whatever the case, after listening to the tape we weren't able to analyse what we'd heard, evaluate the result or start strategic planning. I think we were confusing sound spectrums with musical content in our minds. One thing's for sure, though: If the content on the magnetic tape had been convincing, we would have had a finished album at that point. A mix that manipulates the relative volume levels, frequencies and physical surroundings of the instruments and vocals doesn't change the idea on which the music is based, only the sound spectrum of the mix. Leaving aside extreme interventions, that is. A mix is a mix – no more and no less. Essentially, we knew intuitively at that time that the session had been a failure, but we were in a difficult situation – like comic characters who have stepped off a cliff with their feet still running in mid-air . . .

The Reinvention of Techno Pop

We talked about the New York mixes. Something had to happen but there was no solution in sight. Sadly, we didn't return to our tried and tested method of free improvisation, but instead started editing 'Techno Pop'. There were some elements we wanted to keep, others we wanted to replace with new things. Basically, we took our orientation from the way remixes were done, the latest craze at the time. Having worked with the old tracks for some time, we changed our minds again. We set up a new tape and started over from the beginning. Ralf spent a lot of time live-mixing the recorded tracks, creating more and more new combinations. They sounded good for the moment but they were fleeting – they slipped through our fingers like sand. There were simply too many options.

Over the next few months, we worked exclusively on the new version of 'Techno Pop'. Even on Christmas Eve and New Year's Eve, in fact even on 1 January 1984, the first day of the Orwellian year, we met up at the studio and made adjustments to the track. Every new detail was cause for debate, sometimes argument.

At the beginning of February, I heard that 'Tour de France' had climbed to number 4 in the US Billboard dance charts. That good news put a little wind in our sails, but we soon ran out of steam again. Even though we worked every night apart from Saturdays, we had no idea in what direction we wanted to take 'Techno Pop' – three years after the release of *Computer World*.

Increasingly, our shifts at the Kling Klang Studio didn't begin until after eight at night. We simply couldn't liberate ourselves from 'Techno Pop'. Looking back, I think it wasn't a mixing problem – though that might have been the case with 'Tour de France' – it was more a problem with our composing technique, which was developing more and more towards montage, due to all the sampling we were doing. We had long since stopped making music together. It seemed like we'd forgotten that was exactly how our music had come about in the first place.

Boing Boom Tschak

Without a doubt, Florian's main interest during our time together in Kraftwerk was speech synthesis. That included experiments with his own voice, too. So Ralf and I weren't particularly surprised when he spoke a few onomatopoeic words into the emulator during one session. Boing, boom, tschak, bang and pssst and similar sounds – all perfectly Florian-esque. As soon as he animated the samples rhythmically on the keyboard, the content-free words turned into musical form. And that was pretty funky from the word go. This phonetic material contained the first really promising further ideas for our 'Techno Pop' track for a long time. We initially regarded it as a kind of intro and added it to the beginning of the multitrack. It was a good match for the existing artificial speech.

As always, the idea didn't come out of a cultural vacuum. There had been a few recent hits featuring nonsense words or syllables, and they still reverberate with me to this day: Trio's world-famous 'Da Da Da' (1982), 'Din Daa Daa (Dum-Dum)' (1983) by another German artist, Georg Kranz, and not to forget 'Beat Box' (1983) from The Art of Noise with its rhythmized phonemes. The tradition dates back many years, to Ernst Jandl's speech poetry, sound poems by the Dadaists and Futurists, all the way to Lewis Carroll's influential nonsense rhymes and word creations. Rock'n'roll also made use of the method, thinking of 'Wop-bop-a-loo-bop-a-wop-bam-boom' for instance. The roots of these vocal pop acrobatics go back to the doowop style of 1950s America and even further, to the scat singing of the 1920s.

But aside from that, nonsense words and melismatic vocals – meaning a melody sung on a single syllable – are among the traditional means of expression in folk and art music. Every child in the German-speaking world knows the whimsical lyrics 'sim sa la dim bam ba sa la du sa la dim' from the song *Auf einem Baum ein Kuckuck* (1838), for example. Or there's *Die Vogelhochzeit* (1470) with its fun refrain 'Fidirallala, fidirallala, fidirallalalala', another beloved tune. Papageno also comes to mind, the bird-catcher who introduces himself in Mozart's *The Magic Flute* (1791) with the words 'Der Vogelfänger bin ich ja, stets lustig, heissa, hopsassa!' And in the second aria by the Queen of the Night, 'Der Hölle Rache', we hear the world's most famous 'aaahs'. Going even further back – for instance to Bach's *St Matthew Passion* (1727), unthinkable without melisma, and past the Italian Renaissance composers – let's say Orlando di

426

Lasso (1532–1594) or Palestrina (1525–1594) – we reach the liturgical songs of the early Christian church. The Old Orient had a huge cultural head start. Under the influence of Jewish ritual music, simple note sequences came about that already used occasional melisma. The best known example today is Gregorian chorals, a direct descendant. Without instrumental accompaniment and sounding unusually unisono to our ears, the voices would float almost timelessly in the echoing space of the church. Over long drawn-out syllables – such as in the circuitous intonation of a 'hallelujah' – the monks sang plentiful ornaments using melisma, as if trying to recreate the sound of eternity. All that has survived is early church music. What, where and how else people used to sing around the world, we don't know. The ordinary people of those times left nothing to remind us of them – but the monks did. I admit I'm not all that familiar with Hebraic music, and I can hardly imagine how the people of Mesopotamia made music three thousand years before the Christan era. But I wouldn't be surprised if several notes have always been sung on one vowel everywhere since the dawn of time. That's my take on nonsense words and melismatic vocals – making no claim to completeness, of course. Boing, boom, tschak!

Filming by the Rhine

The film with the historical cycling footage appeared not to have been all that helpful for promoting 'Tour de France'. Interestingly enough, Ralf and Florian decided to make another film a year later featuring us doing the cycling ourselves. As you probably know, the Tour de France is held every year in July, but we'd missed our chance to make a film reflecting the sporting event's atmosphere – summer, heat, blue sky and all that. It was the cold and foggy end of February when we met up late one afternoon at the Rheinstadion. The mood was very much grey on grey.

The four of us wore tight-fitting black bodysuits, revealing how slim we all were. We wore our helmets over the suits' tight hoods. And although we only cycled short distances wearing gloves and lined cycling shoes, we froze half to death even during the initial shots.

The song is only 2:30 minutes long, which doesn't leave a lot of scope for major experiments in terms of camera angles and editing. Bearing in mind that Günter Fröhling only had a short time until dusk, he got the very most out of those minutes. In his camera settings, Fröhling goes from the drawn portraits of the draft for the *Techno Pop* album cover to details of the bikes to material filmed in various odd perspectives from a moving car.

Fröhling spliced in flashes of photos from the session on 5 August 1983, showing us resting in summer outfits, four friends laughing as we sat on the ground under a tree. Then at around the two-minute mark, Florian greets the viewers in his typical friendly manner – my absolute favourite sequence. The end shows us four cycling down the exit of the Theodor Heuss Bridge. Fade to black.

Rebecca Allen and her Virtual Creations

In mid-May, Ralf and Florian went to Paris for a weekend. Ralf had the ambitious plan of cycling the 265.5 kilometres of the classic spring Paris–Roubaix Challenge. I can't remember his report from the 'hell of the north' but I do know he and Florian met the American multimedia artist Rebecca Allen in Paris. They had come across her during their research into possibilities for 3D animation. She was working on simulating human movements and facial expressions, and had already been involved in making several music videos. She was definitely one of the pioneers of that form of digital technology. Allen had just moved to the Computer Graphics Laboratory at the New York Institute of Technology, regarded as the birthplace of 3D animation. The university had already agreed to work with Kraftwerk.

Ralf and Florian invited Rebecca to Düsseldorf. She was about my age, I estimated when we met at the studio. To judge by the great atmosphere, Ralf and Florian were in the midst of charming her. Personally, I couldn't envision how she would transform us into virtual creations. Before Rebecca returned to New York on 1 June, she explained how she worked. We could imagine her first steps would take some time.

In the mid-eighties, animating bodies on computers was a major technical challenge. To model the virtual figures, Rebecca started by getting us to send her the four heads of our showroom dummies. We also recorded video footage of our skulls from various angles with Günter Fröhling. After digitalizing these sources, she could add a few elements of our physical faces – like our eyes, for instance – when designing the avatars.[4]

In the summer of 1984 I took stock of our progress, looking both back and ahead. We had first talked about calling our new album *Techno Pop* on our 1981 world tour. After producing the four central tracks, we placed a mysterious teaser in *Select* magazine in May 1983. At around the same time, EMI

Electrola announced the upcoming album with a catalogue number in *Musikmarkt*. For the July 1983 Tour de France race, we released our advance single with a slight delay, which was an unsurprising flop in France but got to number 22 in the UK and 47 in Germany. In February 1984, 'Tour de France' was at number 4 in the US dance charts. Up to that point, so many different versions of the song had been released – German, French, instrumentals, versions with extended percussion parts, etc. – that I had trouble telling them apart. In the UK the track would eventually spend an impressive 23 weeks in the charts – two weeks longer than our number 1, 'The Model'/'Computer Love.'

The 'Tour de France' song was developing an unexpected dynamic – but the planned *Techno Pop* album had lost all momentum. The original cover looked jaded thanks to the parallel use of the cyclists on 'Tour de France' and it had also gone out of style. At that point, the new look of digital 3D animation symbolized the cultural and technological zeitgeist. Being modern – or even being considered a synonym for modernity – had always been important for Kraftwerk, and now it was our main concern. Kraftwerk should be perceived primarily as innovative and pioneering, as a mirror of the technological age. So it was the perfect time for Rebecca to come along with a video clip that would communicate that image of modernity.

Flüela Pass – 2383m

For the next four or five weeks we went on working, now usually meeting between nine and ten at night in the social and media room. Ralf was doing daily cycling training and was in top physical form. And a year after our first attempt, A.S.O. did use our track as the signature tune for the Tour de France. When the peloton of cyclists was running late one day, our song was played non-stop on loop for a whole hour.

I wasn't at all surprised when Ralf suggested going to Switzerland for a week of cycling in July. Florian graciously declined but Willi Klein wanted to come along. By this time, Ralf was doing an excessive amount of cycling, training up to 200 kilometres a day in summer.[5] As I saw it, sport had become his number-one priority, before everything else. But I still harboured the hope that we'd find our way back to making music together. So I decided to accompany him on his trip to the Alps, to revive our relationship. I normally just cycled any which way, not thinking much about it. That had to change now, though. My preparations began three weeks ahead, with regular training: I swam a kilometre in the Rheinstadion and cycled at least fifty kilometres a day to get halfway fit for the mountains.

We'd be stopping at Zürich, St Moritz, Livigno and Davos on our trip. Ralf could hardly wait to start cycling the Alps. That was no problem for Willi Klein either, but for me it was really tough following them across the Flüela and Albula passes, both over 2300 metres high. On the way up, I noticed that my old Koga Miyata weighed almost ten kilos, and downhill it reached the limits of its stability. Always just about to lose my balance after minutes of constant shaking, I kept the brakes on as I coasted down the mountainsides. The guys would wait for me at the bottom.

Willi and I took a day's break in Livigno, spending it in an indoor swimming pool with a view of the Alps. Ralf used the day to cycle up and down the same pass several times over. The whole trip was for training purposes, after all! He was definitely entitled to the polka-dot jersey . . . Nonetheless, the mood on our little sporting excursion was friendly. I came to the conclusion, though, that I wouldn't get through to Ralf by taking part in his cycling tours either. My approach to physical culture was very different to his. I wanted to use sport to support and accompany my life with and in music, not the other way around. In the pool at Livigno, I promised myself to get regular exercise to counteract the stress of music production.

Back in Düsseldorf, a moderate form of triathlon seemed like the best way to get in shape. Alongside swimming and cycling, I began running every day, starting slowly and building up to ten kilometres in an hour. The outdoor pool closed in the autumn and cycling's not much fun in the cold either. But pounding the pavement is. By the end of the year, I knew that running was my thing. The only equipment I need is a pair of shoes – and I'm happy to go without cycling's designer jerseys and helmets. There was no traffic in the forest or on the riverside road to Kaiserswerth, and I soon grew to love the strange floating state of mind that sets in after running for a while, in which I experience a new quality of thought.

Musique Non-Stop

The language lab had become the key part of the studio for Florian. With the aid of the team from the Bochum Faculty of General Electrotechnology and Acoustics, he had not only got the speech synthesizers DECtalk and Infovox talking; over time, they had developed regular workflows. When using speech synthesis for music, the key task is to define the phonemes' pitch, length, volume and timbre; that is, the inflection, to set the text into the desired timescale and increase comprehensibility. Without human emotions, comprehensibility is essential, especially because Kraftwerk often use acoustic pictogrammes like 'Pop' or 'Tekno' or, in fact, 'Music Non Stop – Techno Pop'. Sounds complicated? Yes, it is, in its way. As I see it, Florian profited hugely from the university project's competence for the specific uses he had in mind.

The DECtalk speech synthesizer had several impressive pre-programmed expressionless voices. *Betty*, for example, radiated a fascinating artificial presence. The first time she spoke the 'Techno Pop' lyrics in Studio A, we were all crazy about her. Irresistible! The perfect female android voice. In the course of our further voice castings, we also discovered a French bass or baritone. The track eventually got the name 'Musique Non-Stop'.

The Downward Spiral

In the fourth year of production work on the *Techno Pop* album, things started looking more and more desolate. No one turned up at the studio before late in the evening, and one or other of us kept making our excuses. If the three of us were there at the same time, we'd often get stuck in front of the TV, sinking deep into the sofa and chairs only to head home again after a few hours of getting nothing done. Our morale was at an all-time low.

At least François Kevorkian's visits dragged us out of our lethargy for a short while. Ralf and Florian had invited him over for the first time in the spring of 1984, to mix the latest version of 'Techno Pop' at Soundstudio N in Cologne, which was followed by further sessions at Kling Klang. The fifth and last occasion for the moment was in September 1985. That time, he brought along a Sony PCM-F1. A relatively affordable portable stereo recorder, it could change analogue into digital signals, record them on a video recorder and play them back in astoundingly good sound quality (16 bit, 44.1 kHz sampling rate).

Our schedule was made up of 'Techno Pop' and 'The Telephone Call'. François soon set up shop in Joachim Dehmann's workshop office on the opposite side of the courtyard, from where he called up all kinds of numbers all over the world to record telephone signals: dial tones and engaged tones, automatic messages about holding loops and wrong connections. 'The number you've called is wrong. Please call Information' and that kind of thing. At one point during the session, I even lugged the mixing desk from my home studio over to Kling Klang to use it as a sub-mixer for our thousands of effect machines.

During that visit, the Kling Klang Studio was temporarily transformed into a veritable anthill of productivity. François was making phone calls and recording in Joachim's workshop, Ralf and I were putting things together in Studio A, and Wolfgang Kulas was shuffling phonemes with Florian in the language lab. Yet even after the fifth session with François, we still didn't have a finished album to show for it.

All around us, the market for electronic studio equipment and instruments was exploding, business buzzing like crazy. It was a real gold-digger atmosphere. Everyone thought they'd fall behind if they weren't up to date on the latest technology. As of 1982, there was the industry standard MIDI (Musical

434

Instrument Digital Interface), to connect all the different manufacturers' instruments in the studio like in a telephone network. It had enormous potential, resulting in fantastic possibilities in music production.

The most astounding thing for me was the method of recording this MIDI data, for instance on a device I bought myself in September 1985: a LinnSequencer that cost an incredible 5800 Deutschmarks. In the mid-eighties, this new technology was nothing short of revolutionary. If you connected a MIDI-compatible keyboard like the DX7 – the first commercially affordable digital synthesizer – to a data recorder like the LinnSequencer, you could record and save the data of a musical performance and then play it back.

The DX7 soon became a staple instrument and was now installed in the Kling Klang Studio. We also added a TX-816 rack, consisting of eight DX7 modules. The device used an algorithm for frequency modulation synthesis (invented by the American John Chowning in 1967), which was remarkable at the time for its realistic imitation of acoustic sound creation. Now, when I brought my LinnSequencer along to the studio, we could control several instruments at once to produce polyphonic sound and arrange the music before it was recorded on magnetic tape. That was amazingly effective.

Looking back, the new instrumentation on most of the album tracks in autumn 1985 tells us a lot. It seems like we considered analogue sound production outdated. With the violin presets on the DX7 and TX-816 racks, suddenly digitally imitated orchestras of centuries gone by were determining the sound of our music. To put it ironically, the innovation of FM synthesis led to a more modern form of nostalgia.

'Progress likes to assume the mask of lack of alternatives,' writes the German philosopher Richard David Precht in his 2018 book *Jäger, Hirten, Kritiker*, a brilliant observation on our digital society.[6] In 1985, we were in fact convinced that digitalization would simply make everything better in the music world. And many things did indeed change. But was that change for the better? Essentially, the manufacturers' R&D departments focused on automating the music production process through new technology – increasing efficiency. Perhaps that was always the way, but with digitalization, the processes took on a new dimension and split up into a million tiny units. At that point in time, I wasn't aware of how this huge technological change would influence our work. Far less could I imagine how radically it would transform the entire music business.

The next few weeks slowed right back down again. When Ralf and Florian broke off for Christmas holidays on 13 December, I went on working in my home studio.

Electric Cafe

At the end of February, Maxime turned up at the Mintropstrasse studio. He was developing a new music format for French television. The programme was to be given the evocative name of *Electric Cafe*. What if Kraftwerk were to write a song for him to offer as a signature tune? I instantly thought of Maxime's amazing coup in 1976, when he persuaded Jean-Loup Lafont from the Europe n°1 radio station to use 'Radioactivity' as a jingle. Perhaps he could pull off something similar again.

The track composed itself so quickly that I can barely remember any details. My favourite part was Florian's electronic soap bubbles, which floated up to the studio ceiling and burst with a plop. I can still see him piling up a few analogue synthesizers and a sequencer in one of the emptied consoles and connecting them up with patch cables. Florian was suddenly unexpectedly supple and agile. He bustled around, plugging in patch cords and adjusting the synth modules, not letting up until the archetypal electro-sounds filled the room. His set-up was so clever that we could synchronize it to the music's metre and insert the sound objects into the musical form. The synthesizer riff came about off the cuff, and for the second section we used the motif of an earlier version of 'Techno Pop'. Ralf's decision to speak the lyrics in French made perfect sense. Why did he only translate it into Spanish as the music went on? I think the words sounded so good in this second Romance language that he chose to do without German or English.

We recorded the instruments using my LinnSequencer and transferred the loops one by one to the multitrack. Even though we were still only in the studio in the evenings, the whole thing took less than a week. Today, the production seems to me like a kind of acoustic commando operation: get in, get the job done, get out.

As luck would have it, Maxime didn't manage to sell his concept in the end; all the channels turned it down. But his idea had given us a push for an unusually productive week, during which we came up with a song that gave its name to the album, instead of *Techno Pop*. For a while, at least.

437

The Plan

We were still making sporadic trips to Cologne to listen to our music on the Moroco club's sound system. After that, we'd talk again about how to go on with our mixing sessions. The idea came up to work with a sound engineer from closer to home. I remembered a guy I'd studied with, Henning Schmitz, who I'd met years ago at an end-of-term party in the Robert Schumann Conservatory's sound studio. I quickly got hold of his phone number and we agreed to meet at the Kling Klang Studio in mid-April. At our first meeting, I thought we'd get on well with Henning and I recommended to Ralf and Florian that we should give him a try. Only a week later, we mixed the new orchestral version of 'Sex Object' with Henning at Kling Klang. The six-day session went well, but after that our work came to a total standstill.

In this gridlocked situation, I had to find some way to keep myself above water mentally. I needed an outlet to tackle my frustration, and sport was the only solution. I came down with an acute case of running fever, covering almost ten kilometres a day in the spring. A few readers might remember the end of April and beginning of May 1986. Back then, I regularly checked the news before going out running, to find out about possible nuclear fallout. In late April 1986, the largest reactor disaster of the era had happened in the Ukrainian town of Pripyat, at Chernobyl. The consequences were all over the German media, more than any other news item. Radioactive rain fell over Germany and I wasn't about to go running at high levels. For the first time, everyone had a concrete realization of the real dangers associated with the peaceful use of nuclear energy.

As you can imagine, we now saw our song 'Radioactivity' very much in the light of this event.

But at some point, we turned our attention back to our half-finished record production. We asked ourselves what options we had left to get the album, now renamed *Electric Cafe*, done. The long production time had exhausted us. Ralf came to the conclusion that we wouldn't get where we wanted with the technology available in Germany, and suggested another mix in New York – two and a half years after his last attempt. An interesting idea. At the beginning of the album, a trip to New York might have been inspiring, might have influenced our compositions, but now? There was hardly any scope left. Then again, at that point we'd ground to a total halt in Germany. At least relocating to New York would make something happen. Aside from that, there was a much more pertinent reason, at least for me, to support Ralf's suggestion: he wouldn't be able to cycle in Manhattan. And that – or so I hoped – might play a key role in getting our album finished. I was firmly convinced there were two things Ralf needed in this situation: quitting cycling cold turkey and pressure. Pressure would build up there anyway, simply because a day in a New York studio cost inordinate amounts of money.

I did keep my calendar but I avoided counting how many days we'd been working on the album so far. Writing this book, I totted up that we'd had about 750 sessions together in the Kling Klang Studio, from the starting point in October 1981 up to our trip to the USA. That's not counting the month Ralf spent doing the first mixes at Power Station. On 31 May 1986, my 34th birthday, the three of us set off. I thought: aren't a lot of victories in the Tour de France won on the finishing straits?

Mixing in New York City

When we landed at JFK Airport at 3:30 in the afternoon on Sunday, 1 June, there was a terrific storm raging. Well, electricity is certainly a fitting motif. My last visit was a few years back, but in the limo from the airport to the Hotel St. Moritz I immediately got that strange feeling of being in the secret capital city of the world again. We probably wouldn't stay more than two or three weeks, I thought, but I'd packed my running shoes and a few sports clothes just in case. On that very first day, I circled Central Park twice in 110 minutes.

Over the next few days, we took a taxi downtown to François Kevorkian's Axis Studio near Canal Street around noon. The building also housed the Gramavision Studio, where we planned to do the overdubs later on. We were still missing a few speech samples for 'Sex Object' and 'The Telephone Call'.

A colleague of François' also helped on the production side: Fred Maher. He was a musician who'd grown up in Manhattan, and we found out by the by that he'd already played with Bill Laswell and Lou Reed, despite only being in his early 20s. But the way I see it, he brought something much more interesting into play than his great references: a piece of software on his portable computer. Fred explained he was a beta-tester for Octave Plateau Electronics, a company that had developed a music software program by the name of Sequencer Plus in 1985. He was testing its version 2.0. A little like my LinnSequencer, the program could record MIDI data. But while my machine represented the recorded music in numeral form and let me organize it into patterns, the new software supported our work

440

through a graphic user interface. Every musical event was represented on a time axis. What I saw on the portable computer screen and heard at the same time almost took my breath away. It was Igor Stravinsky's dream come true: a sounded score. I got hold of the software's red handbook to take a closer look. It was absolutely clear: I had to have that program! One of the things I liked about Fred was the extremely laid-back way he integrated himself and his Sequencer Plus software. Later, his involvement as an operator was called 'data transfer' on the album cover. Fred was happy with that.

In the first week, we met up every day at François' project studio in the early afternoon. That gave me an opportunity to take my run around Central Park in the mornings. Then I'd shower, change and get breakfast in the coffee shop around the corner. One day, Donald Sutherland sat down next to me at the counter in a green army jacket and ordered a coffee. Perfectly normal – that's just what everyday New York life feels like.

After one of the sessions, we went to the Area nightclub on Hudson Street, one of the hippest Manhattan clubs at the time. Someone smuggled us in past the crowds at the door. The mix of guests wasn't bad at all: anonymous middle-class people, girls dolled up in taffeta, businesswomen, college kids, faces from the media and music biz, a few artists – and the celebrities allegedly met up in the Silver Bar. I think that was where I first met Hubert Kretzschmar. Hubert is a German artist who'd been living and working in New York for some time. He'd designed the cover of the Rolling Stones album *Some Girls*, for example. And we wanted him to help with the artwork for *Electric Cafe* as well.

Even though I was never a pioneer in terms of nightlife, I did get to know other clubs apart from Area. The Limelight in the Episcopalian church on Sixth Avenue was one of the absolute hotspots. The place was crazy and a whole lot of fun. Above the club kids' heads, there were cages suspended over the dancefloor, where go-go girls put on their show. The eccentric eye-patch-wearing Canadian Peter Gatien was the unchallenged 'King of Nightlife' at the time. He ran not only the Limelight but also the Palladium, where we occasionally hung out. Another hip place was Danceteria, which boasted several floors. The Video Lounge showed a mix of music videos, experimental movies and found footage.

On 11 June, we moved to the Right Track Studios directly on Times Square. François was supported by Ron Saint Germain and Fred Maher was on standby for any overdubs. The mix began – including Times Square deli breaks, delivery service, 'power dinners' and baseball viewing sessions. Once all the preparation work was done, François and Ron started mixing 'Sex Object'.

At the end of that week, the three of us went to the Computer Graphics Lab on the campus of the New York Institute of Technology. Rebecca Allen had made several trips to Düsseldorf over the past two years to keep us in the loop. Now we wanted to take a look at the latest iteration of her computer animations. Showing us around the lab, she also pointed out the gigantic computer cabinets humming away to store data.

In the Right Track Studios, François and Ron were still cranking the levers on 'Sex Object' when someone put on Janet Jackson's 'Nasty'. Talk about a cold shower – our mix sounded unconvincing in comparison. Another time, François and Ron were listening to the hit tune 'Sledgehammer' on the big speaker when we got to the studio. Peter Gabriel's sound spectrum was an impressive demonstration of where we stood with our mix. The mood barometer fell below freezing and Ralf disappeared for a few hours. When would this nightmare come to an end? We'd been in New York for almost a month when Emil showed up at the studio, with Lothar Manteuffel in his wake. And the Kling Klang lawyer Marvin Katz also put in an appearance at Right Track. Everyone made a real effort to radiate positive energy and relaxed vibes, but the situation remained tough.

In our free time, we watched Prince's strange movie *Under the Cherry Moon* at the cinema – filmed by Michael Ballhaus – and then went out on the town again. New Order were playing a gig at the 1018 Club, we heard. Cool. How would they get 'Blue Monday' across live? Their equipment was buzzing brightly on stage but sadly, the band was several hours late and we left again. It was to be a few more years before I saw Bernard, Peter, Stephen and Gillian live.

Time passed. On 3 June, after a good month at Right Track, Florian said his farewells. I could understand him; things had certainly gone better than they were going at that point. But the cause of our problem lay in the Kling Klang Studio, not at Right Track. It was too late to turn back now. If the new album was ever to happen, we had to pass through the eye of the needle. Every individual at the New York studio was definitely qualified to produce an album that sounded very good, so it wasn't down to the team that we were having so much trouble. I felt torn. On one hand, it made sense to compare our production's sound spectrum with other artists'. On the other hand, our music has its own significance. It's a product of our invention, playing, programming, orchestration and arrangement – it breathes and sounds in its own way.

On 21 July, a Monday, we finally made it – the songs were all mixed. Ralf would do the final few edits to the masters in François' project studio, for instance the montage of the 'suite' on the A-side: 'Boing Boom Tschak' – 'Techno Pop' – 'Musique Non-Stop'.

With two months of New York City behind me, I booked a flight back to Düsseldorf at the Lufthansa bureau. Ralf volunteered to take me to the airport – in a chauffeur-driven stretch limo. But before my departure, we visited a branch of New England Digital to get more information on the Synclavier. We'd already had a demonstration of a Fairlight CMI. As the limo pulled up to the terminal, Ralf told me he'd decided to buy a Synclavier; state-of-the-art technology would make music production easier for us again. Was that really the solution for our problem . . . ? I got out of the car and we said goodbye. Before I passed through the revolving doors into JFK, I took one last look back. The stretch limo seemed to me like the broom wagon at the Tour de France.

Düsseldorf Layover

On my flight back, I expected the burden to fall from my shoulders. It didn't. The hard work and tension of the past few weeks, the past few years, was still weighing me down. Bettina came to collect me from the airport in the morning and we celebrated my return at home. After that, I fell ill for an entire week. Bettina had finished her degree while I was away and gave me a copy of her master's thesis, complete with a dedication that almost brought tears to my eyes. To clear our heads, we took a short trip to Berchtesgaden. Something was pulling me back to the town where I was born.

A little later, I talked to Ralf on the phone. It turned out he was back in the studio with François to edit a suspicious offbeat. Alright, it could have been worse. I called twice more in August to find out what was taking him so long. More edits were needed, he hinted. Ralf didn't come back to Germany until 6 September, and we agreed to meet up for a listening session at Willi Klein's place. Hearing the finished album, I had no illusions: we hadn't managed to create a great work of art.

Still, the show must go on. The computer models from Rebecca's video formed the basis for the album artwork. The close-ups of the polygonal surfaces of our faces give the front cover its unique aesthetic. Hubert Kretzschmar was in charge of designing the record sleeves. The inside sleeve shows our bodies in a preliminary stage of 3D computer modelling, as wireframe graphics.

As we now know, 'Musique Non-Stop' wasn't a huge hit. And yet Rebecca's video, which she and her team worked on for two years, is regarded as a milestone in 3D computer graphics. It won a number of awards and was shown on the music channels up until the mid-nineties. The ad campaign for the album was also based entirely on Rebecca's work.

Like on *Computer World*, Ralf and Florian mainly avoided using specialist terminology in the credits. There's a mix of companies, names, neologisms and technical job descriptions, which makes the credits more reminiscent of acknowledgements in a book than something you'd find on an industry-produced record. For instance, there's no mention of copyright details on the CD. I refrained from commenting, though. After all the years of hard work, I was relieved we'd managed to put out a product at all.

Electric Cafe was released in October 1986. The record got to number 23 in the German album charts and fell out again in January 1987, after ten weeks. Rebecca's 'Musique Non-Stop' video was shown on the country's then most important music show *Formel 1* to coincide with the launch. Five weeks later, the track made the leap to the German singles charts. It stayed there for twelve weeks, making it to number 13. In the two weeks *Electric Cafe* spent on the British charts, it made number 58.

During this period, I visited Wolfgang in his GAF Studio on Kaiserswerther Strasse. He and two colleagues were doing pretty well designing and building furniture. I think at that time he was still interested in going on tour with Kraftwerk, but it grew less and less likely with every year that Ralf and Florian would ever do it again.

'Ralf was always putting it off until the next year,' Wolfgang recalls. 'I didn't know what else to do with my life, started suffering from depression and having nightmares. That made two things I wanted to get rid of. So I just stopped going to Kling Klang and joined the furniture studio.'

Wolfgang will have made sure he caught the video on *Formel 1*. He liked Rebecca's animations, especially the virtual stage set, which reminded him of a miniature model he'd once made for our set on the *Computer World* tour, with all the little details. There were even four tiny plastic figures from a toy shop standing

446

behind their consoles. The model had been in our media room since the tour. The video's stylized wireframe backdrop really did look similar to Wolfgang's physical model. When he asked me: 'Is that Kraftwerk now?' all I could say was: 'You'll have to ask Ralf and Florian.'

Remix: The Telephone Call

In mid-November, our American label approached us with the magnificent idea of buying in a remix of 'The Telephone Call' – by Steve Thompson and Mike Barbieri. The two producers were totally hip at the time, remixing their way to fame and fortune among the top names in the business. Only a week later, Ralf and I were back on a plane across the Atlantic. We landed at JFK on a Saturday and spent the rest of the weekend in New York's clubs.

At the start of the week, we turned up at Media Sound Studios, where Steve and Mike were already working on the remix. The next few days flew past and Ralf and I turned night into day on the following weekend as well. Arriving in the studio on Monday, we were really pleased with the great bassline the remixers had come up with. But then they dubbed an 808-cowbell onto the track. It may have been all the rage, but other than that it wasn't a great idea . . . Just to help readers understand, perhaps: you could hear the TR-808 drum machine on countless hits back then. Its electronic 'cowbell' was the latest fashion, clearly recognizable. The sound had become ubiquitous, which made it absolutely taboo for us. After a short break, Ralf decided not to continue our work with the star remixers.

We talked to Florian back home to discuss what to do next. François and Ron were mentioned again. When Ralf and I got to Right Track Studio on Sunday morning, François and Ron were just starting to set up 'The Telephone Call'.

I suggested using the 'Numbers' beat as the track's rhythm formula, and that was what we did. Then François and Ron developed the bass sound. After a fourteen-hour session, we listened to the results late at night in the Palladium and knew straight away that we were on the right track (pun intended). The next day was another fourteen hours non-stop, and then we checked the mix in the Area club. After several long sessions and various club tests, we got the remix done in just under three and a half weeks.

UFA Again

It'll come as no surprise that we needed a video for the second single, 'The Telephone Call'. In the MTV era, bands didn't exist without film material. It didn't look like any more footage would be forthcoming from Rebecca Allen's lab, but it wouldn't have suited the song's subject matter anyway. The artwork for the maxi-single matched the album cover's aesthetic, though. At that moment, Ralf remembered the tried and trusted UFA look. Fine. But hang on . . . where was Wolfgang? We persuaded him to join in, and the four of us met up for filming with Günter Fröhling again.

As always at times like these, Wolfgang managed to bring out the positive side of our group dynamics. Suddenly, we were Kraftwerk again, a relaxed band in an excellent mood. Our outfits were black polo necks and leather gloves. Only Wolfgang hadn't been able to find his polo neck. The 'plot', such as it was: We make a phone call. No, actually, we only pick up the phone, dial a number, listen with emotionless faces, and hang up again. That's it. Looking up a number in the phone book also fitted into the screenplay. We see Ralf playing a piano-shaped telephone and later operating a reel-to-reel tape player while sitting in front of a microphone. In one scene, Florian is wearing headphones. Also featured: the telephone operator. In this case she provides the information: 'The number you have reached has been disconnected.'

Fröhling also filmed us using a small camera dolly that ran on rails, which made the tracking look extremely smooth. In the editing process, the footage was combined using hard cuts, soft fades or swipes – very much in the old-fashioned film style.

Even though it's me singing this title in the original – the first and only time on a Kraftwerk song – I wasn't allowed to act that out in the video. It was up to Wolfgang's silhouette to lip-sync the chorus at one point. Why? Hard to say. I do at least hammer away at a mechanical Torpedo typewriter on the line 'You're so close but far away' – wearing gloves, naturally, as befits the Fritz Lang motifs. It was the last time we filmed together.

The recording and editing really didn't take long, but we were still too late for any decent promotion, sadly. The single had died in the UK on 12 March, having reached only number 89. In the US dance charts, at least, the 12-inch maxi-single 'The Telephone Call'/'House Phone' with the by then rather tired 'Numbers' beat did get to number 1.

Reviews of Electric Cafe

I asked myself: Had we ever got fewer reviews and reports on an album release than for *Electric Cafe*? The established media ignored us. Even the timing of our few interviews was wrong. The promotion campaign went nowhere. What had we been working for, all those five years?

After the long silence, our music seemed not to meet the reviewers' high expectations. In its laconic record review, *Die Rheinische Post* wrote: 'The four men from Düsseldorf [. . .] can hardly cover up the fact that they've long since run out of steam, even lagging behind artists like Rheingold or Orchestral Manoeuvres in the Dark who can show them a thing or two.'[7] 'Great video, deadly dull record,' wrote *ME/Sounds*, branding us with laziness or inability or ivory-tower nostalgia, or all three at once.[8] For the Ruhr region magazine *Marabo*, Kraftwerk's new album sounded in many places 'veritably old-fashioned'.[9] Ralf's two-page interview in the May 1987 issue of *Fachblatt* is illustrated with a series of stills from our video for 'The Telephone Call'. The album's Tamara de Lempicka aesthetics seemed to have been forgotten already.

1981–1986: A Techno Pop Odyssey

In the 1970s and 1980s, the dancefloor was an important site of music culture. 'Soft machine tests' – as Chris Bohn once called them – were fairly commonplace. By getting DJs to test our mixes on disco crowds, we were automatically in competition with the music played in that context. The feedback looped back into our work and prompted a reaction. No one would ever accuse me of having any objection to music with strong rhythms, but in retrospect, I can't help but conclude that this focus on the dancefloor didn't do our development much good. On the contrary, it hugely limited the spectrum of our musical expression.

Pianist and conductor Daniel Barenboim says: 'Every work of art has "two faces", one directed towards eternity and the other towards its own time.'[10] To apply his metaphor to pop music, on *Techno Pop/Electric Cafe* we looked too much at our own time and its fashions and technical innovations, instead of focusing on putting together our very own musical elements. During this phase, we morphed unnoticed from independent composers into music and sound designers. Looking back at the origins of the 'Numbers' beat illustrates how we'd worked before this production. I never thought for a second about a particular format that had to be met. Ralf and I turned the feeling we had about life in that moment into music. And if Florian hadn't had the presence of mind to press the red 'record' button, that instant might have been lost forever. We were absolutely free in that act of creation. And we didn't head off to Cologne to test out the recording in Moroco. Perhaps the drum pattern might not have fitted into the soundscape of the time. And if all the 'soft machines' had left the dancefloor, that would have been it . . . Would we have cast aside the beat for 'Numbers'?

During our production of *Techno Pop*, we forgot the method we'd used in our writing sessions, where the three of us improvised freely and kept coming up with diverse pieces of music and recording them. We would pick pieces from various

451

sessions – often recorded months or years apart – and blend them into a synthesis, an organic whole. Instead of remembering how our most authentic and probably therefore most successful music had been made, we fixed our gaze on the mass-market music zeitgeist. But comparing our own ideas to other people's work was anti-creative and counterproductive. We were no longer capable of looking further than the end of our own noses. It didn't help if we discovered elements of our own musical DNA in other artists' songs. We weren't interested any more in inventing our music – all we wanted was to sound better than others, or not worse. We'd forgotten our night-time sound rides, where all that counted was whether the music spoke to us or not.

There was another circumstance that made this production into an odyssey. We recorded new ideas directly onto the multi-track machine without playing with them together beforehand. Through this tape-focused approach, however, we committed ourselves far too early. Once recorded, the scheme of the music couldn't be changed. And then when we did have to rework the ideas, we spent way too much time editing minor details. That had little influence on the pieces as a whole, however, so it was mostly ineffective. We also concentrated on a small number of musical ideas without considering alternatives. And the more time we invested in our scant resources, the less probable a new start became.

Over the course of the five-year production, we had lost sight of our trusted set-up of analogue synthesizers and drums. The same applied to the Synthanorma and the Triggersumme. Our interest was focused increasingly forwards, on what we perceived as technical innovations. But no matter whether with the old set-up or the new digital equipment – what was missing was our free improvisations, during which we pursued no other purpose to begin with than making music together, translating our thoughts and emotions of the moment into music.

Through the easily accessible sound fragments of sampling technology, our approach to music altered. Specific sounds and rhythmic sonic collages had always marked out Kraftwerk's compositions. But previously, they were either used as a form of audio drama ('Autobahn') or integrated into the music as musicalized effects ('Pocket Calculator'). Electronic imitation by synthesizer was another key element ('Autobahn', 'The Robots'). The use of these concrete and electronic sounds, however, had always been linked to the idea of the music and then brought into the composition. Thanks to sampling, concrete sounds often became the starting point for building our songs. That meant our music had developed over the past few years into a perpetual sequencing of rhythmic patterns of speech and sounds, noise structures in the sense of *musique concrète*, which remind us permanently of reality. That led to very specific units of meaning: dial tone, rotary dial, rotary dial, rotary dial, call signal, call signal, engaged tone, engaged tone, engaged tone, push-button tone, push-button tone, push-button tone, push-button tone, push-button tone, push-button tone . . .

Our form of expression, once shaped by polyphonic elements, transformed into a form of sequenced events that had more in common with the serial system than with the original idea behind our music. Hadn't our guiding thought once been to transform technology into music? Now it felt at times as though technology had absorbed our thoughts.

Even almost forty years later, the odyssey of *Electric Cafe* – which once began full of hope as *Techno Pop* with authentic artwork – seems to me like an unsolved riddle. After a promising start, we stumbled on the pre-release single 'Tour de France' and got so bogged down in detail that we didn't manage to give the album a consistent and coherent feel. Then we lost hold of the most important track and the original artwork through that first single release. Three promotional videos – two attempts for 'Tour de France' plus 'The Telephone Call' – were filmed in the UFA-inspired black-and-white aesthetic that matched the artwork of the lost *Techno Pop* album stylistically. But those films had nothing at all to do with the aesthetic of the computer animation for 'Musique Non-Stop', which also formed the basis of the cover design for *Electric Cafe* with its two single releases. Essentially, the release after the years in production was a crash-landing, a write-off from our ideas factory.

We were simply lacking an objective analysis of our situation. It appears we weren't capable of reaching that point. We found things like planning, coordination and organization extremely difficult. We were on the move with no order, no conventions and no compass. Aside from that, we had lost our process for opinion-forming as a group, partly due to the fact that audience and media reactions to our concerts and records no longer fed into our work. And sadly, during the course of the production we had also forgotten how to immerse ourselves entirely inde-pendently in our most important activity: composing. We didn't even think about how to reach that state of 'flow' because we didn't notice we'd lost it. Instead, the latest products on the music market, the loss of our USP, and rapidly developing technology distracted us hugely, blocking our view of our specific capital: autonomous imagination.

NOTES

1. 'It will always go on – music as bearer of ideas.'
2. 'Somebody within the record company went out and did a pre-order, we were working on the sleeve and some marketing idiot did this.' Ralf Hütter. Interview by Stephen Dalton, *The Scotsman*, March 2004.
3. 'Le phénomè KRAFTWERK associé à la légende du Tour de France. Après *Radio Activity, Trans-Europe Express, Man-Machine et Computer World* ils poursuivent leur concept homme-machine cette fois-cisur des vélos aérodynamiques et avec le thème le plus cher à notre pays et universellement aimé. Une tube puissant et solide pour un cadre léger. L'hymne de l'été, qui est cette année le thème officielle du Tour . . .'
4. Rebecca Allen: 'I had to input all these into the computer and put them all together. So, that was a huge ordeal. Then you have the wireframe, and then you have them standing. We used models that I had done for another commercial piece that we did at our lab, because, again, building human figures was a really hard problem as well. Then I just modified those models so they were more to the body style of Kraftwerk. Then we used those models and put the heads on top of them.' David Buckley: *Kraftwerk – Publikation.* Omnibus Press: London 2012, p. 221
5. 'Kraftwerk – Menschmaschine.' Interview by Teddy Hoersch, *Keyboards*, July 1987
6. Richard David Precht: *Jäger, Hirten, Kritiker: Eine Utopie für die digitale Gesellschaft.* Goldmann Verlag, 2018
7. 'Boing Boom Tschak.' By Hans Hoff, *Rheinische Post*, October 1986
8. 'Kraftwerk: Electric Cafe.' Review by Rolf Lenz, *ME/Sounds*, October 1986
9. 'Techno-Pop in Rheinkultur.' By Peter Erik Hillenbach, *Marabo*, October 1986
10. Daniel Barenboim: *A Life in Music.* Weidenfeld and Nicholson, London, 1991, p. 57

13

THE MIX

*Zen and the Art of Synclavier Maintenance. Kling Klang
Construction Site – Part Two. Swanky Dinner with Bob Krasnow.
Back on Hold. Marathon. The Sounding Score. Robovox. Sacrilege.
New Beginning. The Wall Falls. Wake-Up Call. Whiplash.
Argument. Christmas Party. Italian Journey. A Visit to London.
Utopia. Cause and Effect. Death Mask. Over.*

Zen and the Art of Synclavier Maintenance

As I opened the door to the Kling Klang Studio on Friday, 16
January 1987, I rubbed my eyes in amazement. The metal stand
that once held Ralf's chrome case containing the Minimoog,
Polymoog and Orchestron was now the home of the New
England Digital Synclavier. With its special grey paint-job, it
looked to me like an expensive piece of designer furniture. I
positioned myself at the top-class keyboard with its 6⅓ octaves
and discovered a large display panel and a barrage of red-lit or
flashing buttons.

The computer-controlled audio system's legendary reputation
was down to its sound quality, and above all its price: depending
on the set-up, it cost several hundred thousand US dollars.
Included in the delivery was a massive monitor, which just about

456

fitted into one of the grey consoles. And Joachim Dehmann was to make a special room with its own cooling and ventilation system directly next to the studio door, to house a huge tower consisting of the processing unit and several hard drives.

To understand the New England Digital (NED) business model, you have to mentally beam yourself back to the 1980s. At the time, conservative parties were setting the parameters of politics and business in the West. 'Less state – more market' was their credo. It was the beginning of digitalization, the time of investment bankers and yuppies. Cocaine was part and parcel of the lifestyle. Never was so much money made in the music business as during the MTV era, including in the booming electronic instrument market. So, what could be more logical than giving yourself an advantage over the less solvent competition with the latest technology in music production? I think NED aimed its products explicitly at a clientele for whom money was no object.

The Synclavier II was a digital synthesizer and sampler with a 'direct-to-disc' option. It enabled sixteen-track hard-disc recording, every music producer's dream. One key sales argument was the very high resolution on audio recordings and playback. The only limit to the length of samples was hard-drive capacity. That was what determined the boundaries of technical possibilities at the time, and also the epic price tag. The hand-made, velocity- and pressure-sensitive wooden keyboard gave it something approaching the haptics and luxury of a Steinway grand piano. In practice, however, it turned out the machine's architecture was not yet fully mature; updates took a long time to come and then arrived at outlandish prices. The internal sequencer also wasn't up to the standards of a 1987 software equivalent. Despite these 'minor' drawbacks, the new device held an incredible fascination for us. By buying the Synclavier, Ralf and Florian focused on the means of production. Couldn't better music be made with better machines?[1]

In my early years with Kraftwerk, our different social backgrounds had been clear enough, but music made me forget the inequality. Now, though, our writing sessions and concerts were years back and material thinking had long since become the all-determining factor. I began to feel the contrast ever more acutely.

I've described my childhood in the first few chapters of this book: the frugal conditions of the postwar years, but also the fact that I wanted for nothing. Later, at the conservatory, what I cared about was practising and learning. The focus was on music. It was no place for pumped-up egos and they weren't 'produced' there either. I never had the feeling of belonging to an elite in any way, neither socially, financially, intellectually nor artistically. I had to seek my own place in the world and I was hugely fortunate to find fulfilment in music. Perhaps that's the reason why it's so important to me. I think it does make a difference if you grow up aware of being part of an elite. In that case – at least according to the Eton College chronicler Adam Nicolson – 'success is the measure of all things'[2] and the road to that success is a means to an end.

These days, I see the purchase of the Synclavier as a symbol of the different ways of life and thinking in Kraftwerk. It presumably didn't fit in with Ralf's self-image to make something that fizzled out as unspectacularly as our last product. By investing big in digital equipment, my bandmates wanted to get back on track for success. I believe that's what we call entrepreneurial thinking. As I saw things, we were increasingly losing our grounding in reality, and I began to grow more and more uneasy.

On the purely technical side, the Synclavier's high sampling rate didn't impress me. The irony is that high resolution is mainly noticeable when recording acoustic instruments, not necessarily with instruments recorded without making the air vibrate. Besides, we sampled many of our sounds from our old multitrack tapes – and some of those were 8-bit samples. All in all, I didn't get the hype over this alleged super-machine. But apart from all that, the expensive technology would soon be overtaken by similarly good and significantly cheaper devices. The fast-paced progress in the IT sector soon began to cause difficulties for NED, and the company disappeared from the market towards the end of 1992. Around then, people were beginning to realize that the development of electronic information and data processing is not a linear curve but an exponential one.

Kling Klang Construction Site – Part Two

So now the magical box was in the Kling Klang Studio, but the backdrop no longer met the latest demands. There was no doubt about it: If we wanted to produce and mix tracks here in future, the acoustics had to be improved. And so Ralf and Florian decided to remodel their studio once again. Joachim had been talking for years about changing the position of the speakers and the MCI console in the room – finally, that day had come. A studio design company in the USA was hired and Joachim followed their construction plan to make the required alterations, including soundproofing, completely new wiring and the installation of a cold-storage room for the Synclavier.

The new production device called for new technical skills. The many spec sheets and manuals delivered with the 'Clav', as its fans affectionately called it, had to be read, understood and applied. All that plus expert communication with the manufacturer . . . Ralf had more of an intuitive approach to music, though. The haptic feedback of his analogue instruments, like the Minimoog or the Orchestron, suited his natural feeling for sound. Interacting with those instruments enabled him to make full use of his musical abilities. With the Synclavier, that was different. The way of dealing with sound suddenly took on a much more distanced structure because you had to start by learning a new logic and its ordering principles. They were more like administrative, bureaucratic activities,[3] meaning Kraftwerk needed an administrator for the Synclavier and all its challenges.

Once again, I thought of my old fellow student Henning Schmitz, who had helped us out for a few days of mixing on *Electric Cafe*. When I asked Henning if he could imagine working regularly for Kraftwerk as a sound engineer and Synclavier operator, he recommended Fritz Hilpert, who he'd studied with. Fritz was not averse to the idea and, in the end, we met up at Mintropstrasse in late January: Ralf, Florian, Joachim, Fritz and me. I vaguely remember about a dozen thick handbooks lying around somewhere, which Fritz was supposed to read. At the beginning he was working freelance as a sound engineer, but he would keep popping by for a couple of days over the course of the year to get into the material. Together with Ralf and Florian, he also took part in a Synclavier workshop in the States. After that educational trip, Fritz started to sample sounds from the sixteen-track tapes in Studio B, where the equipment now was. And that was how three graduates of the sound engineering degree at Düsseldorf technical college – Joachim Dehmann, Henning Schmitz and now Fritz Hilpert too – came to work at the Kling Klang Studio.

Personally, I found myself once again in a strange limbo. During the months to come, we met up sporadically at the building site. We hung out in the rooms facing onto Mintropstrasse, lounged on the leather couch and chairs in the media room, stared at the Sony screen and gave a running commentary on whatever was on TV – sometimes it was funny but not always. Our calendar was structured around sporting events: winter sports at the start of the year; ski jumping and downhill racing; in April the Paris–Roubaix, followed by the Giro d'Italia in May and July's Tour de France. Time passed. When Ralf and Florian went on holiday for four weeks in August – Ralf exploring Corsica on two wheels – I had little choice but to take on the job of 'studio manager' and write cheques for Joachim and Fritz's work. But I never felt particularly comfortable in the role. I guess I don't have a good head for business. Nonetheless, I was beginning to have more and more misgivings about the company strategy. I couldn't get my head around why we were constantly investing in extremely expensive high-end technology. Especially as one thing was abundantly clear by now: the more capital went into allegedly optimizing the means of production, the less music came out at the other end.

Swanky Dinner with Bob Krasnow

After Ralf and Florian got back, we met up at the end of September with the head of our US label, Elektra, for a meal at a posh Düsseldorf hotel. Robert Alan 'Bob' Krasnow – according to David Geffen one of the smartest and most talented executives working in the music business – turned out to be a remarkable fellow. The evening really had its eccentric moments. Eventually, as a dessert of berry compote was served, Krasnow talked about our next record and whether we could imagine a 'Best of Kraftwerk'. A concentrated blast like that with a tour to go with it would take us a long way in the USA, he said. In my view, it was a good idea. It seemed like an appropriate measure, at just the right time to finally establish the band as a live act in the USA. And there was no denying its financial potential, either.

Parallel to this product, I could have imagined a collection of 12-inch maxi-singles: a veritable remix frenzy by the usual suspects on the scene. Perhaps also a box-set of 7-inch singles and various CD editions. Special products – you know the score.

We could get the studio remodelling done and go on tour while it was going on. A world tour with a 'Best of Kraftwerk' album, and additional MTV presence with all the stops pulled out certainly wouldn't have harmed Kraftwerk as a band. At last our focus would be back on people and music, I thought. As well as that, it would have been the ideal moment to collate the work of the 'analogue' years in a retrospective of our own design, and then to set off together into the digital age that had long since dawned.

But Ralf and Florian simply couldn't imagine a conventional best-of album. They presumably found it a retrogressive gesture, whereas Kraftwerk stood for progress – or that was how it was communicated, a number of times. It appeared the concept was too unsophisticated for them, not intellectual enough. And then start gigging again . . . ? Whatever the case, after dessert and business talk with Bob Krasnow, Ralf and Florian made the decision to accept his ideas – but in a 'slightly' modified version. Instead of a greatest-hits collection, they planned to produce selected tracks from the band's repertoire in the form of Kraftwerk's own remixes.

Back on Hold

Whether a DIY remix album would have a similar impact to a best-of album, I couldn't really say. One thing was clear, though: new compositions weren't on the to-do list for the time being. While Joachim Dehmann remodelled the studio, Fritz Hilpert put together the library on the Synclavier. Both were bureaucratic tasks that took a long time – which meant I was back on hold. I wouldn't exactly describe my mood at the time as euphoric. Once again, our work together was on ice. Over the next few months, we would meet sporadically at the studio – to watch TV and find out how the building work and the sampling were going. We'd occasionally eat out in various combinations at the Ristorante da Bruno around the corner on Mintropplatz. Our classic pick was spaghetti aglio e olio and salad.

Ralf was living entirely in his cycling world. Our common language was peppered with cyclist-speak like, 'Got the legs,'

'Made good time today' or 'I need to make weight'. It seemed to me as if Ralf was using the cycling conversations as a kind of verbal cloak of invisibility, so that he could talk about something without really saying anything.

Now and then when we were alone, we did 'talk' about how things were going. It wasn't usually about music, more about strategy and tactics. A brief synopsis from my perspective: If you want to race in Formula 1 you have to get to the starting line in the right car. Better machines = better sounds. With the modernized studio, we'd be back in a good starting position. We may have had an amazing reputation, but live appearances were pointless without a new hit. Our advantage was that people in the business knew we weren't hungry. All we had to do was keep calm and carry on. Ralf's monologues gave me the impression he was holding imaginary press conferences.

In his function as our spokesman, his rhetoric had grown ever more mysterious over time. You could say he'd evolved into a personal PR virtuoso. For instance, he would style himself as a scientist, music worker, machine lover, explainer of society, understander of progress, seeker of truth and a cycling philosopher, among other things. My efforts to recognize our real lives and working conditions in his Kraftwerk storyline were in vain. I believe the nature of narrative manipulation is that you not only pretend to others but at some point, also to yourself. Eventually, felt, experienced and factual reality start to mingle and are romanticized into myth.

No matter if it was a private setting or a published interview, my bandmate made it difficult for me to follow his deliberations. He criticized the man-versus-machine struggle, for example – impressively brought to the screen by Fritz Lang in *Metropolis* or by Stanley Kubrick in *2001: A Space Odyssey*. Society's way of dealing with machines seemed to him 'like a battle of man against our own inventions,'[4] which he considered 'a catastrophic misinterpretation of the situation' to which we allegedly 'set a counterpoint with our work.'[5]

In December, I fell pretty ill. I couldn't move my head, suffering extreme neck pain like whiplash after a car accident. Except I hadn't had an accident. Not even a thorough check-up with X-rays, ECG, blood tests and all the rest brought a diagnosis. My doctor prescribed me mud-pack treatment and massage, and that continued in the background from then on.

I remember New Year's Eve of 1987 well. Ralf, Volker Albus, Willi Klein, Bettina and I headed to Cologne with no fixed plans, in search of the right place to see in the New Year. Florian had disappeared somewhere or other. At first, we wandered the streets of the city, not knowing where to go, and towards midnight we ended up in an otherwise empty Turkish kebab shop, sitting at a brown plastic table and following the celebrations on the TV screen mounted above the counter. What a dreary moment. It wasn't until Bettina and I got back home and opened a bottle of champagne that the dark clouds cleared.

Marathon

There wasn't much point in going to the Kling Klang Studio in 1988. After the odyssey of *Techno Pop* – oops: *Electric Cafe* – there was no way I wanted to surrender myself again to what was going on there, or rather what wasn't going on. During this phase, running gave me something to hold onto in life. It was the constant factor in my life, basically – aside from Bettina and music, of course – that kept me in balance. September was the most intense training month of the year, with 460 kilometres under my belt.

My long runs were firmly integrated into my daily routine, like a ritual. They got me out of bed in the morning and kept me distracted. One day, I got it into my head to run a marathon. Or at least I wanted to manage the distance of 42.195 kilometres. I had no problem with 20 kilometres by this point, and I chose a stretch in the Grafenberg Forest that brought me back to my starting point after around ten kilometres. I'd park my car there, with water and muesli bars and everything I needed after a circuit. The plan seemed doable. And I was right: on 6 August 1988, I ran my first marathon! To be precise, it was 42.4 kilometres, which took me 3 hours and 55 minutes. Not really anything to write home about in terms of timing, but I was only running for myself. Speed and sporting competition weren't remotely important to me.

To this day, running is a moment all to myself, in every season, all kinds of weather. There are certainly good health reasons for pursuing an endurance sport like long-distance running. But to be honest, that's just a useful side effect for me. In fact, the key factor for me is the range of impressions on my senses during a run. And also what goes on in my mind in the process. Unlike many sports-enthusiast musicians, I've never been able to think about music while I run. Instead, I listen to my body: my breathing, puffing, occasional groaning and panting – how does my body sound as a whole when I'm pushing it? When I'm running, I concentrate on the motoric rhythm of my steps and the changing sounds of the world around me.

Such a multisensory spectacle is hard to beat. That's why I often wonder why so many runners add a soundtrack via an MP3 player and in-ear headphones to the running experience. I'd probably end up fixed to the spot because I'd always feel the need to concentrate on the music. I can't do it. And no one climbs on a treadmill to make music, do they?

When I'm running, thoughts fly past without structure, but I usually get caught up in a monotonous loop that accompanies me for a while, or an idea flashes up and vanishes again as if I was in a William Burroughs cut-up text, and then if I run for long enough I really can't think of anything any more. At last.

The Sounding Score

Ever since our mix in New York, I had been learning the ropes of the Sequencer Plus program. I was thrilled by the digital development of music-making machines; in fact, I saw the technology as a revelation. Like in a musical score, the various sound sources were arranged vertically, one above another. On the horizontal timeline each track held a grid of dots representing empty measures. Measures containing notes or other MIDI data were designed as boxes, which you could zoom into for a closer look at its content. Inside the chosen measure, you saw the pitch levels vertically and the length of the events horizontally. The recorded data could be manipulated; that is, all four dimensions of a tone – pitch, length, strength and colour – could be changed. What a huge step in the eighties! From the very beginning, I found it absolutely natural to design music on the timeline of a computer, with the representation of the tones as bars equally logical and helpful.

And yes, I've always been interested in the graphic represent-ation of music. Music has been part of our culture for millennia, but it originally relied on oral tradition. The invention of modern musical notation in the Middle Ages made the mathematics on which music is based visible and accessible. All at once, musical structure could be designed and altered. Gradually, polyphonic music came about. That means several voices progressing together in time – independently and yet tuned to each other – linked in new and beautiful patterns. As a result, the processes for working with musical ideas developed in previously unimagined direc-tions, and that unleashed music up to the modern age . . .

It's almost superfluous to mention, but just as a musical score can only deliver a graphic representation of music, the order of events on a computer timeline is no more than a collection of data, which still has to develop into music. How do the two media differ? Unlike sheet music, the computerized score has a sound and can also be manipulated, almost like word processing.

Hell-bent on continuing my experiments, I got myself an IBM Personal Computer XT, the classic cream model with an incred-ible 20 MB hard drive and a floppy disk drive. I slapped down a five-figure cheque for this beauty – a fortune for me at the time. And I spent the next few months falling down a hole every morning like Alice, finding myself in a completely new environ-ment once I landed at the bottom.

I was really thrilled by the idea of working with this new graphic representation of music on the computer. These days, there are free apps offering similar functions for any mobile phone. But back then, it felt really uplifting when I went to my computer's timeline, zoomed into a melody and edited its param-eters with a couple of keyboard commands.

468

Few will deny that computers have changed the world – but music is still music. And when we listen to it and our brains are flooded with sound, it stimulates regions where 'social, primeval and abstract emotions'[6] are seated, as the neuroscientist and music scholar Daniel Levitin writes. That's why we have strange sensations, feel moved and often speechless. It's no wonder; music is a matter of life and death – and of immortality. With music, we experience the fleeting nature of the moment, but also a world beyond time. There is music, after all, that exists only in our thoughts. All that is something computers know relatively little about.

In July 1988, I began writing down the Kraftwerk songs as lead sheets – meaning the simplified notation of a piece of music, consisting of melody, lyrics and chords – and entering them successively into the Sequencer Plus. I used the live recordings of our last tour for orientation. I also added 'The Man-Machine', 'Showroom Dummies', 'Tour de France', 'Sex Object', 'The Telephone Call' and 'Musique Non-Stop', because I thought they belonged in the possible selection.

As a medium for playing the tracks, I had three samplers, all ridiculously cheap compared to the Synclavier. I sampled many of our sounds – for instance the percussion and the electro sounds – from the Synclavier library. In the other direction, we transferred a number of 8-bit and 16-bit samples to the Synclavier over the course of production. That was how I gradually put our live repertoire together using my samplers and computers.

469

Robovox

Florian spent most of his studio time in the language lab. The speech synthesizers were still his mission. Like in football, in art it's extremely important to spot free spaces and run into them before the ball gets passed there. Very early on, he recognized that vacant space of the synthetic voice in music, and occupied it with skill and determination.

I remember once running into Florian in the studio kitchen, where he casually handed me a 19-inch device. He had commissioned a four-voice Robovox system and had a few of them made, he told me light-heartedly. I could now control the phonemes on my computer via MIDI and insert them into a composition, he explained. Based on the Votrax SC-02 speech synthesizer, this 'system for and method of synthesizing singing in real time' was even patented under his name for a while. But then the development took a different path – electronic speech synthesis sounded too robotic for general use and was also difficult to understand. These days, it can be difficult to tell artificial and human speakers apart. The IT moved away from the original synthesis of the speech signal, and concentrated on linking recorded speech segments to optimum effect. That's fine, but I'm still a fan of Florian's Robovox.

When I turned up at the studio with my sampler on one occasion, he persuaded me to sample a number of phonemes in his voice, to make the raw material for a speech synthesis program. So we sat down with microphone and sampler in his language lab and he recorded 32 phonemes. This rudimentary version of speech synthesis sounds pretty strange. You can hear it on the remake of 'Radioactivity': 'Chernobyl, Harrisburg, Sellafield, Hiroshima'. After that, I used the same method with my own voice and called it 'Newspeak'.

Another day, Florian came to visit me in my home studio with his electronic flute. He took a curious look around and registered all the stuff I had in there. I was working on a new track at the time. Although I hadn't come up with any lyrics yet, I had given it the working title 'TV'. The song was running in a loop but I turned it off so we could talk. My new digital synthesizer was hooked up and Florian plugged into my system with the flute – which had been MIDI-fied by this point – and played a few of his typical rising and falling scales. As he said goodbye, he told me with a laugh that the synth had convinced him – he'd get one too now. These were moments when we got along well. It seemed that way to me, at least.

Sacrilege

My relationship with Fritz Hilpert was very collegial, as we say in Germany. Fritz was born in Bavaria, which gives us common geographical roots. He's four years younger than me to the day, and was a great sound engineer even then. And also a friendly person who had plenty of social contacts, so we immediately got on well. The timing for his joining the Kraftwerk crew couldn't have been better; our repertoire had been written and the creative phase was over, or almost at any rate.

Now was the time to manage the material. The skills needed to do that for Kraftwerk were a perfect match for Fritz's portfolio. At this point, engineers were more appropriate to Ralf and Florian's needs than musicians and writers. Thanks to his technical understanding, Fritz became Ralf's tutor on the Synclavier. But his personal qualities and his objectivity also brought a little bit of outside-world reality back into the Kling Klang Studio.

At some point while I was working on it, I played my song 'TV' to Fritz. I guess he thought the track was pretty good, and he made a spontaneous offer to mix it for me. We got in contact with Stefan Ingmann from Düsseldorf's renowned Klangwerkstatt sound studio, and when a gap came up in their bookings in March 1988, they let us use it for free. We weren't interested in much more than playing around with a mix on their excellent equipment.

When we met up at the Kling Klang Studio the Monday after, Fritz talked about our session with a huge grin. Even as he was talking, I saw the look on Florian's face change. I don't remember the conversation that followed precisely, but I perceived it as Florian evaluating our mixing session as betrayal, or even sacrilege. The very consideration of such a thing appeared to be beyond the realms of his imagination.

At that point, Fritz was not yet entirely familiar with the unofficial Kraftwerk GbR behavioural code – the 'tacit agreement' that you worked exclusively for Kraftwerk. The situation couldn't have been more embarrassing. I think Florian found our actions highly disloyal.

The storm blew over after a while. But Fritz and I never again worked on my music together after the incident. The rest of 1988 passed in an unspectacular manner. With construction work on the studio taking its time, we still couldn't make music.

472

New Beginning

In January 1989, after two years of remodelling, Joachim connected up our equipment in the studio. We now started meeting up to work on stuff at Kling Klang again. Our sessions were something like warm-ups to set up our working environment. I installed my IBM PC so that I could programme arrangements flexibly with the Sequencer Plus software.

Ralf worked with his Clav in his own way, loading the samples Fritz had produced from the library onto the machine's internal memory, playing the weighted keyboard and testing out the internal sequencer's LED buttons. Florian's new set-up consisted of his Robovox and an Atari computer.

During these first few sessions, something else happened. Once Joachim had finished remodelling and rebuilding the studio, communication with him began to deteriorate rapidly. Ralf and Florian, it seemed, were no longer happy with his work. Things had been simmering between them for some time, and after the construction work was done they reached boiling point.

Joachim Dehmann: 'For the remodelling of Studio A from January 1987, I was asked to manage and instruct new technical assistants. Although Ralf and Florian hadn't talked to me about changing or even ending my job, I couldn't escape the impression that I was supposed to train these people, who were paid by Ralf, to take over my function in the studio.

Once certain remodelling work was completed in Studio A and the machines were connected, I wrote my final

473

invoice on 15 March 1989. There were differences of opinion over it, which led to a rupture between me and the two of them, and we eventually ended up in court.'

Joachim had made himself available to us around the clock for the past ten years. This abrupt ending was a bitter pill for him to swallow, especially as his workshop and office were directly opposite the Kling Klang Studio. I think he feared for his financial existence because of it. The last verbal dispute in the courtyard of the building complex ended very, very badly. What shocked me the most, though, was how little this dramatic event affected Ralf and Florian. They seemed not to have the slightest hint of a guilty conscience.

The Wall Falls

On Wednesday, 9 November 1989, Ralf, Florian and I met up at the studio at six to continue work on *The Mix*. Leaving the studio after midnight, we were pretty amazed to see a never-ending procession of hooting cars driving around the 'millipede' and increasingly blocking the city centre. People were leaning out the windows of their cars, yelling and cheering. What on earth had happened?

Since August, it had been impossible to overlook the fact that something big was approaching. Thousands of East Germans had sought asylum in the West German embassy in Prague. The West German foreign minister Hans-Dietrich Genscher had spoken from the embassy balcony on 30 September, a historical milestone. On 3 November, the Czechoslovakian authorities then allowed their East German guests to leave for the West unchecked.

We paid less intense attention to the GDR opening its borders on 9 November. I'd be lying if I told a sentimental story, adding a fake nostalgic tint to my emotional involvement in German reunification. I didn't cry like the East Germans now allowed to travel to the West, but I was happy for them and with them. I much prefer a unified Germany to a divided one. On 9 November 1989, it felt right and good, and we Germans couldn't be grateful enough for the approval of Russia and our European neighbours. Back in my youth, I'd never have believed I would experience such a thing one day.

Wake-Up Call

That same month, I got a letter from the Düsseldorf tax office: a bill for back tax. In conjunction with my advance tax payments, it took me to the financial brink and for a moment, I lost my grip. Something had clearly got out of hand. Thankfully, I was able to pay the bill, but the fundamental dilemma was much worse. I had been in Kraftwerk for almost fifteen years, regarded myself as a member of the band, had invested time, passion and creativity, only to one day come down to earth with a bump and find myself at a dead end. The community in the Kling Klang Studio ended, I felt, where financial interests began. Ralf and Florian wore the trousers and I had to ask for everything: writing credits, a share of licensing fees, advances.

As long as we brought out records and went on tour I managed somehow, but the long production time for *Electric Cafe* and the past couple of years on hold had been gruelling – and they also had financial consequences. It made a big difference whether I worked exclusively for two, three, four or more years for a certain percentage of the licensing fees.

The whole situation came like a wake-up call. I got more and more mistrustful and started asking myself questions: Were the licensing fees shared fairly? How many record sales were we actually talking about? Why were our individual contributions not clearly defined on the albums, but instead referred to by descriptions like hardware and software? And why was it normal for many agreements to be made only verbally? Once I started thinking about it, I was at a complete loss about what to do.

Whiplash

In mid-November 1989 I flew to Paris to speak to Maxime Schmitt about my situation. He listened attentively as I explained my problems. I told him I regarded myself as an integral part of the band, on one hand, and still believed in our music, but on the other hand saw how the partners in the GbR were no longer the slightest bit predictable. They may have had their reasons for their concepts and ways of working, but I couldn't understand their actions any more.

His answer was not only wise, but also very helpful. Even though he was a good friend of Ralf's, he still managed, in his emotionally intelligent way, to remain absolutely neutral and objective and to place my problem in a general context. His advice, in my own words, was this: the only thing that counts in life is being happy. And if you don't feel comfortable in a

476

setting of any kind, you have to leave it, otherwise you'll end up damaged and ill.

Hmm . . . I was starting to think the whiplash that had been plaguing me for some time might have psychosomatic causes. The symptoms weren't constant; they came in waves. The massages I'd been prescribed again weren't really helping. They didn't make a difference at all.

In my desperation, I contacted Willi Klein. It was the first time I met him in his function as senior consultant in the rheumatic arthroscopic surgery department, and he came across very differently in his white coat. But his warm-hearted character was still there. Professor Klein examined my whiplash using every trick in the book, and found: nothing! Willi then talked to me about my mental state, touching on the real sore spot. But Willi was another good friend of Ralf and Florian's.

Once again, I became aware of how inescapable my situation was. All the people I respected and could ask for advice were also friends with Ralf and Florian, and so couldn't pass independent judgement. If I told them about my feelings of alienation, they'd end up in a conflict of interest. After my visit to Maxime in Paris three weeks previously and the check-up with Willi Klein, I felt calmed and concerned at the same time.

Argument

Arriving at Mintropstrasse the next day, I found the studio empty. I walked through the workshop and kitchen to the media room at the front, just catching Ralf and Florian finishing up a

477

telephone call in the office. Business. I would have liked to go on believing in our 'mission' but the uncomfortable feeling of seeing things more realistically for the first time was growing stronger and stronger. A lot of emotions had built up inside me, and yet I still found it extremely unpleasant to confront the two of them with my doubts about their decisions. It will have sounded something like this:

We've been stuck for another three years now and we're not making any progress. Do you know what I don't understand? Why can't we just work regularly during daylight hours like normal people? We've missed out on the entire eighties and you're taking it easy. But I'm caught up in it, with my life plan. I wouldn't have the slightest problem with your management if you didn't insist on me working exclusively for Kraftwerk.

Ralf and Florian appeared surprised at my apparently suddenly awakened interest in company planning and policy. But my complaints bounced off them. I think they found my words inappropriately clear and felt they had to assert their authority – which makes sense from their point of view. The GbR was a successful company, after all, and it was me, Karl, who had a problem they couldn't understand.

Florian let out his annoyance emotionally, saying I wasn't entitled to make that kind of criticism. I interpreted his words to mean he was accusing me of ingratitude, along the lines of: A company clerk was happy to work forty years for a firm and then retire with a gold watch, so why wasn't I?

Ralf stayed under control and argued objectively. I think what he said was: A Mercedes employee can't work for Opel at the same time. The record would be finished when it was finished. Work was going on in the Kling Klang Studio, and progress was

478

visible. They also had global connections – and the most difficult thing was establishing a brand name. In short, he used the corporate rhetoric of a multinational digital company to sketch out the big picture.

While we exchanged arguments, I realized I had to set a limit to this drama, or it would go on this way forever. I remember how much I hated to say it, but in the end I did: 'I've had a different opinion on the planning and organization of our work for some time, and still I've supported everything we do, with all my energy. But if nothing changes here in the near future you'll leave me no choice but to jump into the deep end and leave.' I translated Florian's closing statement as something like: That didn't matter anyway, because all the music was now in the Synclavier. After that we went back to the studio, where Ralf played us a couple of short sound sequences he'd recorded for 'Computer Love' with the Synclavier sequencer . . .

There are three things I wish had happened: a fast and constructive reaction to my criticism with the introduction of an open communication style, making processes, plans and decision-making transparent through background information. A schedule for the album we were working on and the live projects connected to it. And finally, reliable information on the past foreign licences and copyright finances. Instead, I received another mysterious advance against my future income from Kraftwerk, to be offset at a later date, while effectively being exhorted to 'keep calm and carry on'. There was no question of ending my unofficial exclusivity clause. Everything went on as before. I programmed the tracks on the computer and we worked on the arrangements of our repertoire for *The Mix*.

Christmas Party

Willi Klein lived in a split-level penthouse and had invited the 'old gang' to dinner: Ralf, Florian and his girlfriend, Bettina and me. Perfectly normal. But when we sat down at the long table, I registered a certain air of dissonance. There was nothing specific, no words or gestures, but the atmosphere felt forced and awkward. Something had changed and everyone seemed to sense it. Bettina and I were part of the circle – as always – but somehow also not part of it. Might this feeling be the effect of my criticism of Ralf and Florian's management? What I noticed clearly that evening was the extreme speechlessness behind the all-too familiar phrases, the nerdy cycling talk. Nobody could accuse my two colleagues of taking a passionate interest in other people's lives. Without letting it show, Bettina and I played along half-heartedly. And so that little Christmas party didn't turn into the crowning celebration of 1989 we'd hoped for.

Back at home, we were still tense and nervous. Bettina threw herself onto an armchair and announced: 'Those people! I never want to go to another evening like that with Ralf and Florian. It's so uptight and it's no fun at all anymore.' That was easy for her to say; it didn't affect her directly. After graduating, Bettina started work as a journalist, got around a lot and had her own friends. It made no difference whether she took part in Kraftwerk activities or not. I envied her independence.

I myself felt alienated from my spiritual home, which was increasingly upsetting me. The business conversations with Ralf and Florian had been extremely drastic and strenuous. That weighed on my mind. And it seemed we no longer had a common denominator in our private lives either. Things were getting worse and worse. What would happen next? Would nothing of what had once been good ever return?

Italian Journey

The announcement that our booker Ian Floogs had organized a handful of test gigs in Italy caught me on the back foot. Why now? Eternal lateness seemed to have become a distinctive characteristic not only of Ralf, but also of Kraftwerk as a whole. But never mind; perhaps a few concerts would have a positive effect on our mood and put a bit of oomph into the proceedings – who knows? Either way, we could use them to test our new system.

That same evening, I called up Fritz, Maxime and also Wolfgang, to tell them the good news. Wolfgang's reaction was laid-back: 'Yeah, a tour, I know,' he said calmly. 'Florian came by the furniture studio at the beginning of the year.' 'And what did he say?' I enquired. 'He was very cheerful and he talked about you guys working on a new album in the studio and going on tour soon. Then he wanted to know what I thought about joining again.' 'And what did you say?' I asked impatiently. 'I told him I couldn't imagine it anymore and I'd rather stick to making my designer furniture.' 'Are you sure, Wolfgang?' I pressed him. 'Karl, I don't get anything out of running around with those two these days. There's nothing left between us. It'll never make me happy. I have a lot more fun with my new workmates. Plus, I have to make a bit of money and I can't spend years waiting around for those two gents.'

Wolfgang's farewell to Kraftwerk didn't happen from one day to the next. Sometimes, though, I think it might have gone differently if he'd come along on that little tour . . .

The next few weeks consisted mainly of preparation for the five gigs booked for us. From 1 to 4 February, we rehearsed in Cologne. Seeing as Joachim Dehmann was no longer working for Kraftwerk, Fritz took care of the technical side. Alongside his function as sound engineer, he was now supposed to stand on stage to the left of me, where Wolfgang's place had been. That meant these concerts would change Kraftwerk's outward appearance as well.

But we were also facing a reorientation in terms of technology. For the live gigs, we tried to translate the manual influences on analogue technology into a digital setting. The idea came up to integrate pre-programmed loops into the songs. For that purpose, we'd put together a few short sequences that could be switched on or off synchronously, for example on 'Computer Love', 'Home Computer' and 'Metal on Metal'.

The idea was good, but as you might expect, the decision between sound blocks A, B and C didn't lead to free improvisations or any new form of musical expression. As soon as a sequence that sounds good is found in a modelling kit like this, it makes sense to reproduce it. Electro-acoustic sound collages were always a key element of our music. Now, they were rhythmically varied and extended into a new, universal design principle. But that meant our repertoire lost its dramatic structure, diversity and bandwidth.

With respect to Kraftwerk, people often claim that digitalization finally brought technology to the developmental level needed to put our musical ideas into practice. In fact, the opposite was the case. Up to that point, the band had composed all of its work on analogue instruments. Now we had spent years transferring to digital, managing and cataloguing the data, and reproducing and reshaping our music. But while we were programming we stopped listening to each other. We lost our physical feeling, no longer looking each other in the eye, only staring at the computer monitor. The interface between man and machine was the PC keyboard or the mouse, held by one of us while the others more or less passively watched what happened on the computer screen.

In this situation, 'copy and paste' became our manifesto. Copying and duplicating data didn't have nearly the power required to supersede the artistic spirit of composition with the musical content created in this way. Alongside the predictable music design, constructed as if using templates, we also struggled with the obvious disadvantages of early sampling technology. The bass riff on 'Autobahn' played on the analogue Minimoog sounded different to the separate sampled tones – no matter whether triggered manually or by computer. The digital Moog samples stayed the same every time, unchanging, static, dead. Digital aids did make our music rhythmically perfect – superhuman, so to speak – but it was also sterile, as if it had been chemically cleaned three times over. The songs lost their aura, their poetry, they lost precisely what can't be captured in words . . .

On 5 February, we boarded a bus to Bologna, ready to perform our first concert two days later. That was followed by gigs in Padua, Florence and Genoa, where we concluded our mini-tour at Sgt Pepper's Psycho Club on 11 February 1990. It was my last Kraftwerk concert. The venue's name has stayed in my mind, if nothing else. We headed back to Düsseldorf on the 12th.

Even though these were the last gigs I played with Kraftwerk, I can barely remember a thing about them. Only that Florian kept kicking a football at the mixing desk in one of the auditoriums. Otherwise, it all remains a blur. I can't recall the nature of his role at these concerts; he had said a mental farewell to the band. But I too felt more like a visitor to the whole thing, not like I was playing an active part. Our communication was limited to the bare necessities, with no conversations beyond the purely functional level.

Back home, I was completely wiped out. It's perfectly natural for different people to take over set functions in human organizations. Nobody is unreplaceable; we all know that. But when it comes to Kraftwerk, it was not nearly the same without Wolfgang.

A Visit to London

After our test gigs in Italy, my feeling of being in a dead end intensified. Did I have a future with Ralf and Florian? The two of them seemed to have a clear vision of how they planned or in fact didn't plan their careers – and that was unlikely to change. That was up to them, of course. But how would my life in music go on? I apparently thought I hadn't yet tried everything to bring about a change in our working situation. Where there's life, there's hope.

My network at the time was made up of a handful of people: Wolfgang in Düsseldorf, Emil in the Caribbean, Maxime in Paris and Michael Mertens, who was now living in London. I picked up the phone and talked to all of them, and Michael invited me on a spontaneous visit. He'd had enough of the opera orchestra and joined the German band Propaganda with Claudia Brücken in 1983, previously made up of Ralf Dörper, Andreas Thein and Susanne Freytag. The British ZTT label signed them up and brought out their song 'Dr. Mabuse' in 1984. Their very successful album *A Secret Wish* came out in 1985, and also the remix album *Wishful Thinking* – an impressive six years before *The Mix*.

I was feeling a dire need to talk to other musicians, so I was happy to accept Michael's invitation to London at the end of February 1990. He was working on Propaganda's second album at the Abbey Road Studios and living on Ladbroke Grove in north Kensington. When I arrived, he opened the door to Flat E with a good-humoured flourish and we were soon planted in two armchairs in front of an artificial fire. Equipped with cups of tea and biscuits, we spent hours talking shop. Michael told me about his experiences with Trevor Horn and his ZTT label and about his current production.

We partook of a couple of the new tracks as well. 'Have a listen to 'Only One Word', it's got David Gilmour from Pink Floyd playing the guitar solo,' Michael told me. 'And he joined in just like that?' I asked in amazement. 'He sure did, it's all great fun for those guys. Derek Forbes and Brian McGee – out of the Simple Minds line-up – are in the band now,' Michael said, 'and Ian Stanley and Chris Hughes – you know, the Tears for Fears producers – are producing the album. I reckon we're doing pretty well, eh?'

Then it was my turn to reel off a couple of anecdotes from our Italian tour, and Michael told me about his experiences in the music business. How deals are done, how advances are paid, how music publishing companies work, how copyright fees are collected and that kind of thing. He showed me standard international licensing and copyright account statements. 'Aha, so that's what they look like,' I thought.

We kicked off the next day with a full English breakfast. Then Michael took me along to the Abbey Road Studios, where they were working on the new album. I explored the place with a child's curiosity; I'd only ever seen photos of the studio.

It did me a lot of good to communicate with a musician like Michael, who looked back on a comparable biography to my own, thought similarly to me and presented me with a relatable attitude to life and music. On board the return flight to Düsseldorf, I felt I'd found my way back to inner balance.

Utopia

Our booker, Ian Floogs, came to visit us in March. As you can imagine, reliable planning is the bedrock of a booker's job, and he wanted to find out the best point in time for our next gigs. It's hard to say how Ralf and Florian felt about that. I certainly couldn't make out any concept behind their reaction; they remained non-committal and Ian flew back home with no specific dates. Farewell, tour!

The leaden atmosphere of the past few years was getting me down. The protracted studio conversion and our work on the samples library – which I now think we lost control of completely – were behind us or were going on forever. It was still not clear when our remix album would be finished. No one was thinking about new songs any more. But there were still irregular episodes when I believed I could change things. In my view, what we needed was a reset, a return to the values that had made us productive and successful.

On 8 June 1990 – some three and a half years after *Electric Cafe* – another opportunity arose to talk fundamentals. That warm summer day, Ralf and I made a spontaneous trip to the café at the main station. Ralf was looking great – tanned, excellent competition weight, calm and collected. It was no wonder; after his daily cycling training he had an estimated resting heart rate of less than 50 beats per minute by the evening. But I'd also been running that morning and was feeling pretty relaxed.

Over our second slices of cake, we talked over how our Italian gigs had gone. I mentioned Florian's 'reserved' performance, then summoned up my courage and said I couldn't imagine Florian felt very inclined to play live in the future. He clearly didn't enjoy working on stage anymore, and reproducing musical content wasn't his thing either. Aside from that, he had been withdrawing more and more into his specialist field of speech synthesis, even during *Electric Cafe*, and keeping out of the musical side. 'It's not working anymore,' I said. 'We practically never talk music.' Then I suggested to Ralf: 'How about you and me work out a really good live concept. Why can't Florian stay at home, like Brian Wilson?'

I tried to explain to Ralf that I considered him an extraordinary artist but thought he was losing his profile because he was clearly no longer interested in making music. 'We can write great songs together, I reckon we can get another two or three albums done. I know we will – so let's not lose any more time.' Almost as I was saying it, I realized this attempt was bound to blow up in my face. Ralf reacted as I feared, saying – as I understood it – that he was 'wedded' to Florian on the business level and they couldn't restructure their company. Plus, people wanted to see Florian on stage. Kraftwerk was absolutely unthinkable without Florian – it wouldn't work and it wouldn't be credible either.

Despite our contradicting opinions, our conversation was calm, not angry or argumentative. Afterwards we went back to Mintropstrasse and played around with 'Pocket Calculator'. Ralf had made a couple of short house loops in the style of Lil Louis' 'French Kiss' on the Synclavier's sequencer, which he played to me at the touch of a button. We went straight back to business as usual. But at least I can say I tried. Florian stayed with Kraftwerk until 2008, almost another twenty years, before finally leaving the band officially.

Cause and Effect

On a July afternoon, we meet up at 3 p.m. – an unreal time of day for a Kraftwerk session. I turn up at the studio and say 'hello'. Fritz looks up and answers 'hi', or something. We're here to record the vocals for the 'Trans-Europe Express' remake. He explains that the living-room algorithm on the new reverb machine is an excellent fit for Ralf's recitative style. I can well believe it. Ralf is reading *L'Équipe* on his mobile chair in the back corner of the studio, wearing shorts that reveal his shaved, oiled legs. He seems so absorbed in his newspaper that nothing else registers.

I think back to the recording session for *TEE* with Peter Bollig – how the mood has changed since then. My first few years with Kraftwerk sped past: the *Autobahn* tour, *Radio-Activity*, *Trans-*

Europe Express. From *The Man-Machine* on, I was credited as a co-author. Ralf and Florian were completely mad about music and impressed me with their dynamics. We laughed a lot. I remember a snappy, humorous exchange of opinions. Our writing sessions were the epitome of our communication. I've always been interested in this type of teamwork composition; that's what makes pop fundamentally different to classical music. Sometimes it seemed like the Kling Klang Studio was a forum into which we brought our skills, thoughts, opinions and knowledge, coming out every day cleverer than we went in. That combination of musical work and cultural awareness meant a great deal to me. During the *Computer World* phase with the subsequent world tour, we reached our peak as the 'classic line-up'. But then electronic pop music became more professional and established, and Kraftwerk lost its USP. We couldn't ignore the other artists' and producers' work. In fact, it was the opposite: we used them as reference points.

Ralf is almost entirely concealed by *L'Équipe* and now consists only of the French sports paper and his cyclist legs. He doesn't seem to have noticed me yet. Fritz is scurrying around to prepare for the recording.

After *Computer World*, we started on the production of *Techno Pop*. 'Tour de France' – the uncoordinated pre-release single – turned out to be a total marketing disaster, torpedoing the album's entire concept. The aesthetic of Rebecca Allen's computer animation became a 'new lens' through which we saw the project as a whole. We turned into avatars as Rebecca's video beamed us into virtual space. Once we got there, though, we didn't know what to do. The unexpected return to the UFA look in the promo film for 'The Telephone Call' is a perfect illustration of our problem – nothing matched up any more. We had lost the thematic coherence of the earlier albums. During the *Techno Pop* odyssey, Ralf completed his evolution into an extreme athlete, making cycling the focal point of his life. That changed his consciousness and influenced his character. Not to our advantage, though; a tired mind always makes different decisions. Our productivity declined and our work processes became more and more attuned to competitive thinking. We held countless listening tests, comparing our music to other people's productions in nightclubs, which couldn't help but change our musical output. The dancefloor led the way. We became music designers, manufacturing consumer music oriented only towards 'winning' against the other 'contestants'. Without us noticing, our imagination lost its autonomy. After 'Tour de France' we used our last reserves to release *Electric Cafe*.

Ralf grips *L'Équipe* with his left hand and clenches his right into a fist. With his third finger stretched out slightly, he massages his calf muscles. Fritz flits back and forth and casts a friendly glance over at me. 'Be ready in a mo,' he says in passing. It looks like Ralf still hasn't noticed I'm in the studio.

After that album, we took our eyes off the ball for the rest of the 1980s. Were we out of the game because Ralf was reading *L'Équipe* – or was he reading *L'Équipe* because we were out of the game? Was there even any link? Why were we recording our songs all over again?

In retrospect, the decision to produce an album of remakes after *Electric Cafe/Techno Pop* was a logical step for Kraftwerk. *The Mix* marks the point at which Ralf changed from an independent artist to the designer and curator of the Kling Klang back catalogue.

490

My new life: Klangwerkstatt on Stockkampstrasse, 1990. BETTINA MICHAEL

ELEKTRIC ⚡ MUSIC 05/93

spv Records

a division of **spv** G M B H

1992: Camera on – press photo with Lothar for the *Esperanto* album.

Beatles tour in Liverpool: Andy McCluskey (OMD) showing me Penny Lane, 1992.

1995: Love and marriage. RÜDIGER NEHMZOW

1996: (left to right) Johnny Marr, me and Bernard Sumner in Hamburg during the promo for Electronic's *Raise the Pressure*. FOTEX/SHUTTERSTOCK

The story of a message – my storyboard for the film *I'm the Message* (2003).

Me – a DJ? Why not! With Robert Baumanns at the Cologne Kickzone 1999, and from there around the world. JENS HARTMANN

Back in New York City: filming the video for the single '15 Minutes of Fame' (2000).

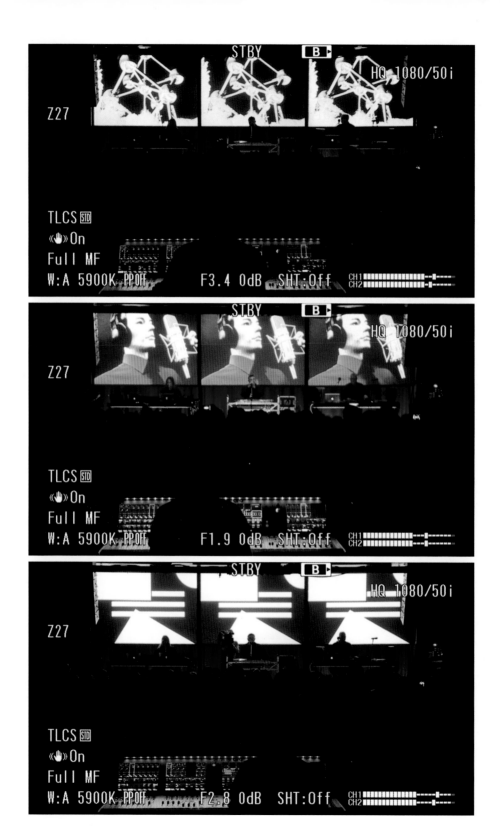

'Atomium', 'Without a Trace of Emotion', 'Rhythmus' – screenshots from the
live video of the *Off the Record* concert at Postbahnhof Berlin, 2014.

Live crew 2014: (front, left to right) Mathias Black, me, Robert Baumanns; (back, left to right) Rüdiger Ladwig (Trocadero), Michael Ochs, Sven Mouhcine, Dominik Sebald (a2b2c) at Steintor-Varieté, Halle/Saale. BETTINA MICHAEL

Photo session with Sascha and Robert before the opening concert for the 'Robots' exhibition at DASA Dortmund, 2015. PATRICK BEERHORST

A visitor from Manchester: during the Hamburg Reeperbahnfestival 2015 with New Order's Bernard Sumner.
BETTINA MICHAEL

Let's see what the future brings... MARKUS WUSTMANN

Ralf will go on reading *L'Équipe* and massaging his oiled legs until Fritz calls him over to the microphone, that much is clear. Florian is sitting in front of his Robovox with headphones on, tapping away at his Atari computer. I can't tell exactly which track he's working on. Florian looks up, grins and says hello; he's in a good mood. He seems to enjoy lining up the phonemes in the Robovox, as you can hear on the tracks 'The Robots', 'Dentaku', 'Autobahn', 'Radioactivity' and 'Home Computer' on *The Mix*. Florian is busy and I can't see any reason to disturb Ralf's reading. So I say goodbye to Fritz. My home studio is where the music's playing. My piano is waiting, the computer is waiting.

Death Mask

Preparations continued for the live shows, planned for an undetermined date. Seeing as the line-up had changed, we needed a plastic doppelganger for Fritz. I've no idea whether the legendary showroom dummy-maker Heinrich Obermaier was still alive by then, but Fritz's head wasn't modelled in the same style as the others. Someone had the idea of making a plaster cast of each of our four faces – like a death mask.

Off I went to an artist's studio in Mönchengladbach. Having the plaster applied to my face and the feeling as the material gradually hardened was an unusual experience. Not particularly pleasant, I'd say. My eyes and mouth stayed closed as I breathed through a straw in each nostril. The plaster grew heavy and pulled my features downwards, the major disadvantage to this type of mask. A modelled face has a completely different quality to it. As I lay under the stiffening plaster, an indefinable fear arose inside me. After what felt like an age, I was liberated from the mask – and my fear vanished into thin air. Once all the remaining traces had been removed from my face, I set off for the Kling Klang Studio.

Over

In the past few months, I had made several attempts to talk to Ralf and Florian. But whatever I said, none of it got through to them. It was uncertain how long they wanted to go on working on the remixes. Open end. From my perspective, our production was veering off course – yet again. And there was nothing I could do about it. I felt powerless and was getting more and more unhappy.

We were still working on *The Mix* – including on 23 July 1990. At some point during our session, I screwed up my courage and made another attempt to convince the two of them to change our production processes and modalities. They reacted with incomprehension. We were stuck fast in our positions.

Through all the trials and tribulations of the past few years, I had stayed loyal to Ralf and Florian. But that day, the way we communicated made it clear to me once and for all that my time with Kraftwerk had run out. I explained to them that I was quitting, deposited the studio keys on the mixing desk, said a brief goodbye and left the Kling Klang Studio without a backwards glance. Outside in the courtyard I got in my car, and as I steered through the gates and turned right onto Mintropstrasse, I was driving back into my own biography.

NOTES

1. Ralf Hütter: 'With better machines, you will be able to do better work, and you will be able to spend your time and energies on a higher level.' In: 'Kraftwerk: The Final Solution to the Music Problem? Lester Bangs Vivisects the German Scientific Approach,' by Lester Bangs, *New Musical Express*, 6 September 1975.
2. W. E. K. Anderson, Adam Nicolson: *About Eton*. Long Barn Books Ltd 2010
3. Ralf Hütter: 'We're not uber-programmers; the bureaucratism dominant in a lot of this computer music – pressing "Event" every eight bars – that's somewhere too . . .' In 'Kraftwerk – Die Frequenz der Events im Zeitfenster,' by Dirk Scheuring, *SPEX*, July 1991, p. 18
4. Ralf Hütter: 'In society, the way we interact with machines often seems like a battle of man against our own inventions. Our work sets a counterpoint to this catastrophic misinterpretation of the situation.' In: 'Science Fiction ist schon lange Realität,' by Michael Fuchs-Gamböck, *Wiener*, 7 July 1991
5. Ibid.
6. Levitin, Daniel: *This Is Your Brain on Music: The Science of a Human Obsession*. Plume (Penguin): New York, 2007

14

MY NEW LIFE

Prelude. Musical Manoeuvre. Full Speed Ahead. Esperanto. The Castle. The Northern Sky. Hamburg Calling. Guitar on the Brain. Roberto in Play. Live. Visual Music. 15 Minutes of Fame. Expo Gigs. Gesang der Jünglinge.

Prelude

It's hard to describe my mental state after saying farewell to Kraftwerk. I certainly didn't take the split lightly. I was hurt and disappointed – but at the same time I was euphoric. What I felt was an indescribable flood of relief at finally being able to regain control of my own life.

Things were set to change in my private life too: Bettina and I decided to move in together. The new flat didn't have enough space for a home studio, though. Which was where my contact to Klangwerkstatt – the place I'd committed 'sacrilege' with Fritz – came in very handy. The boss, Stefan Ingmann, suggested emptying out a storage room in the basement of his studio complex. If I liked the look of it, I could set up a project studio in there and work around the clock, and the monthly rent wouldn't be a problem either. So I accepted the generous offer with no beating about the bush.

494

Once again, it was time to design a technical setting for myself. Wireless imagination[1] did exist as a Futurist manifesto, but you still had to connect up all the equipment in those days. Not to mention configuring the patch panels. The analogue world, so it seems, started turning digital at an almost sedate pace. Towards the end of the summer, a sense of normality returned to my life, or perhaps more an everyday routine. I would run my circuits in the Grafenberg Forest first thing, and arrive at Klangwerkstatt around noon. The big studio was always busy. I have fond memories of the miraculously crowded little kitchen with the coffee machine. It was fun to be around other people, chatting easily about music and other subjects. Sometimes Stefan would play me his current production from behind the mixing desk. Then I'd head down to the basement with my cup of coffee and tinker with my equipment in search of new music.

I was all fired up to record an album of my own in the fore-seeable future – what else? First of all, though, I had to find out what Karl Bartos actually sounds like. The question wasn't all that easy to answer – up to that point, my musical lifeblood had flowed mainly into Kraftwerk compositions.

Pablo Picasso's famous quote comes to mind: 'It took me four years to paint like Raphael, but a lifetime to paint like a child.' I may not be able to paint like Picasso, but for me that childlike feeling is also a guiding principle behind my work. What I aim for is to see the world from a child's perspective as I create, and to immerse myself in play with objects – in my case the elements of music. Mostly, anyway. And how was it with Kraftwerk? In the early days, I experienced making music, improvising and composing with Ralf and Florian as a new, inspiring conjuncture of creativity. For a brief time, it seems, we had a shared approach

495

to music. And then it was all over . . . Childlike feelings and calculation aren't really all that compatible.

Essentially, I was now starting over from scratch. Mentally and materially. But I wasn't too worried about money matters; the music business was booming in the early 1990s. The A&Rs at the record companies and music publishers were always on the lookout for new artists. With a little luck, I ought to be able to pick up a record deal. The wind of confidence in my sails, I sat down at my instruments and started improvising. I'd often spend all day tinkling the keys. Lothar Manteuffel, part of the Klangwerkstatt crew, lent me his support. Especially in the early phases, we had a lively exchange of ideas. Now and then, friends, acquaintances and former colleagues would knock at my studio door too, for instance Wolfgang and Emil, but also Fritz Hilpert, Bodo Staiger, Klaus Dinger, Michael Mertens and Karl Hyde from Underworld.

Our first business trip together took Lothar and me to New York in the spring of 1991. We booked into the Mayflower Hotel for a week. One of our appointments was with Doreen D'Agostino, who we knew from her EMI days. She was now working for the Big Life label. Later, we headed for the Rockefeller Center. I wasn't there to visit the attorney Marvin Katz, who took care of business for Kling Klang Inc. – as you can imagine, I had no wish to pay him a courtesy call. Instead, I wanted to get a slot with Bob Krasnow, the head of Elektra, who were based in the same building; a pretty naive undertaking. Sent packing by his secretary even before I could knock at his door, I felt like an absolute beginner. It was the first time I became aware of my status as a total nobody. Ah well, that's life. All the more reason to keep trying! Starting from this solid position, I could begin to build something new.

496

I spent a long time thinking about what to call my project. A friend advised me to work under my own name. That's always a possibility. But somehow it didn't feel right for me. In the end I had the idea of using the name of my music publishing company as a band name: Elektric Music. I hoped that would be easier to identify with for Lothar and also Emil, who was working on graphic design and lyrics.

Lothar was by my side for the production of my first demo. Aside from renovations, studio work and conceptional matters, he helped me with the lyrics for several songs and I recorded his vocals for the song 'TV'. Back then (as now) I saw myself more as a composer, musician, sound director, producer and less as a lead singer. Apart from that, it's not necessarily wise for a film director to star in his own screen debut.

When SPV made me an offer, Stefan Ingmann negotiated the details as my newly appointed manager. I suggested to Lothar that the two of us both sign the record contract. Now we were in business.

The record company planned to release a single to start off, so I had to come up with a track quick-sharp. Somewhere in New York I'd picked up the phrase 'There's a lot of crosstalk going on,' which seemed the perfect description of my current situation and became the theme. Emil kicked off with 'Cut the superstition,' Lothar and I joined in and together we came up with the words to our first single, 'Crosstalk'.

I put the music together out of a number of fragments, and SPV also wanted a remix. Remix, remix, remix – how I hated the bloody things! Why should I remix one of my own songs? But never mind, remix it was. We booked the Heartbeat Studio in Cologne for three days and Stefan Ingmann did the final mix for both songs there.

'Crosstalk' landed absolutely unexpectedly on the US dance charts in April as a 'hot dance breakout club play' and in May at number 43. It doesn't really mean a thing but it's still cool, isn't it?

Musical Manoeuvre

In October 1991, Düsseldorf was plastered with posters for the Kraftwerk concert in the Philipshalle. At the last gig in Düsseldorf, Wolfgang, Emil and I had all still been in the band. Incredibly, that was ten years ago! I decided to sit this one out. Instead, I went to an OMD gig at the E-Werk in Cologne a few days later. It looked like they'd had a reshuffle, too: Paul Humphreys had left the band and Andy had recorded the *Sugar Tax* album under the name OMD. It included a remake of 'Neon Lights', which I thought was really great. After the gig, Andy and I loosely arranged to stay in touch.

And he meant it. Come March 1992, he and I were sitting in the Klangwerkstatt studio kitchen, drinking tea and talking ourselves silly until Andy suggested we compose a song together. I quickly put together a cassette for him with a couple of rough mixes of my latest 'audio crimes'. At that time, I was recording something almost every day, not thinking too much about it.

We had a date for dinner with Wolfgang in his fabulous flat on Hofgarten. As luck would have it, Emil was currently in Düsseldorf, and for the first time in ages the old Berger Allee

498

flatmates were reunited around the table – plus Andy McCluskey from Liverpool. As you might imagine, Emil was not unaffected by the turmoil at the Kling Klang Studio, and we ended up in an epic conversation about music in general, the changes in OMD and the future of Kraftwerk, which somehow tied the four of us together. Emil had dealings with Chris Blackwell's Compass Point Studios in Nassau and regaled us with a couple of anecdotes. Names dropped like rain: Paul McCartney, Robert Palmer, Sade, the former Talking Heads members Chris Frantz and Tina Weymouth and at some point . . . up popped Julio Iglesias. Plus sun, sea, beaches and abandoned Colombian planes – with best regards from Pablo Escobar.

In October, I accepted Andy's invitation to Liverpool. As I glanced out of the window of his house, a fox was strolling across the garden. English country life. I sat down at the mixing desk for a moment at Andy's studio Pink Museum, and we had great fun on a Beatles memorial tour, with him showing me Penny Lane, Strawberry Fields and the Cavern Club on, or rather under, Mathew Street.

And then Andy played me a song which kept picking up on one of my melodies: 'Kissing the Machine' sounded rather like hit material and promptly ended up on my first album. More than twenty years later, the track was to reappear on the OMD LP *English Electric*.

We wanted to come up with more tunes but the next opportunity wasn't until September 1994. This time we met up in Ireland, where he had just moved. We kicked off in his rehearsal room: a pulse, a rhythm, a sequence – and before I knew it I came up with the chords to 'The Moon and the Sun', with Andy singing along in an imaginary language. Driving around autumnal Dublin after the session, Andy's melismatic vocals evolved into the opening line: 'The autumn leaves were falling as we raced against the sun . . .' There's not much in the world that can top the feeling of creating music with someone who knows their stuff. 'Pure magic', Karlheinz Stockhausen would probably say. Andy once described it laconically as: 'We threw a few ideas into the computer.' He took another improvisation from those few days and turned it into a song about Mathew Street. 'The Moon and the Sun' came out in summer 1996 on the OMD album *Universal*, and the single 'Walking on the Milky Way' with our joint B-side 'Mathew Street' entered the UK Top Twenty. Not too shabby!

Not long after that, I paid him another visit – but this time the journey was a little longer, since Andy had moved to L.A.; he seemed a little restless to me. By day we cruised around in the car like Chuck Berry, with no particular place to go. And by night we sat at the window of his bungalow in the hills and looked down on the city's never-ending sea of lights.

I also made a point of visiting the two former Tangerine Dream members Christoph Franke and Paul Haslinger in their impressive studios. Moving to LA is apparently essential for anyone planning to get into the American movie business.

These days, an occasional email flutters into my inbox from Andy or from Paul, who re-joined the band in 2007, saying hello or inviting me to meet up at a hotel or a venue before a gig. One of these days we're bound to throw some more ideas into a computer.

Full Speed Ahead

Writing songs with Andy was terrific, but I knew only too well that OMD was an established and very successful project. Andy was doing his thing and I was only just starting to reinvent my life and my music. I thought it would make good strategic sense to get in the swing of things with a couple of jobs: a cover version, a remix, producing another band – that kind of thing. I wanted to get back in the game.

There was a jam session in Düsseldorf with Gez Varley and Mark Bell from LFO, which sadly didn't produce anything usable. That was a shame because the band's eponymous track is dynamite! I became a firm fan. Two other productions did turn out results, though. I would never have had the idea to do a remix of 'Planet Rock' of my own accord. But for Afrika Bambaata's label, Tommy Boy, it seemed like a no-brainer, and in less than a week my two mixes were winging their way to New York. Another pretty unusual offer came from *NME*. For the magazine's charity record *Ruby Trax*, they invited a selection of artists to remake a UK number 1 hit of their choice. For some reason, Lothar, Stefan and I picked up on 'Baby Come Back' by Eddy Grant, incidentally, on Andy's recommendation. Our version was the only contribution from Germany to make it onto *Ruby Trax*. And SPV also put the remake on the 'Crosstalk' single.

Then one day Paul Robb, mastermind of the American band Information Society, was sitting in my Düsseldorf studio. They'd had a breakthrough single in 1988 with 'What's On Your Mind (Pure Energy)', which reached number 3 on the *Billboard* Hot 100.

Now I was to produce two songs for their new record. In April, the band booked François Kevorkian's Axis Studio and I flew to New York for the recording sessions to, um . . . well, why was that? It was just how things were done back then, to get to know each other and discuss the production. When an opportunity came up I played François my new tracks and asked if he could imagine mixing them. François's reaction was very diplomatic. He explained that he couldn't, sadly, because he was friends with Ralf and Florian and felt obliged to them. Everyone has their reasons. I think his mix would have been great, but of course I didn't put any pressure on him. No problem.

My next trip to New York was not much later. Doreen D'Agostino had arranged a place for me on a dance music producer panel at the New Music Seminar, alongside Juan Atkins, Kevin Saunderson, Joey Beltram and Todd Terry, if I remember rightly. When I joined them on the podium the whole auditorium stood up and applauded. I wasn't prepared for that kind of hero worship and it put me at a bit of a loss for words, I have to admit. After the panel, I could barely get out of the room for people thronging around me and trying to shake my hand, thanking me for my music. It seemed like a farce come to life when a man from the audience asked me with tears in his eyes (no kidding!) if he could kiss my hand. I said no, I'm afraid. Kraftwerk reverence in this dimension would take some getting used to. On the last day of my trip, I caught an appearance by Underground Resistance at the Limelight Club. 29-year-old Jeff Mills showed off his skills on a 909 drum machine and the turntables. He chucked the vinyl records he didn't need any more behind him just as he took the next one out of its sleeve. Talk about nonchalant!

502

Esperanto

Alongside these production jobs and enquiries, I never lost sight of my own music. I can't ever say exactly what I want when I start something new. But I know pretty precisely what I don't want. The stupid thing is, inspiration's usually not there when you need it, so it makes no sense to rely on it. In art, selection is an important method for organizing work. If you eliminate the irrelevant and concentrate on the essentials, you make progress. That means it's sometimes helpful to have a concept for an album, because that sets a direction for your thoughts and it's not as easy to lose focus. Neil Postman's 1985 book *Amusing Ourselves to Death* had been on my mind for a while, a critical examination of the media. That was my starting point. Postman's 'peek-a-boo' world is full of terms like 'message', 'information', 'news', 'image', 'politics', 'performance', which in turn inspired me to new chains of thought. For example, I came across the international auxiliary language Esperanto, invented way back in 1887 to give all of humankind a universal language. It reminded me of the secret of music, and became the title of my album.

As always when composing, I drew on my sound archive, found rhythms, melodies, harmonies and lyrics I'd once worked with before. Like the 1987 song 'TV'.

Sometimes pure coincidence lent a helping hand. Looking for a radio station on an old ghetto blaster, I suddenly heard strange signals. These odd electronic noises were known to German radio nerds as 'wave spaghetti', a really bizarre racket – caused by Eurosignal, a long-since defunct paging system that used the lower frequencies on FM radio. I recorded a couple of them and broke them up into a variety of samples. That was the starting point for 'Overdrive'. Essentially, the entire track is made up of cranked-up voices, electronic drums and these Eurosignal samples, which I use to improvise electrojazz.

I shared the album's lyrics with Lothar and Emil. Andy McCluskey contributed 'Kissing the Machine' and part of 'Show Business'.

All the tracks went through the beta-version method I came up with back then, and still use to this day. I start by improvising the first fragments and developments, and trying to imagine the complete album. This stage of the process really calls for imagination. Then I record the first acoustic sketches in a rudimentary beta-1 version. A provisional track list usually comes about at the very beginning. Next, I work more or less simultaneously on the titles, which go through several generations of beta versions. Using this method, I avoid spending too much time on one particular section of the album and losing sight (or sound) of the rest. I was all too familiar with that problem and I had no wish to get lost in a sound labyrinth ever again. Once all the tracks have reached the beta-4 or beta-5 level, the musical context and cohesion, final track list, keys and tempos have evolved almost automatically.

Although I don't need external incentives to organize my work, there was no avoiding a deadline. And so, from December 1992 to early March 1993, I produced the first Elektric Music album in Cologne's Heartbeat Studio and my own project studio in parallel. Emil used a room in the Klangwerkstatt complex as his workspace, designing our record covers and working on promo films. I abandoned my initial idea of depicting a map of the world on the album cover and instead used the imperial Japanese army's red-and-white 'flag of the rising sun'. Perhaps not the best stroke of genius of all time, but that was what I chose. In the old days everything took forever, but with this album everything went far too quickly.

I was gaining first-time experience in another area, too, because over the next three months, Lothar and I were obliged to promote *Esperanto*. It wasn't easy for me to talk to the media about my music. All the journalists saw in me was an anonymous ex-member of a weird band, and I had to explain who I was. All in all, the album and the 'TV' single were much better received in Britain than in Germany. We even managed to get a short interview with MTV in London. Sure, all the media made comparisons to my old band, but often not to my detriment. 'The album is a solid, pleasant surprise, with its fun stylistic range – all cast within a synth-pop milieu,' wrote *Billboard*,[2] *Melody Maker* spoke of 'fabulous music,'[3] and *NME*[4] noted: 'TV' drifts by with simple tuneful grace.'

On the whole, most reviews motivated me to keep going. But there was one thing I had to bear in mind: I couldn't escape Kraftwerk's shadow. It would pursue me wherever I went. If I wanted to leap over it, I'd have to come up with something – certainly no easy task.

The Castle

At the start, my diverse productions and collaborations, along with the work on my debut album, kept me far too occupied to look back at my past, but the subject kept coming up automatically.

505

Wolfgang and Emil would occasionally stick their heads around my door. The two of them had just started reappraising a few things in relation to Kraftwerk. They were getting legal advice, prompting animated correspondence between various lawyers. And that opened up something of a Pandora's box. It was only then that I became aware of the consequences of the years of opacity in our business relationships and record-cover credits.

My own former status as a freelancer and co-author with a share in the revenue was both evident and vague. For instance, neither written agreements on my share of the licences nor publishing contracts existed. From today's point of view, our behaviour seems negligent to me. I too now wanted to see things clarified. My efforts to clear up the matter by direct means were in vain, however, so lawyers took over the talking for me.

During the legal dispute, *The Mix* was released in June 1991. The album with the death-mask robots got to number 15 in Germany. 'The Robots' – the single taken from the album – reached number 20 in the British charts. I never found out what happened to the record in the USA. I bought both the album and the single and put them on a shelf. There were a few of 'my' tracks on there, after all. The album credits were creatively cryptic, as usual. But I was amazed to find I wasn't even credited as an author on the CD. In the end, I was assured that Messrs Schneider and Hütter would not oppose the addition of copyright allocations on the album's second production run. I never checked. To this day, I have very mixed feelings towards *The Mix*.

The legal dispute proved to be long-running, extensive and draining. It took binders and binders to document the correspondence. I'll spare myself and my readers the details here. In 1993, the episode seemed to come to an end, and Ralf, Florian and I signed an agreement covering open questions. I now hoped to get a bit more calm in my life. I was to be wrong, however. Sadly, renegotiations began and dragged on for years. Years in which – like the protagonist K. in Kafka's *The Castle* – I couldn't put the subject to rest.

The Northern Sky

Yet there was also another world out there. Soon after leaving Kraftwerk, I made a professional contact that was to blossom into several genuine friendships stretching all the way to the present day. In mid-1992, I was strolling around the Popkomm music trade fair in Cologne – at that time, one of the most important meeting points in the international music business and a must for every musician. Suddenly, someone called my name. An eccentric-looking, strangely dressed man introduced himself with a slight English accent as Mark Reeder. In a couple of sentences, Mark mentioned the keywords Manchester, Bernard Sumner/New Order, Johnny Marr /The Smiths – and their new project, Electronic. Then he asked me what I'd think of meeting the two musicians.

Electronic's first album is filled with brilliant pop songs from beginning to end. They instantly triggered positive connotations in me, with everything sounding so skilled, playful and familiar, and yet the music had an unknown quality to it that made me curious. Aside from that, I also knew how successful the album had been in the UK, of course. So I let Mark know I'd be thrilled to meet the band. Then I went back to my journey of discovery around the endless record-label booths.

Not much later, in the middle of the *Esperanto* mixing session, I really did receive a fax – at that time the standard means of fast written communication – from Bernard Sumner in Manchester. He and his partner, Johnny, would like to work with me on a few tracks for the new Electronic album, he wrote, and he suggested visiting me in Düsseldorf to discuss it in more detail.

Bernard and Johnny had founded the Electronic project at the end of the eighties. On their eponymous debut album (1991), they worked with Neil Tennant and Chris Lowe from the Pet Shop Boys. And now they were coming to me? It seemed they wanted to give their music new impulses by adding variables to the band's line-up. And that was how Bernard Sumner and Johnny Marr came to land at Düsseldorf Airport in April 1993. As they got into my car – a silver Golf C with a tremendous 40 PS – I spotted Bernard inspecting my 'vintage' vehicle with interest. We drove straight to Klangwerkstatt. I showed them my studio, played a bit of piano in the recording room, and we chatted about this and that. I could already make out a similar sense of humour, and the three-way communication seemed familiar. Musicians can usually tell pretty quickly from their first conversation whether it's worth intensifying the contact or not. By the time the two of them set off the next day, our first writing session was firmly planned.

I flew to Manchester in the last week of October 1993. Bernard greeted me with a dramatic 'Welcome to England.' It sounded solemn but also pretty funny. Johnny lived to the south of the city, in Cheshire. In the sound studio in his basement, I met Andrew Berry, an old friend of Johnny's. He was actually a hairdresser, he told me, but he was working as the studio

508

manager for this production. As time went by I found out a bit more about him, for instance the story of his pilgrimage to Düsseldorf to visit the Kling Klang Studio. Andrew had astounding musical skills. And a gorgeous-sounding Martin acoustic guitar also played a role at the beginning. Johnny reminded me that at the start of our session I picked up his D-28, which was lying around in the studio, and bashed out Arlo Guthrie's 'Alice's Restaurant Massacree'. I think my little acrobatic show was the final ice-breaker. Then we started the session, just like that. The producer Owen Morris was also part of the team at the beginning. Not much later, though, he switched to an unknown Manchester band by the name of Oasis. But that's another story . . .

The lads were already working on a Mac. But although there was only ever one person holding the computer mouse here too, it never caused a logjam. We saw the computer as a recording medium – no more and no less. In the pre-computer era, no one stared at the reel-to-reel tape recorder for hours on end, either. The focus was clearly on the music, not the technology. We looked each other in the eye, talked to each other and made music.

Bernard and Johnny were obviously pretty experienced song-writers who knew how to make hits. But there was something else I noticed: although we don't have a direct translation in German for the idea of 'leftfield thinking', I've always associated the term with them ever since.

Having heard the fantastic 'Get the Message' from the first Electronic album, I could hardly believe how rarely Johnny played 'normal' guitars. Instead, he experimented with a selection of guitar synthesizers, pre-amps and other electronic magic boxes. He had no fear of modern technology; in fact, he seemed pretty good at dealing with computers, samplers and synths, which really surprised me. The Smiths hadn't been exactly famous for their electro sound, after all. Bernard also nerded out on the machines during our sessions. I would sit down at the keyboard and play a couple of motifs or chords I had in my head, or lay down a few electro beats. We were getting to know each other musically, little by little – improvising or practising the craft of composing, depending on how you see it. And we never stuck stubbornly to the first idea that popped up. The DAT tape has the world's greatest track names on it, similar to the ones every musician probably writes on session recordings: 'Guitar Song', 'New Track Bass Tech', 'Hacienda Disco Track', 'High Energy'.

Between 1993 and 1995, I flew over for a total of seven sessions. I felt absolutely unselfconscious; the undogmatic communication and the lives of the Sumner and Marr families seemed to be in perfect harmony with musicians' ways.

In July 1994, Bettina and I met Mark Reeder, Bernard and his wife, Sarah, in Berlin. Along with almost a million people, we joined in the Love Parade on Kurfürstendamm. We somehow lost all sense of time and ended the day at eight the next morning in the legendary Tresor Club. The very next day, Bernard and I were on the plane back to Manchester. At the end of that session, we all went to London together for Neil Tennant's 40th birthday. The first thing Neil told me was that 'Computer Love' was his favourite Kraftwerk track. He didn't understand why it hadn't been a huge hit. The author and cult journalist Jon Savage was sitting near me in a burgundy velvet jacket, looking like someone out of the Kinks. In the early hours, we all ended up in a hotel room – spread all over the furniture – talking and chatting in an 'Easy (Like Sunday Morning)' kind of mood. Absolutely exhausted, I promptly plunged into a magnificent hangover. I don't regret a minute of it!

Our next writing session, in Cheshire in November, was to last three weeks. While we were working, *The Best of New Order* came out. Bernard took me along to a New Order party for the release, and introduced me to Peter Hook and Stephen Morris. It was impossible to overlook the compilation's positive effect on their group dynamics. After a long time-out, all the band members grew closer again. So it is possible, sometimes.

Everyone in the business knows Peter Gabriel's Real World Studios, his production complex in Box, Wiltshire. Clients can stay overnight there like at a hotel, eat their meals in a dining room and roam the grounds, watch swans and geese in the adjacent By Brook, and generally recuperate from the stress of recording. The dining room is a place of fascinating encounters. Over dinner at the latest, all kinds of production teams, bands and other music-makers come together.

In the summer of 1995, Bernard and Johnny lined up a few recording sessions for us there. As well as the recordings, I have good memories of driving along the typical country roads with Bernard in his sports car to swim a few lengths at a thermal bath. I'm just wondering whether Bernard's hair got wet while we were swimming . . . Never mind. Afterwards, we leaned against the side of the pool, our arms draped along the edge, gazing through the big windows at the landscape of Bath and North East Somerset. As you can probably tell, recording was pretty damn tough for all of us. Now and then, Grand Seigneur Peter Gabriel would look in, exchange a few words with us and then vanish again. After the session we spent a weekend in Manchester, and from mid-July Electronic booked the Metropolis Studio in Chiswick. Interestingly enough, the address is: Metropolis Studios, The Power House, 70 Chiswick High Road, London W4 – revealing that the building is a former power station. OK, that might not be all that important but it certainly sounds good, doesn't it?

Mixing an album is always a ritual that's hard to explain to anyone who wasn't there. Please forgive me for not even trying, in this case. But I do remember a few chance encounters on the margins. For instance, Noel Gallagher came over to the studio after the Brit Awards. Johnny played him a few tracks and the two of them had an animated conversation in broad Mancunian – which sounded to me like a language from a different galaxy. In the studio café, I met Claudia Brücken and Michael Mertens or Andy McClusky, who was in town at the time. Brian May put in an appearance, his hair lovingly preened and his shorts astoundingly short, and on one weekend we met up again with Neil Tennant for a tour of the Soho clubs. It was pretty full-on!

The remix album *The Rest of New Order* came out in August, and at the end of the year we had our last session to work on a few Electronic titles back at the Real World Studios near Bath.

When Bernard and Johnny came to Hamburg to promote their album in 1996, we celebrated its release. That was the year when the first singles 'Forbidden City' and 'For You' got to number 14 and 16 and the album to number 8 in the UK charts. It was a high point for me, although I knew the two of them were already thinking about their next record. My biggest regret is that we never played live together. But you can't have everything.

Hamburg Calling

While I was commuting between Germany and the UK for almost three years, my work in Düsseldorf continued. At the time, I was eager to play concerts again and I tried hard to get into the business. Playing live corresponds to music's ephemeral nature. Just like life itself, music takes place in the flow of time. Because time only moves in one direction – forwards – it can't be repeated. That's what makes a live performance unique, and the most primordial way to experience music. When we record music, we capture a moment on a medium, rather like film. We can listen to this document of a time over and over. Not unusually, the result is an artistic product of astounding force of expression, but – and this is due to the nature of the thing – it is simply a different animal to the vibrant venture of a concert.

Early in 1994, we got the opportunity to appear at an event organized by the Franco-German channel Arte at the Bataclan in Paris. While we played 'TV' live to half-playback, Emil painted the test card from the single cover on a canvas at the edge of the stage. The song is relatively short and he only just managed to colour in two or three stripes. Probably no one understood what he was actually trying to do. Oh, Emil . . .

In the spring and summer of that year, we played a few gigs in Scandinavia as Elektric Music. But there was something not quite right about us. I spent a long time thinking about what it might be. In the end, I realized that Lothar and I and the young electro-craftsman Ralf Beck, who was playing with us for a while, simply weren't a band and never would be. Even Emil with his underground videos and the multi-functional Stefan couldn't do anything to change that. We didn't have much to say to each other. The whole project, I saw now, was an illusion. All those involved apparently had a different idea of what it was meant to be. We simply weren't pulling together as a team. And so, in the bright light of a Swedish summer night at the Arvika Festival, the pluralism I'd been striving for – unmistakeably a reaction to the formalistic Hütter–Schneider capitalist model – dissolved into thin air, as did the music itself. Back in Düsseldorf, I lugged my equipment from Klangwerkstatt to my flat. Once I got there, I sat among all my music machines and thought about what to do next.

It was a turbulent time. Bettina was now working as managing editor of a city listings magazine, commuting to Cologne and back every day. It's not a huge distance but it did get her down in the long run. We ended up asking ourselves what was keeping us in Düsseldorf. We wanted to leave. But where should we go? Moving a few kilometres to Cologne seemed too unspectacular – and then Hamburg came into play. In the mid-nineties, the port city was Germany's top media location. All the important magazine and music publishers, the NDR TV channel and the big record labels were based there. When Bettina and I got married in April 1995, we decided to move north. And in June, at the end of my sessions with Electronic, we set off with all our worldly goods.

Our first place was off Elbchaussee near the River Elbe. The typical turn-of-the-century brick villa had real style, and we could hear the creaks of the cranes in the harbour and the big ships' low horns. The big wide world was at our feet, complete with all the clichés about Hamburg. We explored the terrain like children. It was great fun – the Reeperbahn, the Star-Club, quick trips to the Baltic Sea or the North Sea island of Sylt.

Incidentally, although northern Germans are famous for being aloof, we never found that unpleasant or disturbing – even though we Rhinelanders are well known for our sociable nature. For us, Hamburg was a real change of scenery, a liberation on many levels. Life in this Anglophile city is great.

Guitar on the Brain

Strumming Johnny's black-and-white Rickenbacker in England had taken me back to the sounds of the vinyl records Lance Corporal Peter Hornshaw brought into my teenage world all those years ago. I think my psyche was beginning to free itself around that time. Just as moving from Düsseldorf to Hamburg had a positive effect on my mental balance, I wanted to change my musical address for a while and produce an album containing the sound of my childhood.

It was about then that my manager Stefan got a record deal with SPV for the Swedish band the Mobile Homes. The label offered to sign me up to produce the album. Hans Erkendal, Per Liliefeld, Andreas and Patrik Brun had come from Stockholm to Düsseldorf in a camper van in April 1992 to record a song at Klangwerkstatt, and we'd stayed in touch since then. I was most interested in making my own album, but producing the Swedes was sure to be an absorbing task as well. I wondered if it might be possible to work on two records at the same time. The Mobile Homes were an electronic band, though. I've always been enthusiastic about different types of music, but I didn't think I was schizophrenic enough to produce electro music and guitar pop side by side. So I suggested they also shift their sound slightly towards guitar pop. That seemed to be OK with them. I really don't know what came over me, but I accepted the offer.

I couldn't manage it all on my own, that much I knew. Through a friend, I met the Frankfurt-based Markus Löhr. Markus, part of the successful Neue Deutsche Welle trio Hubert Kah in the eighties, had made a name for himself as a songwriter and music producer. Conveniently enough, he's also a very accomplished guitarist. He was surprised when I first talked to him about the projects, but he still agreed to support me as co-producer and also help make the Mobile Homes record. Markus lent me one of his electric guitars, on which I came up with compositions and layouts. He then played most of the solos and guitar parts. The computer was amazingly good at reproducing the tricks of the sixties' magnetic-tape era. I also 'played' the drums by computer mouse, until it sounded like I'd been drumming live.

There's one term I associate with that first summer in Hamburg: lust for life. The feeling of sea air, the blue skies, the light, the ships, the gulls, the sound of the harbour . . . in this mood, I wrote a song for the Mobile Homes' album: 'You Make the Sun Shine'. I think that summer's atmosphere translated itself directly into music.

After that, I sank up to my neck into an eighteen-month composing and producing phase, commuting between Hamburg and Frankfurt and finishing up with mixing sessions at Düsseldorf's Skyline Studios. That was the first time I worked there with Mathias Black. Mathias – a couple of years younger than me – had studied video and audio engineering at the Düsseldorf technical college and qualified as a sound engineer. His training, of course, also included instrumental lessons at the Robert Schumann Conservatory. Sadly, we missed each other

516

there by a few years. When I found out my former teacher, Ernst Göbler, had taught him percussion, we were instantly on the same wavelength. The result was a whole lot to talk about, and we immediately bonded.

Mathias knew his way around the entire musical spectrum. Whether he was recording a band in the rehearsal room with adventurous equipment, mixing a 48-track production on a high-end console, or making a remix with a couple of samplers and a computer – he adapted to each situation and engineered the sound with the same calm competence seen in captains of large passenger planes. The two of us have a similar ability to see musical content as a construction, regardless of genre or personal taste, so it's not hard for us to analyse music and talk about its elements. But our opinions don't cancel each other out – as happens occasionally in egomaniac studio struggles – they complement and intensify each other. When we get together in the studio, we're on the same level, and the results are pretty good. Over the years, Mathias became my closest and most important collaborator.

Looking back, it seems to me as if the mega-production of *The Mobile Homes* and *Electric Music* was not 23 songs, album mixes, singles mixes, remixes and additional versions, but a 'drone', one long constant sound that contains all the tones, noises and voices created within that window of time. Both albums came out in summer 1998 on the same record label. Everyone there clearly saw the greatest hit potential in 'You Make the Sun Shine', and they made a video for the track. There wasn't a budget for similar promotional activities for my own album, however. *Electric Music* only got through to a few print media outlets, which were either perturbed by the unexpected guitar sound or praised the songs' poppy character. One thing soon became clear beyond that: the almost simultaneous release of the two similar products, both of which had something to do with me, confused the record company, the retail stores, the media and lastly the fans. People also seemed to think of me in terms of electronic sounds. I was evidently far too unknown as a person for anyone to take an interest in the depths of my sound biography. My guitar experiment was doomed to fail. Mea culpa.

Roberto in Play

In May 1998, Bettina and I relocated to the west side of Hamburg. There was a very practical reason for the move. The sessions in the Düsseldorf studio had ended up not only exhausting but also pretty expensive. The logical consequence was to set up my own studio. Only in my own production space would I be able to work economically. We bought a house on the edge of the city, where I built a studio in the basement – which is where I also worked on this book, incidentally.

And business really did begin to pick up in the new place. After our move, Stefan Ingmann withdrew from my management and my new Hamburg manager Jens-Markus Wegener put me in touch with several record companies, including the Sony label Epic. Via this contact, I met the Munich-based Austrian action artist Wolfgang Flatz, and went on to compose several songs for his debut album and work on the lyrics with him. Writing and pre-producing the record kept me busy for a few months in 1999. *Love and Violence* and the single 'Wunderkind' came out in the summer of 2000.

In parallel, regular enquiries about remixes and demo productions landed on my desk, some of which I took on with Markus Löhr or the Hamburg music producer and DJ Gerret Frerichs, for example, a remix of the single 'Little Computer People' by the Frankfurt electro artist Anthony Rother. I liked the track and I spent three days working on the remix with Gerret. I did enjoy playing around with existing songs, but it didn't quite satisfy me. After this last intensive phase in the record business, I came to realize it would never be my second nature to remix or produce other artists' music. From then on, I would concentrate only on the music that comes out of my own mind.

One day, the Cologne journalist and DJ Robert Baumanns called me; we had met while I was promoting *Electric Music*. He asked me if I wanted to appear at a music festival in Cologne in August 1999. I hadn't played live for ages – so Robert suggested I could just DJ. Me, a DJ? I wouldn't have thought of it in my wildest dreams. In the end, I accepted on condition that Robert supported me. That was fine by him and he said I could call him Roberto in future – just like Karlheinz Stockhausen did. Stockhausen? It gradually emerged that Robert and the genius composer were friends.

So I played my very first DJ set at the Kickzone Festival in Cologne's Müngersdorf Swimming Stadium on 21 August 1999 – along with Roberto. I remember a large audience, a lot of applause and the immense joy that Roberto and I felt. As we left the stage, I shouted in his ear with a laugh, 'I bet this isn't the last time we two do something together!' And it was in fact the beginning of our musical collaboration, which has continued ever since, developing into an unshakeable friendship.

Live

Although electronic music more or less gave way to an all-encompassing DJ culture and music curation generally came to be understood as a form of music-making, I couldn't shake the old-fashioned idea of a musician who plays an instrument. There were, and still are, convincing economic reasons to play pre-recorded music to audiences, but I was looking for a compromise that linked the old concept of a musical performance with that of a DJ.

While I was thinking about a live strategy, I received an offer from Warner Special Marketing in 1998. They wanted me to contribute the Kraftwerk track 'Tour de France' to a compilation CD scheduled to tie in with the Tour de France, from 11 July to 2 August 1998: *21 Racing Tracks – Tour de France*. It would never have occurred to me to produce a Kraftwerk song, but now I saw it – quite literally – as a sporting challenge. So I slipped into my studio and recorded my breathing and groaning and the sound of my racing bike's wheel turning. The marketing people gave the remake the name 'Tour de France '98'.

The compilation release prompted a sign of life from my former bandmates: an approximately three-metre-long fax from a lawyer acting on behalf of the Kraftwerk company. They seemed to have a problem with the term 'ex-Kraftwerk' that Warner had used next to my name. It didn't bother me, seeing as I'd neither asked them to do it nor knew anything about it, so I forwarded the communication to Warner Special Marketing. I never heard another word about it.

Programming 'Tour de France' on the computer for this

production was no more than a routine task. To avoid objections by my co-authors, I had to stick to every detail of our original. Yet this purely technical work on the track did trigger something inside me. All of a sudden, the question came up: would it be legitimate for me to perform the Kraftwerk repertoire? After all, Ralf and Florian were still playing the songs we'd composed together, even though I'd left the band. At the same time, I was thinking of a possible visual level, though not following any precise plan. I asked my music publishing company to check the legal situation, to be on the safe side. Was I allowed to perform 'my' Kraftwerk songs live along with self-produced films, or might such a performance violate other people's rights? It was absolutely unobjectionable, came the answer. Right, then. Now I could keep thinking along those lines.

And so I began programming the repertoire, from autumn 1999 to the spring of 2000. I didn't have any trouble recreating the authentic sound because I'd worked on the songs in the first place, and also owned most of the original equipment.

Essentially, I followed the performance practice of live inter-pretation and playback, for which the term 'musique mixte' had been established at the beginnings of *musique concrète*. I used the original versions as my orientation – which I still think are the best, incidentally. The albums *The Man-Machine* and *Computer World* formed the core of my selection – and I recorded both of them in their entirety, plus 'Tour de France' and 'The Telephone Call' from the *Techno Pop* phase. And as I also feel part-responsible for 'Trans-Europe Express' and 'Hall of Mirrors', I had a go at those two tracks as well. To break down the stark predictability of our structural forms, I got rid of repetitions of verses where it made sense to me.

521

I abridged unnecessarily long passages and transposed 'Computer Love', for example, into a key that better suits my vocal range, created bridges between the songs, and much more along those lines. As a medium for the supporting tracks at the live electronic concerts, I chose a digital sixteen-track hard-disc recorder, on which I'd recorded my last album. Mathias, who also had a machine of the same type, ordered the sound tracks and took over the sound-engineering side of the recording process.

Via my management, I met a group of media artists at the time, who'd given themselves the programmatic name of Bauhouse. DJ Clemens Wittowski and the two VJs[5] Fabian Grobe and Alexander Koch combined electronic dance music – house, dub, acid – with a very rhythmic visual level. We wanted to put something together and the guys arranged a couple of gigs in Leipzig, Dresden and Berlin. While I played my electronic set, Fabian experimented with different film sequences to accompany my tracks.

I was fascinated by the enormous effort they put into their computer terminals and self-written software. The interesting thing about Fabian's performance was that he didn't run films to the music, but improvised like a jazz musician with film sequences. I was blown away by this visual music. Of course, I didn't have the slightest idea how it was made, but I simply got stuck in and picked up the necessary hardware, like three video recorders, ten second-hand TVs of various sizes, a video camera and a video mixer. I spent many an arduous day trying to combine the components and get them up and running. Often, the only resort was a call to Düsseldorf, where Mathias got me jump-started with his technical skills.

As I didn't have any editing software, I filmed longer sequences – for instance television material, fairy lights, pictures or traffic – mixed various sources and recorded them again with my camera. The video mixer could create split screens and digital effects. Interestingly, like in electronic music, artefacts – images randomly generated by signal distortion – promptly came about, which flowed into the material. These experiments were exciting and I soon had over a hundred VHS cassettes and at least as many DV cassettes piled up in my recording room. But I needed support. Via a recommendation, I met the art director Karsten Binar, who worked for the WDR television channel. I managed to convince him to produce a couple of films. For the song 'TV' for example, he filmed a fairly long loop of test cards, for 'Metropolis' a motorway junction, for 'Numbers' . . . you guessed it: numbers moving in all manner of ways. The plan was for Karsten to sync the videos to the music from the side of the stage at our future live shows.

Our first official booking was scheduled for my 48th birthday, 31 May 2000: the Electronic Beats Festival in the Cologne Palladium. By the by, I found out the whole festival programme would be broadcast live on MTV2: from zero to hero at the very first show.

The white-painted BARTOS on our flight cases wasn't quite dry by the time we arrived at the venue. I'd done it by hand that morning with a roller and stencil. I felt unsure of myself in front of the phalanx of cases on stage; I still had to get used to using my own name as a group or product title. We were fairly low down the billing in the festival line-up. Bartos, what Bartos? The stage manager did a fine job of ignoring us but we still managed to try out two or three songs. Róisín Murphy, at the festival with her then band Moloko, applauded from the balcony as I kicked into 'Computer Love' with the Düsseldorf musician and sound engineer Dave Anderson, who I'd persuaded to join me for the live show. All we had for the visual loops were a couple of large TV sets, which were standing around somewhere like they'd been left behind by accident. All of a sudden, the festival crew broke off the soundcheck. Thanks, lads! The afternoon passed me by – completely deleted from my memory. At last, we stepped on stage with leaden stomachs. Nailed to the floor behind the keyboards in the cameras' focus, we played our set: 'Numbers', 'Computer World', 'Metropolis', 'Home Computer', 'TV', 'Neon Lights', 'The Model', 'Computer Love', 'The Robots'.

After that cold shower, our next bookings were in Riga and at the Arvika Festival in Sweden, both of which worked far better – apart from the fact that it simply didn't get dark enough in the Swedish summer for the films to be properly visible . . . But still, there was no point in Karsten controlling the films from backstage like a video technician at the theatre. He had to be visible for the audience. So I chose a triptych form for the visuals and placed one of us in front of each of the screens: Dave on the left with keyboard and vocoder, me on another keyboard in the middle, and on the right-hand side I constructed Karsten's workplace, conveying a similar atmosphere to a vision mixer in a live TV studio with a table, mixing desk and control monitors. I wanted the audience to be aware of his monitors and follow the mixing of the media. Apart from his skills, Karsten brought along a laptop plus professional video editing software to the new media work station. Now we were ready to go.

Visual Music

In the old days, I had never been consciously aware of the rhythm of moving images. The visual level was important for Kraftwerk, but more in the sense of a backdrop, as an element of a scenic space. There was no real interaction between sound and images. It was only when I switched between two image sources to music or moved the fader back and forth to fade them, that I learned of the power inherent to the picture edit. A whole new world opened up for me, a thrilling place I wanted to know everything about.

In the 1990s, TV and various channels showed hours of techno music and visuals, all of which adhered to a certain aesthetic. The visuals mainly worked by distorting clear images using video effects. It's amusing when you're behind the mixing desk yourself, doing the modulations. On the eye level, they more or less concentrated on repetitions – just like the music itself – which evolved on a linear track by using altering effects. I wasn't interested in that form of image processing. Repetitions of film sequences have a very different effect to musical loops. But I was convinced by the idea of understanding films in the same way as music and improvising with the images. *Visual music* was an entirely new idea. From that moment on, I researched the concept and where its roots lie. The techno visuals seemed superficially related to the psychedelic liquid slide shows and avant-garde films of the sixties – prompting memories of psychedelic lightshows by Velvet Underground, Grateful Dead and Pink Floyd. But to get to the beginnings of modern audio-visual design, I had to go back to the first half of the twentieth century, when painting was becoming ever more abstract and the artists were interested in music, which is of course essentially abstract itself.

In the 1920s, Wassily Kandinsky was one of the artists working and teaching at the Bauhaus. He set out to translate musical characteristics like dynamics, rhythm and simultaneity onto the spatial plane. At around the same time, artists such as Walter Ruttmann, Hans Richter and Viking Eggeling were interested in the new medium of film and wanted to bring its speed and rhythm into their own work. Richter's *Rhythmus 21* and Eggeling's *Diagonal-Symphonie* are classics to this day. As different as their techniques were, they all led to squares, triangles, circles and lines coming alive through the dimension of time. Walter Ruttmann's *Lichtspiel Opus 1* was the first abstract film shown in public. Ruttmann, Richter and Eggeling would have been surprised to learn what recognition and admiration their avant-garde experimental films elicit today, since their work gained little attention during their lifetimes. Not at all like the films of Oskar Fischinger, which were popular and successful by comparison. His experimental animated films treated image and sound equally from the very beginning. Alongside his purely artistic works, Fischinger made advertisements such as for the Muratti cigarette brand (1934/35), which ran before the main features. Blithely leapfrogging the next forty years, I end up at Andy Warhol's film experiments, Nam June Paik's video art and the Fluxus movement, and then at the music industry's promo videos, music TV and the clubs and raves of the techno and house scene, where a new youth culture evolved in the nineties. It was within this movement that the first video artists began experimenting. They combined a wild mix of sources: Super-8, commercial films, TV material, ads, camera recordings. This visual content – often labelled 'found footage' with affectionate naivety – was understood and processed by them like music.

Today's computers are fast enough to manipulate moving images in real time. And we can now improvise with those images, like jazz musicians. How does it work? I cut a sequence of a few seconds out of a film, producing a snippet devoid of all context. Let's say, Karl Bartos driving a convertible around Hamburg. It doesn't matter where he's come from or where he's going. He becomes an abstract figure doing something that has no significance, makes no sense. But we can work with this visual fragment like with music. We can repeat it, imbue it with rhythm, run it slower or faster, stop and start it, play it backwards, enlarge it, minimize it, mirror it, invert or filter the colours, revolve it around its own axis, and much more. The visual level – which we generally grasp with our intellect – is now perceived emotionally. To really understand this development – which I've just presented in cross-section and fast-forward – I needed time to think and try things out, and so I essentially spent the next few years gathering this information, studying it and putting it into practice.

15 Minutes of Fame

The Millennium Bug may not have happened, but the new millennium did bring change on the business level for me: in July 2000 I signed a contract for my first album under the name of Karl Bartos with the Hamburg label Orbit, which distributed its products with Virgin. From then on, I only wanted to work under my own name. After my years of experimenting, it simply felt right.

At the beginning of the writing phase, I contacted Anthony Rother. His track 'Little Computer People' was still an inspiration to me. The Frankfurt-based electronic musician made real-life music with machines and published a whole load of records on his own label. I went right ahead and invited him to Hamburg. We spent two days in my studio 'throwing a few ideas into the computer,' one of which evolved into pop music.

While I was working on the new song, I read the book *Famous for 15 Minutes: My Years with Andy Warhol*[6] by Isabelle Dufresne, a.k.a. 'Ultra Violet' from the inner circle of Warhol's Factory. I was interested in his underground movies, his strange books and statements. He really wanted to be a robot, and he held other views that were oddly familiar. Warhol seemed to have been something like a sociopath – or was he just playing a sociopath? With his quote 'In the future, everyone will be world-famous for 15 minutes' in mind, I sat down to write the lyrics for the song and went on tweaking at the arrangement.

This was around the time that the new casting show format was launched on TV. I couldn't explain their high viewing figures (or I didn't want to). One thing's for sure: the only people making money out of them were the producers and the A-, B- or C-list celebrity judges. It was probably these shows that gave me the idea to play with the phenomenon of modern celebrity culture, which had fascinated Warhol and before him Marshall McLuhan. I took a look at the phenomenon and collected key terms – 'stars', 'celebrities', 'fame', 'religion', 'paranoid', 'it-girl' – to put together a kind of trash-collage text in reportage tone. Just like a camera adopts a subjective viewpoint in film, the perspective switches to the aspiring superstars for the refrain. They proclaim their credo: 'We want 15 minutes of fame.'

My new label boss Sascha Basler liked the song. Impatient as label bosses can be, he suggested not waiting for the album but releasing it straight away. I couldn't help thinking briefly of our head-over-heels 'Tour de France' single, but then I went along with the idea. As you might expect, I needed the obligatory music video to go with the single. And what made more sense than filming an Andy Warhol pop theme in New York? We set off on 12 September. *We* meaning a small film crew consisting of the producer Ulrike Licht, director Stefanie Sixt, the label's product manager and, of course, yours truly. Once again, I spent just under a week at the Mayflower. We filmed all over the city. I think we'd forgotten to get a permit, so we had to make sure we didn't get caught. I enjoyed letting Stefanie direct me in front of the camera. On her request, I climbed onto flat roofs with their typical water tanks, clambered up fire escapes and ran several carefree laps of the World Trade Center, which collapsed almost exactly a year later after the inhumane Al Qaida attacks. I strolled through Little Italy – pursued by the director in a rickshaw with a Super-8 camera – bumped into Germany's then foreign minister Joschka Fischer in Central Park and took the subway downtown.

Despite the trendsetting title and the enthusiastic support of the people of Manhattan, selected representatives of whom joined in the refrain, the video almost never aired on MTV. I managed to contain my annoyance, though, because when Virgin decided not to extend their deal with Orbit there was no prospect of promotion for the single anyway. It didn't matter that the tune was on its way into the British charts – all the problems solved themselves.

Expo Gigs

Out of the blue, the Expo 2000 organizers made me an offer to play on two October evenings as part of the world exhibition. Expo 2000? Hold on, that rings a bell! The previous December, Ralf and Florian had actually released new sounds: the signature tune for the world exhibition in Hannover. Lasting only a few seconds, the German jingle – which was translated into five other languages – made major waves in the media. Rumour had it a relatively high fee had changed hands for the job. It caused quite a storm, but the media teacup soon calmed down again. At any rate, Kraftwerk were apparently busy and couldn't perform at the Expo 2000 opening on 1 July.

On receiving the offer, I instantly thought of the Paris World Exhibition of 1889, where Claude Debussy first came into contact with music from other cultures. He is said to have been incredibly impressed by the sound of a Javan gamelan ensemble. And although the event may have become less significant in times of globalization, it is still my first thought when I hear 'world exhibition', 'world's fair' or 'Expo'.

I said yes, obviously! But I did wonder what would happen when it was me and my collaborators kicking off at the fair and not Kraftwerk. We were playing partly the same repertoire, after all. Would we be booed off stage? I had mixed feelings at the performances on 2 and 3 October, but what happened? Nothing.

There was no negative reaction, at any rate. We reaped applause, and plenty of it. The two nights in Hannover were two good gigs – the first time I sang 'The Young Urban Professional' live, the first track from my last album. After that I swore never again to compose pieces with long lyrics I'd have to learn by heart.

Gesang der Jünglinge

Whenever I spoke to the Mobile Homes singer Hans Erkendal on the phone, I got breaking news from Stockholm, and this time was no different. 'I think I've got something interesting here for you,' he said. 'Have you heard of the Polar Music Prize?' 'Nope,' I admitted. 'Man, it's the unofficial Nobel Prize for Music, and they've just chosen three recipients: Bob Moog, Burt Bacharach and Karlheinz Stockhausen. You've been asked to make the speech for Stockhausen next year at the ceremony. The Polar Music Prize is a big deal over here, Karl, it's broadcast live on Swedish TV. A big song and dance with the king and all the stops pulled out,' my excited friend told me. And then he asked: 'What are you doing next May?' I instantly pricked up my ears. Alongside the honour of giving the lauditory speech, there was another thing that made me happy. We were planning a small Scandinavian tour and the gigs in Copenhagen, Malmö, Stockholm and Göteborg happened to have been booked for just after the ceremony. It was perfect timing. What else could I say but: 'Great, let's do it'?!

Bettina and I landed at Arlanda Airport in Stockholm on the early afternoon of 12 May 2001. We were chauffeur-driven straight to the venerable Grand Hotel, where the prize-winners

531

and the musicians holding their speeches are traditionally put up. Looking out of our window at the Stockholms ström, Norrström and the Strömbron bridge, I realized how beautiful and quiet Sweden's capital is. We had an invitation to the American embassy for 7:30 that evening. Two of that year's award-winners were Americans, after all: Robert Moog and Burt Bacharach, and the ambassador was throwing a party in their honour. The embassy was heavily guarded but large and magnificent. Stockhausen and his entourage were also among the guests. I spent some time standing next to a blonde lady who was quietly watching the proceedings, like myself. It was only on second glance that the penny dropped: none other than Agnetha Fältskog from ABBA was right there beside me.

The next day, we attended a seminar at the conservatory, at which the Stockhausen composition 'Aries' was performed. After that Mr Bacharach also presented excerpts of his work. And what a body of work that is! He sat at the piano in a pale-blue tracksuit, 73 years old at the time, and gave a relaxed rendition of his all-time classics like 'Raindrops Keep Fallin' on My Head', 'I'll Never Fall in Love Again' and 'That's What Friends Are For'.

Later that evening, the German ambassador invited everyone involved in the award ceremony to dinner. This gathering was much smaller and more intimate than the one at the US embassy. Instead of finger food, we dined around a table and chatted by the fireside. That was my opportunity to talk one-to-one with the 72-year-old Karlheinz Stockhausen. His eyes shining with pride, he told me his music was soon to be premiered in Denmark. I followed up.

'Herr Stockhausen,' I began hesitantly, 'I've always wondered how you get to stage such big-budget performances?' 'Och, you know,' he replied in the finest Rhineland sing-song accent, 'it's no secret: I talk to the directors or the politicians, introduce them to my work, and now and then I actually get to present it.' He gave me a cheerful look, apparently very amused . . . presumably by the things he didn't tell me in his answer. Unfortunately, there was no time to talk to him about Burt Bacharach's music. What would that conversation have been like? I know very little about his views on popular music but he certainly came into close contact with it. In a number of interviews, he talks about how he financed his studies from the end of the 1940s until well into 1950s by playing popular music and Cologne carnival songs in pubs and bars, also accompanying the well-known magician Alexander Adrion on one of his tours around Germany and abroad. I think even at the time when he was composing his highly significant mass for electronic sounds and voices, he was still playing in Cologne bars.

Stockhausen was to present his key early work, *Gesang der Jünglinge* (*Song of the Youth*), during the award ceremony. The rehearsal was scheduled for noon the next day in the Berwaldhallen. I absolutely had to be there! Dressed all in white, the master stood behind a mixing desk in the middle of the hall, directing several stagehands who were on a mobile ladder to set up the four groups of loudspeakers around the seating. He kept in eye contact with the technicians and gave them clear signals in one or other direction, like a policeman directing traffic. Absolutely immersed in this communication, for him the angle of the speakers, every degree, every centimetre was important. *Gesang* is, after all, one of the first examples of electronic music-in-space in the world. Stockhausen included the direction of the sound and its motion in the space on their own level of his composition in the mid-fifties, creating a completely new dimension for the aural experience.

I stayed as long as I could, watching the preparations as if hypnotized. Despite the bright lighting, when the first sounds floated through the hall, the incomparable effect produced by the work was instantly present, drawing in anyone who has learned how to listen.

At some point, I had to tear myself away from the soundcheck because there was a short practice for my little speech, and then it was off to get changed into my finery. The hall slowly filled up, and when King Carl XVI Gustaf of Sweden, Queen Silvia and Crown Princess Victoria made their ceremonious entrance, the official occasion began at 4:30 with the honouring of Robert Moog, the youngest of the laureates at 66. His speech was held by Manfred Mann, whose hits like 'Do Wah Diddy', 'Mighty Quinn' and 'Fox on the Run' had rung out in my childhood bedroom from Radio Luxembourg in the sixties.

I'm not easily ruffled, but then I was announced as the speaker for Karlheinz Stockhausen and I nervously watched the projected film, in which I was walking around in a red shirt as a Kraftwerker. It seems I'm destined to remain a robot, second from left, for the rest of my life. The presenter did at least introduce me as a former member of one of the most influential bands in pop-music history – OK, I'll take it. Someone beckoned me to the rostrum. Was my voice perhaps trembling slightly? Objection: Hearsay! After my brief words, the king presented the prize to the composer, who thanked him and proudly announced he would be using the award money to train young musicians. Then he dashed off stage and popped up not much later from the auditorium with the words: 'Listeners, I'm sitting now at the center of the ground floor at the sound projecting table. We will hear my electronic music *Gesang der Jünglinge*. It is a composition of new sounds and angelic voices. If you close your eyes every now and then you might even see these angels. I wish you a good time.' Whether anyone did see angels during the sound projection, I'm not sure. What I am certain of is that everyone in the building was entranced by the composition. After the performance, Elvis Costello held the speech for Burt Bacharach, and the Stockholm Symphony Orchestra and Sweden's best vocalists filled the Berwaldhalle with his songs, heavenly sounds of a very different kind.

After the ceremony, everyone – including the royal family – was taken back to the Grand Hotel on beautifully decorated boats for the official banquet. First, though, there was an aperitif with the Bernadottes on one of the hotel's top floors. Even though we're not exactly enthusiastic monarchists, we did feel a little nervous. A lady-in-waiting gave us a few tips on how to behave and then they all appeared – Carl XVI Gustaf of Sweden, the queen formerly known as Silvia Sommerlath – who graduated from a Düsseldorf high school in 1963 – Crown Princess Victoria, her sister Madeleine and brother Carl Philip. We said polite *hej*s and *hello*s, shook hands, took symbolic sips of champagne. And before it got too painful, the chamberlain rapped his ceremonial staff three times on the floor, the signal for us to head straight to the banqueting hall. When we got down there, all 200 invited guests were standing patiently behind their chairs – no one was allowed to sit down before the royal family had taken their seats. Pretty strict etiquette . . .

Bettina and I sat at one of the countless tables, with our Swedish friends Annika and Hans Erkendal and the great Manfred Mann and his wife. During the banquet, Mr Mann made me the kind offer of playing a keyboard solo on one of my next tracks. Nothing came of it in the end, but I have the best of memories of him – what a gentleman. Two more musical performances followed after dinner. First we heard an excerpt from the composition 'AVE' from Stockhausen's opera *Montag aus Licht*. Suzanne Stephens and Kathinka Pasveer – the composer's partners – performed a delicately choreographed duet for alto flute and basset horn, wearing indescribably imaginative costumes. In this combination, it couldn't have been any more extraordinary and exciting – like exotic birds, the two virtuosos played and danced around each other, as though Stockhausen had composed the piece especially for them. And then as the night drew in, Mr Burt Bacharach stepped up to the grand piano and sang a few of his songs with his very own elegance and gravitas.

NOTES

1. Filippo Tommaso Marinetti: 'Destruction of Syntax – Wireless Imagination – Words-in-Freedom,' 1913
2. 'The album is a solid, pleasant surprise, with its fun stylistic range – all cast within a synth-pop milieu.' *Billboard*, 12 June 1993
3. ' . . . there is some fabulous music there,' '*Elektric Music*.' Review by Dave Simpson in *Melody Maker*, 3 July 1993
4. '"TV" drifts by with simple tuneful grace.' 'TV.' Review by David Quantick in *New Musical Express*, 31 July 1993
5. A Visual Jockey is a video artist who improvises with visual content in real time.
6. Isabelle Dufresne: *Famous for 15 Minutes: My Years with Andy Warhol*. Harcourt Brace Jovanich: New York 1988

15

COMMUNICATION

9/11. Communication in Progress. Artwork by Weissraum. Bad Timing. Surreal Experience in Miami Beach. Live at the ICA. UK Blitz Tour. The Internet: Curse and Blessing for the Music Industry. A Life in Pictures. The Call. Guest Professorship in Auditory Media Design. Muzak. Frequent Traveller. New Releases Out Now! Florian Schneider, Ex-Kraftwerk. My Thoughts about Sound.

9/11

My fellow musician Dave Anderson paid me a visit in Hamburg in early September. During our gigs in Sweden, we'd arranged to spend a few days in the studio together. The weather was still summery, so we started off by cycling to an idyllic restaurant in the nearby Klövensteen nature reserve to get us in the mood. With the blue skies of Hamburg above us, it was a perfect but relatively insignificant day. What happened in New York City a day later – on 11 September 2001 – was to change the world, however. As Dave and I entered the studio I switched on the TV, on mute, as I always do. The screen revealed an inferno: the north tower of the World Trade Center engulfed in flames. Horrified, I turned up the volume and heard the newsreader reporting a plane crash in New York. A few minutes later, we watched live as a second plane rammed into the south

537

tower. There was no way we could think about music. We spent the rest of the day glued to the television screen, as if paralyzed. Watching thousands of people die. Live. All the channels went live around the clock. Television has always done live reporting, of course, but perhaps that 11 September will go down in media history as the date when live broadcasting entered a new era. The full extent and the context came to light gradually, on the day that would come to be stored in our collective memory as 9/11. I think the import of the apocalyptic images was so huge that they are the only explanation for the depth of mental confusion and disturbance the events triggered in many people.

Communication in Progress

That new visual element also had a lasting influence on me. Once I began writing the music for my new album, under the shadow of 9/11, my mind revolved around the ideas of acoustic and visual communication. Sound was my starting point, but the current events imbued electronic media images with more and more significance for me. They play a key role in determining our view of the world. However, there was another, more profane reason to produce an album: I needed a larger repertoire for my live show.

To start with, I looked for an overture, a 'corporate identity' song – similar to 'Alexander's Ragtime Band', 'Sgt. Pepper's' or 'The Robots' – as a brief introduction for the audience and a summary of the main audio-visual elements of the performance. I called the song 'I'm the Message' and used self-referential telegram-style language: 'Look at me / I am the message / In sound and vision / Here and now / Listen to me / I am the message / In sound and vision / Here and now.'

I had highlighted the phenomenon of media culture on the *Esperanto* album – and now I wanted to go into greater depth. Susan Sontag's 1977 essay *On Photography* was to be the entrance point and compass for 'The Camera' and its extension 'Camera Obscura'. The American writer opened my eyes to a new view of photography as a medium. For instance, she points out that, through photography, the world 'becomes a series of unrelated, freestanding particles; and history, past and present, a set of anecdotes and *faits divers*'[1] (events). The bassline is of course an adaption of the 'Robots' riff, which I consider the best Minimoog riff of all time.

For 'Reality', I found a formula for drums and bass that works like a car engine: get in, turn on, drive off. The lyrics again reference Susan Sontag, who notes that the camera atomizes reality. 'Electronic Apeman' describes us humans at the beginning of the digital age. Almost unnoticed, the future has begun, one in which we appear to be increasingly losing orientation. In my song, technology itself – in the form of a computer voice – bolsters the electronic apeman's courage and tells him, rather naively, to pull himself together.

When Bernard Sumner invited me to a New Order concert in Berlin that November, I leapt at the chance. Back in 1986, Ralf and I didn't want to wait all night in New York's 1018 Club for the band to turn up, but everything was very different now. We met for dinner and then made our way to the sold-out Columbia-Halle together. I experienced the backstage atmosphere as a mix of intelligence, emotion and nonsense. Pretty much the setting that makes good pop music possible in the first place. I actually really missed being on the road with a band. New Order had just brought out their album *Get Ready*, and when they played 'Crystal' at this gig I thought: Right, that's how to do it! Back in my Hamburg studio, I wrote another song for my new album: 'Life'.

After the release of *Communication*, I spoke to Bernard on the phone while he was at the Real World Studios with New Order. They had just been listening to 'Life', he said, and Peter Hook noticed how similar my vocals are to Bernard's. Whether our voices have a comparable timbre, I can't say; we hear ourselves through a psychological filter. One thing's for sure: I can't change my cadence, I'm not a voice impersonator. But our vocal range is similar and I've been familiar with Bernard's unmistakeable effortless way of singing for many years. And we also have a great deal of musical consensus. After all, we've known each other for ages and didn't become friends for no reason.

My first encounter with the term 'cyberspace' was in the mid-eighties, in William Gibson's novel *Neuromancer*. The book revolves, very generally speaking, around the main character Case – these days we'd call him a hacker – who logs into a gigantic data space that the writer calls 'cyberspace'. A matrix, a world of data that humans can visit with their intellect and imagination, but not their physical bodies. Years later, a new technology by the name of 'virtual reality' was first demonstrated at a 1991 computer show in Boston. People could travel into cyberspace by means of specially constructed computer clothing. You strap a TV in front of your eyes like diving goggles, slip into a data glove, quasi-glide through the TV monitor and find yourself in an interactive virtual 3D setting, an artificial world.

540

Sure, in the eighties there'd been the Disney film *Tron* and the TV series *Max Headroom*, but they were nothing more than simulations of a computer-mediated simulation. By the beginning of the nineties, virtual reality had clearly become just that: reality. In essence, though, parallel or illusory worlds have existed since time immemorial, as sites of desire in our imaginations. For instance, in our nightly dreams we experience the boundaries of space and time disappearing, the laws of nature and logic losing their significance. In mythology and the world's religions, such a place is defined as paradise – Elysium, Nirvana, Jannah – where the immortal spend eternity. But we also enter different worlds through artificial paradises created by drugs. As a child, I made my own 'rooms' in the drawers in my bedroom, places I occasionally dived into mentally – a procedure now described as 'immersion'. Books, theatre, film – all media takes us away for a while into fantasy worlds if we immerse ourselves in it. And because music is another catalyser for our imagination, the title 'Cyberspace' is very apt – even though it sounds like science fiction at first – for a song on this album.

I had long been wanting to write Dada-style lyrics, connecting words apparently randomly. No plan, only coincidence and caprice. A little like trying to put into words what I recognize in a fraction of a second when I'm zapping through the TV channels. The whole 'Interview' track is oriented around a sequencer riff that seems like it's straight out of a seventies disco. I didn't bother adding a modulation to a different key, or perhaps I simply forgot.

The scenario for 'Ultraviolet': a man is sitting apathetically in front of the TV at home, talking to himself. It doesn't matter

541

how long he's been there. Over the past few days, he's read Bret Easton Ellis's *American Psycho*, which has rendered him unbalanced. The metaphor of 'ultraviolet light' expresses his mental state. The character appears to feel the TV takes him for a fool. Suddenly, it occurs to him – like the protagonist of *American Psycho* – that he has to bring a couple of tapes back to the video store. Yep, there were still video shops on every corner back around the turn of the millennium, and the German ones, at least, always had a rather grubby air to them because of their porn sections. As far as possible, I avoided formal symmetry on this track, as well. Instruments are switched in and out. It's all about motor skills and the fragile state of mind of some guy in some city, who wants a new life but can only describe that life using a colour sequence.

On the album's epilogue – 'Another Reality' – I try not to let the metre get tangible, aiming to create a state of Gregorian weightlessness. In practice, that proved incredibly difficult. Composing and producing the track took an astoundingly long time. While working on the album, I kept diving more and more into visual music, and it was via these abstract, rhythmic film experiments that I arrived at narrative cinema. I asked myself: How are films actually made? For a long time, a Jean-Luc Godard quote revolved in my mind like a mantra: 'The cinema is truth twenty-four times per second.'[2] And that was how I got to the aphorism 'Every second you can see / Twenty-four pictures of reality,' which I assembled out of the phonemes of my 'Newspeak' collection.

By the summer of 2002, I had put together sixteen tracks and chosen ten for the album, which I produced with Mathias Black. The label's advance enabled me to buy production equipment, including a digital mixing desk. Mathias's technical concept united all the advantages of digital production with the possibilities of analogue instruments and signal processing. The computer and mixing desk were connected up digitally. That meant everything we programmed could be reproduced. In addition, we integrated the synthesizers, outboard equipment and my vocals into the set-up via the mixer's analogue channels. Mathias brought along his analogue equipment to Hamburg, and my studio soon looked like a submarine command centre. Over those few days, we developed work processes and sounds that we still use today.

A day in the studio lasted from noon until midnight, and passed extremely quickly. When I went upstairs to bed, Mathias would usually spend another hour or two communing with the computer. Including mastering, between August 2002 and January 2003 the two of us spent over two months in my control room over five sessions, with considerable headwind from the speakers.

Artwork by Weissraum

For the cover, I was thinking of pictograms. These black-and-white symbols have the task of imparting information, making them predestined for the album's concept. I borrowed several books on the subject and stumbled over the pictograms designed by Otl Aicher for the 1972 Olympics. When I saw the symbols for the sporting disciplines spread out in front of me, they looked to me like a film. A miniature movie in my mind! My imagination leapt from one contest to the next. Thanks to my discount card for a local copy shop, I put together an archive of hundreds of pictograms, then used a paper cutter, scissors, glue and a whole lot of time and effort to choose four that somehow fitted together and also told a vague story: pedestrian – telephone – camera – aeroplane.

I think I surprised my label of the time with this *idée fixe* but the boss Sascha Basler seemed to trust me. In any case, he introduced me to Lucas Buchholz and Bernd Brink. The two of them run a visual communication agency with the programmatic name of weissraum.de(sign)°. We got on well at our very first meeting. Taking the four first pictograms as a starting point, we developed a lively exchange of ideas, which then led to the familiar design of the album and all the accompanying media in their various shapes and forms.

Our label, which had meanwhile switched to Sony Music and now called itself Home Records, incidentally, decided to release 'I'm the Message' as a single. We wanted to produce an animated film for the promo video. But what should the storyboard be? Cup of coffee in hand, I stared at the demo version of the album cover, which I had propped up on my chest of drawers. It was like those mysterious optical illusions concealing another image, which you can only make out after staring long and hard, if at all. From one second to the next, I saw a storyboard in the four pictograms. Starting with the pedestrian, I developed the story clockwise. The little man was to take on the role of a reporter in the film, who receives a call (telephone) from his newspaper. His editor-in-chief tells him to fly to England (aeroplane) to do a photo story (camera) about a football match.

I spread out all my photocopies of the countless pictograms – car, escalator, the Information symbol, and so on – and drew the storyboard. Once I was done, I faxed the three pages to the label and suggested commissioning the Weissraum guys to make my idea reality. No sooner said than done – Lucas and Bernd produced and directed the pictographic animated film with the aid of Florian Bruchhaeuser, who programmed the moving images. We were all crazy about the finished product. The design perfectly suited my album, but it was also characteristic for Lucas and Bernd, so it was no surprise that they won the Red Dot Award for it, and a great deal of praise and plaudits for the overall album artwork. The three of us have worked together on various occasions since. Admittedly, there are times when our communication feels like a competition for the best idea, the next step, a new perspective. But that's exactly why our intellectual exchanges are always exciting and productive.

Bad Timing

We were planning the release of *Communication* for 8 September 2003, when rumours went around that Kraftwerk would be putting out a new album in August: *Tour de France Soundtracks*. Another 'Tour de France?' That sounded familiar . . . Some time previously, the legal adviser at my music publishing company had informed me of an enquiry from Sony Music Publishing – the company that administered Kraftwerk's copyrights – as to whether I would agree to a change in the lyrics on the track 'Tour de France'. I asked whether I could hear what they were actually talking about, and I also let them know I'd appreciate discussing the matter personally with Ralf and Florian. I heard not a word from Sony Music Publishing after that, and the lyrics never did get changed, as I established later.

Our label tried to postpone the upcoming release of *Communication*. If *Tour de France Soundtracks* came out on 4 August, we could forget media coverage for *Communication* on 8 September. No one would care about the Bartos album any more. But Sony Music couldn't or wouldn't push the date back.

As predicted, almost all the media reported on the new Kraftwerk album and showed no major interest in *Communication*. But we didn't give up. Maxime Schmitt had thought up amazing release parties for my former band's products back in the seventies. The trip to Reims on the fake *Orient Express*, the *Soirée Rouge* in the Tour Montparnasse – I still remember them very well. We thought about how and where to arrange a cool, spectacular album presentation. It was then that I remembered Johnny Marr mentioning a London venue that was an excellent fit for events of this kind – the Institute of Contemporary Arts (ICA). Founded in 1947 directly on Trafalgar Square, the institute has a well-earned reputation as a centre of the British avant-garde and interdisciplinary arts scene. Gilbert & George first presented their *Singing Sculptures* there, Damien Hirst premiered a solo exhibition, and musicians like Kate Bush and Laurie Anderson launched their own projects on the premises.

Along with our label, we thought about presenting the album to the public at the ICA – live on stage, of course. It had to be possible to fly a few journalists over. It was certainly ambitious, but luckily Home Records was into that sort of gimmick, and dipped into petty cash to make it happen.

Surreal Experience in Miami Beach

In the middle of preparations for the London launch, we received an offer to play at the Magical Maydaze Festival in Miami. My band was made up of Dave Anderson on keyboards, Karsten Binar as VJ, Mathias Black as technical director, Uwe Kanka as technician, and me. The booker at our agency, Thomas Köster, would be coming along as our tour manager. I knew we'd be fine, but I still asked Bettina to come with me.

We landed in Miami in mid-May. Just as we were fetching our cases from the luggage carousel, a highly motivated drug-detecting beagle caught sight of us, launched itself at my bag and tried its hardest to open it. You can imagine what came next . . . Like in an American TV series, we suddenly made the acquaintance of narcotics agents and police officers, who barked instructions at us. There was no doubt they meant what they said. Not only did we get thoroughly searched; our luggage was also completely unpacked and taken for X-rays. It might sound amusing after the fact, but in reality, it was pretty intense. While we were getting checked, I remembered I'd transported several bags of dry dog food in my travelling bag before our trip to Florida, when Bettina and I went on holiday with our new housemate Winnie, a black Pyrenean Shepherd. Perhaps that was why the sniffer dog reacted so drastically. In any case, we managed to pass the extensive police checks with the aid of this explanation.

The festival gig was OK and important as a dress rehearsal for our ICA appearance. What has stuck in my mind more than the concert, though, is the fantastically bizarre hip-hop convention that we ended up in by accident. It was exactly that week when the scene's crème de la crème and their friends and fans met up around Ocean Drive to party the nights away. Every inch of the streets and pavements was packed with huge Hummers draped in half-naked ladies, music booming out of every nook and cranny day and night. The beach seemed transformed into a gigantic club, full of the insignia of hip-hop culture. One lunchtime, Bettina flipped out when a flame-red Ferrari stopped outside our hotel and loaded up a bevy of barely-clad beauties, the word 'Wyclef' on the number plate. Oh yes, that's what a superstar's car looks like, absolutely. Wyclef Jean had made it bigger than big a few years before with The Fugees and the album *The Score,* and had now been working solo for a while.

It was certainly a spectacular week! In my memory, our stay in the Sunshine State seems like a surreal episode of *The Sopranos*, in which, after excessive bathing in the lukewarm Atlantic at 40 degrees in the shade, we cruise around the Art Deco neighbourhood of South Beach in an air-conditioned stretch limo with mirrored windows.

Live at the ICA

It was pretty hot in London, too, when we put up our set at the ICA on 22 July. The video beamer and screens were installed by a London-based company and worked just fine. That's always half the battle! A triptych of large screens hung behind us on the stage, with our keyboards arranged in front of them. Dave Anderson on the far left – he played most of the melodies and took on the vocoder parts. On the right was Karsten Binar, who coordinated three VHS recorders, a laptop and a camera, live. I stood in the middle with my synthesizer and wore a headset; in-ear monitors came later. Mathias was responsible for the sound, as the production's technical director. He contributed the necessary experience and collectedness during the set-up and soundcheck, supported by his friend Uwe Kanka, who had also driven the equipment to London.

I have to admit, I was nervous. Would my music hit the spot? At least as nerve-wracking, however, was how the fans would react to my interpretation of the classic Kraftwerk songs.

Doors opened at 7:30 p.m. Alan McGee – co-founder of indie label Creation Records – played a very special DJ set before our show, out of the kindness of his heart. I remember him playing 'She Said' from *Revolver*. It was a really cool gesture – hey, thanks a lot, Alan!

The ICA gradually filled up and then we finally started off, with 'The Camera'. While the Minimoog riff kicked in and the audience greeted us with cheers, we hooked into the system. At the first chord and the onset of the drumming, the applause felt like it increased by 20 decibels.

I looked out at the audience and spotted dozens of Kraftwerk and Elektric Music T-shirts. The venue was packed, even though we hadn't had much time for promotion. After the 'la la la's at the end of the song and the fade-out, we were knee-deep in applause. But the show must go on! We stuck to the running order on *Communication* and counted into our second number: 'I'm the Message'. A world premiere! Karsten played the film of the travelling sports reporter directly from his

549

laptop. Best male lead: the pedestrian pictogram, an Oscar-worthy performance.

When we started the third track, '15 Minutes of Fame', a few geeks couldn't help holding a spontaneous air-synth contest, or that's what it looked like from where I was. The rhythm, the drive, the groove got under everyone's skin. Movement came over their bodies, enthusiasm at every turn. That carried over to us and helped us relax. After 'Reality' and 'Electronic Apeman', a wave of approval lifted us off the floor. Then we got to 'Life'. I blocked out everything around me and concentrated on my vocals. It was only the roar of applause after the last 'I have to get on with my life' that brought me back to reality. By then, we had played about half of our planned 60 minutes. The London audience reacted to every song with applause, whoops and whistles.

But what would happen in the second half of the show? The last time I'd appeared in the UK with Kraftwerk was 1981, an incredible 22 years previously. How would the fans react now to my versions of our repertoire? Would they even accept me, the guy who left the band, playing our electro classics? I had at least co-composed them. But did anyone know that? We played 'Computer World', 'The Model', 'Trans-Europe Express', 'The Telephone Call' and as an encore 'Tour de France', which a few people saw as an ironic reference to the new Kraftwerk album. I didn't mean it that way, to be honest. After a good hour, we ended our showcase amid frenetic applause. I felt a huge sense of relief.

Immediate online reactions were a new phenomenon at that time. I was surprised to be guided by a search engine to umpteen websites reporting on our showcase, shedding a light on how the fans in London felt about it. On one blog, I read with amazement: 'Bartos was so alive, so amiable, appreciative and in touch with the crowd, giving each and every one a personal show. Classical training showed – it was all so effortless.' Sure, that's just one person's opinion, but there were lots of them along those lines. Negative reviews? Nope. The venerable *Guardian* also wrote about the almost hysterical reaction to our performance, noting that an ICA organizer said there were 200 applications for the guest list, even though there were only a few free tickets. And some disappointed fans apparently even sent money and asked for posters.[3] This initial feedback, the positive reaction from the audience and the press, was important to me. I thought if the Londoners understood my concert, people everywhere would. Kraftwerk's *Tour de France Soundtracks* got to number 21 in the British charts in August 2003, even hitting the top spot in Germany. That did feel pretty strange – I had been involved in the making of the original 'Tour de France' track, and now it was the album's title song. Things looked bleak in comparison for my own release: *Communication* charted in Germany at number 85 on 22 September 2003. That same week, *Tour de France Soundtracks* fell to number 76.

The Kraftwerk release took up the column inches, but I tried as best I could to promote my own album. A few reports did come about: the broadsheet *Die Welt* regarded my mentions of current bands as a 'major gesture',[4] the *Süddeutsche Zeitung* newspaper portrayed me as a 'romantic'[5] and *Spiegel Online* declared I had to be 'explained anew with every album'.[6] The occasional reviews in the British press were also largely positive.

UK Blitz Tour

Following the sensational reception at the ICA, a London concert agency wanted to put together an extensive European tour. First, though, we were to play Manchester, Glasgow and London in October. For timetabling reasons, I had to vary the line-up for this UK trip slightly, and now Rick McPhail came along as video operator instead of Karsten Binar. Rick comes from the wonderful town of Maine on the East Coast of the United States, and ended up in Hamburg many years ago. The fact that he played guitar in the German band Tocotronic didn't stop him from accepting a job in our little media circus. His laid-back demeanour brought a certain pop component into our group, and always relaxed the mood.

At that time, I'd been hearing a lot about the British band Client, essentially consisting of Kate Holmes and Sarah Blackwood. Their electro sound and chic uniforms – a hybrid of an Aeroflot stewardess outfit and the East German People's Police uniform – really made an impression. So I was very pleased when they asked me whether they could perform at our gigs as support band. And their performance really did work very well before our set.

My only memory of the Manchester gig is that nobody turned up. And that I left the B&B we'd been put into in the middle of the night and checked into a more trustworthy hotel – I couldn't sleep in the disastrous bed and the night porter was in an extremely altered state. At King Tut's in Glasgow, however, the Scottish audience gave us an emotional welcome that totally impressed me. I think it moved all of us. The small club was bursting at the seams, the audience almost standing on the stage, but the warmth and joy emanating in our direction overwhelmed us. The University of London gig also went well. Aside from the depressing bed and breakfast in Manchester, we had a good time in the UK. The average ticket sales were well below my expectations, however. And apparently, the agency felt the same way – they cancelled our planned European tour after the three gigs, with no further comment.

The Internet: Curse and Blessing for the Music Industry

That was the first time an agency dropped us without a word, and it hit me pretty hard. After all, if you don't play any gigs with a new album, it puts a huge damper on things. So I pulled the hand brake, switched on the hazard lights and got off the tour bus. Alright, I looked around for a new agency. But in February 2004, we got another piece of bad news: our label Home Records was leaving Sony – or perhaps you could say it was left by Sony – and wouldn't be able to make the next Karl Bartos album. They simply didn't have the financial means.

Once again, the music industry was in a time of turmoil. Only a few years before, they'd been throwing money around by the billion. The music business had reached its peak in 1999, making 26.6 billion dollars[7] in international turnover. And then came the MP3, and the facade began to crumble. Developed at the Fraunhofer Institute in Erlangen, Germany, in the early nineties by two computer scientists, the practical music compression format was initially popular with younger listeners. It made it

553

possible to shrink down music data from recording media and put it on the internet, where users then swapped to their hearts' content – leaving the music industry empty-handed.

It was in fact the first branch of culture to be shaken by the internet. And it happened out of arrogance – the music bosses were apparently unable to imagine their business model ever going out of style. They thought music listeners would never be willing to go without the haptic experience of playing a vinyl record or flicking through a lavishly designed CD booklet. Expensively produced videos would only ever be watched exclusively on a handful of music channels. And all this would be financed by the juicy income from selling records and CDs. That meant they missed their chance to work together on a legal infrastructure and offer user-friendly legal downloads themselves. Which was what enabled the illegal sharing portals to make such a killing. Exchanging and sharing music, getting it for free, was not only a lot of fun for cash-strapped teenagers, but simply became a normal way of handling the medium right across all the generations and classes.

When I got my hands on internal statistics showing the illegal downloads of my album *Communication* during that time, it took my breath away: the six-figure numbers were in no relation to the sales of the usual CD and vinyl formats – and of course, not a penny went into my or my record label's account.

Like a rabbit caught in headlights, the music industry profited little from Apple boss Steve Jobs launching iTunes in 2001, the first commercial download shop, where anyone can buy individual tracks or whole albums for a relatively small sum. It took the business more than ten years to adjust to the technological developments. During that time, it forfeited almost half of its worldwide turnover – a landslide from 23.8 billion dollars in 1999 to 14.3 billion in 2014.[8] The tide didn't turn until 2015, when sales both in Germany and around the world began to pick up – albeit minimally – and reached 15 billion US dollars in 2016.[9] The reason for that improvement: the internet! The technology that once broke the neck of the music industry now started creating rising turnover, through streaming, music on demand, flat-rates. At home, on the road, on the computer or smartphones. Anywhere, at any time.

The clear beneficiary of the streaming boom is the record companies. Not only do they collect monies for usage rights; they also pay the artists according to the old scheme of things – even though streaming does away with many costs, such as the production of physical media, their storage and distribution, and even performing right society fees.[10]

An artist receives less than one euro-cent per stream from Spotify, for instance. You can add up how many clicks would be necessary to make anything approaching a living.[11] In most cases, though, the artist isn't Spotify's client, it's their record company, which in turn takes off its own percentage, as contractually agreed in the past – and for most of the 30 million songs on Spotify, that contract dates back to pre-download or streaming times. In that case, the artist gets only part of the already tiny rate. The term 'million-selling record' suddenly has a very different meaning.

But back to the year 2004: illegal downloads, no budget for a new album, no tour – the music industry crisis hit me straight between the eyes. My mood was below sea level. I started asking myself if all the energy I was putting into my musical work was worth it in the first place. Then again, what was the alternative?

Music is what I'd always wanted to do. So I had to keep going, learning, moving with the times, no matter how confusing it was at the start.

It was the right decision, as it turned out. Business gradually picked up again. I was one of the protagonists in an image film for Deutsche Telekom, gave a lecture at Promax in Rome – a conference for TV and video production companies – a new concert agency in Frankfurt arranged gigs for us in Moscow and St Petersburg; I was a judge for the Oberhausen International Short Film Festival alongside the marvellous artist Pipilotti Rist, and we played at the Wave-Gotik meet-up in Leipzig for an entirely black-clad audience. I made an effort to forge as many contacts as I could, in all directions. Things moved along.

A Life in Pictures

In the summer of 2006, the award-winning TV director Hasko Baumann reached out to me. We'd met a few years previously when he filmed an episode of the ARTE series *Durch die Nacht mit . . .* in Paris with me and the French musician Benjamin Biolay. Now he asked me: 'Do you know Jean Giraud?' I had to pass on that one. 'Moebius, maybe?' he went on. Negative. Then he brought up the comics anthology *Métal Hurlant* and all of a sudden, I was in the picture, quite literally. Emil had always had a few issues of *Métal Hurlant* floating around his studio on Berger Allee. When Hasko then mentioned Giraud had written screenplays and concepts for numerous science fiction and fantasy films, such as *Alien, Tron, The Abyss* and *The Fifth Element*, the penny finally dropped. The Frenchman is one of the most famous and influential comic artists and writers ever. Hasko got to the point: 'I'm making a documentary about Giraud to be shown on ARTE next year, and I wondered if you might like to compose the soundtrack.'

Dramatic music? Of course I wanted to! However, there was a slight organizational problem: the film hadn't been made yet. To get into a workflow, we started by discussing the opening sequence. For the opening titles, Hasko suggested using 'I'm the Message' as orientation. So I put together a similar rhythm track and came up with a melody that fitted the mood. Then filming began. As soon as the team had a couple of sequences in the can, they put them on their server to provide me with impressions. We talked about appropriate music on the telephone. It went well.

I composed and produced the music in October and November. The first time I saw the finished seventy-minute film, I was amazed at how masterfully Hasko had cut and synchronized my music to the images. The premiere was held at the Cinestar cinema on Berlin's Potsdamer Platz in January 2007. *Moebius Redux – A Life in Pictures* has since been screened at many international festivals and is regularly shown on TV all over the world.

The Call

An academic position at a conservatory or university had never occurred to me during my time with Kraftwerk or the years that followed. I did get occasional offers, including from Düsseldorf, but there was always something else to do.

Then again, I'm forever interested in new settings and contexts, so in summer 2001 I accepted an invitation from Dr Holger Schulze to take part in the Berlin University of the Arts' conversations series SoundXchange. The idea was to discuss the shape of a new degree course, combining training on working with sound and an examination of modern auditive culture. Almost exactly a year later, they surprised me with the offer of a guest professorship in Sound Studies. I was thrilled, but the timing wasn't right because I was producing the *Communication* album. For better or for worse, I had to turn it down, but we kept in touch. When Sound Studies first presented itself to the public at a symposium in October 2003, I went to Berlin to listen to all the talks. The team was very welcoming and showed an interest in recruiting me as a lecturer.

And that's how it happened: in 2004 I received the call to the Berlin University of the Arts (UdK) as a guest professor of Auditory Media Design. On this occasion, the timing was perfect. The guest professors first met up for a colloquium on 10 June 2004.

There have always been scholars who take joy from music and enjoy making it themselves. The most prominent examples are probably Albert Einstein and his fellow physicist Heisenberg. The former played the violin, the latter piano. Science and art are sometimes a perfect match. When it comes to Kraftwerk's alleged scientific approach, though, I never understood it – neither during my active years with the band, nor afterwards. Perhaps that was one reason why I felt increasingly uncomfortable with various written materials from the past, at the beginning of my professorship. As luck would have it, most of the Ralf Hütter interviews had been published in the print media back then, and weren't available on the internet. It seemed much of it had dissolved into thin air. It turned out people at the UdK didn't connect me to our former PR expert's mysterious statements, to my relief, but saw me as a classical musician.

I had full autonomy on what to teach. Recently, my interest had shifted to the visual music of club culture. The abstract films of the 1920s had also left a lasting impression on me. My own cinematic experiments, which I filmed in my studio and in public, were exciting, and I was getting better at creating loops for our live show.

However, I didn't feel sufficiently qualified in visual communication to make it the basis of my teaching concept. Looking back, it makes sense that I began to take an interest in the virtual sound world of film, to expand my curriculum. My initial thought was of 'scoring', writing music for movies. I did some more research and soon immersed myself up to my ears in the articles and lectures of Walter Murch.[12]

One of his examples that really impressed me comes from *The Godfather*, among my all-time favourite films. Murch uses a sequence from Francis Ford Coppola's masterpiece to explain how a sound with an invisible source can express a character's mood, stance and emotion. His example, however, refers not to traditional film music, but to a screeching metallic noise audible in the background before Michael Corleone shoots the 'Turk' Solozzo and the corrupt cop McCluskey in an Italian restaurant and McCluskey's head falls forward onto his plate of veal – according to Solozzo, the best veal in town.

Although we don't see the sound's source, we viewers subconsciously allocate it to a train rounding a corner on an elevated railway. The setting is the Bronx, of course. Over the course of the conversation, the sound gets louder and louder, mirroring Michael's mental state shortly before he commits his first murder. Murch points out how effectively the sequence builds up between what we see and what we hear. Michael's placid, almost impassive face, revealing no emotions, and the constantly intensifying screech of the train create increasing tension, which is released with the gunshots that kill Solozzo and McCluskey. When I watched the film sequence again with Walter Murch's analysis in mind, I now heard and saw what I'd previously perceived unconsciously, as a deliberate acoustic layer, as sound design.

What fascinated me about this world of film sound is the creativity and cleverness with which people work in the field. What we hear in a film influences our perception of the storyline, without us even realizing. This new perspective has made me experience and assess films in a completely different way. The convergence of sound and image became my most important topic. I wanted to learn everything about the art of filmmaking, more about films' development and conception, and about film sound. Over time, I read not only the work of Walter Murch and Michel Chion, but also books by Claudia Gorbman, Barbara Flückinger, Jörg Lensing and others. And of course, at some point I ended up at Sergei Eisenstein's *Battleship Potemkin* (1925). My consolidated smatterings of knowledge and above all my own practical applications helped me to add extra content to my curriculum at the UdK for Auditory Media Design. This new input created a feedback loop that altered my perception of music in general. It was – I remember it precisely – as if I had opened up a whole new chapter of my biography in sound.

560

Guest Professorship in Auditory Media Design

Every time my train from Hamburg to Berlin stopped in Spandau on the northern edge of the capital, I couldn't help thinking of the Nuremberg Trials and the convicted men who served long terms in the war criminals' prison there. The building was demolished after Rudolf Hess's death in 1987, but the place name will probably forever be linked to the end of the Second World War. Zoo Station in the Charlottenburg district was the last stop on my regular journey. I would head towards Kurfürstendamm, cross the swanky shopping street at the Kranzlereck café and walk on to the University of the Arts building on Lietzenburger Strasse. The master's degree in 'Sound Studies – Acoustic Communication' was launched in April 2006.

I promptly brought Mathias on board as a lecturer, and the two of us drew up the final curriculum for Auditory Media Design together.

The first aptitude tests I took part in as a member of the teaching staff were exciting and educational. If I remember rightly, almost a hundred people applied for the course and one of the rare degree places. In the first round, the prospective students had to put their impressions on paper of a sound walk that took them along Kurfürstendamm and around the nearby Memorial Church. These notes and a subsequent interview showed us how well developed their perception of sound was. The biggest problem was having to decide on thirty applicants in the end. The tests took a whole week, but then we had our starting year students together.

561

On the first day of teaching, I attended an orchestral rehearsal conducted by Sir Simon Rattle at the Berlin Philharmonic, along with all the students. Afterwards, we sat outside on the grass and talked about our impressions. We looked at a few musical scores, placed the notation in relation to a music software time-line, and talked for example about the orchestral instruments' timbre. It was a very special day, not only for the students but for me as well, and I couldn't help but think of my audition back in 1974, when I was young and fresh and had my whole life ahead of me. It felt like things had come full circle.

Winter semester 2008/2009. I had been teaching in Room 318 all day and now I was alone. My head was buzzing. Automatically, I switched off half of the bright overhead lights and looked out of the window. It was already growing dark outside. In the distance, the famous illuminated Mercedes symbol was rotating on the roof of the Europa Center mall.

The plan was to head straight to Zoo Station to catch the next train to Hamburg. But just then, Holger Schulze – the professor heading up the degree course – came bowling into the room. He had a young man in tow – in his early 30s, I guessed, shorn hair, casual clothing – who he introduced as Sascha Wild from Frankfurt. Sascha might make a great addition to my specialist area as a lecturer, he suggested. Apparently, he was an excellent musician and very experienced in digital signal processing. Holger was right: I could use some support. And here was Sascha. The buzzing in my head was getting louder, I was tired and almost incapable of speaking. But we managed to talk somehow, and then I headed off to the station.

Considering the unfavourable circumstances of our first meeting, it's astounding how well we got on. Sascha had a degree in instrument teaching in the jazz field, played percussion and piano, was absolutely top-rate at electronic media, and knew his way around pop music. And although he was still young, he made an impressive lecturer. But our work was to go beyond that – as we'll soon see.

I met a lot of people with outstanding skills at the UdK, who impressed me with their creativity and motivation. My time there broadened my horizons to an incredible extent. But after a few years, the constant commute between Hamburg and Berlin started to drag, and I also noticed I was missing something key. I was focusing entirely on explaining things, putting them in context, saying who did what, when and where. My mind was filled with history and theory. And although we did keep going back to what lies below, the essence of music, I felt the lack of making music, I really did. I missed starting at zero, me alone with a blank sheet of paper, sitting down at a piano or an empty screen and creating new music. In the summer semester of 2008, I held a seminar entitled 'The Abbey Road Recording Sessions.' However, in the following year I ended my guest professorship at the UdK Berlin.

Muzak

My many train journeys to and from Berlin had been a good opportunity to prepare for my teaching. I was usually reading several books at once, scattering their pages with adhesive notes and scribbling remarks all over them. It was during these train rides that I also wrote the first sketches for this book. I always had something to do while travelling. The annoying thing was that the other passengers in the carriage seemed to enjoy nothing more than talking on the phone: MPs chatted to their party-political buddies, lawyers to their colleagues or clients, businesspeople had relocated their offices to our carriage and had their secretaries line up appointments for the next day, advertising execs explained campaigns to someone or other. Grandparents informed their grandchildren they'd soon be arriving, husbands and wives asked what was for dinner, lovers exchanged heated verbal missives, and friends discussed their emotional issues for hours on end. Almost everyone spoke absolutely freely, casually and with no regard for anyone around them.

My most amazing experience was with a judge. Although I was sitting less than a metre away from her, she told the person on the other end of the line all sorts of details of a court case that clearly shouldn't have been aired in public. Then she dictated a letter, including file number. When she simply didn't stop, I started reading aloud at the same volume from Barry Truax' *Acoustic Communication*. All of a sudden, she seemed to remember my existence, grabbed her bag and coat and left the carriage, pretty annoyed but not interrupting her monologue. As a consequence of all these ridiculous situations, I soon got a hearing aid technician to fit me with ear plugs, to give me some protection from the cacophony in the train carriages.

Alongside the telephonitis, I also noticed more and more people wearing on-ear or in-ear headphones in public. They decoupled themselves from acoustic reality and created their own soundtrack for their surroundings, independent of time and place. Although it was obviously voluntary, in a strange way

564

it reminded me of 'elevator music', which I'd first heard on our initial tour of the States. Back then, the generic name for so-called background music in departments stores, hotels, airports and lifts was 'muzak'. The Muzak company spent decades working on manipulating human behaviour – for example employees or customers – by playing music at them. The actual danger of this constant backdrop sound is that while we do hear something, we don't listen to it consciously. This acoustic garbage does nothing but block up our nervous systems. Real listening, in contrast, means paying attention to what's going on and following it mentally.

These days, music is omnipresent. In public space, at the supermarket, in a taxi, on a plane, at a restaurant, on hold while calling the dentist: we're constantly exposed to music, like it or not. We don't get to choose it. What is communicated via this permanent acoustic pollution is the message that music is a minor issue. So minor that we can even get it (almost) for free on the streaming sites.

We can demonize streaming or come to terms with it; that's up to every individual. It seems we're currently experiencing the next developmental stage of music consumption. And yet we shouldn't underestimate the fact that streaming has altered the general understanding of pop music. Streaming has an influence on how we hear and understand music. And that in turn changes music itself: there are new criteria for what is a success and what isn't.

Streaming sites make decisions on behalf of listeners – they curate the 'soundtrack to your life'. Their aim: 'To find the right music for every moment – on your phone, computer, tablet and other devices' (Spotify). Music for daydreaming, for falling in

565

love, to banish heartbreak and keep amateur athletes moving. The job is mostly done by algorithms, which filter moods out of collected data. It's an exception for humans, perhaps even musicians, to compile these recommendation lists. Curated music is tailored to the individual and their 'individual needs', and the individual then listens to it in isolation, via headphones. More and more, one thing is being pushed into the background – the very thing pop music used to stand for: shared human experiences. Music in the streaming age is no longer the medium that connects me up with an idea, gives me an identity, expresses my life and my generation, the way pop music was ever since the days of rock'n'roll in the fifties. It appears that music has become a by-product with no value. In a sound cosmos in which I can listen to all the music in the world, randomly and therefore with no meaning, music loses significance, becomes arbitrary. It becomes muzak.

Everyone can take their own stance on the matter, but I think it certainly wasn't this business model that made music an essential element of human culture.

Frequent Traveller

During my time teaching at the UdK Berlin, our live business gradually began to pick up. We played at the Roskilde Festival in Denmark, where I waded ankle-deep in mud as tradition demands. Another booking for the Arvika Festival in Sweden was cancelled at the last minute – the organizers had booked Kraftwerk as well, and they seemed unable to imagine us both together . . . We flew to Bogota in Colombia, where we spent a week around an amazing pool in a James Bond-style hotel at tropical temperatures, we got lifted onto the stage of the Frankfurt Opera House by elevator while playing 'The Model', and performed open air by night in Tenerife, under a full moon. At some point we were even guests at a festival in Caracas, Venezuela, at which Roberto involuntarily made the acquaintance of ecstasy, slipped into his drink. His stage show certainly impressed me. Our 'travelling circus' really got around.

A tour of Germany took us to Berlin, playing at the historic Haus des Rundfunks. In the almost sold-out broadcasting house, the presence of my UdK colleagues was a special challenge. On top of that, I was told, my former Düsseldorf bandmates' concert agent was sitting in the front row. By this point, Kraftwerk had mutated into a touring band. Had they started to miss contact with the audience, having fans close at hand? Record and CD sales had shrunk considerably, and only live appearances could compensate for that once free-flowing income stream. All the bands hit the road again. It wasn't without irony for me to see Ralf and Florian suddenly developing an unbridled lust to play live.

In the summer of 2005, we performed at the audio-visual festival Optronica in London. The duo Addictive TV gave a virtuoso VJ performance, which inspired me to take control of the visual layer at future live appearances. I felt there was far greater potential in musically abstract images than in musical arrangements, so I decided to give up my position on keyboards and operate only on the visual level. Improvising live with film clips was new and exciting, and doubtlessly the intuitive and enjoyable side of working with visual media. But I also got to know the other side, the preparation of the visuals, which took

567

up more and more time. I was continually expanding my film archive, teaching myself how to work the film editing programs necessary for creating the visual level. And I was gradually getting better in practice.

So as to be able to react flexibly to booking enquiries, along-side the audio-visual live show with Roberto I put together a DJ/VJ set, which we toured with. Unbeatable in terms of economics. After a few gigs, we found that people wanted me to play either my own music or 'my' Kraftwerk songs, rather than a curated programme of my favourite electronic dance music tracks. So I changed the repertoire to give them what they wanted.

Roberto took on the DJ part, and I fired up the films live and sang or spoke live to a couple of songs. Over time, I expanded the set-up and Mathias took over from Roberto. Mathias' job on stage included sound direction, oops, I mean DJing, mixing the various sources – by this point we were using several laptops and HD recorders – and the live vocoder vocals. To optimize our workflow on the road, we added the sound engineer Sven Mouhcine to the team. That meant we were always certain of having good sound.

The three of us criss-crossed the world during the second half of the 2000s. Our bookings took us to Austria, Scandinavia, Britain, Luxembourg, Poland, Hungary, Russia, Italy – and we occasionally worked in Germany, too. We went on a mini-tour around Brazil and Asia, where we travelled via Bangkok to Japan and played in Osaka, Tokyo and Ibaraki. We usually stuck to hand luggage, containing our laptops, HD recorders, DI boxes, cables and the bare necessities for our personal needs. I remember the endless hours we spent in airports and hotels. And then the inescapable security checks, where I had to keep unpacking my bag and putting everything on the conveyor and was regularly waved over to a special, window-less room for intensive checks on all the electronics. The world has never been a simple place, but after 11 September 2001, travel in particular got more and more complicated. At least for someone like me, who lugged all sorts of electronics around with him.

It was only a question of time until I got upgraded to 'frequent traveller' status and was entitled to hang out in airport VIP lounges, sipping ginger ale and coffee. I soon worked out that the verb 'to travel' is derived from the French 'travailler', to work. Nonetheless, there was no way to overlook the fact that air traffic was constantly increasing, even then. And I was very much aware that flying is no good for the environment. That didn't mean I felt guilty at the time, though. In this context, I'm reminded of a booklet that fell into my hands at the Robert Schumann Conservatory back in the early 1970s. I flicked through it in the canteen and put it aside without a thought, not knowing at the time how important it was: *The Limits to Growth*. A report on the situation of humankind, commissioned by the Club of Rome.[13] Thankfully, today's young people aren't as indifferent as I was back then. Fifty years on, I do wonder what CO_2 footprint my generation has left behind.

Like many of us, I've begun thinking more and more about the state of the world. For instance, about the curious alliance that business and democracy have entered into in the West. We now have brutally globalized capitalism and the myth, repeated ad nauseum, that our wellbeing depends on unceasing growth. We're still trusting in the 'invisible hand' of the markets,

569

which allegedly regulate everything in all our best interests. The influence of radical market-focused thinking, now referred to as neoliberalism, has us firmly in its grip. The state ought to keep out of matters of the economy – or at least that's what the wealthy say, the businesspeople, bankers and economic-liberal politicians. From the perspective of radical market-focused economists, the dynamo of successful business is the selfishness of homo economicus, who weighs up every decision rationally according to its benefit to him. To go by this theory, every person is the architect of his own fortune – profits and increasing wealth are a well-earned reward. The less successful among us are to blame for their own misfortune. This established system is also nourished by belief in technical innovations, with their new digital business models and global competition. The only thing is: would growth even take place if the true costs of business for society – or rather, for humanity – were factored in, for example in energy production? So far so good; or so bad, depending on how you see it. However, 'we', the *homo economicus* species, have become rather too successful. As we've known for some time now, our marvellous civilization is radically destroying the prerequisites for life on our planet.

As I write, the cultures of the world are fighting against coronavirus (Covid-19). For some scientists, this pandemic is only 'one element in a matrix of evidence that what we face with this virus is not a rare event, but the emerging visibility and tangibility of systematic problems. These are based on the mutually intensifying interplay of societal and technological dynamics and the rapid deterioration of the global environmental situation.'[14]

Climate change is proceeding at full speed and we can predict the date when it will have a significant effect on life on earth. Too pessimistic? Am I a doom merchant, a querulant, a nihilist, a misanthrope? No idea . . . It came as no surprise to me that the Volkswagen CEO called for another major government stimulus programme for the automotive industry in the face of the collective corona lockdown. What else would he do? It's capitalism. Strangely enough, the state suddenly comes back into play in crises of all kinds – the 2008 financial crisis springs to mind immediately. We're told it's all about preserving jobs. In truth, the implementation of neoliberal philosophy means nothing other than a permanent redistribution, from bottom to top. There's one guiding principle: if the big guys are pacified, the little people might catch a few crumbs from their table.[15]

Looking at future elections in Germany – where might they take us? Will we still be governed by parties whose politicians and lobbyists continue to preach uncontrolled growth as if hypnotized, simply going on as before – possibly until the system crashes entirely? We really are living in strange times . . .

New Releases Out Now!

Back to 2005: in June, a live Kraftwerk double album came out with the title *Minimum-Maximum*. Alongside all the usual formats, it was also released on DVD. It contains – or so it says on the case – gigs recorded in 2004. It's certainly not my most burning task to comment on the content of this release. But as you might imagine, I was pleased about the unexpected output, because I have a share in ten of the tracks as co-writer. However, my joy was mitigated when I heard from people in the know that the album wasn't exactly a bestseller – it seemed to be gathering a lot of dust on a lot of record-shop shelves.

When design concerns and artistic skills form a unit, they grant better prospects for aesthetic success. The British band Coldplay is a good example. One of their singles played in a different league, not only commercially. The band appeared to have experimented with the hookline from 'Computer Love', developing it into their song 'Talk'.

The release in December 2005 didn't come unexpectedly, as Coldplay had got official permission via the music publishing companies some time beforehand. I liked the song and I was happy with the deal. It meant the melody I'd come up with many years ago, on a piano in the Krefeld Music School's pavilion, became a small part of a new composition with seven co-writers: Guy Berryman, Jonny Buckland, Will Champion, Chris Martin, Ralf Hütter, Emil Schult and Karl Bartos.

The Coldplay album *X & Y* stayed in the charts around the world from 2005 to 2008 and claimed multiple gold and platinum status. In the UK alone, it went nine times platinum, in Ireland eight times, Australia six times, Canada five times, the USA three times, in Germany three times platinum, and on and on . . .

Florian Schneider, Ex-Kraftwerk

Once in a while, like in November 2008, Bettina and I go to Düsseldorf to meet up with old friends: Wolfgang and his wife Zuhal, Bodo and Brigitte Staiger, and of course Joachim

Dehmann, who still had his workshop on Mintropstrasse, directly opposite the Kling Klang Studio. Everything in the courtyard looked exactly as it always had done. I parked our car in my old spot and switched off the engine. We stayed in the car to discuss a few logistical details, planning our return to Hamburg the next day.

There was an unexpected knock on the window. I couldn't believe my eyes: it was Florian. He gestured and grinned, his radiant blue eyes looking right at me. On the spur of the moment, he suggested a drink in a café on Graf-Adolf-Strasse. Sitting beside us, Florian gave us a buoyant smile and announced he had left Kraftwerk. He seemed to be in a good mood, composed and communicative. We talked for a good while. Ralf had left the Mintropstrasse premises and built himself a studio outside of Düsseldorf, where he was now working with a team of engineers and technicians. Of course he was. It's hard to imagine Ralf without a flock of industrious helpers. As ever, money was a central topic of our conversation, and we also talked about something I knew little about at that point – planned concerts in museums. Florian seemed to reject the idea categorically. The last thing we discussed was our experiences as guest professors – him for two years at the Centre for Art and Media Karlsruhe (ZKM), me for five years at the UdK Berlin. I found out that Florian's father Paul Schneider-Esleben, who had died in 2005, was a friend of the ZKM head Peter Weibel. It was presumably the two of them who arranged the first Kraftwerk gig at the institution back in 1997.

Then we said our goodbyes. It was good to see him again, but also strange, in a way. Even though Florian had kept to the superficial level and not given away what he really thought and

573

felt, I couldn't get our conversation out of my head on the way back to Hamburg. It was to be our last encounter. Florian died on 21 April 2020, shortly after his 73rd birthday.

My Thoughts about Sound

In 2009 the last Kraftwerk product to date, *Der Katalog*, came onto the market: the long-postponed rerelease of the eight studio albums from *Autobahn* to *Tour de France Soundtracks* on vinyl and CD. Curiously, Kraftwerk repeated this *Katalog* idea in 2017 – this time pepped up with 3D animations and so-called live recordings of the most recent concerts. Eventually in 2020 a range of digital releases of the repertoire were available to stream and download.

But back to the first *Katalog* from 2009: the remastering and repackaging of the old records had created a 'new' product, which garnered a positive reaction from fans and the media. I too was among the buyers of the box. Once again, the credits were written from Ralf and Florian's perspective, heavily featuring their own names in varying functions.

It's clear that Ralf never cared about 'history lessons',[16] 'but about the here and now.' And we know he considered it 'one of the basic faults of society, to look backward and all this fool stuff.'[17] In my opinion, however, a society's history is absolutely necessary for its orientation. After all, we can only tell who we are if we know where we come from. And that's why the past should always be present – at least in our minds. Looking in the 'back mirror'[18] is actually, quite the opposite, highly important for our current existence and for shaping the future.

That holds all the more true today, when the world is facing all-encompassing change.

And what happens if we edit the past? Is truth individual, is objectivity impossible, is everything really a matter of opinion? In George Orwell's *1984*, Room 101 is all about facts and how we interpret them. During Winston's reeducation, the functionary O'Brian recalls the party motto: 'Who controls the past controls the future; who controls the present controls the past.'[19]

Whatever the case: the release of *Der Katalog* prompted a desire in me not to leave the interpretation of my past solely to my former colleagues, and to tell the story of how our music came about from my own perspective. I wanted to do so in a kind of travel journal through time, with the various stops along the way, their content, people and emotions. There were to be no 'unpersons' in my account.

That would be the classic approach to memoir-writing, but I was also interested in another layer. During my years at the UdK, I had often thought about my biography in sound. I imagined a portrait of myself through my musical development. It would include the music I had come across in the course of my life, and I would try to put my thoughts about sound into words. Previously a vague plan, it now started to take shape.

NOTES

1. Susan Sontag: *On Photography*. Farrar, Straus and Giroux, New York, 1977
2. The quote is taken from the 1960 film *Le Petit Soldat*.
3. 'Desperately seeking Kraftwerk.' By Alexis Petridis, *The Guardian*, July 2003

4. 'Kling und Klang.' By Michael Pilz, *Die Welt*, 5 August 2003

5. 'Karl Bartos über Tradition.' By Alexander Gorkow, *Süddeutsche Zeitung*, 30/31 August 2003

6. 'Karl Bartos vs. Kraftwerk – Nichts ist bei mir Deko.' By Stefan Krulle, *Spiegel Online*, 11 September 2003

7. Source: Statista 2017. Online: https://de.statista.com/statistik/daten/studie/ 182361/umfrage/weltweiter-umsatz-der-musikindustrieseit-1997/

8. Source: Statista 2017. Online: https://de.statista.com/statistik/daten/studie/ 182361/umfrag e/weltweiter-umsatz-der-musikindustrieseit-1997/

9. The worldwide music industry's turnover has continued to grow since 2015. In 2020, it hit 21.6 billion US dollars. Some 14.6 billion of that sum came from streaming and digital income, making up 68 per cent of the total turnover. Source: Statista / www.statista.com

10. Tim Renner, ex-head of Universal, explained it as follows: '[. . .] according to the parameters that also applied for CDs or LPs. The price of a recording medium also includes record-company costs, like production, warehousing, shopping, billing, returns – but also the Performing Right Society fee, which the streaming platforms have to pay. With streaming, all these costs fall by the wayside – and the label profits twice over, while the artist gets duped.' In: 'Sind Streaming-Dienste Feinde der Musiker?' By Frank Schmiechen, *Gründerszene*, 23 December 2016.

11. 'Was verdient ein Musiker bei Spotify?' By Sven Grundberg, *t3n-digital pion-ieers*, 4 December 2013.

12. To name one example: Walter Murch: *Sound Design: The Dancing Shadow*. Faber & Faber: London 1995

13. *The Limits to Growth*, Universe Books, New York, 1972. Authored by Dennis L. Meadows, Donella H. Meadows, Erich Zahn, Peter Milling.

14. 'Der Schock hat System.' By Christoph Rosol, Jürgen Renn and Robert Schlögl, *Süddeutsche Zeitung*, 15 April 2020

15. Cf. Friedrich August von Hayek: *The Road to Serfdom*. Routledge Press, 1944.

16. 'For Kraftwerk the world began in the 1920s, with Fritz Lang's utopian cinematic visions of machine-land,' 'Where the scientists and artists are working hand in hand' [. . .] 'We are the children of Wernher von Braun and Fritz Lang. We start from the 20s and jump to the 70s and 80s. We're not concerned with history lessons, we are concerned with today. I think that's one of the basic

faults of society, to look backward and all this fool stuff. It's like, if you are driving a fast car and you look too much in the back mirror you might crash in front. We'd rather watch what we're doing right now, what we could do today or tomorrow.' See: 'Better Living Through Chemistry,' by Toby Goldstein, *New Musical Express*, 24 December 1977

17. Ibid.
18. Ibid.
19. George Orwell: *Nineteen Eighty-Four*. Penguin 1949

16

STATE OF PLAY

The Room where Time Revolved around Itself. Iron Crystal Music. Tokyo in a Major Key. Rhythm in the Flow of Time. Screenings. 90 Minutes. Image and Sound. The Cultural Subject. Progress as a Shining Promise.

The Room where Time Revolved around Itself

Early in 2010, I happened to run into Gunther Buskies. We'd first met at the end of the 1990s, when he was working as a product manager for Universal. In the meantime, Gunther had set up his own business, the indie label Tapete Records, and he also brought out electronic music on his label Bureau B. He asked in passing whether I had any old unpublished sound recordings in my safe. If so, he said, he could put them out on Bureau B. Maybe under the title 'Early Recordings' or 'The Düsseldorf Tapes' or something along those lines.

Originally, I wasn't all that thrilled with the idea. Why look back? I was busy making films for my live show and working on new songs, and things were going well. But Gunther didn't let it drop. And then I couldn't get the idea out of my head either – all of a sudden, it seemed not a million miles away from my plan to write an autobiography in sound. As it turned out,

I did have the recordings, and all the devices required to play them, in my archives. And miraculously, everything still worked perfectly. So I started transferring all my material from the seventies, eighties and nineties into the computer, in chronological order: audio tape cassettes, stereo tapes, multitracks, Betamax video tapes, DAT cassettes, MIDI files, sampler data on diskettes, SyQuest, Zip and Jaz media. Then there were my notes, in handwriting or as musical notation.

For the first time in a long while, I listened to our sound recordings from the Kling Klang Studio. It was a remarkable moment – out of the blue, I thought of the word *Heimat*, home. I don't mean the country I happened to be born in. No, the home that I thought of exists in my memory. It's a place in my mind. I see my mother Rosa and Uncle Sepp there, sitting by the stove in Berchtesgaden and making music together. John Lennon is reading the *Daily Mail*; a half-asleep Keith Richards hears Jack the gardener clumping around; and Ray Davis is watching Terry and Julie at Waterloo Station . . . Elsewhere, I come across Miles Davis, Charlie Parker, Keith Jarrett and all the other jazz musicians. All of a sudden, I'm at the Robert Schumann Conservatory, listening to Bach's *Goldberg Variations*. In my imagination, measures of the *Magic Flute* meld with Beethoven's *Pastoral Symphony*; Franz Schubert tinkles the ivories – the *Tristan* chord floats unresolved around the room; the waves in Debussy's *La Mer* are forever breaking on the cliffs of the Mediterranean; and Igor Stravinsky is drinking tea in Nadia Boulanger's Parisian salon. And precisely in this imagined homeland, this place that contains the things that give my life meaning, I also find our writing sessions. The compositions take me back to the room where we played like children and time revolved around itself on the tape recorder: moments caught as if in a camera's flash, scraps of words, exuberance, enthusiasm, the bright light from above and the sound rides by night . . . It seems our music has withstood alienation, whatever kind it may be.

After reviewing, listening to and ordering the material, I could suddenly imagine continuing a few of my early ideas from today's point of view. I liked the thought of coming face to face with the young musician Karl Bartos. I liked it a lot, in fact.

Iron Crystal Music

The first idea I played around with was a rhythmic orchestral figure in 7/4 time, which I had written down years before. The bitonal chords of Stravinsky's *Le Sacre du Printemps* were wrapped up in it, somehow. To be honest I'd rather not know exactly what goes on in my subconscious. But now and then, something pops up to the surface, and that was the case with these rhythmic sounds. All at once, the Atomium appeared in my mind's eye, the symbolic building in the European capital of Brussels.

I started by loading a few Atomium photos into my VJ software and experimenting with them and the orchestra ostinato. It wasn't long before I found I could create an extremely dynamic series of images using the architectural recreation of an iron crystal. Next, I got hold of a documentary about the 1958 World's Fair, for which the Atomium was first built. The original film footage was so impressive that it pretty much commissioned a composition of its own accord. The building represents the post-war era's naive faith in technological progress, with its great white hope of atomic energy. Nothing could have been further from my mind, however, than writing a song of praise to nuclear power stations. What I wanted was to find a musical equivalent to the Atomium. But how should my iron crystal music sound? I twizzled a few musical building blocks around. And once I found I could sing the word 'A – to – mi – um' in the 7/4 meter, the Atomium – the model of an iron crystal molecule, enlarged 165 billion times – was already almost transposed into music.

It was while I was working on the piece that the terrible catastrophe in the Fukushima nuclear power plant came about, on 11 March 2011. I'm sure everyone remembers the horrific images from Japan. In Germany, the disaster led to a government decision to phase out atomic energy. Fukushima made the great dangers of nuclear power tragically clear, showing us that only renewable energies can secure progress and our very existence. From my perspective, the Atomium stands for the rise and fall of the nuclear industry.

Shortly after that, the question arose: How do I get footage? It wasn't as easy as it might sound – the Atomium is protected by copyright, and the heirs to the engineer André Waterkeyn keep a strict eye on the maintenance of certain standards. A lively email exchange came about, but in the end we got permission to film, and Bettina and I made our way to the Square de l'Atomium in Brussels to capture the building visually.

Photos or films alone can't do justice to the construction's dimensions. That only happens once you're standing in front of the sci-fi-style linked orbs, which seem to have landed in Brussels like a UFO. The nine stainless steel spheres are all 18 metres in diameter, with space for up to 200 people. They are connected by twenty tubes, which we crossed on escalators. In the middle of the 120-metre building, a lift catapulted us up to the panorama sphere.

It was an amazing feeling to wander around the monument, touch the daring constructions and try to capture the unique atmosphere on film. For me, the Atomium – this gigantic model of an iron crystal – remains a symbolic piece of architecture with a breathtaking effect on the observer.

Tokyo in a Major Key

On the subject of huge buildings: isn't it often the case that situations, landscapes, cities seem overwhelming, almost oversized, when you experience them for the first time? And if you return later on, you see everything on a different scale. That was how I felt in Japan in 2011. We were booked for the Metamorphose Festival southwest of Tokyo. It was surely mere coincidence that we were put in the Keio Plaza Hotel. Thirty years had passed since my last visit. In comparison to the *Computer World* days, the hotel no longer looked enormous to me. On closer inspection of the foyer, I was amazed to see that the telephone booths and world time clocks we had posed with for press photos in 1981 had lasted down the decades.

The festival was cancelled due to a typhoon, which gave us a bit of a shock. Thank goodness, the region was spared a major disaster, however. On the next day, the weakened offshoots of the storm dropped their rain on us and the temperature returned to normal. Sleepless and jetlagged, I left the hotel, walked the streets and took countless photos. Out of nowhere, a sound:

I hear a major third. The traffic lights are sonified – Tokyo in a major key.

The festival organizers didn't manage to get a new venue for the headliners, the Flaming Lips, at short notice. Other bands in the line-up, for instance 808 State, were to perform in clubs to make up for the cancellation. Our concert was moved to the Warehouse 274 Club. The lightning-speed internet promotion worked somehow, and the place was bursting at the seams. I think we pulled off a pretty good show. But I was gradually reaching my limits in improvisation with film sequences. The media sets to each song – the reservoirs in which the films are visible as preview images on the laptop and can be called up – were getting ever larger and I needed more and more concentration to harmonize them to my vocals. On top of that, I was missing clever rhythmic cuts and thereby real synchronicity of sound and image. Something had to change, urgently.

Rhythm in the Flow of Time

Directly after my return from Japan, I began producing the films for my new album. Films? It goes without saying that I'll always be a musician, but my way of composing music has changed radically. Essentially, I've been working audio-visually for some time now. The rhythm of the images inspires me more and more often. For instance, I composed the 'Atomium' music like a soundtrack to visual loops that I watched. The whole process only became possible, of course, through the simultaneous use of film and music software on the computer.

583

For the next piece, I came up with a chord sequence and overlaid it with a longer theme. Then I made a bassline to accompany it. When I looped the song structure on the computer and played along, the first line of the lyrics came to me: 'Ich fahr die ganze Nacht / bis ich bei dir bin.' (I drive all night / until I'm with you.) I briefly wondered whether it was cool to use the verb *fahren* – almost forty years after 'Autobahn' – but then I thought: fuck it!

I knew the track 'Nachtfahrt' would form part of the repertoire for our new live show, as would 'Atomium'. So I drew a storyboard for the film. A drive through the night leads automatically to rain and windscreen wipers, doesn't it? It does in my mind, anyway. The movements of the wipers produced a rhythmic element, into which I could cut or superimpose – it would link all the shots together perfectly. And then coincidence came to my aid.

One warm summer evening, Bettina and I were sitting on our patio when it started to rain. Actually, the word 'rain' is an understatement. Masses of water veritably burst out of low, heavy clouds and then one of the most dramatic thunderstorms we could remember broke over us. Fascinated, we gazed at nature's spectacle. Suddenly, Bettina took the initiative: 'We can't miss this opportunity,' she exclaimed, grabbing the camera, and off we set in the car, heading north. I sat behind the wheel and Bettina performed all sorts of acrobatic feats to film me from different useful perspectives. That's what I call an electric session – partly because lightning split the sky above our car every few minutes, which Bettina was determined to capture on film. After an hour, the storm was over and the material we needed for the 'Nachtfahrt' film was in the can.

I originally wanted to compose a purely percussive track for the album – a kind of percussion solo. But I abandoned the idea and instead took my orientation from Hans Richter's 1921 film *Rhythmus 21*. I soon had a line floating around my head, which I adapted literally into a film sequence: 'Das Rechteck, das Dreieck, der Kreis bewegen sich auf der Zeitachse.' (The square, the triangle and the circle move along the time axis.) When I came to think about the music, I remembered an old recording. It was the track I called 'Dom', which we had used as a basis for 'Computer World'. The first demo sounded approximately like the first four bars of 'Rhythmus'. My Polymoog provided exactly the right sound for the motif I discovered in my notebook and developed into a theme. Along with my vocals, speech synthesis and vocoder, I orchestrated the Mellotron's cello and vocal choir. The context called for analogue bass, naturally enough. For the film to go with the song 'Rhythmus', I wanted to build a miniature monument to time, because time of course is what holds everything together. György Ligeti's *Poème Symphonique für 100 Metronome* occurred to me, and as a symbol for musical time, I filmed a rotating metronome.

While I was working on 'Rhythmus' the artist Laurie Anderson performed in Hamburg. Her *Delusion* programme was a personal investigation of death. At one point in her performance, she read out a text she had written on her mother's death. Written and read without a trace of sentimentality, it managed to touch me deeply nonetheless. Perhaps it had something to do with my upcoming 60th birthday; who knows. Generally, we're constructed to block out the thought of death. But I'll admit I have started thinking about it more often, as I get older. A strange melancholy, a feeling I didn't experience as a young man, comes over me. It's probably perfectly normal, just that nobody talks about it.

This is where God comes into play. An estimated 80 per cent of the global population believes in a god. I'm not one of them, but I wouldn't rule out his or her existence entirely. There are things in our lives, after all, that we can't explain or prove. In Kraftwerk we never talked about God, as far as I recall. 'We're all absolutely sober, clear-thinking individuals. God or any other of those supernatural imps has no place in our cosmos,'[1] Ralf once pronounced in his inimitable style, just after I'd left the band.

My impression is that deeply religious people – though I can only speak for Christians – find comfort in their spirituality in times of trouble. Their religious worldview includes eternal life or living in paradise, an idea that seemed suspicious to me even at confirmation class. In the meantime, however, I've learned that for devout Christians, life beyond time begins not on their death, but in the present: God invented time but he himself exists outside of it.

Sacred music has always addressed the wish to understand time as a phenomenon and to overcome its inevitable passage, for instance the seventeenth-century Protestant hymn by Michael Frank, *Ach wie flüchtig, ach wie nichtig* (*Ah, how fleeting, ah how insignificant*), on which Bach based his famous choral cantata, premiered in Leipzig in 1724.

Music and life are similar in many respects, perhaps because both phenomena move forward in time and are ephemeral. I think of the wise Ray Davis, who succinctly compared life to a song. At the end, Davis says, the chorus is repeated several times before it fades out or ends abruptly. No matter how much we might wish to hold onto a moment, we know all the better that it's not possible. The instant, that moment, can only happen in the flow of life.

And yet music has the gift of letting us apparently go back to the past, as Karen Carpenter sang impressively in 'Yesterday Once More' (1973). And when we reconstruct music that's several hundred years old, we also experience an unparalleled journey through time. The music of past ages comes alive again during its performance. It lives on in our minds and is handed down from one generation to the next. Perhaps my perception of music is not exactly equivalent to what many people feel in their belief in God, but for me, it gives us an idea of life beyond time.

Thinking about all this, I came up with more questions than answers – but I did find the lyrics for a new song. A simple melody and a dash of humour bring these big issues down to earth. I borrowed the title 'The Tuning of the World' from R. Murray Schafer.[2] The Canadian composer and scientist's book is about the ordering of sounds.

One good example of how some compositions change over time is 'Musica ex Machina'. In the early 1990s, I recorded a rock-hard piece of music in my Düsseldorf project studio and gave it the working title of 'Bombast'. The track was first performed in 1994 in a quick and dirty version at a handful of Elektric Music gigs. When Bernard and Johnny later invited me to work on their Electronic album, we returned to the unfinished song and 'Bombast' became 'Imitation of Life' and made it onto a single B-side and the album *Get the Message – The Best of Electronic*. For *Off the Record* – that was to be the name of my new long-player – I went right back to the original version, after almost twenty years. My lyrics are on the subject of recording sound, and out of 'Bombast' alias 'Imitation of Life' grew 'Musica ex Machina' – after the book of that name by the musicologist Fred K. Prieberg.[3] What a strange career for a few notes strung together, don't you think?

Outside its coordinates, music means nothing. A tune, a chord, a rhythm is abstract, makes no sense. Music works on the basis of the laws of physics and acoustics. When it sounds out, it creates a broad spectrum of impressions on our senses. But everyone hears and feels differently. Our reactions often have very little to do with the thoughts and emotions of the music's creator. Exactly this – the mysterious nature of musical reception – was what I wanted to capture in my 'Musica ex Machina' film. My concept was to use the sensations reflected in people's faces and gestures while listening to music as my raw material. However, I could never have created this experiment of the senses without Gunther Buskies' enthusiastic help. He managed to drum up more than thirty people who wanted to be in the film. From a toddler to a grandma, from a courier to an artist – they were all kinds of people. Filming in the Bureau B office, they all sat on a chair in front of the camera, wearing head-phones. First I gave each of them a little introductory talk, and then we played them a medley. To provoke clear reactions, I made sure the contrasts were stark, editing together music by the Beatles, the Isley Brothers, Deep Purple, Motörhead and AC/DC. The reaction to 'Highway to Hell' may be particularly noteworthy. A few of the listeners turned into instant head-banging heroes and amazing air drummers. But they also got a taste of Beethoven's fifth symphony and the theme tune to the cartoon series *Maya the Bee*, along with cheesy German pop and march music. My track 'Musica ex Machina' wasn't part of the medley, though.

None of the reactions were predictable; depending on character and temperament, the listeners reacted very differently to the titles, none of which they knew to expect. Quieter types kept their movements more minimalist, while more effusive personalities really rocked out. The cartoon theme tune made some eyes light up with nostalgia, and one young woman weaved her audio experience into an individual dance with her hands, recreating the changing rhythms and melodies. I later edited the film to fit my track 'Musica ex Machina'. The experiment was one of the greatest experiences I've ever had with the medium. At times, I felt like I was playing a kind of 'perception piano'. I've never laughed as much while editing a film. What we see is a sequence of genuinely felt emotions, which incidentally leap across immediately to our audience at concerts, reflected in their faces.

Thanks to the focus on my previous sound recordings, I found myself in a kind of autobiographical mode. In this disposition, I decided to make a fun 'documentary' about my time in Kraftwerk. No matter what context I'm in at any time, people always connect me to the Düsseldorf electro-pioneers. Even after all these years, many still see me in that red shirt and black tie. All my latest output is still measured by the music we made together in the seventies and eighties. There are worse fates in life, but at times it gets annoying, like a shadow I can't shake off. This ambivalence keeps catching up with me, and that was what prompted the idea for a film to go with a song. There could be no better leading actor than my showroom dummy with the head modelled by Heinrich Obermaier, which I had christened

589

'Herr Karl'. Using my alter ego, I could effortlessly cite all the recording artist clichés: the dress code, golden records, front pages, sound studios, paranoia . . . Herr Karl remains, as you might expect, 'Without a Trace of Emotion'.

To make the 'documentary', I transformed the room we use as a library into an amateur film studio for about a year. We made our own backdrops, installed props and spotlights, and eventually we blocked out the daylight. I think we produced a total of more than twelve hours of film for the song, which is a whole three and a half minutes long.

The 'plot' begins with me – human Karl – walking towards Hamburg's Reeperbahn from the Indra Club, along Grosse Freiheit. Past the Kaiserkeller and the Star-Club, the venues where all the famous bands played in the early sixties, including the Beatles. I get to the Reeperbahn, turn left onto it, and walk past the Davidwache police station to the Panoptikum waxworks. Clang! I spot a portrait of my showroom-dummy doppelganger on a poster. Next comes a flashback, in which I visualize my numerous roles and transformations using Herr Karl: as a photographer in the style of David Hemmings in the film *Blowup*, as a robot performer, with a trench coat like in the *TEE* film, in a Tour de France outfit, on the telephone, reading the *Melody Maker*, holding a vinyl record, reflected in a mirror, admiring an Oskar Fischinger animation, clutching a Super-8 camera and raising a champagne glass at the end. I must have forgotten a pocket calculator – or there was no room for it. My favourite scene is the press conference. In a flurry of camera flashes, Herr Karl stands in front of a wall of golden records, speechless – just like me during my time with Kraftwerk. Then he gets the bus home.

In the middle of filming 'Without a Trace . . .' we were hit by a gigantic avalanche of information: Kraftwerk at the New York Museum of Modern Art! On eight consecutive evenings, Ralf and his Kraftwerkers presented a programme of the eight central albums from *Autobahn* to *Tour de France Soundtracks*. For the German curator Klaus Biesenbach, these gigs took 'the form of a classic museum retrospective: looking back, chronology, reassessment of the oeuvre'.[4] Biesenbach, an expert networker, succeeded in igniting an unprecedented level of public interest. He skilfully staged the pop event and grabbed the attention of the global media. But why a retrospective? Alongside the music from the eight albums, the current Kraftwerk line-up was performing a greatest-hits set. The focus of the presentation was on newly produced 3D projections.

Screenings

That was all well and good, but I had to take care of my own presentation. Seeing as *Off the Record* is an audio-visual work, Bureau B supported us in organizing a screening at Hamburg's Robert Morat Gallery in January, to present it to the press. As you can imagine, we invited along a few friends who helped us empty a couple of crates of Astra beer and sparkling water. Roberto and Mathias came along of course, as did the Sennewalds and even Claudia Schneider-Esleben.

While my looped films ran on five giant flat screens, the sound was pumped out simultaneously via headphones, provided by Sennheiser's 'Silent Disco System'. That enabled people to see and hear the material but didn't disturb communication inside

591

the gallery. At the sixth viewing and listening station, we ran a twenty-minute loop of my original acoustic diary. To my surprise, people took great interest in these recordings, and the question came up of whether I might want to publish them. It's a good idea – I'm working on it . . .

After the screening, I set out on a small promo tour of Europe. Once again, there was a counterpoint to my activities: Kraftwerk's performances at the Tate Modern in February 2013. The media were fascinated by the event and I was asked about it again and again in my own promotion work. I was surprised Kraftwerk were continuing their museum gigs – it seemed to contradict what Ralf had been saying for decades about 'institutionalized culture'. As far as I know, Florian only once commented on Ralf's ambitions after he left the band: 'Kraftwerk has become historic and is now exposed in museums,'[5] was his official view.

Reflecting on music in museums was not at the forefront of my mind, however; I simply had a lot to do. For the album release in March, my label organized the same audio-visual installation with screens and headphones as in Hamburg, only this time at Rough Trade East in London. It was open to the public, which meant not only old friends and acquaintances like John Foxx, Françoise Lamy and Graham Daniels from Addictive TV and Kate Holmes from Client came by, but also lots of fans. It was a great day, rounded off in fine tradition with a trip to the pub.

It was only once the Bureau B label boss Gunther Buskies had got out of our cab that night and waved a cheerful goodbye that Bettina came out with some information everyone had been keeping from me all day, so as not to spoil my mood. Bang on time for the album screening and release, a certain Mr Günter

Spachtholz, acting on behalf of the Kraftwerk company/Ralf Hütter, had registered a copyright infringement with Amazon for the album *Off the Record*: the product, he objected, had not been licensed by Kraftwerk. In the end, the whole thing proved to be nothing more than an empty threat.

90 Minutes

I couldn't shake the thought of illustrating every song in my live repertoire with a film. After putting a large amount of effort into the media for the last album, for me at least, I found it difficult to go on generating the visuals in real time. My tracks are relatively short and call for a fast-moving visual language. So I took the unavoidable step from improvised VJing to storyboards. I wanted to link up individual short films, their themes tied in to one another, to make a ninety-minute episodic film.

Years previously, the Weissraum agency had produced the video for 'I'm the Message' with a budget from Sony. My financial means were limited, though. All I had to film the set-list of more than twenty titles was a digital camera, my computer, an editing program and my own labour. It soon turned out: what looked like a mammoth task really was one, I have to be honest. But I was obsessed with the plan, I suppose.

My starting material, for example, was music programs for which I animated their functions ('Home Computer'); I brought pictograms to life ('Reality') or sent artists who have inspired me – from George Martin to Jeanne Moreau – gliding across the screen ('Interview'). I had a whole lot of fun filming for 'Pocket Calculator', spending weeks playing the song in front of a fixed camera on each of the instruments included in it, then followed the musical events in the song structure for the edit. As the end result, the filmed musician Karl Bartos makes music on screen alongside the real Karl Bartos on stage.

All this work kept me occupied for some time, but by some point every one of the short films had been shot, edited and put together in a 'perceived' narrative framework. Without a doubt, the central element that connects them all is the harmonic musical language, which enables me to place tracks such as 'The Model' and 'I'm the Message', 'The Robots' and 'Atomium', 'Life' and 'Computer Love' side by side.

Shortly after that – in August 2013 – our new live programme premiered with my ninety-minute film at the Brussels Summer Festival. We played open air on the central Mont des Arts square between the Gare de Bruxelles and Warandepark. It was great to see the audience's fascination as they watched the artificially provoked confrontation of sound and apparently unrelated images, while an effect unfurled and the poetic spark leapt across to them. There were actually a few staff members from the Atomium watching, and as we kicked off the track I saw and felt their resonance.

Image and Sound

In the spring of 2013, I had met Rüdiger Ladwig, head of the artist agency and record company Trocadero. His agency takes care of young niche artists with the same enthusiasm as established stars. Rüdiger had been staging concerts since his youth, and founded the Trocadero label. His belief in music's power to connect has survived all the unpredictable intricacies of the changing music market. In short: we got on right away, and although I can't pass for either a newcomer or an established star, we decided to work together. And we got off to a great start.

Since *Communication*, we had travelled halfway around the world with our various shows, but the last concert in Germany was an inconceivable eight years back. Rüdiger rolled up his sleeves and got stuck in. He organized gigs for January 2014 in Cologne, Stuttgart, Frankfurt, Halle, Nuremberg, Berlin and Hamburg. Another night in Copenhagen was added at the last minute. Just as we had the dates finalized, news popped up again of my obligatory shadow: Kraftwerk, we heard, would be receiving a Grammy for their life's work, the Lifetime Achievement Award. Ralf was to be honoured in Los Angeles on 25 January of all days – the day we started our German tour in Cologne. Once again, it seemed like there was an involuntary counterpoint between my activities and Kraftwerk's.

For the media, it was a welcome opportunity to keep asking me about the subject in interviews on the tour. There's no question that the Grammy is really great, and I do feel acknowledged in a way as a co-author, but I didn't know quite how to categorize the award. After all, it was essentially recognition for Kraftwerk as a brand, and not for the team of writers or the members. And so the Grammy passed me by, somewhere in faraway LA. Instead, preparing for my own tour kept me busy.

And then off it went: Cologne's Live Music Hall. A full house. The atmosphere was electric; I've rarely experienced such tense excitement. I think everyone in the venue expected something unusual, but no one could imagine what it would be. There was

595

a certain nervous mood in the team, as well. The first gig of a tour is always a challenge, even for Mathias, who has decades of experience of live events. Roberto paced to and fro, inspecting the backstage area at least a hundred and twenty times. Admittedly, him being a well-known journalist in Cologne meant the upcoming performance was a particular test of his nerves. I had a few interviews to give that afternoon, which usually keeps me nice and distracted, but even so I couldn't escape the general sense of stage fright.

Suitably, ahead of the concert's start, we put on Karlheinz Stockhausen's *Gesang der Jünglinge* to announce our imminent arrival. The best reference I could imagine, it was an homage and a genuine sign of our admiration. But it was also a little bit cocky. I hope the master will forgive us if he ever gets wind of it – you never know . . . Once the *Gesang* had faded out, Mathias started the 'Numbers' beat and we stepped on stage.

Our set kicked off with Kraftwerk evergreens and songs from *Communication*. Then we played a few tracks from my new album. Just as the audience has its eye on the stage, I like to watch them back during a performance. Perhaps *watching* is not quite the right word; it's more of a scan of the atmosphere, trying to ascertain the emotional temperature in the venue.

The synergy of seeing and hearing films is well known: the more conscious, rational perception of the visual level mingles with the rather unconscious, emotional experience of the sound. To illustrate this mix of intellect and emotion, I recommend underlaying a film sequence – for instance a view of a bustling city – with different types of music and observing how the city's atmosphere changes depending on the music's character. Sustained minor chords awaken a melancholy impression, while a cheerful major melody lends the city a positive outlook. Even though – and this is key – it's all the same sequence. Although we don't project feature films with consistent plots onto our triptych of screens during our performances, the concepts, thoughts and ideas do communicate with the audience – or at least that's what is reflected in people's faces and reactions. This surprising effect might be due to the way – unlike in a cinema screening – the visual level is sustained by the music. The two codes – visual *and* musical – are perceived consciously and meld together to produce a common impression on the senses.

When we inserted a few sequences of Cologne Cathedral between the views of Düsseldorf during 'Life' in the final segment of the show,[6] we didn't reap mere applause but frenetic cheers. In case you don't know, the cities of Cologne and Düsseldorf have been rivals ever since the Battle of Worringen in 1288. When Düsseldorf was made capital city of North Rhine-Westphalia in 1946, despite being far smaller than Cologne, it didn't exactly improve matters. So it might be strange for a boy from Düsseldorf, but ever since my first concert in the WDR Sendesaal, I've loved playing in Cologne. The locals are lively, heartfelt, really emotional, they let the music move them. Although the audience can't intervene directly in our show, they can take an active part by responding – hopefully with understanding, ideally with applause . . . like they did in Cologne on this occasion. The fact is, we musicians are influenced by that reaction. I learned that way back in my first semester at the Robert Schumann Conservatory: interaction with the audience is part of the nature of performance. In my view, precisely that is still an essential reason to give concerts.

Someone persuaded me to sign records for half an hour after the gig. I'm always in a bit of a strange mood when I come off stage, but for some reason I like the atmosphere when signing records. But the crowd in Cologne was so big, the audience so excited that the table with the products got pushed aside . . . Within minutes, the situation threatened to get completely out of control and I had to make my escape. Get me out of here! Strangely enough, that crowd reminded me of a gig in Liverpool, so many years ago now.

As Roberto steered me through the crush like a bodyguard, I felt pretty helpless. We eventually made it backstage, where I could spot everyone's relief that our new live concept worked. All of a sudden, I was surrounded by countless companions. My old colleague Wolfgang and his wife Zuhal hugged me, the Synthanorma inventor Hajo Wiechers showed me his LED tie with a burst of laughter, Wolfgang Kulas, the grandmaster of speech synthesis, patted me on the back and former opera house colleagues smiled over at me: 'Remember how we drummed the stage music for *La Bohème*, Karl?' There was a joyful hubbub of voices and chat.

Carried on a wave of goodwill, this eight-city tour was one of my most important experiences of recent years. I looked to the future with optimism.

Immediately after the trip, we received an offer to play live at the opening of the exhibition *Die Roboter* at the DASA Working World Exhibition in Dortmund at the end of 2015. It was a definite technical and acoustic challenge, as the steel hall is gigantic and contains exhibits like trams, smelting furnaces and structural engineering equipment, all behind long glass facades. What it doesn't have is a stage, or any possibility to hang screens.

Just as preparations were at their zenith, news broke of my former bandmate – unbelievably, Ralf's Kraftwerk would be playing on exactly the same date as our Dortmund concert, only thirty kilometres away in Essen.

The Cultural Subject

In times gone by, pop stars were mainly solo artists like Bing Crosby, Frank Sinatra or Elvis Presley, who were accompanied by a big band or orchestra at their concerts. Then a few Liverpool lads banded together, called themselves the Beatles and conquered the world with their music. 'En route to their first record, in Hamburg they invented a new cultural subject, one that was to become incredibly influential: the band.'[7]

Along with digitalization, contemporary production conditions made their way into the music business – many people were euphoric about what they called the democratization of the means of production. Unfortunately, though, the computer also put paid to many processes based on division of labour, like making music as a group, listening and playing at the same time, sharing sparks of inspiration, and fun. What was ultimately lost was the idea of how great it can be to hang out with a few friends and look for a sound that reflects you for an instant, and the whole world along with you – I'll just call it pop music. It's perfectly clear to me that having partners on stage and in the studio is always an advantage. Perhaps a band is an anachronism, but if you belong to a small group of let's say two, three or four people who stick together and don't drive each other insane, you've got a pretty good hand in this game. A team is

599

far superior to an individual, even if that person owns the world's most modern computer with the very latest inescapable operating system update.

After leaving Kraftwerk, I was lucky enough to work with fantastic musicians, but my major wish of being part of a band again was never fulfilled, sadly. One key characteristic of such a community is mental and geographical closeness. The great plan of 'let's send a few files back and forth' rarely turns into anything substantial. There are certainly long-distance relationships between musicians that do work, but it's highly likely that shared interests will gradually pale when they're so far apart. To say nothing of experiencing music together. I've learned that you have to be close to one another to make music. And by that, I mean intellectually and physically close.

My parents gave me the gift of imagination, for which I am grateful. But I was never a dreamer. So I see my current music group in realistic terms, and I see that geographical distance is a problem for us, too. Bearing that in mind, I can count myself lucky that our community hasn't dissolved into thin air over the years. Our point of commonality, as I see it, is our interest in serious cultural undertakings. And perhaps it's an advantage that each of us has his own focus in life and we're financially independent of each other.

My exchange of ideas with Sascha Wild, who was such a great support at the UdK, was going in a good direction. We stayed in contact after Sascha moved out of Berlin. Now back in Frankfurt, he teaches at the music school, lectures at several universities, writes film soundtracks and is involved in the city's Polytechnic Foundation, promoting jazz and improvised music. He rather reminds me of myself, of the time when I moved up

600

and down all the levels of culture like an elevator. The two of us have become friends without ever planning to. Sascha came along with us on our German tour, and we celebrated his official onstage premiere at the DASA gig in Dortmund.

The inner circle includes Roberto, of course, our man in Cologne, the journalist and DJ Robert Baumanns. I was pretty surprised when I realized he's been by my side for almost twenty years. The same applies to my friend Mathias Black, with whom I've travelled the world, whose technical and musical skills amaze me over and over again, and who I trust unconditionally. We all have different characteristics and visions, but we couldn't look back on such a longstanding collaboration if our ideas didn't overlap.

The gig in the industrial surroundings of the DASA exhibition turned out to be really spectacular for me and my friends. I think the large audience also had a good time. One German newspaper even referred to the parallel events in Dortmund and Essen as a 'long-distance musical duel'.[8] We played the last concert of that season at Berghain's Panorama Bar in Berlin – sold out.

Progress as a Shining Promise

It's over forty years ago that we presented *The Man-Machine* to the press at a *soirée rouge* in Paris's Tour Montparnasse. We started work on *Computer World* not much later. Even in those days, people were afraid of the consequences of digitalization. German headlines at the time included 'Progress Breeds Unemployment',[9] 'The Power of the Robots'[10] or 'Computers for Home Use'.[11]

In the 2020s, it's impossible to imagine our lives without digital machines. Their flat screens and displays symbolize progress – at least, that's what we're supposed to think. Everywhere – and I mean really everywhere – we see people of all ages, apparently oblivious to the rest of the world as they interact with their devices. Smartphones are omnipresent, keeping their users in a constant state of suspense.

Digitalization and globalization accelerate the speed of our lives, create gigantic growth rates, generate billions in revenue – and divide society into winners and losers. Structural change – a rather harmless-sounding term for what is actually happening – plays into the hands of nationalism and presents enormous challenges for democracy. In view of the complexity of all this radical transformation, politicians appear out of their depth, to put it mildly.

Optimists on the future believe technological progress provides its own solutions to all problems. That was the case at the dawning of the electrical age, and it applies all the more in the twenty-first century with its fantastic possibilities. Digital technologies are seen as a magical promise for the future. Yet it is not at all clear even how to cope with the deluge of data and where to source the energy to do so. Just think of all the data and electricity consumption to be expected of networked, self-driving cars on our streets. However, we can hardly expect objectivity in assessing the future of mobility. It's a paradox situation that reminds me of the debates about nuclear energy of the 1970s and 1980s, when the question of where to dispose of radioactive waste was dismissed as left-wing environmentalist waffle.

As far as I'm aware, this problem still hasn't been solved. There appear to be more important things to do. Business has to boom.

And that's why our new digital copy of capitalism still applies the rule that caught out Orpheus in the underworld: We look forward, not back. The high-tech corporations have now managed to sell the terms 'innovation' and 'progress' to the general public as synonyms – which I find disturbingly backward, bearing in mind the climate change we can already see and the expected collapse of our ecosystem. 'Many prerequisites have changed,' the philosopher Richard David Precht warns. 'We can no longer see the future as we did in the past.'[12]

I have been on the internet since the end of the 1990s. To be honest, I never would have thought, back then, that I would see the address bar of a browser as an interface between me and a machine. Now, a virtual space exists alongside our physical world, a place we can go no matter where we are, at any time. Some experts say we have access there to the whole of human knowledge. Even today, information machines and the internet generate a volume of data I cannot possibly imagine, hard as I try.

The centre of the Western IT and high-tech industry is on the Pacific coast of California. Silicon Valley is home to Stanford University, Google, Amazon, Facebook, Apple and many other digital corporations. And even Microsoft, headquartered in Washington, has now set up its own Silicon Valley Campus in the Bay Area. With the market economy's obsession with efficiency and growth in mind, and with their investors' money, they set out and became pioneers in the development of information technology. As we know, anything and everything can be traded on the net: physical objects, services, communication, entertainment. What makes the digital business model, known as platform capitalism, so successful, is offering free services while collecting and evaluating personal data. Users' motion profiles can be effortlessly bought and sold. By this means, however, the customers themselves become the product without even realizing it. Data trading seems to be one of the most bizarre and successful business models of all time.

Certain people in Silicon Valley regard humans and animals as a kind of protein-based computers, which can calculate and reproduce by chemical means.[13] By methodically and systematically collecting data, their behaviour can be predicted – and eventually manipulated. This method pays reference to the American mathematician Norbert Wiener, who in 1943 founded cybernetics: the science of controlling and regulating machines, living organisms and social organizations.[14]

Wiener was aware, however, of the dangers inherent to observing and analysing human behaviour. He rejected commercialization of his findings – for instance through expert manipulation of individuals. Yet like many others, he also saw automation as a chance for humanity to liberate ourselves from the burden of reproductive labour. In his opinion, machines should be 'used for the benefit of man, for increasing his leisure and enriching his spiritual life, rather than merely for profits and the worship of the machine as a new brazen calf.'[15] Wouldn't it be interesting to hear his thoughts on the big data business of our times?

Thanks to sophisticated social technology, people today are willing to reveal everything about themselves and their surroundings – voluntarily, because it's fun. That's probably for the best, say the advocates of the billion-dollar data-marketing industry. It's more difficult to hide evil intentions if you don't have a private sphere, they tell us. One thing's for sure: the search engines and social technicians (not to mention the intelligence services, of course) have more information about us than democratically legitimated governments are ever allowed to store officially. And since Edward Snowden's disclosures, no one can say they know nothing about it.

The business school of the digital economy, Silicon Valley's Singularity University, has been making waves since its foundation in 2008. By its own account, the university studies how exponentially growing technologies can be used to solve humankind's greatest challenges. The co-founder, aeronautical engineer Peter Diamandis, makes perky prophecies such as: 'We will become god-like. People don't like to hear it but we have a mission, a mission to know anything, plugging your brain into Google, you're omnipotent. Being able to control something on the other side of the world, be omnipresent. Know the thoughts of someone in Japan or Hawaii or wherever they might be, at any time. To unplug yourself would be so lonely.'[16]

The forward-thinkers and sales managers of the San Francisco Bay Area have taken it upon themselves to freshen our planet up a little – as they see fit, of course. For example with the Internet of Things, which German Wikipedia sums up neatly as 'a global infrastructure that enables the interconnection of physical and virtual objects'. Everything is carried out, as long as the targets of commercial usefulness, patent law and assessable demand are met. Often enough, digital corporations and start-ups aim to get rid an existing phenomenon so as to replace it with something new. Economists talk about the theory of disruptive technologies.

For another of Singularity University's co-founders, the all-rounder Ray Kurzweil, ours is above all 'an exciting time for entrepreneurs'.[17] The world is, at least, about to step up to the next level of digitalization, and if we believe the experts, then artificial intelligence (AI) will very soon accelerate technological progress so drastically that life on our planet will change radically. The melding of man and machine, referred to as singularity, is allegedly not far off. Without doubt, the advantages will initially be so overwhelming that no one can resist them. And yet, the human body is also a breathtaking market of the future, as if made for our consumerist lifestyle. As we know, the Californian experts are not the first to cultivate scientific progress as a type of surrogate religion.

Is it not tempting to believe in these blessings? Even more tempting is the assumption of profiting from scientific and technological innovations – provided one can afford to play the game. This technical and societal utopia was also Kraftwerk's ideology and business model. As in the Silicon Valley strategy, the new was always more significant than the old. Provocative soundbites such as, 'We are machines. Man is heading towards a more robotic existence,' or 'Individuality has been exaggerated in the twentieth century,'[18] were strikingly unusual in general reporting in the pop media. Or there was the witty coming-out statement: 'As for ourselves, we love our machines. We have an erotic relationship with them.'[19] The band countered musical tradition with the effortless reproduction of music by machine. 'The guitar,' I read to my surprise, 'is an instrument from the Middle Ages.'[20]

Usually cryptically formulated, this glorification transferred the fascination that technical innovations held for my former colleagues to the Kraftwerk brand. Aside from the illusion of being able to make music for the times solely on electronic devices, however, this eccentric Futurist rhetoric had little to do with our daily work. Certainly, the instruments sounded modern for a millisecond, but playing a melody on a synthesizer doesn't change the grammar of how we hear it in the Western world. In fact, we did invent our music in the traditional way, using compositional skills, dedication and emotion, and not artificial intelligence, for instance, but our own natural intelligence. That was just as much the case, incidentally, when we developed the musical idea of a *Computer World*.

To quote Daniel Barenboim, 'Music is the physical expression of the human mind'.[21] In my view, we had set out with this understanding to launch an assault on the cultural norm of the musical artform, to expand its definition – or at least to try – and to invent the music of the technological age by viewing ourselves as a man-machine and musicalizing technology. As far as I can judge, all those involved agreed on this approach.

Our writing sessions in the Kling Klang Studio were very focused. We would forget everything around us, sometimes including ourselves, while we improvised. I think we wanted to find out how the elements of music become an organic whole. Our mutual search for new artistic expression made us feel happy – or at least me. Psychologists refer to this state of mind as 'flow'.[22] And because we felt this pleasure in our actions, the feeling of creative passion, we kept doing it again and again. I think everyone has experienced this phenomenon at one time or another.

The creative process continued with the synthesis of the existing, the selection of our elements, the integration of random artefacts, and another round of changes. Over the course of time, the challenges grew and we got better. It was fun, it was fulfilling, and we learned something along the way. At the end of the process, we produced a result in which we all recognized ourselves, like in a mirror.

In the 1970s, we realized what previously unknown possibilities for expression were harboured by microelectronics. The aestheticizing of technology was part of our design concept, but only a part. As I see it, in their best moments our compositions are a testament to our search for the poetry concealed in the sound of the machine.

In the mid-1980s, the digital society imagined on *Computer World* became a reality in our daily work. Computers entered the studio and we transferred our music from an analogue world in a time continuum, into virtual space. Later, our spokesman rhapsodized about our 'collaborative co-existence with the machines,' and how they enabled the 'greatest possible creative freedom' for us.[23]

Nonetheless, each of us had a different perception of our creative work, by this point. That happens to the best of us, and it wouldn't have been the end of the world, had we had an official version of our views to present to the outside world. But we had decided to go without such a corrective measure. Through public communication, to which there appeared to be no alternative, a cryptic machine cult developed over the years, which fed back into our circle and ultimately led to a cult of the non-human.

Looking back, I have to say that digitalization did not change my understanding of music in any fundamental way. After all, musical notation also arranges the temporality of sounds in a linear, graphically represented system. It is the prerequisite for musical thoughts to be picked up later and made present

608

again – perfectly normal artistic work. For me, as I've said, a computer's music software is an audio score. A universal tool like the piano, the guitar, the pencil and the five lines of the notation system or sound recording.

In our studio, however, we felt something like awe-inspired euphoria. We were now in possession of the most-hyped machine in the world of music production. The extremely expensive acquisition, in combination with our unerring faith in modern technology, temporarily increased our confidence in our own prowess. Without Electronic Data Processing (EDP), it would be impossible to put all our ideas into practice, it was said, and the present era was a great time for musicians in particular. Ralf claimed to be certain that computers exceeded the senses-based experience of a traditional musical instrument, 'because you have more sounds to choose from' and touch 'buttons, switches, dials'.[24] It was enthusiastically claimed it was 'not about playing any more'. At last, some thought, machines are liberating us from the trivial work of making music. 'All this mechanical stuff from the past is totally off the agenda.'[25] In other words: 'It's more fun to compute!'

Regardless of this euphoria, the entrepreneurial machine dream – that the total quantification of our music would have a positive effect on our creative energy – did not come true. Instead, our thoughts received an operating system and our imaginations a program, with algorithms to predetermine 'a clear regulation for action to solve a problem or a class of problems'[26] for us. Our joint work process in the 'Kling Klang Future Lab' soon became nothing but technical operations and the administration and storage of data. We interacted with the digital machines by typing and clicking (swiping hadn't yet been

609

introduced) and our verbal communication was reduced to an exchange of information about technical procedures. To make matters worse, the sophisticated systems were increasingly maintained by external engineers, establishing a layer of experts that became ever more important and entirely rationalized our thinking. The increasingly short intervals between alleged improvements in software and hardware also rigorously blocked our access to the music. What we lost was the practice of making music, the bodily aspect, the free thinking and association, the spontaneous use of our creativity as we improvised, the sense of humour – all the skills we previously valued in each other. In brief, digital machines had replaced the analogue ones and changed the way we thought and behaved. In this sterile technosphere, all the prerequisites for our creative art were extinguished, without us being aware of it.

One might say that the studio had finally adapted to the legend around it. All the mechanical stuff of the past – the way we had once invented our music – really was totally off the agenda. Instead, we scanned analogue signals and translated them into digital data, technically optimized them and sorted them into neat categories. Then we programmed – often independently of each other – imitations of the musical elements and shapes of our originals.

The vocabulary of computer science produced a technical image of our work for public consumption: 'Through every new experience, we gain a new identity; the old one dies. In computer language, that's called an 'open program': only a basic foundation of genetic material remains in place, and otherwise any change is possible!'[27] In this data matrix of ones and zeros, the human aspect appeared irrelevant. Economic rationality now set the tone, instead of music. 'So now there's more sound, more electronics, programming and sound engineering,'[28] was the credo of the digital business model.

Whatever happens . . . when dealing with computers, you should never forget where the off switch is. It's really very simple: we musicians have to play our music the way we think it and feel it, as well and as intensely as we can – that's all that counts. In my understanding, art is not something that can be subjected to algorithms, but a concept and its marketing can. And thus, our music, formerly the product of our minds, bodies and senses, was turned into a program – frozen in the technical patterns of its reproduction.

NOTES

1. 'Science Fiction ist schon lange Realität' by Michael Fuchs-Gamböck. *Wiener*, 7 July 1991

2. R. Murray Schafer: *The Soundscape – The Tuning of the World*. Arcana Editions: Ontario 1977

3. Fred K. Prieberg: *Musica Ex Machina. Über das Verhältnis von Musik und Technik*. Ullstein: Berlin 1960

4. 'Die Kunst der guten Freunde' by Moritz von Uslar, *Die Zeit*, 14 April 2012

5. Quoted from: 'Kraftwerk's co-founder made this track to save the oceans.' By Daisy Jones, *Dazed*, undated. Online: http://www.dazeddigital.com/music/article/28760/1/kraftwerk-s-co-foundermade-this-track-to-save-the-oceans

6. Many thanks to Hermann Rheindorf, koelnprogramm.de

7. I have taken the idea of using the 'cultural subject' as a term from Tobias Rapp's outstanding essay 'Yesterday' in *Der Spiegel*, issue 48/2018, 24 November 2018 (Original quote: 'Auf dem Weg zu ihrer ersten Platte erfinden die Beatles in Hamburg ein neues kulturelles Subjekt, das ungeheuer einflussreich werden wird: Die Band.')

8. 'Karl Bartos und Kraftwerk – Großer Elektropop im Doppelpack.' By Stefan Reinke, *WAZ*, 23 November 2015

9. *Der Spiegel*: 'Fortschritt macht arbeitslos. Die Computer- Revolution.' By Monika Zucht, issue 16/1978, 17 April 1978

10. *Die Zeit*: 'Die Macht der Roboter.' By Rudolf Braunburg, No. 46/1979, 9 November 1979

11. *Der Spiegel*: 'Computer für den Hausgebrauch,' issue 36/1978, 4 September 1978

12. Richard David Precht: *Jäger, Hirten, Kritiker – Eine Utopie der digitalen Gesellschaft*. Goldmann, Munich 2018

13. Quote from the campus of Singularity University San Francisco, in: *Un monde sans humains?* documentary film by Philippe Borrel, France 2012, 22 November 2012, https://www.youtube.com/watch?v=gOv4602fK2k 58:08:00 ff.

14. Norbert Wiener: *Cybernetics or Control and Communication in the Animal and the Machine*. Paris. (Herman & Cie) & Camb. Mass. (MIT Press) 1948

15. https://en.wikipedia.org/wiki/The_Human_Use_of_Human_Beings   See: Norbert Wiener, *Cybernetics: Or Control and Communication in the Animal and the Machine*. Paris, (Hermann & Cie) & Camb. Mass. (MIT Press), 1948, 2nd edition 1961, p. 11.

16. Peter Diamandis in: *Un monde sans humains?* Film by Philippe Borrel, 2012, 01:12:54 ff.

17. Ray Kurzweil in: *Mensch 2.0 – Die Evolution in unserer Hand*: Film by Basil Gelpke and Alexander Kluge. Dctp.tv NZZ-Format

18. Ralf Hütter: 'You're never alone with a clone.' By Tim Lott, *Record Mirror*, 29 July 1978
    Ralf Hütter: 'People say, we have no souls. But classical musicians – do they have a soul? And yet they are machines. They perform what is written down for them many years before. We are machines. Man is heading towards a more robotic existence.' [. . .]
    'We think of uniforms in relation to society. We are suggesting that Kraftwerk is a unit, that we have just come from a machine, mass produced. individuality has been exaggerated in the twentieth century. Everybody wants so much to be different. But individuality is just wishful thinking. It is a sales argument to stimulate commerce.'

19. Florian Schneider: 'Rockers Cybernétiques.' By Yves Adrien, *Rock & Folk Magazine*, June 1978

612

Rock & Folk: 'Let's talk about *Man-Machine*. Is the man in *The Man-Machine* submissive to the machine?'

Florian Schneider: 'I don't think so. It's rather a more sophisticated relationship. There is an interaction. Interaction on both sides. The machine helps the man, and the man admires the machine. (Showing the Sony tape recorder) This is the extension of your brain. It helps you remembering. It's the third man sitting at this table. As for ourselves, we love our machines. We have an erotic relationship with them.'

20. Ralf Hütter: 'Blubber von der Datenbank.' *Der Spiegel*, issue 24/1981, 8 June 1981

21. Daniel Barenboim: *Musik ist alles und alles ist Musik*. Berlin Verlag: Berlin 2014

22. Flow: This state was described in 1975 by a Hungarian psychologist with the near-unpronounceable name of Mihály Csíszentmihályi. He is regarded as the outstanding scientist in the field, but was not actually the first to discover the concept (cf. Kurt Hahn 1908, one of the founders of expeditionary education, with his 'creative passion', the doctor and educationalist Maria Montessori with 'polarisation of attention' (on the senses and actions) and the psychologist Abraham Maslow with 'peak experience'.)

23. Ralf Hütter: 'Science Fiction ist schon lange Realität.' By Michael Fuchs-Gamböck, *Wiener*, 7 July 1991

'The machines enable the greatest possible creative freedom for us. We experiment with the machines and the results, contingent on the devices' own lives, are completely new and amazing. "Progress through dialogue" is our manifesto: We enter into a collaborative co-existence with the machines and venture into unknown territory . . .'

24. Ralf Hütter: 'Kraftwerk – Menschmaschine.' By Teddy Hoersch, *Keyboards*, July 1987

Keyboards: 'Is there an equivalent to the sense-based experience of playing the piano, the touch, the pressure on the keys, etc., when you're operating machines?'

Ralf Hütter: 'The sense-based experience is even greater, because you have more sounds to choose from. Apart from that, I do touch the machine – buttons, switches, dials. You can play anything with these electronic instruments. The only boundary is the creativity of the person sitting in front of the machine.

It's not about playing any more. If I want to, I can program the Minute Waltz so that it plays in 59 seconds or half a minute. All the mechanical stuff from the past is totally off the agenda.'

25. Ibid.

26. Charles E. Leiserson, Ronald L. Rivest, Clifford Stein: *Algorithmen – Eine Einführung.* Oldenburg Verlag, Munich 2010

27. Ralf Hütter: 'Science Fiction ist schon lange Realität.' By Michael Fuchs-Gambock, *Wiener,* 7 July 1991
'Through every new experience, we gain a new identity, and the old one dies. In computer language, we call it an "open program": Only a basic foundation of genetic material remains in place, otherwise any change is possible!'

28. Ralf Hütter: 'So now there is more sound, more electronics, programming and sound engineering going on.' 'Kraftwerk: Robopop.' By Simon Witter. *New Musical Express,* 1991

EPILOGUE:
'WE ARE STILL BORN
IN DO RE MI'

Like many musicians before me, I had begun to write my life story. The past exists only in our imaginations. For that reason, I started by entering the real content of my pocket calendars from the late 1960s to the present day into my computer, day by day. The result was a chronology so rich in information that it was hard to see the wood for the trees.

Then I had the idea of interpreting my life as the timeline of a musical score, and approaching writing via the musical form. The similarities between music and our lives are obvious: music rings out, unfurls in space and time, and fades away. For a few of the book's chapters, I really did draw up timelines depicting various tracks, rather like music software – except that the regions they presented weren't musical content but weeks, months and years of my life. Very active phases in the 1970s and 1990s stood out in the graphics, as did long periods with little output in the 1980s. This way of presenting my life helped me move away from thinking in terms of calendar days, to sketch out the narrative strands on various themes that run through the book in polyphonic form. This is very close to how I think about my life in music.

In actual fact, while my thoughts were fully occupied by the past, there were times when I felt the same way as I do when playing old music. But the past is not by nature a musical score to be read in a single sitting, nor is it an audio-visual medium that can be rewound or fast-forwarded to watch a sequence over and over. Instead, the past is made up of many different fragments of time, sometimes years apart, which nonetheless add up to a coherent picture in our memory. It consists of individuals we meet in our short lives, who play a role for a time and then disappear, perhaps popping up again decades later, out of the blue. Others die unexpectedly, leaving us behind in our pain and unable to make sense of it all.

Looking at my past, I make out patterns. For instance, I seem not to have been a very good judge of character. I kept making the mistake of assuming other people were thinking the same way as I did. Which, of course, underlines the importance of mutually open and honest communication. The constant factor in all these years has been my wife Bettina Michael, with whom I have been through life side by side for so many years, and without whom I would not have become who I am today.

I have managed to make sense of the past – but I can't imagine how the future will play out. Everything is seemingly defined via technical progress. Yet that progress occasionally trips over its own feet and we all have to live with the consequences . . .

Isn't it uncanny how the profiteers of the progress business model believe unerringly that modern technology can solve the world's problems? That is just as much a mistake as assuming that computers would create spaces for creativity, with which we could invent a new kind of music. So far, however, the main thing the digital revolution has brought us is a fundamental shake-up in the distribution of music, rather than lending us creativity and the development of new musical content.

616

And so, I am on the side of Pierre Schaeffer, who says: 'In music there are new things – synthesizers, tape recorders etc. – but we still have our sensibilities, our ears, the old harmonic structures in our heads, we're still born in Do Re Mi.'[1]

Although I came up with a musical analogy for my life, and although thinking about music has always been a significant part of my work, writing hasn't come easy to me. Sense and lunacy, happiness and unhappiness, closeness and growing apart – things that are in contrast in life – are often only a few words apart on the pages of this book, and I've repeatedly come up against the boundaries of what I am capable of expressing in language.

Yet despite all the difficulties of reconstructing my life in the past, I never felt lost there or left alone, and never without a perspective. For aside from all the facts and images in my head, there is an absolutely reliable source that provides information on everything I cannot say in words, and that source is music.

NOTES

1. Pierre Schaffer in: 'An Interview with Pierre Schaeffer – pioneer of Musique Concrète.' By Tim Hodgkinson, *Recommended Records Quarterly* magazine, Volume 2, Number 1, 1987. Online: http://www.timhodgkinson.co.uk/articles.html schaeffer.pdf (2 May 1986)

LITERATURE

The following books have accompanied me through my sound biography, influenced me or given me exciting ideas. In one way or another, they have found their way into this book. I have quoted from some of them, others helped me to research particular subjects, and there are some that I can only recommend reading. I have sorted them by subject area.

Classical Music & Musicology

Barenboim, Daniel | **Die Musik – mein Leben** – List, 2004

Barenboim, Daniel | **Klang ist Leben** – Pantheon, 2009

Barenboim, Daniel | **Musik ist alles und alles ist Musik** – Berlin Verlag, 2014

Barraqué, Jean | **Debussy** – Rowohlt, 1964

Baumeister, Mary | **Ich hänge im Triolengitter: Mein Leben mit Karlheinz Stockhausen** – Edition Elke Heidenreich bei C. Bertelsmann, 2011

Cunningham, Mark | **Good Vibrations – A History of Record Production** – Sanctuary Publishing, London 1998

Decsey, Ernst | **Debussys Werke** – Leykam-Verlag, 1948

Eimert, Herbert & Humpert, Hans Ulrich | **Das Lexikon der elektronischen Musik** – Gustav Bosse Verlag, Regensburg, 1973

Kaegi, Werner | **Was ist elektronische Musik** – Orell Füssli Verlag, 1967

Kunstmuseum Basel | **Strawinsky: Sein Nachlass. Sein Bild.** 1984

Levitin, Daniel | **This Is Your Brain on Music: The Science of a Human Obsession** – Plume (Penguin): New York, 2007

Lemacher/Schröder | **Formelehre der Musik** – Gerig, 1962

Maler, Wilhelm | **Beitrag zur durmolltonalen Harmonielehre** – F. E. Leuckart, 1931

Prieberg, Fred K. | **Musik des technischen Zeitalters** – Atlantisverlag, 1956

Prieberg, Fred K. | **Musica ex Machina** – Ullstein, 1960

Ross, Alex | **The Rest Is Noise** – Piper Verlag GmbH, Munich, 2009

Schaeffer, Pierre | **In Search of a Concrete Music** – University of California Press, 2012 – **A la recherche d'une musique concrète** – Paris, Éditions du Seuil, 1952

Schafer, R. Murray | **The Soundscape: Our Sonic Environment and the Tuning of the World** – Destiny Books, 1977

Schmidt-Garre, Helmut | **Oper: Eine Kulturgeschichte** – Arno Volk Verlag Cologne, 1963

Spitzer, Manfred | **Musik im Kopf** – Schattauer, 2002

Stockhausen, Karlheinz | **Texte zur elektronischen und instrumentalen Musik** (Volumes 1 – 6) – DuMont Verlag, Cologne, 1952–1984

Stravinsky, Igor | **Poetics of Music in the Form of Six Lessons** – Harvard University Press, Revised Edition, 1 July 1974

Pop Music

Boyd, Joe | **White Bicycles: Making Music in the 1960s** – Serpent's Tail, London, 2006

Brown, James with Tucker, Bruce | **The Godfather of Soul** – Mac Millan Publishing Company, New York/London, 1986

Clapton, Eric | **The Autobiography** – Fischer, 2009

Davis, Ray | **X-Ray** – The Overlook Press, 2007

Dawson, Julian | **Nicky Hopkins: Eine Rock-Legende** – Edition Elke Heidenreich bei C. Bertelsmann, 2010

Hook, Peter | **Unknown Pleasures: Inside Joy Division** – Metrolit, 2013

Marr, Johnny | **Set the Boy Free** – Century, 2016

Mason, Nick | **Inside Out – A Personal History of Pink Floyd** – Phoenix, 2005

Richards, Keith | **Life** – Heyne, 2010

Savage, Jon | **The Kinks: The Official Biography** – Faber and Faber, 1984

Savage, Jon – Pepper, Terence | **Beatles to Bowie: The London 60s** – Schirmer/Mosel, 2009

Smith, Patti | **Just Kids** – Kiepenheuer & Witsch, 2010

Sumner, Bernard | **Chapter and Verse – New Order, Joy Division and Me** – Penguin, 2015

Sting | **Broken Music: Die Autographie** – Fischer, 2005

Wyman, Bill and Coleman, Ray | **Stone Alone** – Goldmann Verlag, 1990

The Beatles

Emerick, Geoff and Massey, Howard | **Here, There and Everywhere** – Gotham Books, 2006

Lewison, Mark | **The Complete Beatles Recording Sessions: The Official Story of the Abbey Road Years 1962–1970** – Hamlyn Publishing, London, 1988

Martin, George with Hornsby, Jeremy | **All You Need Is Ears: The Inside Personal Story of the Genius who Created the Beatles** – St. Martin's Press, New York, 1979

Martin, George with Pearson, William | **Summer of Love: The Making of Sgt. Pepper** – Macmillan London Ltd 1994

McDonald, Ian | **Revolution in the Head: The Beatles' Records and the Sixties** – Fourth Estate, London, 1994

Miles, Barry | **Paul McCartney, Many Years from Now** – Secker & Warburg, London, 1997

The Beatles Complete Scores

Hal Leonard Publishing Corporation and Wise Publication, USA 1993

Jazz

Dümling, Albrecht and Girth, Peter | **Entartete Musik** – Düsseldorf, 1988

Sander, Wolfgang | **Keith Jarret** – Rowohlt, 2015

Futurism

Apollonio, Umbro | **Der Futurismus. Manifeste und Dokumente einer künstlerischen Revolution 1909–1918** – Cologne: DuMont Schauberg, 1972

Baumgarth, Christa | **Geschichte des Futurismus** – Reinbek bei Hamburg. Rowohlts deutsche Enzyklopädie, 1966

Nautilus Moderne | **Drahtlose Phantasie. Auf- und Ausrufe des Futurismus** – Nautilus/Nemo Press, 1985

Schmidt-Bergmann, Hansgeorg | **Futurismus. Geschichte, Ästhetik, Dokumente** – Reinbek/Hamburg: Rowohlt, 1993

Instruments

Block, René – Dombois, Lorenz – Herltling, Nele – Volkmann, Barbara (eds.) | **Für Augen und Ohren. Von der Spieluhr zum akustischen Environment. Objekte. Installationen. Performances** – Akademie der Künste, Berlin, 1980

Buchner, Alexander | **Vom Glockenspiel zum Pianola** – Artia, Prague, 1959

Mansfield, Joe | **Beat Box: A Drum Machine Obsession** – Get On Down, 2013

Media and Cultural Criticism

Kittler, Friedrich | **Grammophon. Film. Typewriter** – Brinkmann & Bose, 1986

Postman, Neil | **Amusing Ourselves to Death** – Viking Penguin, 1985

Postman, Neil | **Technopoly** – Alfred A. Knopf, Inc., 1991

Sontag, Susan | **On Photography** – Penguin, 1977

Werkmeister, Otto K. | **Zitadellenkultur** – Hanser, 1989

Society

Benjamin, Walter | **The Work of Art in the Age of Mechanical Reproduction** – Createspace Independent Pub, 2009

Friedman, Thomas L. | **The World Is Flat. A Brief History of the Twenty-First Century** – Duglas and McIntyre (2013), 2007

Göpel, Maja | **The Great Mindshift** – Springer International Publishing, 2016

Göpel, Maja | **Unsere Welt neu denken** – Ullstein Buchverlage, 2020

Meadows, Dennis L. | Authors: Dennis Meadows, Donella H. Meadows, Erich Zahn, Peter Milling | **The Limits to Growth** – Universe Books, New York, 1972

Precht, Richard David | **Jäger, Hirten, Kritiker: Eine Utopie für die digitale Gesellschaft** – Goldmann Verlag, 2018

Precht, Richard David | **Künstliche Intelligenz und der Sinn des Lebens** – Goldmann Verlag, 2020.

Wiener, Norbert | **Cybernetics or Control and Communication in the Animal and the Machine** – Paris. (Herman & Cie) & Camb. Mass. (MIT Press) 1948

Wiener, Norbert | **The Human Use of Human Beings – Cybernetics and Society** – Cambridge: Cambridge University Press, 1950

Historical Figures

Neufeld, Michael J. | **Wernher von Braun. Visionär des Weltraums – Ingenieur des Krieges** – Siedler Verlag, 2009

Wagner, Jens-Christian | **Produktion des Todes: Das KZ Mittelbau-Dora Hrsg. von der Stiftung Gedenkstätten Buchenwald und Mittelbau-Dora** – Göttingen, 2001

Politics

Kraushaar, Wolfgang (ed.) | **Die RAF und der linke Terrorismus,** (2 Volumes) – Hamburger Edition, 2007

Film

Bogdanovich, Peter | **Fritz Lang in Amerika** – Studio Vista, 1967

Buñuel, Luis | **Die Flecken der Giraffe** – Ein und Überfälle. Berlin: Wagenbach, 1991

Ballhaus, Michael | **Bilder im Kopf** – Deutsche Verlags-Anstalt, 2014

Chion, Michel | **Audio-Vision: Sound on Screen** – Columbia University Press, 1994 [1990]

Eisner, Lotte H. | **Die dämonische Leinwand** – Fischer, 1955

Eisner, Lotte H. | **Ich hatte einst ein schönes Vaterland – Memoirs** – Fischer, 1955

Gorbman, Claudia | **Unheard Melodies: Narrative Film Music** – BFI Publishing, London, 1987

Jungk, K. | **Wie ein Tonfilm entsteht** – Verlag von Wilhelm Knapp, 1952

Moritz, William | **Optical Poetry: The Live and Work of Oskar Fischinger** – Indiana University Press, 2004

Murch, Walter | **In the Blink of an Eye** – Silman-James Press, 2001

Murch, Walter | **Sound Design: The Dancing Shadow** – Faber & Faber: London, 1995

Oumano, Ellen | **Filmemacher bei der Arbeit** – Fischer, 1989

Reihe Film 7 | **Fritz Lang** – Carl Hanser Verlag Munich, Vienna – p. 94 footnote 5: La nuit viennoise. Une confession de Fritz Lang. [continuation] in: Chahiers du Cinéma 179, June 1966

Riess, Curt | **Das gab's nur einmal – Die große Zeit des deutschen Films** – MTV. Molden Taschenbuch-Verlag, 1977

Sonnenschein, David | **Sound Design** – Michael Wiese Productions, 2001

Schreier, Dirk | **Film und Rhythmus** – Verlag Werner Hülsbusch, 2008

Spinard, Paul | **The VJ Book** – Feral House, 2005

Literature

Clarke, Arthur C. | **2001: A Space Odyssey** – ROC, 1976

Hesse, Hermann | **Steppenwolf** – Penguin, 1965 [1927]

624

Hoffmann, E.T.A. | **Der Automaten-Mensch. E.T.A. Hoffmanns Erzählung vom Sandmann** – Verlag Klaus Wagenbach, Berlin, 1976

Jandl, Ernst | **Gesammelte Werke** (3 Volumes) – Luchterhand, 1985

Orwell, George | **Nineteen Eighty-Four** – Penguin, 1954 [1949]

Pirsing, Robert M. | **Zen and the Art of Motorcycle Maintenance** – William Morrow and Company, 1978

Von Harbou, Thea | **Metropolis** – Ullstein, 1978

Art

Isabelle Dufresne | **Famous for 15 Minutes. My Years with Andy Warhol** – Harcourt Brace Jovanich: New York, 1988

Kunsthaus Zürich | **Der Hang zum Gesamtkunstwerk** – Verlag Sauerländer, 1983

Lissitzky-Küppers, Sophie | **El Lissitzky – Maler Architekt Typograf Fotograf,** 1967 – VEB Verlag der Kunst Dresden, 1976

Museum für moderne Kunst Bozen | **Ludwig Hirschfeld-Mack: Bauhäusler und Visionär** – Hatje Cantz Verlag, 2000

Kraftwerk

Barr, Tim | **Kraftwerk, from Düsseldorf to the Future (with Love)** – Ebury Press, 1998

Buckley, David | **Kraftwerk: Publikation** – Omnibus Press, 2012

Bussy, Pascal | **Kraftwerk: Man, Machine and Music** – SAF Publishing, 1993

Bussy, Pascal | **Neonlicht – Die Kraftwerk Story** – Bosworth Edition, 2005

Flür, Wolfgang | **Ich war ein Roboter** – Egmond, 2004

PICTURE CREDITS

01 + 02. The classic Christmas photo – Marietta and me in the town where I was born, Marktschellenberg near Berchtesgaden, in 1953; below: posing in the snow, 1954.

03. In Düsseldorf's Flora Park, 1956.

04. My parents, Rosa and Hans-Joachim Bartos, in the early 1960s.

05. Friedenstrasse in Düsseldorf-Bilk: my entire world in the 1960s.

06. On holiday with my beloved sister Marietta in Berchtesgaden – in lederhosen, naturally.

07. 1962, with Marietta and my mother.

08. Christmas 1962 with my grandparents Martha and Alfred Bartos (left).

09. I had a happy childhood!

10. 1965 – Brits at the Bartos base: Lance Corporal Peter Hornshaw played me my first Beatles record: A Hard Day's Night.

11. Even back in 1966 we knew a press photo was essential. Marietta took the picture in my bedroom – with me are (left to right) Jürgen, Heiko and Karl 2.

12. My first drum kit, 1967.

13. The first time I played in front of an audience, on 2 February 1967: The Hotbacks in the Jugendtanzcafe on Bilker Allee. With me on stage: Hans-Joachim (left) and Adolf.

14. The Anthonies' String Group's famous flower-power bus, 1969: Jörg (James), Franz, Brigitte, Günther and me (top to bottom).
Friedhelm Holleczek/NRZ

15. Professional: The Jokers at a Social Democratic Party election event, 12 November 1969.

16. My gigs with The Jokers paid my living expenses as a student: (left to right) me, Reiner, Klaus, Wolfgang and Franz.

17. Woodstock was still in our collective memory: 1971 with acoustic guitar in our shared flat on Nordstrasse in Düsseldorf-Derendorf.

18. Sinus 1971: (left to right) Rainer, me, Peter and Bodo – from jazz improvisation to twelve-tone music.
Rainer Sennewald

19. + 20. Sinus plus dance ensemble: poster for the theatre concert in December 1972. On the floor (left to right) me, Rainer, Peter. Standing (left to right): Margot, unknown, Frank, Marlis, Conrad, Angelika, unknown, Karin, Georg.
Rainer Sennewald

21. I think this is the only photo of me on timpani: in 1974, the class of Ernst Göbler (back right) performed Carl Orff's Carmina Burana in the Robert Schumann Hall.

22. My first music room of my own in Oberkassel, 1974.
Rainer Sennewald

23. + 24. Capriccio für Schlagzeug und Orchester by Friedrich Zehm. The conservatory orchestra in the Robert Schumann Hall, 1975. On xylophone and percussion: Karlheinz Bartos.

25. First gig with the classic lineup: Kraftwerk in the Forum Leverkusen on 27 February 1975.
KSTA/Holger Schmitt

26. 'Now I'm inserting the special film!': photo session at Foto Frank on Blumenstrasse in Düsseldorf, 1975.

27. A performance at Alex Cooley's Electric Ballroom in Atlanta, Georgia, 21 April 1975.
Tom Hill / Getty Images.

28. Before our gig at the Olympia, Paris, 28 February 1976: (left to right) Angelika Sendner, Maxime Schmitt, Emil Schult, Ralf Hütter, Draga Kuzmanoviç, me, Florian Schneider.

29. Vibraphone solo at a Sinus gig in Kunsthalle Düsseldorf, May 1976.
Rainer Sennewald

30. All smiles on the sofa in Rotterdam, 1976.
   Gijsbert Hanekroot/Redferns

31. Second from left: September 1976, rehearsing for the Belgian TV show *Follies*.
   Erik Machielsen

32. December 1977 in Munich: the legendary showroom dummy artist Heinrich Obermaier modelling 'Herr Karl'.

33. Bettina as Salome.

34. 13 April 1978 – album presentation for *The Man-Machine*: invitation to our Soiree Rouge on the 56th floor of the Tour Montparnasse.

35. The Mephisto experiment: test polaroid during filming for 'Neon Light'.

36. 1980: In my first studio on Taubenstrasse by the Hofgarten park.
   Bettina Michael

37. In the writing sessions days in the Kling Klang Studio.
   Joachim Dehmann

38. Two pages from my notebook . . .

39. 'I'm the operator with my pocket calculator': 1981 in The Ritz, NYC.
   Laura Levine/Corbis via Getty Images

40. 'Red shirt, black tie': 'Pocket Calculator' with Wolfgang 1981.
Bob King/Redferns

41. The Alps or Paris-Roubaix weren't my thing – I was happy with the left bank of the Lower Rhine. I trained regularly in 1985.
Bettina Michael

42. While Joachim Dehmann was rebuilding the Kling Klang Studio between 1987 and 1989, the equipment was kept in Studio B. Front right: my midi vibraphone.

43. My new life: Klangwerkstatt on Stockkampstrasse, 1990.
Bettina Michael

44. 1992: Camera on – press photo with Lothar for the *Esperanto* album.
SPV

45. Beatles tour in Liverpool: Andy McCluskey (OMD) showing me Penny Lane, 1992.

46. 1995: Love and marriage.
Rüdiger Nehmzow

47. 1996: (left to right) Johnny Marr, me and Bernard Sumner in Hamburg during the promo for Electronic's *Raise the Pressure*.
FOTEX/Shutterstock

48. The story of a message – my storyboard for the film *I'm the Message* (2003).

630

49. Me – a DJ? Why not! With Robert Baumanns at the Cologne Kickzone 1999, and from there around the world.
Jens Hartmann

50. Back in New York City: filming the video for the single '15 Minutes of Fame' (2000).

51. 'Atomium', 'Without a Trace of Emotion', 'Rhythmus' – screenshots from the live video of the *Off the Record* concert at Postbahnhof Berlin, 2014.

52. Live crew 2014: (front, left to right) Mathias Black, me, Robert Baumanns; (back, left to right) Rüdiger Ladwig (Trocadero), Michael Ochs, Sven Mouhcine, Dominik Sebald (a2b2c) at Steintor-Varieté, Halle/Saale.
Bettina Michael

53. Photo session with Sascha and Robert before the opening concert for the 'Robots' exhibition at DASA Dortmund, 2015.
Patrick Beerhorst

54. A visitor from Manchester: during the Hamburg Reeperbahnfestival 2015 with New Order's Bernard Sumner.
Bettina Michael

55. Let's see what the future brings . . .
Markus Wustmann

ACKNOWLEDGEMENTS

Writing an autobiography, you suddenly remember people who have accompanied you in life – for short or long periods – and given you differing amounts of input. There were some I'd completely forgotten, and I had to rediscover them and their roles at various times. Others still influence my thoughts and feelings to this day. I was surprised how many people I wanted to thank in these acknowledgements. My gratitude goes out to you all!

Rebecca Allen, Dave Anderson, Martha and Alfred Bartos, Rosa and Hans-Joachim Bartos, Sascha Basler, Hasko Baumann, Robert Baumanns, Hans-Joachim Bauer, the Beatles, Patrick Beerhorst, Matthias Bischoff, Mathias Black, Ira Blacker, Peter Bollig, Rebecca Boulton, Sabine Breitsameter, Michael Briel, Bernd Brink, Lucas Buchholz, Gunther Buskies, Anja Caspari, Holger Clausen, Marietta and Hans Czerny, Doreen D'Agostino, Graham Daniels, Joachim Dehmann, Klaus Dinger, Rusty Egan, Jürgen Engler, Hans Erkendal, Klaus Fiehe, Ian Floogs, Wolfgang Flür, John Foxx, Günther Fröhling, Ernst Göbler, Eva Gössling, Bianka Habermann, Kurt Halfmann, Friedbert Haus, Margot Heimbuchner, Günther Hilgers, Fritz Hilpert, Heiko Hoffmann, Hanna Holder, Philipp Holstein, Andrea Hornshaw, Peter Hornshaw, Paul Humphreys, Ralf Hütter, Vela Huber, Erica Hynot, Lisa Immensack, Stefan Ingmann, René Junge, Josef K., Ulrike Kamps-Paulsen, Uwe Kanka, Jakob Keusen, Jenny and Heiko Krüger, Wolfgang Keller, Claas Kielhorn, Willi Klein, Frank Köllges, Bettina Köster, Thomas Köster, Zuhal Korkmaz,

Franz Krähhahn, Wolfgang Kulas, Reiner Kunz, Rüdiger Ladwig, Francoise Lamy, Hans Lampe, Sepp Lankes, Jean-Marc Lederman, Adrian Leverkühn, Markus Löhr, Fred Maher, Lothar Manteuffel, Johnny Marr, Andy McCluskey, Richard Arthur McPhail, André Medow, Michael Mertens, Rolf Meurer, Manfred Mirsch, Claudia, Rose and Erwin Michael, Robert Morat, Sven Mouhcine, Marius Müller-Westernhagen, Rüdiger Nehmzow, Sean Newsham, Rainer Nickel, Reinhold Nickel, Michael Ochs, Jean-Hervé Péron, Helge Peters, Conny Plank, Rüdiger Plegge, Jonathan Potter, Sönke Prigge, Mark Reeder, Martin Renner, Ondrej Ritter, Jan Rimkeit, Hermann Rheindorf, Klaus Röder, Anthony Rother, Michael Rother, Ralph Rotzoll, Klaus Rybinski, Florian Schneider, Claudia Schneider-Esleben, Marko Schmidt, Maxime Schmitt, Emil Schult, Holger Schulze, Michael Schwabe, Thomas Schwebel, Heiko Schwenke, Dominik Sebald, Marlis and Rainer Sennewald, Ilse Siegle, Andrew Slegt, Günter Spachtholz, Brigitte and Bodo Staiger, Karlheinz Stockhausen, Bernard Sumner, Teja, Asmus Tietchens, Nicolas Villeminot, Kathrin Wagmüller, Rainer Weichhold, Otto Weinandi, Carl-Frank Westermann, Hajo Wiechers, Paul Wilkinson, Sascha Wild, Karin and Peter Wollek, Sabine Wolde, Markus Wustmann, Klaus Zaepke, Jürgen Ziemer, Olaf Zimmermann.

Translating an autobiography into another language and getting across the tone, the feel, and the author's sense of humour and character is a great art. My translator Katy Derbyshire has done all that incredibly well. This is exactly how I'd have written the book if English was my native language. I can't thank her enough!

I also owe special thanks to my editor David Buckley. I met him in 2009 when he was writing a book of his own about

Kraftwerk – a good one, as we now know – and contacted me for his research. What began as a purely professional interest developed into a continuous electronic dialogue, marked out by our shared passion for music and a very special sense of humour. I was all the happier that this Liverpudlian lad found the time and energy to edit my book. David's Northern view of things, his expert scrutiny of my manuscript and his wise comments have made my autobiography richer, and also brought it down to earth at some points. Thanks a lot, Mr Buckley!

I'd also like to thank the whole team at Omnibus Press, and especially Managing Editor David Barrraclough for his negotiating persistence and his calm hand during the production process.